ISSUES IN BIOMEDICAL ETHICS

Children in Medical Research

Lainie Ross presents a rigorous critical in⬛⬛⬛⬛⬛⬛⬛⬛⬛⬛⬛ ⬛f
policy governing the involvement of childr⬛ ⬛⬛⬛⬛⬛⬛⬛⬛ ⬛. ⬛ne examines the shift in focus from protection of me⬛ ⬛⬛⬛⬛⬛⬛ ⬛⬛⬛ subjects, enshrined
in post-World War II guidelines, to the current era in which access is
assuming greater importance. Infamous studies such as Willowbrook
(where mentally retarded children were infected with hepatitis) are evidence
that before the policy shift protection was not always adequate, even for the
most vulnerable groups. Additional safeguards for children were first implemented in many countries in the 1970s and 1980s; more recent policies and
guidelines are trying to promote greater participation. Ross considers
whether the safeguards work, whether they are fair, and how they apply in
actual research practice. She goes on to offer specific recommendations to
modify current policies and guidelines.

Ross examines the regulatory structures (e.g. federal regulations and institutional review boards), the ad hoc policies (e.g. payment in pediatric
research and the role of schools as research venues), the actual practices of
researchers (e.g. the race/ethnicity of enrolled research subjects or the decision to enroll newborns) as well as the decision-making process (both parental permission and the child's assent), in order to provide a broad critique.
Some of her recommendations will break down current barriers to the
enrolment of children (e.g. permitting the payment of child research subjects;
allowing healthy children to be exposed to research that entails more than
minimal risk without requiring recourse to 407 panels); whereas other recommendations may create new restrictions (e.g., the need for greater protection for research performed in schools; restrictions on what research
should be done in the newborn nursery). The goal is to ensure that medical
research is done in a way that promotes the health of current and future
children without threatening, to use the words of Hans Jonas, 'the erosion of
those moral values whose loss ... would make its most dazzling triumphs
not worth having'.

Lainie Friedman Ross holds appointments in the departments of Paediatrics,
Medicine, Surgery and the College at the University of Chicago. She is the
Carolyn and Matthew Bucksbaum Professor of Clinical Medical Ethics, an
Associate Director of the MacLean Center for Clinical Medical Ethics, and the
Director of the Ethics Consultation Service that provides both clinical and
research ethics consultation.

ISSUES IN BIOMEDICAL ETHICS

General Editors
John Harris and Søren Holm

Consulting Editors
Raanan Gillon and Bonnie Steinbock

The late twentieth century witnessed dramatic technological developments in biomedical science and in the delivery of health care, and these developments have brought with them important social changes. All too often ethical analysis has lagged behind these changes. The purpose of this series is to provide lively, up-to-date, and authoritative studies for the increasingly large and diverse readership concerned with issues in biomedical ethics—not just health care trainees and professionals, but also philosophers, social scientists, lawyers, social workers, and legislators. The series will feature both single-author and multi-author books, short and accessible enough to be widely read, each of them focused on an issue of outstanding current importance and interest. Philosophers, doctors, and lawyers from a number of countries feature among the authors lined up for the series.

Children in Medical Research: Access versus Protection

LAINIE FRIEDMAN ROSS

CLARENDON PRESS · OXFORD

OXFORD
UNIVERSITY PRESS

Great Clarendon Street, Oxford OX2 6DP

Oxford University Press is a department of the University of Oxford.
It furthers the University's objective of excellence in research, scholarship,
and education by publishing worldwide in

Oxford New York

Auckland Cape Town Dar es Salaam Hong Kong Karachi
Kuala Lumpur Madrid Melbourne Mexico City Nairobi
New Delhi Shanghai Taipei Toronto

With offices in

Argentina Austria Brazil Chile Czech Republic France Greece
Guatemala Hungary Italy Japan Poland Portugal Singapore
South Korea Switzerland Thailand Turkey Ukraine Vietnam

Oxford is a registered trade mark of Oxford University Press
in the UK and in certain other countries

Published in the United States
by Oxford University Press Inc., New York

British Library Cataloguing in Publication Data
Data available

Library of Congress Cataloging in Publication Data
Data available

Typeset by SPI Publisher Services, Pondicherry, India
Printed in Great Britain
on acid-free paper by
Biddles Ltd., King's Lynn, Norfolk

ISBN 978–0–19–927328–7 (Hbk.)
      978–0–19–923042–6 (Pbk.)

10 9 8 7 6 5 4 3 2 1

I dedicate this book to the two professors who inspired me to think about human subject protections:

In memory of Paul Ramsey, PhD (1913–1988)
Harrington Spear Paine Professor of Religion at Princeton University;
and

In honor of Jay Katz, MD (1922–
Elizabeth Dollard Professor Emeritus of Law, Medicine and Psychiatry
and Harvey L. Karp Professorial Lecturer in Law and Psychoanalysis at
Yale University

Acknowledgements

I owe a debt of gratitude to many individuals and institutions who supported me in this project. First, I want to express my appreciation and admiration for the two individuals to whom this book is dedicated: the late Paul Ramsey who changed my career at Princeton in 1982 and Jay Katz who was a mentor and guiding light at Yale from 1989 to 1994, and continues to be a source of inspiration.

This book began as a number of mini-projects looking at empirical data regarding research ethics. It took shape into a book with the support of the National Library of Medicine which provided me with funding October 2001–September 2004 (NLM 1 G13 LM07472, Children in Medical Research: Ethical and Policy Challenges). Of course, every book comes in overdue and over-budget. I thank the University of Chicago MacLean Center for Clinical Medical Ethics and the University of Chicago Department of Pediatrics for additional protected time.

The book is strengthened by numerous experiences on human subjects committees. During the past decade, I have served on the University of Chicago Institutional Review Board, several Data and Safety Monitoring Committees (DSMCs), and the Internal Organizational Advisory Group (IOAG) for the Policy and Ethics Committee of the Collaborative Network for Clinical Research on Immune Tolerance (also known as the Immune Tolerance Network (ITN)) sponsored by the NIH. A heartfelt thanks to all of these colleagues from whom I learned so much.

Academic medical centers are not accustomed to single-author book-length manuscripts. In this vein, many of the chapters were first written as articles. I thank numerous peer reviewers, both named and anonymous, for their comments on various versions of these chapters. I also thank the many editors and journals that have permitted me to reprint these articles with revisions.

Converting articles into a full-length manuscript was more difficult than I had expected. Publishing in law journals, medical journals, and bioethics journals required an ability to discuss these issues with many different audiences, but the articles themselves required different formatting and different endnote styles. Of course, Oxford University Press has its own style. But the real difficulties were in revising the chapters so that the themes flowed without redundancies, and that the development of ideas progressed in a coherent fashion. In this regard, I owe a special thanks to Ellen Wright Clayton, MD, JD, Walter Glannon, PhD, (Robert) Skip Nelson, MD, PhD, and Ann

Dudley Goldblatt, JD, LLM for agreeing to read the entire manuscript as well as two reviewers from Oxford University Press. Their perspicuous comments have significantly improved the flow and content of the chapters.

The book has also been supported and encouraged by colleagues and friends whose contributions lie beyond the text. A special thanks to Stan Goldblatt, JD, Mark Siegler, MD, Herb Abelson, MD, and John Lantos, MD. I also want to thank John Harris, PhD and Søren Holm, MD, PhD, the series editors at Oxford, for their support and suggestions.

Five chapters began as short articles and editorials for the *American Academy of Pediatrics Section on Bioethics Newsletter* of which I was editor from November 1999 to October 2004. All of these were then revised into longer articles and published in the medical and legal literature as will be described below. They were revised and expanded with the permission of the American Academy of Pediatrics. 'Children in Research: Access versus Protection', *American Academy of Pediatrics, Section on Bioethics Newsletter*, 6–8, September 2000, was a brief overview of the policy changes that are now described in Chapter 1. 'The Use of Placebos in Clinical Research', *American Academy of Pediatrics, Section on Bioethics Newsletter*, April 2001, pp. 5–7 is now revised and expanded in Chapter 13, Clinical Asthma Trials. 'Research Ethics on Trial: Lead Studies in Maryland', *American Academy of Pediatrics, Section on Bioethics Newsletter*, Autumn 2001, pp. 3, 8–10 was revised and expanded and is now a part of Chapter 12, Lead Abatement Studies. 'How many parents should be needed to consent to a child's participation in medical research?' *American Academy of Pediatrics, Section on Bioethics Newsletter*, May 2002, pp. 1 & 4 is now revised and expanded as part of Chapter 5, Informed Consent in Pediatric Research. 'Research Not Otherwise Approvable', *American Academy of Pediatrics, Section on Bioethics Newsletter*, Autumn 2002, pp. 2 & 7 was modified and is now part of Chapter 14, 'Research Not Otherwise Approvable: A Look at One Protocol'.

Three chapters are based on articles that I wrote with colleagues. I thank Eric Weil, MD and Skip Nelson, MD, PhD for agreeing to use our original data on IRB review and informed consent in pediatric research for Chapter 7. I thank M. Justin Coffey and Benjamin Wilfond, MD for allowing me to use our data on asthma for Chapter 12. And I thank Catherine A. Walsh, MD, Michael L. Kelly, and Paul Ackerman for agreeing to let me use our original data on race and ethnicity in Chapter 2.

Many of these chapters are based on articles that have been published previously. I thank the journals and the publishers for allowing me to revise, modify, and reprint many of the ideas presented in those articles. Chapter-by-chapter acknowledgments are enumerated below.

Introduction: Section 1 of the Introduction is based on the Introduction of '(Women and) Children First: Applicable to Lifeboats? Applicable to

Human Experimentation?' It was co-written with M. Justin Coffey for the *Journal of Health Care Law and Policy*, 2002; 6(1): 14–32. Reprinted and revised with permission. The remainder of this chapter is original.

Chapter 1: From 1966 to 2005: Balancing Protection and Access in Pediatric Research. This chapter is revised from, 'Balancing Protection and Access of Children in Medical Research: Has the Pendulum Swung Too Far?' *Perspectives in Biology and Medicine*, 2004; 47: 519–36. It has been expanded to include international policy changes. It is revised and reprinted with permission of the Johns Hopkins University Press.

Chapter 2: Access versus Protection: Minority Representation in Pediatric Research. This chapter is based on two large empirical data collections during the summers of 2002 and 2003. Catherine Walsh was principally involved in the data from 2002 and earned three publications. Michael Kelly and Paul Ackerman both worked on data collection from 2003. Mike continued his work in this area for his BA thesis. The data come from three articles: (1) Catherine A. Walsh and Lainie Friedman Ross, 'Are Minority Children Over- or Underrepresented in Pediatric Research?' *Pediatrics*; 2003; 112: 890–5; (2) Paul D. Ackerman, Michael L. Kelly, Catherine Walsh, and Lainie Friedman Ross, 'Do Institutional and Editorial Policies Affect the Reporting and Discussion of Race and Ethnicity in Pediatric Research?' *Accountability in Research*; 2005, 12: 17–31; and (3) Michael L. Kelly, Paul D. Ackerman, and Lainie Friedman Ross, 'The Participation of Minorities in Pediatric Research', *Journal of the National Medical Association*; 2005: 97: 777–83. Parts of the text are revised and reprinted from Lainie Friedman Ross and Catherine Walsh, 'Minority Children in Pediatric Research', *American Journal of Law and Medicine*, 2003; 29: 319–35. Revised and reprinted with the permission of my co-authors, *Pediatrics*, Taylor and Francis (publishers of *Accountability in* Research), the National Medical Association Journal, and the American Society of Law, Medicine, and Ethics.

Chapter 3: Overview of the Common Rule and Subpart D was written exclusively for this book.

Chapter 4: Should We Provide Healthy Children with Greater Protection in Medical Research? This chapter is revised from, 'Do Healthy Children Deserve Greater Protection in Medical Research?' *Journal of Pediatrics*, 2003; 142: 108–12. It has been revised and reprinted from the *Journal of Pediatrics*, 142, 108–12, 2003 with permission from Elsevier Publishers.

Chapter 5: Informed Consent in Pediatric Research. This chapter is revised from: 'Informed Consent in Pediatric Research', *Cambridge Quarterly of Healthcare Ethics*, 2004; 13: 346–58. Revised and reprinted with permission from Cambridge University Press.

Chapter 6:   Phase I Research and the Meaning of 'Prospect of Direct Benefit'. This chapter is revised from, 'Do Phase I Trials Offer the Prospect of Direct Benefit?', *Journal of Pediatrics*, 2005; 147: supplement, forthcoming. Revised and reprinted from the *Journal of Pediatrics* with permission from Elsevier Publishers.

Chapter 7:   Human Subjects Protections in Published Pediatric Research. This chapter is based on a publication with two colleagues: Eric Weil, Robert M. Nelson, Lainie Friedman Ross, 'Are Research Ethics Standards Satisfied in Pediatric Journal Publications?' *Pediatrics,* 2002; 110: 364–70. Revised and reprinted with permission from both of my co-authors and the journal, *Pediatrics.*

Chapter 8:   Payment in Pediatric Research. This chapter was written as an invited article for *Michigan State University Journal of Medicine and Law*, 2005; 9 (1): 1–24. Reprinted with permission.

Chapter 9:   Research in the Schools was written exclusively for this book.

Chapter 10:   Minimizing Risks: Diabetes Research in Newborns. This chapter is revised from, 'The Ethics of Predictive Diabetes Screening Research in Newborns', *Archives of Pediatrics and Adolescent Medicine*, 2003; 157: 89–95. Reprinted and revised with permission of *Archives of Pediatrics and Adolescent Medicine*, 2003; 157 (1): 89–95 copyright © 2003, American Medical Association, all rights reserved.

Chapter 11:   Diabetes Prediction and Prevention Research in Childhood. This chapter is revised from, 'The Ethics of Type 1 Diabetes Prediction and Prevention Research', *Theoretical Medicine and Biology*, 2003; 24: 177–97. Reprinted and revised with permission of Springer-Verlag publishers.

Chapter 12:   Lead Abatement Research. In Chapter 12, I examine the controversial lead paint studies undertaken in the early 1990s by the Kennedy Krieger Institute. This chapter was originally published in 2002 as, 'In Defense of the Hopkins Lead Abatement Studies', *Journal of Law, Medicine, and Ethics*, 2002; 30: 50–7. After this article was published, I was contacted by the Kennedy Krieger Institute and asked whether I would agree to be an expert witness on their Appeal. I agreed to review the records to see whether I could support their position, and did accept the role. For the record, the documents confirmed my belief that the research was ethical and that the court was mistaken in its criticism. To ensure that I would not disclose any confidential information I received as an expert witness, I chose to minimize any substantive changes in this chapter. I have also added a denouement to inform the reader that the case was eventually dismissed with prejudice. This article is revised and reprinted with the permission of the American Society of Law, Medicine and Ethics.

In the original article, I examine two additional concerns about the court's ruling: (1) that institutional review boards (IRBs) are in-house agents that are unable to protect research subjects; and (2) that research relationships can create special relationships that give rise to special duties. Both issues are important in the context of human subject protections and I recommend the reader to the original article. I have excluded these sections from the chapter to focus on those aspects of the decision germane to Subpart D of the federal regulations (the regulations written to protect children as research subjects). Specifically I am focusing on (1) the relevance of having a 'disorder or condition' to the permissibility of research involving children; and (2) the appropriate risk to which children can be morally exposed.

Chapter 13: Placebo Controlled Asthma Trials. This chapter is based on work by Justin Coffey. We designed this project for a BA thesis in the HIPSS department at the University of Chicago. Justin then spent the summer finding all of his own mistakes and expanding the project. Justin received guidance from Ben Wilfond. This chapter uses the data from the project but is rewritten and updated. See M. Justin Coffey, Benjamin Wilfond, and Lainie Friedman Ross, 'Ethical Assessment of Clinical Asthma Trials Including Children Subjects', *Pediatrics*, 2004; 113: 87–94. The chapter is also derived from a law review article that Justin and I wrote together. See Lainie Friedman Ross and M. Justin Coffey, '(Women and) Children First: Applicable to Lifeboats? Applicable to Human Experimentation?' *Journal of Health Care Law and Policy*, 2002; 6(1): 14–32. The Tables are reprinted from *Pediatrics* with permission. Thanks to the *Journal of Health Care Law and Policy* to allow me to reprint and revise from this article. And thanks to my colleagues, Ben and Justin.

Chapter 14: Research not Otherwise Approvable: A Look at One Protocol: This chapter is revised from, 'Convening a 407 PANEL for Research Not Otherwise Approvable: Precursors to Diabetes in Japanese American Youth as a Case Study', *Kennedy Institute of Ethics Journal*, 2004; 14: 165–86. Revised and reprinted with permission from the Johns Hopkins University Press.

Chapter 15: Evolution of the 407 Process. This chapter is reprinted with permission from, 'Lessons to be Learned from the 407 Process', Health Matrix, 2005; 15: 401–421.

Finally, my acknowledgments would not be complete without a special thanks to my husband John and our two daughters, Geri and Maddi. One could argue that parenting is a form of human experimentation. With love to my co-investigator and our two experiments-in-progress.

Contents

Introduction

1. From First to Last and Back Again

The phrase 'women and children first' refers to the rescue policy on a sinking ship. Its origin is credited to the brave action of Lt. Col. Alexander Seton and his men on the HMS *Birkenhead*.[1] On 26 February, 1852, the HMS *Birkenhead* hit a rock just off Danger Point near southern Africa and its metal hull was torn open. Those soldiers who did not drown in their sleep rushed on deck and attempted to free the lifeboats. Three lifeboats were released, and the women and children were ushered onto them. As the ship began to sink, Captain Seton drew his sword and ordered his men to stand fast because he feared that if the men rushed the lifeboats, the women and children might perish. Over two-thirds of the men died.[2]

By contrast, in medical research, the traditional policy was 'women and children last'. The justification was paternalistic: women and children needed protection. But with this protection came a drawback: health issues unique to women and children were understudied and underfunded.[3] In 1990, the Office of Research on Women's Health was established to ensure that 'women's health research is part of the scientific framework at the National Institutes of Health (NIH) and throughout the scientific community.'[4] The NIH began to require the participation of women in NIH-supported research or a justification for their exclusion. The moral justification was simple: if competent adults have the right to decide for themselves what risks they are willing to bear for particular benefits, then this holds for both competent men and competent women. The exclusion of women from the frontlines of medical research could not and cannot be justified morally.

The policy of children last, however, was morally justified on the grounds that children cannot consent for themselves and are therefore more vulnerable than competent adults. This position was articulated clearly by the National Commission for the Protection of Human Subjects of Biomedical and Behavioral Research (National Commission) in the *Belmont Report*. In its discussion on the selection of subjects, the National Commission concluded: 'Thus it can be considered a matter of social justice that there is an order of preference in the selection of classes of subjects (e.g., adults before children).'[5] Likewise, in its report *Research Involving Children*, the National Commission stated that 'whenever possible, research involving risk should be conducted first on animals and adult humans in order to ascertain the degree of risk and the likelihood of generating useful knowledge.'[6] The National Commission was clear that this 'children last' policy was not always desirable nor feasible such as when the research is designed to study disorders or functions that have no parallel in animals or adults.

Harry Shirkey was one of the earliest advocates for greater access of children to participate in medical research. He argued that children would be 'therapeutic orphans'[7] unless government and industry supported pediatric drug investigation. His position was strengthened by historical events: most of the laws empowering the US Food and Drug Administration (FDA) to regulate drugs were passed in response to adverse drug reactions in the pediatric population.[8] Thirty years later, the pendulum has swung to emphasize access. In June 1996, the American Academy of Pediatrics (AAP) and the National Institute of Child Health and Human Development (NICHD) sponsored a workshop on the 'Inclusion of Children in Clinical Research'[9] in which the theme was that current policy may be too little, too late.[10]

Part of the support for increasing pediatric participation in research, particularly in pharmaceutical research, is that major advances have been made during the past half century in adult medicine, but only more modest advances in pediatrics. Consider, for example, that more than 80 per cent of drugs prescribed to children have never been tested on them.[11] The danger is that unless drugs are tested in children, every child's treatment remains an experiment because there are no data for safety or efficacy and no guidelines for dosing. Policies promulgated in the 1990s by the National Institutes of Health (NIH), the FDA, and US Congress attempted to overcome this knowledge gap by offering carrots and sticks that would promote the participation of children in research.[12] One such policy was the passage of the Children's Health Act in October 2000 that included a Pediatric Research Initiative (Title X).[13] Importantly, the Act also required the Department of Health and Human Services (DHHS) to conduct a review of Subpart D (the regulations written to provide additional protections for pediatric research subjects) and to consider 'any modifications necessary to ensure the adequate and appropriate protection of children participating in research'.[14] This book is my response to that challenge.

While I support a policy of 'children first' on sinking ships, I reject this policy for medical research. I question whether the pendulum has swung too far; that is, whether the new initiatives place too much emphasis on access and not enough emphasis on protection. Let me assert that I do support pediatric research. But I realize that research may place some children at risk—sometimes for their own potential benefit; other times for the potential benefit to others. My goal is to ensure that risks and harms are minimized. One way to minimize harms is to limit research with children, and to use, when possible, animals and adults.

In this book, then, I offer a critical view of the current pendulum position on access. It is written from a US perspective, although the push towards access is occurring internationally. My criticism about the current over-emphasis on access, however, is not the book's sole focus. Rather, my goal is to look at what is being done right, what needs to be done better, and possibly what should not be done at all. To strengthen my arguments I have collected data about (1) who participates in pediatric research with respect to race and ethnicity (Chapter 2); (2) whether children are harmed by placebo-controlled trials using asthma as a case study (Chapter 13); (3) whether the policy to include children in research with adults promotes pediatric medical knowledge, again using asthma as a case study (Chapter 13); and (4) whether researchers who do research involving children conform to research ethics standards (Chapter 8).

This book has its origins as a chapter in my first book, *Children, Families and Health Care Decision Making*.[15] In Chapter 5, 'The Child as Research Subject', I addressed 'the moral questions of whether and when children can serve as subjects of human experimentation'.[16] My goals were to show that (1) children can participate morally as human subjects (a topic to which I return in Chapter 1) and (2) limitations in the federal regulations (a topic to which I return in sections 2–4).

In the seven years since this book was published, my position about how decisions should be made for children in various health care settings has evolved, but the philosophical underpinnings remain the same. I argued then, and still believe, that parents are and ought to be the primary deci-sion-makers about their child's health care. To make these decisions in a way that reflects their values and beliefs, parents need wide latitude. The child, too, has a role in health care decision-making. In my first book, I proposed a standard, 'constrained parental autonomy', that would limit parental discre-tion and would modulate the child's role in decision-making depending on the type of decision being made, the risks involved, and the child's own develop-ing personhood. For example, in the research setting, particularly when the research involves risks and is not intended to benefit the child-subject, the child's voice should be given greater weight than in the therapeutic setting. However, in contrast with the specialized consent statutes that allow adoles-cents to make clinical decisions without parental involvement, I argue that there should be no exemptions to parental participation in the research arena.

Examining the role of parents and children in the research decision-mak-ing process is necessary but not sufficient for understanding the complexities of the ethical and policy issues raised by the participation of children in medical research. In this book, I go beyond my original methodology to examine the regulatory structure (e.g., federal regulations and institutional review boards), the ad hoc policies (e.g., payment in pediatric research and the role of schools as research venues), the actual practices of researchers (e.g., the race/ethnicity of enrolled research subjects or the decision to enroll newborns) as well as the decision-making process in order to provide a broader critique and to offer more specific recommendations.

2.   *Book Organization*

The book is divided into five sections. Section 1 is entitled Access versus Protection. The first chapter reviews the last four decades of human subject protections. It begins with the four pediatric cases publicized by Dr Henry Beecher, a professor of anesthesia at Harvard Medical School, as part of his *New England Journal of Medicine* critique on unethical research performed in the United States post-Nuremberg.[17] Unlike Beecher who attempted to preserve anonymity, I cite the references to which Beecher referred. Likewise, in my own case studies, I provide complete references in case the reader wants to examine the primary sources. I do not mean to attack personally any of the researchers whose work I criticize. I do mean to question and criticize how research is being done and how we as a community are protecting and failing to protect our children in research participation.

After reviewing Beecher's cases, I proceed to examine the debate between Paul Ramsey and Richard McCormick, two Christian ethicists, on the ethics of nontherapeutic research* on children.[18] The debate initiated by Ramsey and McCormick continued as the National Commission was charged to examine human subject protections and to develop policy to promote

---

*The phrase 'nontherapeutic research' implies that the research has a purely scientific purpose and offers no prospect of direct [therapeutic] benefit in contrast with 'therapeutic research' which implies that the research offers the prospect of direct [therapeutic] benefit. The distinction is not clear-cut in practice. Although there are research projects that offer no prospect of direct [therapeutic] benefit (e.g., when a healthy volunteer is paid to participate in a study to determine the metabolism and excretion rate of a new compound), many research projects offer therapeutic benefits, even if only indirectly. In addition, activities commonly referred to as 'therapeutic research' often entail procedures which do not directly benefit the subject (e.g., the process of randomization in clinical trials). The National Commission (for the Protection of Human Subjects of Biomedical and Behavioral Research) sought to be more precise by using the notion of research which does or does not offer the prospect of direct benefit. The UK Institute of Medical Ethics Working Group on the Ethics of Clinical Research Investigations on Children found the National Commission's phrases unwieldy and chose to use the terms 'therapeutic' and 'nontherapeutic' for their simplicity and utility (Nicholson, R. H. (ed.)., *Medical Research with Children: Ethics, Law, and Practice*, Oxford: Oxford University Press, 1986, 26–31). Appreciating the limitations but the utility and simplicity of the terms 'nontherapeutic' and 'therapeutic' research, I use them in this book when it is used historically and when its meaning is clear.

protections for human subjects. The focus was clearly on protection. I then consider events in the 1980s and 1990s that have led some to argue in favor of increasing the access of children to participate in research. I also examine the shift in policies with respect to pediatric research guidelines

In Chapter 2, I consider an interesting twist in the debate on access versus protection by examining the participation of minority children in pediatric research. There are many studies that show that minority adults are under-represented in clinical trials.[19] With several students, I examined whether minority children are under- or overrepresented in pediatric research. If one believes that we need greater protection of our children, then one will applaud the underrepresentation of Hispanic children. If one believes that we need greater access for our children, then one will applaud the over-representation of Black children. Alternatively, both those who support greater protection and those who support greater access will be concerned: Why are there discrepancies in participation? Are the discrepancies random or are there only certain types of research in which minorities are over-represented?

The second section of the book is entitled Challenges to the Regulations. Chapter 3 provides an overview of US regulations regarding children as human subjects. The main focus is on the Common Rule (Subpart A) and the additional protections designed for children (Subpart D).[20] Although these regulations are US specific, the regulations regarding children in re-search in the UK are quite similar, although somewhat stricter.[21] Given current attempts to harmonize regulations internationally, one can expect increasing similarity over time.[22] Nevertheless, the international reader may find this exegesis too detailed and may want to skim or skip this chapter. To the extent that critiques in future chapters refer to the US regulations, a brief description of the regulations is provided in the chapter itself.

In Chapters 4–6, I challenge various aspects of the US regulations. In Chapter 4, I examine the policy that allows children with 'a disorder or condition' to be exposed to greater risk than healthy children in nonther-apeutic research. I argue that there is no ethical justification for this distinc-tion, and argue for a uniform level of risk to which it is ethical to expose any child. In Chapter 5, I examine the current consent policies surrounding the various categories of pediatric research. I argue that some of the policies (e.g., two-parent consent) provide no additional protection. I also argue that the dissent requirements need to be revised so that a child's dissent is only sought when the child's refusal will be dispositive. In Chapter 6, I examine what is meant by the concept 'prospect of direct benefit' by looking at phase I pediatric oncology testing. If phase I research offers the prospect of direct benefit, then phase I oncology trials can be approved under CFR §46.405 or 'therapeutic research'. If these trials do not offer the prospect of direct benefit, then the research must be approved under a different classification. I argue that the concept 'prospect of direct benefit' is interpreted as a substantive goal, but that this interpretation is not sufficient because both intent (motive) and substantive goals matter. If I am correct, then phase I research cannot be approved under the CFR §46.405 classification. If phase I research is not defined as offering the prospect of direct benefit, then given the significant risks that it poses such research could only be approved by national review under current federal regulations. (These panels are referred to as 407 panels and are discussed in Chapters 14 and 15.) I propose revisions to the regulations that would allow phase I trials to be approved as non-therapeutic research without having to resort to 407 panels.

In the third section entitled 'Strengths and Limits of Current Regulations', I consider the extent to which the current regulations succeed (Chapter 7) as well as the gaps in current regulations (Chapters 8–9). In Chapter 7, I examine whether pediatric research is being reviewed by IRBs and whether researchers are seeking consent. The data I collected with colleagues confirm that research ethics protections are being upheld. In Chapters 8 and 9, I consider two issues on which the regulations are silent. Chapter 8 addresses the issue of payment in pediatric research. The National Commission expressed concern that payment would lead to 'undue influence'.[23] I consider payment given the current regulatory practices and find that it could be ethical to pay children. Chapter 9 addresses the issue of children as a 'captive population' or children in a 'captive environment'. The National Commission expressed concern about whether prisoners could provide voluntary consent because of their captivity.[24] A major concern is the voluntariness of the consent from subjects who are captive; that is, whether they truly believe that they have the right not to participate and whether their consent can be free and voluntary. I believe that similar consent concerns should be raised in research performed in the newborn nursery (where virtually all infants reside for the first few days of life) and in schools (where virtually all children of certain ages are required to attend) because it is not clear whether the children and/or their parents believe they can refuse to participate. In Chapter 9, I consider the ethical issues of performing medical and behavioral research in schools. I argue that additional protections like those offered to prisoners would be appropriate. In Chapter 10, I consider research on newborns in the newborn nursery.

The fourth section is comprised of case studies. Chapter 10 is entitled 'Minimizing Risk: Diabetes Research in Newborns' and it focuses on what types of diabetes research is morally permissible in newborns. I consider whether the voluntariness of parental consent for research on their newborn is suspect because the newborn nursery is a captive environment. I also argue that the ethical requirement to minimize risk in research would encourage predictive diabetes screening research to be done on older children. In Chapter 11, I continue to examine diabetes research and look at the issue of what types of prediction and prevention research are morally acceptable for children beyond the newborn period.

In both chapters on diabetes research, I examine the concept of what it means to label a child as 'at risk for a disorder or condition'. I continue this examination in Chapter 12 as I examine the Kennedy Krieger lead studies that were condemned as a 'modern day Tuskegee'.[25] To those readers who may be somewhat frustrated at my criticism of current policy and practice, this chapter will be a welcome relief as I argue that the court was wrong and that the lead abatement studies were quite ethical.

Chapter 13 examines placebo-controlled asthma trials and argues that placebo-controlled trials are unethical when a standard of care exists and the subjects are randomized to active drug versus placebo (in contrast with an add-on design). In this chapter, I also show that the new policies that encourage enrolling children and adults into the same trials frequently do not achieve the goal of improved pediatric medicine that they were meant to achieve. Rather, I show that the policies often increase the number of children exposed to research risks without providing benefit to the individual child or children as a class.

In Chapters 14 and 15, I examine 407 panels, national panels necessary to approve research that cannot be approved locally (CFR §46.407). I show how the panels have evolved and what still needs to be done to provide appropriate human subject protections. Most research that undergoes 407 review is nontherapeutic research that entails more than minimal risk and seeks to enroll healthy children. Such research should be prohibited in most other countries because nontherapeutic research on children is limited internationally to research that poses no more than minimal risk.[26] Nevertheless, my research uncovered numerous studies similar to the research undergoing 407 review that were undertaken outside of the US. This should force both US and international reader, to pause and ask how such research was approved.

I conclude with a brief epilogue in which I discuss what is necessary to ensure that access of children to research participation is balanced by the protections that they deserve.

3. Five Caveats

First, this book is written from a US perspective and critiques US regulations. The policy critiques are relevant to the international reader to the extent that their countries have similar policies; and to the extent that there is an attempt to develop international harmonization, particularly with respect to pharmaceutical clinical trials. The tension between access and protection of vulnerable subject populations exists wherever research is performed, even though different communities and different cultures will seek different balance points.

Second, although I discuss research on newborns in Chapter 10, the focus is research on healthy newborns. I do not address the ethical issues of research on ill or premature infants. There are many authors who do, both in the US and internationally.[27] More bioethicists address ethical issues in neonatal clinical care.[28] Why and how neonatal ethics differs from pediatric ethics in the clinical and research arena need greater attention.

Third, at the other end of the pediatric age spectrum is the older adolescent. In the US, the age of emancipation is 18. This means that until age 18, parents are the health care proxies for their children and their permission is required for most pediatric research. To the reader outside of the US where younger adolescents are able to consent for themselves, my arguments should not be interpreted as support for a particular age below which parental permission is required and above which parental permission is not required. There are arguments to support lowering the age limit and even for raising it. My position is that public policy ought to be more consistent.[29] If an adolescent is given the authority to make health care decisions for him- or herself, then the same adolescent should be given the authority to make other important decisions for him- or herself and should be given the appropriate liberties necessary to act upon these decisions.

Fourth, I do not specifically address the 'adolescent alone'.[30] I assume that the child who is being enrolled in research has at least one intimate parent or legal guardian. The federal regulations in the US addresses children who are wards of the state (CFR §46.409). I do not. To the extent that the regulations permit parental permission to be waived if there is an appropriate substitute consent mechanism (CFR §46.408(c), the regulations can accommodate research involving run-away children and adolescents. Critics will argue that some of these children should be emancipated and allowed to consent to research participation for themselves. In Chapter 4, I will argue against this position because it conflates therapy and research.

Fifth, this book covers a wide range of issues, but it is not comprehensive. There are other issues that need further elucidation such as (1) compensation payment for injuries; (2) public health and population-based research; (3) research using stored blood and tissue samples; and (4) the role of siblings as 'normal' controls in research. I hope this book will serve as a catalyst for serious consideration about the topics covered and those omitted.

References

1. Anonymous. 'A Ship Tradition: Women and Children First'. Found on the web at: http://ne.essortment.com/shiptraditionw_rrqb.htm.
2. Ibid.
3. See, e.g., Kolata, G. 'NIH Neglects Women, Study Says', *New York Times* (19 June 1990), C6; Bennett, J. C. for the Board on Health Sciences Policy of the Institute of Medicine. 'Inclusion of Women in Clinical Trials—Policies for Population Subgroups', *New England Journal of Medicine*, 329 (1993), 288–92; and Gross, C. P., Anderson, G. F., and Powe, N. R. 'The Relation between Funding by the National Institutes of Health and the Burden of Disease', *New England Journal of Medicine*, 340 (1999), 1881–7.
4. Office of Research on Women's Health, Office of the Director, National Institutes of Health. *Commemorating a Decade of Progress.* On the web at: http://www4.od.nih.gov/orwh/decade-2.pdf.
5. National Commission for the Protection of Human Subjects of Biomedical and Behavioral Research. *The Belmont Report: Ethical Principles and Guidelines for the Protection of Human Subjects of Research.* Washington DC: US Government Printing Office, 1978, DHEW Publication No. (OS) 78–12. Found on the web at: http://ohsr.od.nih.gov/guidelines/belmont.html; hereinafter referred to as the *Belmont Report*.
6. National Commission for the Protection of Human Subjects of Biomedical and Behavioral Research. *Report and Recommendations: Research Involving Children.* Washington DC: US Government Printing Office, 1977, DHEW Publication No. (OS) 77–0004, 3–4. Hereinafter cited as National Commission, *Research Involving Children*.
7. Shirkey, H. 'Therapeutic Orphans', *Journal of Pediatrics*, 72 (1968), 119–20.
8. Ibid.
9. 'Proceedings of Workshop, Inclusion of Children in Clinical Research', 5 September 1996 (unpublished, on file with author. Supplied by Mona Rowe, Deputy Director, Office of Science Policy, Analysis and Communication, National Institute of Child Health and Human Development).
10. American Academy of Pediatrics (AAP), Council on Pediatric Research 'Meeting the Research Needs of Children and Youth: Research along the Life Cycle' (unpublished, undated manuscript that served as a background piece for the meeting, on file with author).
11. American Academy of Pediatrics Committee on Drugs, 'Guidelines for the Ethical Conduct of Studies to Evaluate Drugs in Pediatric Populations', *Pediatrics*, 95 (1995), 286–94, 286.
12. These policies are discussed in detail in Ch. 1, section 6, 'From Protection to Access'.
13. Children's Health Act of 2000, Public Law 106–310 (2000).
14. Ibid., §1003.
15. Ross, L. F., *Children, Families, and Health Care Decision-Making.* Oxford, UK: Clarendon Press, 1998, ch. 5, 77–110.

16. Ibid., 77.
17. Beecher, H. K., 'Ethics and Clinical Research', *New England Journal of Medicine*, 274 (1966), 1354–60.
18. The Ramsey–McCormick debates in the academic literature took place over seven years. The first piece is a chapter in Ramsey's book, *The Patient as Person*. See Ramsey, P., *The Patient as Person*. New Haven, CT: Yale University Press, 1970. McCormick tried to show that Ramsey's arguments were misguided in 1974. See McCormick, R. A, 'Proxy Consent in the Experimentation Situation', *Perspectives in Biology and Medicine*, 18 (Autumn, 1974), 2–23. The debates continued through 1977 in the *Hastings Center Report*. See Ramsey, P., 'The Enforcement of Morals: Non-Therapeutic Research on Children', *Hastings Center Report*, 6 (August 1976), 21–30; McCormick, R. A., 'Experimentation in Children: Sharing in Sociality', *Hastings Center Report*, 6 (December 1976), 41–6; and Ramsey, P., 'Children as Research Subjects: A Reply', *Hastings Center Report*, 7 (April 1977), 40–1.
19. See, e.g., Smedley, B. D., Stith, A. Y., and Nelsor. A. R. (eds.) for the Institute of Medicine, *Unequal Treatment: Confronting Racial and Ethnic Disparities in Health Care*. Washington DC: National Academy Press, 2003; and Gifford, A. L., Cunningham, W. E., Heslin, K. C., Andersen, R. M., Nakazono, T., Lieu, D. K., Shapiro, M. F., and Bozzette, S. A. for the Cost and Services Utilization Study Consortium, 'Participation in Research and Access to Experimental Treatments by HIV-Infected Patients', *New England Journal of Medicine*, 346 (2002), 1373–82.
20. See Department of Health and Human Services (DHHS), (45 CFR 46 Subpart A), 'Final Regulations Amending Basic HHS Policy for the Protection of Human Research Subjects', *Federal Register*, 46 (26 January 1981), 8366–91; revised *Federal Register*, 56 (18 June 1991), 28003–18, CFR §46.101(b). Hereinafter referred to as the Common Rule and cited by its CFR number in the text; and Department of Health and Human Services (DHHS), (45 CFR Part 46, Subpart D), 'Protections for Children Involved as Subjects in Research', *Federal Register*, 48 (8 March 1983), 9814–20; revised *Federal Register*, 56 (18 June 1991), 28032, CFR §46.401(b), hereinafter referred to as Subpart D and cited by its CFR number in the text.
21. In 1986, the UK Institute of Medical Ethics working group on the ethics of clinical research investigations on children published a full-length manuscript entitled *Medical Research with Children: Ethics, Law and Practice*. The Working Group's recommendations were influential in the revision of the guidelines of the Medical Research Council and the British Paediatric Association, and are quite similar to (and refer frequently to) the recommendations of the National Commission (US).
22. The International Conference on Harmonisation (ICH) is an international collaboration of industry and regulatory bodies that seeks to develop common guidelines and procedures to ensure the safety, quality, and efficacy of new drugs. Information can be found on the web at: http://www.ich.org. The Council for International Organization of Medical Sciences (CIOMS) was created by the World Health Organization (WHO) and the United Nationals Education Social

and Cultural Organization (UNESCO) in 1949. It developed 'International Ethical Guidelines for Biomedical Research Involving Human Subjects' in 1982 which were revised in 1993 and in 2002. The guidelines can be found at: http://www.cioms.ch/frame_guidelines_nov_2002.htm.

23. *Belmont Report*.
24. National Commission for the Protection of Human Subjects of Biomedical and Behavioral Research, *Research on Prisoners: Report and Recommendations*. Washington DC: US Department of Health, Education and Welfare, 1976, 5–6.
25. Ericka Grimes v. Kennedy Krieger Institute, Inc. Myron Higgins, a minor, etc., *et al*. v. Kennedy Krieger Institute, Inc. No. 128, No. 129 Court of Appeals of Maryland 366 Md. 29; 782 A.2d 807; 2001 Md. Lexis 496 16 August 2001, Filed; Revised 28 August 2001. Reconsideration Denied 11 October 2001. The reference to Tuskegee can be found at: Grimes v. Kennedy Krieger Institute, Inc., 782 A.2d 807, 816 (Md. 2001).
26. See e.g., the British guidelines: Royal College of Paediatrics and Child Health (RCPCH], Ethics Advisory Committee, 'Guidelines for the Ethical Conduct of Medical Research Involving Children', *Archives of Disease in Childhood*, 82 (2000), 177–182; the Canadian guidelines: Medical Research Council (MRC), the Natural Sciences and Engineering Research Council (NSERC), and the Social Sciences and Humanities Research Council (SSHRC). 'Tri-Council Policy Statement: Ethical Conduct for Research Involving Humans, 1998 (Updated 2000, 2002)', found on the web at: http://www.pre.ethics.gc.ca/english/pdf/TCPS%20 June2003_E.pdf; and the Australian guidelines: National Statement on Ethical Conduct in Research Involving Humans. Commonwealth of Australia, 1999. On the web at: http://www.nhmrc.gov.au/publications/pdf/e35.pdf
27. In the US, the best-known critic is Bill Silverman. See, Silverman, W. A., *Where's the Evidence?: Debates in Modern Medicine*. New York: Oxford University Press, 1999. There is a wonderful European book edited by Su A Mason and Chris Megone. See Mason, S. A., and Megone, C., *European Neonatal Research: Consent, Ethics Committees and Law*. Aldershot; Burlington: Ashgate, 2001.
28. See, e.g., Goldworth, A., Silverman, W., Stevenson, D. K., and Young, E. W. D. (eds)., *Ethics and Perinatology*. New York: Oxford University Press, 1995; McHaffie, H. E., and Fowlie, P. W., *Life, Death and Decisions: Doctors and Nurses Reflect on Neonatal Practice*. Cheshire: Hochland & Hochland, 1996; Hazel McHaffie, *Crucial Decisions at the Beginning of Life: Parents' Experiences of Treatment withdrawal from Infants*, Oxford: Radcliffe Medical Press, 2001; and Lantos, J., and Meadow, W., *Neonatal Bioethics: A Success Story*. Johns Hopkins University Press, Baltimore, 2006 forthcoming.
29. Ross, *Children*, Ch. 4, 'Respect for the Competent Child', particularly section 3: 'Autonomy Reconsidered'.
30. Blustein, J., Levine, C. Dubler, N. N., *The Adolescent Alone: Decision-Making in Health Care in the United States*. New York: Cambridge University Press, 1999.

1

From 1966 to 2005: Balancing Protection and Access in Pediatric Research

1. Introduction

The modern history of the ethics of human experimentation in the United States begins in 1966 with the publication of Henry Beecher's famous article, 'Ethics and Clinical Research'.[1] One could argue that I should begin two decades earlier with the Nuremberg trials and the Nuremberg Principles of Research Ethics,[2] but as David Rothman, a medical historian notes, 'Neither the horrors described at the Nuremberg trial nor the ethical principles that emerged from it had a significant impact on the American research establishment,' because they did not seem 'directly relevant to the American scene.'[3]

Prior to 1966, children were frequently subjects in research because they were convenient: researchers would often experiment on their children, servants, or slaves.[4] Children could also be recruited from institutions. Alfred Hess, the medical director of the Hebrew Infant Asylum in New York City, explained the scientific advantage of enrolling institutionalized children: it permitted 'conditions which are insisted on in considering the course of experimental infection among laboratory animals, but which can rarely be controlled in a study of infection in man.'[5] Children were also 'cheap' in the sense that they were non-valued or viewed as expendable commodities. One researcher explicitly stated that he used child subjects because they were 'cheaper than calves'.[6] Lederer and Grodin describe the role of children in medical research in the century prior to 1966 as largely one of child abuse.[7]

The concerns expressed by Beecher and others led to the introduction of research regulations in the 1970s. Because of the special vulnerability of children, additional regulations were developed to protect them. These regulations effectively served to restrict participation of children in research. Beginning in the 1990s, however, there has been a movement to include children on the grounds that their exclusion has made them 'therapeutic orphans'.[8] This chapter will examine the changes in policies regarding children in research between 1966 and 2003.

2. Beecher Revisited

In 'Ethics and Clinical Research', Beecher described twenty-two research projects published post-World War II that he found to be of questionable ethics.[9] Beecher noted that these studies were not unique but were chosen to illustrate the wide range of unethical practices (e.g., withholding effective treatment, knowingly exposing subjects to drugs that could be expected to cause serious side-effects, and lack of informed consent). Although Beecher described the studies in enough detail to convince the reader of the ethical problems, he intentionally did not name the researchers, their institutions, or the journals in which these articles were published. Others, however, did.[10]

Of the twenty-two research studies, four involved child subjects. The best known of these is the Willowbrook study, a study that involved institutionalized mentally retarded children at the Willowbrook State School in Staten Island, New York.[11] The study cited by Beecher is one of many studies on hepatitis conducted by Krugman and Ward and colleagues in the 1950s and 1960s at Willowbrook, where they served as consultants in infectious diseases.[12] They were interested in understanding the natural history of hepatitis in order to develop a vaccine. The specific objectives of the study cited by Beecher were (1) to detect viremia during the incubation period, the early icteric phase, and clinically inapparent infection; and (2) to determine the period of infectivity in both stool and blood. To do this, the researchers admitted new residents to the isolation unit where they were given doses of hepatitis derived from other Willowbrook residents either by intramuscular injection or by oral intake. The research confirmed the presence of the virus in infected children two to three weeks before the onset of jaundice and demonstrated viremia in children with subclinical infections, two discoveries that have important implications for the spread of the virus.[13]

Beecher argued that the research design was not consistent with the World Medical Association's (WMA) code of ethics, a code that does not permit 'weaken[ing] the physical or mental resistance of a human being except from strictly therapeutic or prophylactic indications imposed in the interest of the patient'.[14] Beecher did not question the scientific importance of the research but argued against its methodology. He argued that there was no right to risk an injury to one person for the benefit of others.[15] This, I might add, is particularly true of vulnerable individuals who cannot consent to be used in this way.

Despite widespread criticism, Krugman maintained the studies were ethical. In various publications, he attempted to justify infecting the children deliberately on the grounds that most newly admitted children became infected at Willowbrook in the first six to 12 months of institutionalization.[16] In response to criticism that the research took advantage of the overcrowded and therefore unsanitary conditions of the institution,

Krugman responded that 'We were not qualified to deal with the societal problems, but we believed that we could help control the existing medical problem of hepatitis.'[17]

Krugman argued further that he designed the study so as to minimize risk. For example, he only enrolled children between the ages of three and ten years in whom hepatitis was known to be especially mild; and the children were only infected with strains of hepatitis from other residents at Willowbrook, strains that were known to be mild.[18] Beecher rejected these arguments, pointing out that Stokes and Neefe had demonstrated in 1945 the utility of gamma globulin in reducing or ameliorating infectious hepatitis,[19] and questioned why it was not given to all of Krugman's subjects. Of note, Krugman was well aware of gamma globulin and had used it in an earlier hepatitis study.[20]

Beecher questioned the informational content provided to the parents in the informed consent process. Although Krugman repeatedly stated that parental permission was obtained, Beecher noted that 'nothing is said regarding what was told them [the parents] concerning the appreciable hazards involved'.[21] Specifically, Beecher was concerned as to whether parents were told that some children might develop potentially fatal cirrhosis. Although Joan Giles, a pediatrician who worked at Willowbrook throughout the experiments, claimed that she gave as full an explanation as she could, the information she is quoted as providing did not include the potentially serious risks.[22]

Beecher also questioned whether the parents were able to give voluntary consent. In 1954, parents were informed by letter that admission to Willowbrook was closed due to overcrowding. Shortly thereafter, parents received a second letter, advising them that there were vacancies in the hepatitis unit and that, if they would volunteer their children for that study, the children could be admitted.[23] According to Jack Hammond, the administrator of Willowbrook, this was not meant to be manipulative: 'Where do you find new admissions except by canvassing the people who have applied for admission?'[24] Nevertheless, public and professional criticism led to the cessation of this manner of recruitment.

A second study cited by Beecher that enrolled some pediatric subjects involved Triacetyloleandomycin (TriA), an antibiotic used to treat acne. Recent research had found that the drug caused more hepatic toxicity than originally thought. Ticktin and Zimmerman undertook their study to determine the incidence and type of hepatic dysfunction.[25] They enrolled fifty subjects, aged 13 to 39 years, who were residents of Laurel Children's Center (an institution for children who were 'mental defectives or juvenile delinquents') for two months or longer. The subjects were healthy except for acne, and were treated with TriA for three to four weeks. Blood tests were performed on enrollment, at two weeks, at completion of treatment, and at various intervals after the drug was discontinued. Two weeks after the beginning of TriA administration, over half of the patients had evidence of liver abnormalities that worsened with further treatment and resolved within weeks of discontinuing the treatment. Liver biopsies were performed on eight subjects who showed marked liver abnormalities (six of whom had symptoms). Four of the eight patients were given a 'challenge' dose of TriA and were subjected to repeat liver biopsy. Three of the four again developed liver dysfunction. Liver function returned to normal in all three within one week.

The study raises a number of ethical issues similar to the Willowbrook study, in that it enrolled institutionalized individuals, particularly children and those with mental retardation. Enrolling institutionalized children for acne studies may be even more troublesome than the hepatitis research because the knowledge generated from the hepatitis studies would be of particular relevance to institutionalized children whereas the acne studies would not. Fortunately there was no long-term damage, but as Beecher pointed out, '[a]n experiment is ethical or not at its inception, it does not become ethical post hoc—ends do not justify means.'[26]

A third study in Beecher's article involved eighteen children aged 3.5 months to 18 years of age who were to undergo surgery for congenital heart disease.[27] Eleven of the eighteen children would undergo an unnecessary thymectomy as part of the operation; the other seven would serve as controls. They would also undergo unnecessary skin homografts from an unrelated donor. The objective was to study the effect of thymectomy on skin homografts in immunologically competent children. As Beecher noted: 'Total thymectomy is occasionally, although not usually part of the primary cardiovascular surgery involved, and whereas it may not greatly add to the hazards of the necessary operation its eventual effects in children are not known.'[28] As such, the study raised ethical concerns because it subjected the children to the serious and unnecessary risks of thymectomy and skin grafts without any expected therapeutic benefit to the children.[29]

The fourth study to enroll children involved twenty-six healthy newborns (less than 48 hours old). The objective was to determine whether ureteral reflux can occur in the normal bladder.[30] The infants were catheterized and were radiographed while the bladder was filling and during voiding. Six weeks later their urine was reexamined; none had developed infection, although as Beecher notes, the potential long-term risks of the X-ray exposure were not known.[31]

Beecher's concerns were echoed and amplified by Maurice Pappworth, a consultant general physician in the UK who catalogued hundreds of unethical published studies in his book *Human Guinea Pigs: Experimentation on Man* (1967).[32] Pappworth devoted an entire chapter to examples of unethical pediatric research, mainly from the US and the UK.[33] The studies include two articles by British researchers published in the *Lancet* in October 1953. One study investigated the safety of giving large amounts of intravenous ammonium chloride to children to see whether it could be used for the relief of severe alkalosis.[34] The investigators enrolled five infants with pyloric stenosis who might benefit, and two infants with severe hydrocephalus and normal metabolic profiles as controls. The other study examined the relationship between diet and phenylketonuria (PKU).[35] These investigators enrolled a girl with PKU who had responded well to a special diet and was challenged with a large dose of phenylalanine without her mother's knowledge. Her blood and behavioral responses were compared with the responses of a healthy child who was also fed a diet with a large dose of phenylalanine. The former child's blood level and behavior dramatically worsened with the phenylalanine challenge, whereas the latter child's plasma phenylalanine level and behavior were not changed.[36]

The two studies evoked a letter of protest that was published in the next issue of the *Lancet*. Fisher lamented the 'use of normal children (or children suffering from some irrelevant disease) as controls in clinical research'.[37] He argued that children should not be exposed to any risk in medical research 'unless there is a reasonable chance, or at least a hope, that the child may benefit thereby'.[38]

Both sets of researchers responded. Bickel and Gerrard argued that the exposure of a healthy volunteer child subject to large amounts of phenyl-alanine was known to be harmless.[39] In defense of the ammonium chloride study, Holt argued that he was not in major disagreement with Fisher, but that he used a broader concept of benefit: 'no procedure should be carried out involving risk or discomfort without a reasonable chance of benefit to that child *or other children.*'[40] This revision changes the benefit: risk analysis from the individual to the group level. In a follow-up letter, Leys rejected the revision, arguing that research not designed with the sole intention of providing benefit to the individual can be performed only on competent adults who freely give their consent.[41]

The studies can also be criticized on other grounds. The ammonium chloride study can be criticized for its use of disabled children as controls merely because they were available.[42] The PKU study can be criticized for not seeking the mother's consent. The mother was not even informed that a challenge dose would be given. She was described as 'distressed that her daughter had lost in a few days all the ground gained in the previous ten months'.[43]

Other studies criticized by Pappworth included nontherapeutic cardiac catheterizations, both in children with cardiac disease (e.g., to show that active rheumatic carditis interferes with the functional efficiency of the heart, a fact already well established) and in children without cardiac defects (to determine normal pressures in the pulmonary artery during the first few months of life).[44] Pappworth also documented several studies investigating vesico-ureteric reflux in healthy infants published in the 1950s.[45] The vesico-ureteral study cited by Beecher was published in 1964.[46] The redundancy of the data makes it even more ethically questionable.

3. Ramsey and the Ethics of Nontherapeutic Research

In 1970, Beecher published *Research and the Individual*, a more comprehensive critique of current research practices.[47] He described the critique as one offered by an investigator and stated that there was a 'pressing need for a philosopher's approach, but only by one so wise that he can competently resolve the enormous complexities of the problems involved'.[48] The philosophical approach was provided that same year by Paul Ramsey, a moral theologian who had just spent a year as a visiting scholar at Georgetown Medical School. In 1970, Ramsey published an examination of the ethical problems in medicine, problems he described as consonant with (and only a particular case of) the ethics of a wider human community.[49] He argued that the major task of medical ethics 'is to reconcile the welfare of the individual with the welfare of mankind; both must be served'.[50] Ramsey was concerned that medical research had developed a momentum and life of its own. He believed that there could be situations where one would have to choose between knowledge and morality 'in opposition to our long-standing prejudice that the two must go together'.[51]

Ramsey argued that medicine and medical ethics demanded 'a determination of the rightness or wrongness of the action and not only of the good to be obtained ... Medical ethics is not solely a benefit-producing ethics even in regard to the individual patient, since he should not always be helped without his will.'[52] The patient's will was expressed by a free and adequately informed consent. In medical research, consent allows researcher and subject to become joint adventurers in a common cause and serves 'as a canon of loyalty expressive of the faithfulness-claims of persons in medical investigation,'[53] thereby placing 'an independent moral limit upon the fashion in which the rest of mankind can be made the ultimate beneficiary of these procedures'.[54]

Ramsey was not the first non-physician to venture into medical ethics. Over a decade earlier, Joseph Fletcher, another Protestant theologian, had published *Morals and Medicine*.[55] Fletcher analyzed ethical issues in health care from the patient's point of view. He argued that for individuals to act as responsible moral beings, they needed information to make an informed choice. In trying to understand why Fletcher did not stimulate dialogue but Ramsey did, Rothman argues:

[T]o bring outsiders into medical decision making, to have philosophers take a place at the bedside, in effect to substitute bioethics for medical ethics would require far more than one man adopting a new approach. It would demand nothing less than a revolution in public attitudes toward medical practitioners and medical institutions.[56]

As Rothman notes, such a revolution in attitudes was precisely what was occurring in the 1960s, epitomized by the patients' rights and civil rights movements.

Ramsey, like Fletcher and Beecher, placed great emphasis on informed consent. Ramsey argued that the need for consent raises particular problems for those individuals who cannot give consent, such as young children:

[C]hildren, who cannot give a mature and informed consent, should not be made the subjects of medical experimentation unless, other remedies having failed to relieve their grave illness, it is reasonable to believe that the administration of a drug as yet untested or insufficiently tested on human beings, or the performance of an untried operation, may further *the patient's own recovery*.[57]

Ramsey did not deny that parents had moral authority to consent on behalf of their children, but he argued that their moral authority was limited: 'no parent is morally competent to consent that his child shall be submitted to hazardous or other experiments having no diagnostic or therapeutic significance for the child himself.'[58] He noted that Beecher and Pappworth had been criticized for assuming that the failure to mention consent meant that the physicians failed to obtain it. Ramsey went further: it is not a question of whether the researchers obtained parental consent, but rather, 'the point is rather that morally no parent should consent—or be asked to consent to any such thing even if he is quite capable of doing so, and even if in fact his informed consent was obtained in all cases where this fact is not mentioned in the reports.'[59]

The problem, according to Ramsey, is that '[t]o attempt to consent for a child to be made an experimental subject is to treat a child as not a child. It is to treat him as if he were an adult person who has consented to become a joint adventurer.'[60] It is also to treat him solely as a means which violates the Kantian principle of respect for persons.[61] Thus, for Ramsey, research on children was ethical only if it had some relation to the child's own health and informed parental or guardian consent was obtained.[62] This is true even if there is no risk, or no discernible risk, because 'a subject can be wronged without being harmed'.[63] That is, even if the child did not have any interests diminished or defeated by his participation, the child's right not to be used as a means was abrogated. The child was wronged (his rights were violated) whether or not any interests were defeated.[64]

For Ramsey, then, parents must act as fiduciaries and can only authorize their child's participation in research that will promote the child's medical interests.[65] Duane Alexander, a pediatrician and director of the National Institute of Child Health and Human Development (NICHD) since the 1980s, writes about Ramsey's impact on pediatric research: 'Although this position did not receive wide support, it stimulated and stirred debate in the ethics community that brought the issue of children in research to the forefront.'[66]

A lawsuit filed in 1973 made the same claim as Ramsey: 'parents and guardians had no legal authority to consent to the participation of a child or a ward in nontherapeutic research irrespective of the degree of risk.'[67] James Neilsen was an attorney and faculty member at the University of California at San Francisco. As a member of the University's Committee on Human Experimentation, he opposed a protocol that would study the development of allergies and asthma in children whose families had a history of these disorders, as well as normal control subjects from families without an allergic history. The protocol involved drawing blood and administering pharmaceutical agents to the children. When the committee unanimously approved the study at a meeting at which Neilsen was not present, Neilsen sued the committee and his own university. Although the case was never decided, Alexander notes that 'it left investigators and research regulators shivering in their boots, and the shock waves it sent though the research community and the reaction and response it engendered in terms of regulations for protecting children in research cannot be overestimated.'[68]

The primary motivation for refuting Ramsey's position is consequentalistic: excluding children from research will have long-term negative consequences on the well-being of children in general. Ramsey did not deny the danger of prohibiting children from participating in all nontherapeutic research because it would harm children as a class, but his solution was to exhort researchers to 'sin bravely': the trustworthy researcher was the one who did 'not deny the moral force of the imperative he violates'.[69]

4. *The Debate Widens*

The National Commission was established in the 1970s to examine issues revolving around human subject protections. In the National Commission's report, *Research Involving Children*, the National Commission examined the issue of whether the participation of children in nontherapeutic research was morally permissible.[70] The National Commission examined Ramsey's position and counter-arguments that would permit the participation of children in some minimal risk nontherapeutic research.

One such argument was provided by Richard McCormick, a Catholic theologian. McCormick challenged Ramsey's arguments using a natural law approach. He argued, contra Ramsey, that parental consent 'is morally valid precisely insofar as it is a reasonable presumption of the child's wishes'.[71] McCormick held that there are 'certain identifiable valuables that we *ought* to support, attempt to realize, and never directly suppress because they are definitive of our flourishing and well-being.'[72] The child, then, would want to participate as a research subject because he ought to do so. That is, the child would choose to participate because

To pursue the good that is human life means not only to choose and support this value in one's own case, but also in the case of others when the opportunity arises. In other words, the individual *ought* also to take into account, realize, make efforts in behalf of the lives of others also, for we are social beings and the goods that define our growth and invite to it are goods that reside also in others.[73]

McCormick also objected to Ramsey's second argument, that using children as research subjects is contrary to the Kantian principle that persons should never be treated solely as a means, but always simultaneously as an ends, on the grounds that it presumes an atomistic view of humans. Humans are social beings whose good transcends their individual good. Participation as a research subject is consistent with treating the child as an end understood to mean a social being.[74]

Ramsey rebutted McCormick's arguments on the grounds that they were too broad and could require the participation of adults in research projects to which they do not give their consent.[75] While McCormick was willing to tolerate such enforced good Samaritanism,[76] most ethicists and legal scholars are not.

Robert Veatch sought to justify the participation of children by arguing that Ramsey's position takes a highly individualistic understanding of moral responsibility that denies the child's membership in a social community.[77] Although his position is similar to McCormick's, Veatch argues using the language of rights and consent rather than natural law. Veatch acknowledged the 'dangers of balancing individual rights with obligations to serve the common welfare are great especially in cases where consent cannot be used as a mechanism to judiciously waive those rights.'[78] Nevertheless, he argued that 'in cases of minimal risk when information to be obtained would be of great value and can be obtained in no other way, there must be some contribution to the general welfare which can be expected *without consent*.'[79] While Veatch would respect a child's dissent, he believes that where the subject cannot or does not refuse, parental permission should make participation acceptable 'it is reasonable to treat the individual, non-consenting subject as a means to an end, under very limited and circumscribed conditions', [80] Parental approval serves as the best check to make sure that individual rights are not unduly compromised. For Ramsey, the problem with this position is that it presumes a technological imperative at the expense of the respect (and possibly well-being) of the child by subjecting them to risk without consent.[81]

A third argument to support the participation of children in research was offered by Stephen Toulmin. He suggested that the argument should not begin with the question of what children ought to do. Rather, the argument should begin by considering whether there are any presumptions that children could not reasonably object to if they were capable of understanding what is at stake and of making a decision in their own right.[82] Victor Worsfold offered the other side of this argument. Rather than arguing that the child should be permitted to participate in research when he could not reasonably object to his participation, he argued that the child should be permitted to participate in research to which the reasonable child would approve in retrospect. Citing Rawls, he explained:

As we know less and less about a person, we act for him as we would act for ourselves from the standpoint of the original position. We try to get for him the things he presumably wants whatever else he wants. We must be able to argue that with the development or the recovery of his rational powers, the individual in question will accept our decision on his behalf and agree with us that we did the best thing for him.[83]

One problem with both Toulmin's and Worsfold's arguments is the ambiguity of what is reasonable, and how to accommodate an option that some parents would find reasonable and other parents would not.[84] Ramsey did not deny the value of the reasonable person standard, but he argued that it conflates the 'circumstances in which an informed and prudent adult would reasonably be expected to volunteer himself' as the standard for determining 'those circumstances in which a child may be volunteered by someone else'.[85] The reasonable person standard permits a parent to authorize a child's participation in an activity; it does not mean that the option is or ought to be required.

Whereas Ramsey sought to exclude all children from nontherapeutic research, McCormick, Veatch, Toulmin, and Worsfold sought to justify the morality of any child's participation in such research. Others have sought to refute Ramsey by finding a middle ground, arguing for the moral permissibility of allowing some children, such as older children who can express a preference, to participate as research subjects. For example, Beecher argued that parents can authorize a child's participation to promote the child's moral development: 'Parents have the obligation to inculcate into their children attitudes of unselfish service. One could hope that this might be extended to include participation in research for the public welfare, when it is important and there is no discernible risk.'[86] Similarly, Bartholome argued that parents can authorize their child's participation in order to promote their children's moral education.[87]

Both Beecher and Bartholome believed that parental consent was necessary but not sufficient. Beecher argued for both the child's and the parents' informed consent and as such, only permitted children over the age of 14 to serve as research subjects.[88] Bartholome took a more liberal view and allowed for the participation of children with their parents' consent if the children could give assent.[89] By assent, Bartholome meant that the child could meaningfully agree to participate, even though the agreement was not legally binding. The purpose of procuring the children's assent was to demonstrate respect for their evolving personhood and to show that they were not being treated solely as a means.

One objection to the positions of Beecher and Bartholome is offered by Ackerman. Ackerman agrees that parents can authorize their children's participation to serve moral goals. In fact, he contends that parents have a *moral duty* to guide the activities of their children because children rely upon adults for this guidance. Respect for a child requires that parents 'carefully direct his "choices" '.[90] However, unlike Beecher and Bartholome, Ackerman argues that requiring the child's assent makes a mockery both of our duties to children and of their limited present-day capabilities to act autonomously: 'We cannot decide how to intervene in a child's life by projecting what he will come to approve or accept. For what he will come to accept is partly a product of the interventions we make.'[91] In addition, he states that children are usually ill-prepared to refuse requests by their physicians and parents.[92] Instead, Ackerman argues that parents alone can and must decide whether their children should participate as research subjects.

If Ackerman is correct, then we are back to the original positions of Ramsey and McCormick: either it is or it is not morally permissible for parents to decide whether to enroll (any) child in low-risk nontherapeutic research. Ackerman argues that it is morally permissible, but contra McCormick, his argument is based on a broader view of parental responsibility, including the responsibility of teaching children to be contributors to the moral community.[93] Elsewhere, I too have argued that Ramsey's conception of parental responsibility as fiduciary is too narrow and that parents can and should be allowed to enroll their children (of all ages) in minimal-risk research.[94] In brief, I have argued that parental autonomy should be respected unless their decision is disrespectful of the child's developing personhood. Parents who value participation in social projects like advancing science may try to inculcate similar values into their child. Even if the child never shares in these goals, they are goals which responsible parents may try to inculcate.

5. The National Commission and the Federal Regulations regarding Human Subject Protections

The controversy initiated by Ramsey regarding the moral permissibility of the participation of children in nontherapeutic research continued to be debated in the moral, legal, and medical communities as attempts to write federal guidelines began. In 1973, the National Institutes of Health (NIH) convened an outside advisory group of researchers, ethicists, and lawyers to discuss the issues and provide recommendations for research generally and for research involving certain vulnerable populations. Draft regulations for research in general and for research involving children were published in the fall of 1973,[95] but as Alexander explains, '[s]oon thereafter it became clear that there would be a national commission, so no further action was taken until the commission made its recommendations.'[96]

The National Commission published over twenty reports and appendices in the 1970s, the most oft-cited of which is the *Belmont Report*.[97] The National Commission's report, *Research Involving Children*, was published one year earlier.[98] Based on the National Commission's reports, the Department of Health, Education and Welfare (DHEW) proposed regulations in 1978 and 1979.[99] These regulations were finalized in the early 1980s by the newly reorganized Department of Health and Human Services (DHHS).[100] Subpart A of these regulations focuses on human subject protections generally. It is known as the Common Rule because it has been adopted by sixteen federal agencies and departments of the US government, and was most recently revised in 1991.[101] Subpart D provides additional protections for research involving children, and minor revisions were made in 1991.[102]

Although the National Commission acknowledged the need for research on children, it also realized that 'the vulnerability of children, which arises out of their dependence and immaturity raises questions about the ethical acceptability of involving them in research'.[103] To minimize these problems, the Commission established strict criteria that research must satisfy. At a minimum, these criteria require that:

1. The research is scientifically sound and significant.

2. Where appropriate, studies have been conducted first on animals and adult humans, then on older children, prior to involving infants.

3. Risks are minimized by using the safest procedures consistent with sound research design and by using procedures performed for diagnostic or treatment purposes whenever feasible.

4. Adequate provisions are made to protect the privacy of children and their parents and to maintain confidentiality of data.

5. Subjects will be selected in an equitable manner.

6. The conditions of all applicable subsequent conditions are met, including adequate provisions being made for the assent of the child and permission of their parents or guardians.[104]

The National Commission recommended additional criteria depending upon the level of risk and harm that the research entailed, the risk/benefit ratio of the proposed project, and the comparative risk/benefit ratio of the alternatives. Local institutional review boards (IRBs) would be created to ensure that these safeguards were fulfilled, including the adequacy of the consent process.[105] These guidelines, particularly the requirement to conduct, when possible, studies enrolling less vulnerable populations first, served to restrict the participation of children in medical research.

6.   From Protection to Access

The justification for the additional guidelines for child subjects was the child's need for protection. This focus on protection, however, may partly explain the underfunding and understudy of the health issues unique to children.[106] In the early 1990s, various governmental agencies shifted from an exclusive focus on protecting children from research risks to promoting greater access by children in research. Two reasons for these policy changes are: (1) the concern of the pediatric community that many pharmaceuticals and therapies prescribed to children had never been tested in children;[107] and (2) the response of the Food and Drug Administration (FDA) to the politicization of drug testing and approval by AIDS activists.[108] The AIDS activists successfully challenged a system they deemed too slow and they secured passage of an accelerated approval process.[109] However, the lag time between FDA approval of new drugs, often based solely on adult trials, and the initiation of clinical trials in children results in a persistent delay of pediatric drug information.[110]

One of the early attempts to improve pediatric drug information came in 1994, when the FDA published specific requirements on content and format of pediatric labeling for human prescription drugs.[111] The FDA required drug manufacturers to survey existing data and determine whether those data were sufficient to support additional pediatric use information in the labeling of their drugs. The response was disappointing. New labeling proposals for approximately 430 drugs and biologic supplements were submitted, of which 75% did not improve pediatric use information. More than half simply requested the addition: 'Safety and effectiveness in pediatric patients have not been established.'[112]

An FDA ruling in 1979 required specific pediatric labeling information, particularly if the drug were approved for a pediatric indication. As the FDA noted, however, the rule was self-limited in that 'it neither requires nor is intended to require that studies be performed to develop data for inclusion in prescription drug labeling'.[113] If there were no approved pediatric use, the statement 'Safety and effectiveness in pediatric patients have not been established' was sufficient.[114]

The 1994 FDA ruling went further than the 1979 ruling in several ways. First, the agency acknowledged the difficulties of conducting classic placebo-controlled trials in pediatric patients and allowed for some extrapolation of adult data if 'the FDA found that the course of the disease and the drug's effects are sufficiently similar'.[115] In addition, the FDA maintained its legal authority to compel new pediatric drug studies and required drug sponsors to submit supplemental applications of pediatric information if supported by available data. This change not withstanding, the FDA again clarified that the 1994 rule 'does not add a new requirement that sponsors carry out new pediatric studies'.[116]

In June 1996, the American Academy of Pediatrics (AAP) and NICHD sponsored a workshop on the 'Inclusion of Children in Clinical Research'[117] where it was suggested that current policy may be too little, too late.[118] Part of the support for increasing pediatric participation in research, particularly in pharmaceutical research, is that while major advances have been made during the past half century in adult medicine, only much more modest advances have been made in pediatrics. Almost three decades earlier, Shirkey expressed his frustration with the lack of financial support by government and industry for pediatric drug investigation.[119] Consider, for example, that more than 80% of drugs prescribed to children have never been tested on them.[120] The danger is that unless these drugs are tested on children, there are neither data for safety or efficacy nor dosing guidelines, and every child remains an experiment. Policies promulgated by different government agencies in the late 1990s attempted to overcome this gap.

The FDA proposed the Pediatric Rule in 1997 to increase the number of drugs and biological products for which there is adequate pediatric use information.[121] Finalized in 1998 and effective beginning 1 April 1999, the Pediatric Rule required manufacturers of certain new drugs and biological products to conduct studies to provide adequate pediatric labeling.[122] The Pediatric Rule was not enforced because of the success of the Food and Drug Administration Modernization Act (FDAMA) passed by Congress in 1997.[123] FDAMA provided strong economic incentives for conducting pediatric studies by offering pharmaceutical companies an additional six months of patent exclusivity for testing of medications in children. In January 2002, the law was reenacted for another five years as the Best Pharmaceuticals for Children Act.[124] What studies are needed to earn additional exclusivity are negotiated and may involve pharmacokinetic testing or a phase III clinical trial. Exclusivity can be granted even if the results of the studies are negative or inconclusive.[125] According to a January 2001 status report to Congress, FDAMA has been highly effective in generating pediatric studies on many drugs, although some categories of drugs and some age groups remain inadequately studied.[126]

Although not enforced, the Pediatric Rule was suspended in March 2002 in response to a lawsuit.[127] However, it was quickly reinstated in April 2002 'after members of Congress complained that the FDA was injuring children's health and introduced legislation to force the agency to reinstate the mandate'.[128] In October 2002, the US District Court for the District of Columbia struck down the Pediatric Rule on the grounds that it exceeded the FDA's statutory authority.[129] Congress passed the Pediatric Rule as federal legislation in November 2003.[130]

Whereas the Pediatric Rule requires testing of all new pharmaceuticals, the incentives under FDAMA and BPCA refer only to pharmaceuticals that are still under patent. Pharmaceutical companies do not have incentives to study drugs that are approved but no longer under patent. For this reason, the BPCA provided for government sponsorship of pediatric trials on off-patent drugs. In January 2003, the DHHS announced \$25 million in new government support for research on twelve drugs commonly prescribed for children.[131]

The NIH also issued new policy guidelines in 1998 to increase the enrollment of children in research studies.[132] All NIH-funded research must now include a plan for the inclusion of children, unless there is good justification to exclude them. The NIH encourages compliance by stating on the Frequently Asked Questions (FAQ) section of its Web site that the exclusion of children may affect the priority score given to determine grant funding.[133]

In 1999 and 2000, the Office for the Protection of Research Risks [now known as the Office for Human Research Protections (OHRP)] suspended research at a number of major universities for failure of researchers and institutions to protect human subjects.[134] Possibly due to concerns of institutional reprisal if federal oversight were not sought, the OHRP received over two dozen requests for 407 panels in 2001.[135] CFR §46.407 permits research involving children that cannot be approved locally to be reviewed nationally by a panel of experts convened by the Secretary of DHHS.[136] Although CFR §46.407 had been invoked quite infrequently prior to the year 2000, eleven panels were convened between February 2001 and October 2003, and public comments were sought for six.[137]

In October 2000, Congress passed the Children's Health Act that included a Pediatric Research Initiative (Title X).[138] The legislation was designed to make pediatric research—research specifically addressed at children's illnesses and conditions—a high priority. Nevertheless, although funding for pediatric research is increasing, it is increasing at a slower rate than medical research generally; in recent years, pediatric research has slipped from 12.5% to about 12% of the NIH budget.[139]

The Children's Health Act also provided specific instructions intended to ensure that pediatric subjects would continue to have additional protections. It required that within six months of its passage the Secretary of DHHS 'shall require that all research involving children that is conducted, supported, or regulated by DHHS be in compliance with Subpart D'.[140] In order to comply with this policy, the FDA wrote interim rules in April 2001 that adopted most of Subpart D for all research subject to its regulatory authority.[141] The Act also required DHHS to conduct a review of Subpart D and to consider 'any modifications necessary to ensure the adequate and appropriate protection of children participating in research'.[142] In May 2001, the report was promulgated.[143] It found that 'the current DHHS regulations under Subpart D of 45 CFR Part 46 are sound, effective and well-crafted ... Furthermore, these regulations are robust and flexible, and as such, are useful and appropriate for regulating all types of research involving children as subjects, including biomedical and behavioral research'. [144] In that vein, it recommended that Subpart D not be modified and that DHHS should provide detailed guidance including the clarification of certain terms such as 'minimal risk', 'prospect of direct benefit', and 'minor increase over minimal risk'. It also recommend guidance on whether payment may be provided to children involved in research or their parents.[145]

The responsibility to provide further guidance on these topics was assigned to the Institute of Medicine (IOM) in the Best Pharmaceuticals for Children Act of 2002.[146] The IOM report was released in March 2004.[147] The report seeks to promote access, but it also acknowledges that '[i]n some cases, ethical standards will preclude some otherwise desirable research'.[148] The IOM committee offers two controversial recommendations that could promote access. First, the IOM committee argues in support of payment to children who are subjects in pediatric research (see Chapter 8). Second, the IOM committee argues in support of permitting parental waivers of consent for certain types of research (see Chapter 5).

The actions of Congress, the FDA, NIH, and OHRP in the last decade have been designed to promote greater participation of children in research, despite general concerns regarding human subject protections more generally.[149] The reaffirmation of Subpart D under the Children's Health Act and the convening of 407 review panels by OHRP are signs that the policies to promote greater access of children in research can be accomplished without necessarily undermining the additional protections that were recommended for pediatric subjects by the National Commission and implemented in the federal regulations.

7.   *International Research Ethics*

The World Medical Association (WMA) was founded in September 1947 when physicians from twenty-seven different countries met at the First General Assembly in Paris.[150] The WMA adopted the Declaration of Geneva, an update of the Hippocratic Oath in 1948,[151] and the International Code of Medical Ethics in 1949.[152] In 1962, the *British Medical Journal* (BMJ) published a draft code of ethics on human experimentation that was presented to the General Assembly of the WMA in September 1961.[153] The draft code provided general principles regarding human subjects and examined the different considerations necessary for 'experiments for the benefit of the patient (i.e. therapeutic research) and 'experiments conducted solely for the acquisition of knowledge' (i.e. nontherapeutic research). It was revised and adopted in 1964.[154] As is true of the Nuremberg Code, the Declaration of Helsinki sought to minimize risk, and to ensure that the importance of the objective outweighs the inherent risks and burdens to the subject. In its first revision (1975), the Declaration of Helsinki went further than the Nuremberg Principles in the absolute respect owed to each individual subject: 'In medical research on human subjects, considerations related to the well-being of the human subject should take precedence over the interests of science and society.'[155] A utilitarian calculation that the benefits outweigh the risks to society was necessary but not sufficient; there was also a need to focus on the well-being of each individual subject.

Although the Nuremberg Principles are silent regarding the ethics of children in human experimentation, other countries and international organizations have attempted to examine the ethical issues and develop policies regarding the role of children in human experimentation. In its draft code, the WMA specifically addressed several questions raised if children are to participate in research: (1) whose consent is necessary?; (2) which children can morally participate in research?; and (3) in what types of research can they morally participate?[156] The WMA concluded that parents or lawful guardians should make decisions on behalf of their children and that the informed consent of parents or guardians was necessary. Thus, children in institutions and not under the care of relatives should not be the subjects of human experimentation. With respect to nontherapeutic research, the draft code specifically stated that 'persons incapable of giving consent because of age ... should not be used as subjects.'[157]

There were significant changes from the draft code of 1962 and the Declaration of Helsinki adopted by the WMA in 1964. Two of these changes relate to research on children. First, the ethics of involving institutionalized subjects was no longer mentioned. Second, the WMA specifically allowed for parents or legal guardians to consent for their children's participation in therapeutic and nontherapeutic research.[158] In all revisions, the Declaration of Helsinki permits the participation of children in both therapeutic and nontherapeutic research. More recent formulations of the Declaration make clear that children 'should not be included in research unless the research is necessary to promote the health of the population represented and this research cannot instead be performed on legally competent persons'.[159] In addition, the Declaration of Helsinki now requires both the consent of the legally authorized representative and the assent of the child when feasible.[160] Unlike the US federal regulations, the Declaration of Helsinki does not state if there are particular types of research (e.g., therapeutic research) in which the child's dissent may be overridden.

Other countries have guidelines regarding the participation of children that are more restrictive than those in the US, although they also evolved in the 1990s to allow greater access. In the UK, the Medical Research Council (MRC) explicitly stated in 1962–3 that according to English Law, all children can participate in therapeutic research but children younger than 12 years were not permitted to participate in nontherapeutic research.[161] For children above the age of 12 years, participation in nontherapeutic research was permitted but required the child's full informed consent. Parental permission was also recommended.[162] Beecher contacted the MRC to provide legal citations for their position. Sir Harvey Druitt KCB responded to Beecher by explaining that the MRC statement was based upon his advice although he could not cite any statute or case law.[163] Beecher was not convinced and Curran and Beecher concluded that

There should be strong reasons in professional judgment for the use of immature children (those under 14 years of age) in any clinical investigation where there is no direct benefit intended for the child. However such involvement should not be ruled out as illegal and unethical in all circumstances. Neither American nor English laws demands such a flat and sweeping condemnation.[164]

By 1980, three additional British organizations had promulgated guidelines regarding the participation of children in research. They are more liberal than the MRC statement of 1962–3.[165] The British Paediatric Association (BPA) began its guidelines with four premises, one of which rejected the MRC's position on nontherapeutic research: 'nontherapeutic research' is 'not necessarily either unethical or illegal'.[166]

In 1986, the Institute of Medical Ethics (UK) Working Group on the Ethics of Clinical Research Investigations (Working Group) proposed new recommendations.[167] Their recommendations are quite similar to (and refer frequently to) the 1977 National Commission report *Research Involving Children*. The prime concern of the Working Group was that research should not be 'against the interests of any individual child'.[168] This is in sharp contrast with the MRC requirement that research participation needs to be in *the best interest* of each particular child.[169] However, Nicholson *et al.* argued that children should only be subjects if there is a specific and demonstrable need to perform the research on children and no other route to the relevant knowledge is available.[170] In addition, new procedures were to be tested on animals and adults first.

Like the US National Commission, the UK Working Group chose the age of 7 as the age at which a child's assent must be sought.[171] While the Working Group opined that parents should be allowed to override the refusal of assent by the child under age 14 for therapeutic research, it argued that nontherapeutic research should require the child's assent.[172] Nontherapeutic research for children under age 7 was not considered. For children over age 14, the Working Group argued that their consent was binding for both therapeutic and nontherapeutic research.[173] In addition, it recommended that nontherapeutic research procedures should not be carried out if, using the language of the National Commission, they involve more than a minor increase over minimal risk to any individual child subject.[174]

Revised guidelines for the ethical conduct of medical research involving children were issued by the MRC in 1991,[175] and by the BPA [now the Royal College of Paediatrics and Child Health (RCPCH)] in 1992 [176] and 2000.[177] All three statements reaffirm a preference for doing research on adults. Regarding the participation of children in nontherapeutic research, both of the revised RCPCH statements state that '[a] research procedure that is not intended directly to benefit the child subject is not necessarily either unethical or illegal.'[178] The MRC used the language of the Working Group stating that nontherapeutic research could be ethical if it were 'not against [the child's] interests'.[179] All recommend procuring the assent of the child for all research even when it is not legally required (therapeutic research). The RCPCH statements also recommended against any financial inducements to families, although it permitted expenses to be paid.[180]

Although the British guidelines are more protective than the US guidelines, they are evolving to permit greater access, a policy evolution that one British sociologist, Priscilla Alderson, notes has not been morally examined.[181]

8. *Conclusion: Balancing Access and Protection*

The new policies have encouraged increased pediatric pharmacological testing and have led to some improved pediatric labeling.[182] In Chapter 13, however, I will show some disturbing evidence that the new policies are encouraging the participation of children in research even when the researchers do not plan to do subset analyses, thereby exposing children subjects to risks without providing benefits to children as a class.

In *Strangers at the Bedside*, Rothman shows that many of the research reforms of the 1960s and 1970s that provided greater protection to research subjects were spurred on by the cultural and political changes of the era.[183] Changes in policy and practice since the 1990s reflect a change in attitude from the need to protect persons from research to the need to provide access in response to the cultural and political events surrounding the AIDS crisis. Although US policies regarding the participation of children in research allow greater access than the guidelines and recommendations for children in research in the UK and Europe, one can see a similar trend towards increased access in the guidelines in the UK as well.

Whereas the historical concern was that justice required equitable selection of research subjects to share the research burden; the focus is now on ensuring equity to share the benefits. It is not clear, however, that the data support the decision to abandon the more cautious approach. The clinical AIDS trials of the 1980s, in which only research subjects had access to potentially life-saving medication, are not the archetypical model for medical research. Rather, much research is nontherapeutic, and even therapeutic research is not necessarily designed to promote the medical well-being of *all* the subjects. For example, many clinical trials of 'me-too drugs' are designed as placebo-controlled trials, such that subjects are not even ensured standard of care. I discuss this further in Chapter 13.

In the *Belmont Report*, the National Commission wrote that 'it can be considered a matter of social justice that there is an order of preference in the selection of classes of subjects (e.g., adults before children)'. [184] No compelling moral argument has been offered to justify abandoning this principle. Research involving children should be performed, when possible, only after safety and efficacy studies have been done on animals and adults, and only when such studies are necessary to improve the practice of pediatric medicine. Children should not be enrolled in research merely to expedite the accrual process, but only when the research is specifically designed to provide general pediatric information.

Throughout this book I argue that policies and practices regarding the participation of children must focus primarily on minimizing risks.[185] I will offer specific recommendations to revise Subpart D of the federal regulations to provide greater protection where it is necessary and to remove obstacles that do not provide additional protection but interfere with access. My goal is to ensure appropriate safeguards without compromising access unnecessarily. However, sometimes human subject protections will retard progress. At other times, these protections may make scientific data unattainable. That is the price we must pay to ensure respect for human dignity.[186]

References

1. Beecher, H. K., 'Ethics and Clinical Research', *New England Journal of Medicine*, 274 (1966), 1354–60.
2. Nuremberg Code. See Trials of War Criminals Before the Nuremberg Military Tribunals under Control Council Law No. 10, vol. II. Washington DC: US Government Printing Office, 1948. On the web at: http://www.ushmm.org/research/doctors/codeptx.htm.
3. Rothman, D. J. *Strangers at the Bedside: A History of How Law and Bioethics Transformed Medical Decision Making.* New York: Basic Books, 1991, 62.
   Renewed interest in human experimentation in the 1960s was not unique to the US. According to Nicholson, a deputy director of the Institute of Medical Ethics (UK), public interest in the surveillance of medical experiments in the UK was renewed in 1962 following the thalidomide disaster. See Nicholson, R. H. (ed.), *Medical Research with Children: Ethics, Law and Practice.* Oxford: Oxford University Press, 1986, 3. It led to a statement by the Medical Research Council (UK) in its annual report for 1962–3 entitled 'Responsibility in Investigations on Human Subjects'. See Medical Research Council (MRC) 'Responsibility in Investigations on Human Subjects', *Report of the Medical Research Council for the Year 1962–63.* London UK: Her Majesty's Secretary Office (HMSO), 1964, 21–5. Reprinted in Beecher, H. K. *Research and the Individual*, Boston, MA: Little, Brown & Co, 1970, 262–7. Of note, M. H. Pappworth, a British physician, published *Human Guinea Pigs*, a compendium of hundreds of unethical research studies published in the medical literature the year after Beecher's expose in the *New England Journal of Medicine*. See Pappworth, M. H., *Human Guinea Pigs: Experimentation on Man.* London, UK: Routledge & Kegan Paul Ltd, 1967, reprinted by Penguin Books Ltd, Harmondsworth, Middx., UK, 1969.
4. Lederer, S. E., and Grodin, M. A., 'Historical Overview: Pediatric Experimentation', in M. A. Grodin and L. H. Glantz (eds.), *Children as Research Subjects: Science, Ethics, & Law.* New York: Oxford University Press, 1994, 4.
5. Hess, A. F., 'The Use of a Series of Vaccines in the Prophylaxis and Treatment of an Epidemic of Pertussis', *Journal of the American Medical Association*, 63 (1914), 1007 as cited in Lederer and Grodin, 'Historical Overview', 6.
6. Swedish physician. Humane Society. *Human Vivisection: Foundlings Cheaper than Animals.* Washington, DC.: Humane Society, undated in Lederer and Grodin, 'Historical Overview', 12.
7. Lederer and Grodin, 'Historical Overview', 19.

8. The phrase is often attributed to H. Shirkey. Shirkey, H., 'Therapeutic Orphans', *Journal of Pediatrics*, 72 (1968), 119–20.

9. Beecher, 'Ethics and Clinical Research'.

10. The full citations are reprinted in Appendix A of Rothman, *Strangers*, at 263–5.

11. Krugman, S., Ward, R., Giles, J. P., Bodansky, O., and Jacobs, A. M., 'Infectious Hepatitis: Detection of Virus during the Incubation Period and in Clinically Inapparent Infection', *New England Journal of Medicine*, 261 (1959), 729–34. This is case study 16 in Beecher's 'Ethics and Clinical Research'.

12. See, e.g., Ward, R., Krugman, S., Giles, J. P., Jacobs. A. M., and Bodansky, O., 'Infectious Hepatitis: Studies of its Natural History and Prevention', *New England Journal of Medicine*, 258 (1958), 407–16; Krugman, S., Ward, R., Giles, J. P., and Jacobs, A. M., 'Infectious Hepatitis: Studies on the Effect of Gamma Globulin and on the Incidence of Inapparent Infection', *Journal of the American Medical Association*, 174 (1960), 823–30; and Krugman, S., and Ward, R., 'Infectious Hepatitis: Current Status of Prevention with Gamma Globulin', *Yale Journal of Biology and Medicine*, 34 (1961/2), 329–39.

13. Krugman *et al.*, 'Infectious Hepatitis: Detection'.

14. Beecher is citing the 'International Code of Medical Ethics' passed by the General Assembly of the World Medical Association (WMA), London, 1949. Reprinted in Beecher, *Research and the Individual*, 236–7, hereinafter cited as 'International Code of Medical Ethics'.

   Of note, the Declaration of Helsinki provided ethical guidelines for clinical research. It was adopted by the WMA in 1964, although draft guidelines had existed since 1962. In both versions, the idea that medical research must benefit the patient was incorporated from the International Code of Medical Ethics with minimal modification. See WMA, Ethical Committee, 'Draft Code of Ethics on Human Experimentation', *British Medical Journal*, 2 (1962), 1119 [hereinafter cited as Draft Code]; and 18th WMA, 'Declaration of Helsinki: Recommendations Guiding Doctors in Clinical Research', adopted in Helsinki, Finland 1964 as reprinted in Beecher, *Research and the Individual*, 277–8 [hereinafter cited as 18th WMA, Declaration of Helsinki].

15. Beecher, 'Ethics and Clinical Research', 1358.

16. See, e.g., 'Studies with Children Backed on Medical, Ethical Grounds', *The Medical Tribune*, 20 February 1967, 1 & 23, 23; and Krugman, S. 'The Willowbrook Hepatitis Studies Revisited: Ethical Aspects', *Reviews of Infectious Diseases*, 8 (1986), 157–62.

17. Krugman, 'Ethical Aspects', 158–9.

18. Ibid. See also 'Studies with Children'.

19. Stokes, J. Jr., and Neefe, J. R., 'Prevention and Attenuation of Infectious Hepatitis by Gamma Globulin: Preliminary Note', *Journal of the American Medical Association*, 127 (1945), 144 as cited by Beecher, *Research and the Individual*, 124.

20. Ward *et al.*, 'Infectious Hepatitis'.

21. Beecher, 'Ethics and Clinical Research', 1358.

22. Beecher, *Research and the Individual*, 125 commenting on the interview with Dr Joan Giles from 'Studies with Children' 23.

23. Beecher, *Research and the Individual*, 126.
24. Jack Hammond cited in 'Studies with Children', 23.
25. Ticktin, H. E., and Zimmerman, H. J., 'Hepatic Dysfunction and Jaundice in Patients Receiving Triaceyloleandomycin', *New England Journal of Medicine*, 267 (1962), 964–8. This is case study 4 in Beecher's 'Ethics and Clinical Research'.
26. Beecher, 'Ethics and Clinical Research', 1360.
27. Zollinger, R. M., Lindem, M. C., Filler, R. M., Corson, J. M., and Wilson, R. E., 'Effect of Thymectomy on Skin-Homograft Survival in Children', *New England Journal of Medicine*, 270 (1964), 707–10. This is case study 6 in Beecher's 'Ethics and Clinical Research'.
28. Beecher, 'Ethics and Clinical Research', 1357.
29. Of note, Beecher was not the first to question the ethics of this study. In response to its publication in 1964, Dr Byron Waksman wrote a letter to the *New England Journal of Medicine* questioning whether the risks were sufficiently offset by the usefulness of the data that could be obtained, and whether 'the long-term hazards, unknown at present, were duly noted and called to the subjects' attention', Waksman, B., 'Thymus Experimentation', *New England Journal of Medicine*, 270 (1964), 1018–19, 1019. Waksman's letter led to an editorial in the same issue which asked, 'How far is it morally proper to go in using human beings for experimental purposes and under what conditions?' The editors stated that '[t]he question is especially disturbing when it involves children...', 'The Ethics of Human Experimentation', *New England Journal of Medicine*, 270 (1964), 1014–15, 1014.

    Zollinger *et al.* responded. They clarified their methodology stating that they 'did not create thymectomized patients but merely chose patients who had total thymectomy as a necessary part of aortic exposure during cardiac surgery'. They noted that the skin-homograft donors were chosen carefully to minimize the risk of hepatitis, and that none of the subjects had developed hepatitis, Zollinger, R. M. Jr., Lidem, M. C. Jr., Filler, R. M., Corson, J. M., and Wilson, R. E., 'Ethics of Thymus Experimentation', *New England Journal of Medicine*, 270 (1964), 1314.

    Clearly their response is ethically inadequate. Although none of the subjects developed hepatitis, good results do not justify unethical means. In this vein, the effect of thymectomy on skin graft survival is also ethically irrelevant. The study found no difference in skin homograft survival between those children who underwent thymectomy and those who did not (Zollinger *et al.*, 'Effect of Thymectomy'). The researchers also did not address the consent issue raised by Waksman about whether the parents understood the additional risks that the research imposed. Consent is not mentioned in the original article nor in the authors' response.
30. Lich, R. Jr., Howerton, L. W. Jr., Goode, L. S., and Davis, L. A., 'The Ureterovesical Junction of the Newborn', *Journal of Urology*, 1964; 92: 436–8. This is case study 22 in Beecher's article, 'Ethics and Clinical Research'.
31. Beecher, 'Ethics and Clinical Research', 1359.
32. Pappworth, *Guinea Pigs*. All page numbers refer to the Penguin Books publication (1969).

33. Pappworth, *Guinea Pigs*, ch. 1, 'Experiments on Infants and Children', 47–61.
34. Doxiadis, S. A., Goldfinch, M. K., and Holt, K. S., 'Alkalosis in Infants: Treatment by Intravenous Infusion of Ammonium Chloride', *Lancet*, ii (1953), 801–4.
35. Bickel, H., Gerrard, J., and Hickmans, E. M., 'Preliminary Communication: Influence of Phenylalanine Intake on Phenylketonuria', *Lancet*, ii (1953), 812–13.
36. Ibid.
37. Fisher, R. E. W., 'Controls', *Lancet*, ii (1953), 993.
38. Ibid.
39. Bickel, H., and Gerrard, J., 'In reply: Controls', *Lancet*, ii (1953), 993.
40. Holt, K. S., 'In reply: Controls', *Lancet*, ii (1953), 993. Italics in original.
41. Leys, D., 'Ethical Standards in Clinical Research', *Lancet*, ii (1953); 1044.
42. The selection of disabled children as controls was not, on my reading, invidious discrimination against disabled children per se, but rather a selection of convenience. Pappworth discusses the common practice of using hospitalized patients as controls for research on conditions unrelated to their hospitalization because of their accessibility. See Pappworth, *Guinea Pigs*. ch. 10, 'Patients as Controls', 127–57.
43. Bickel *et al.*, 'Preliminary Communication', 812.
44. Pappworth, *Guinea Pigs*, 50–5.
45. Ibid., 59–61. The studies were all published in the *Journal of Urology* between 1953 and 1960.
46. See Lich *et al.*, 'Uretovesical' cited as case 22 in Beecher's 'Ethics and Clinical Research'.
47. Beecher, *Research and the Individual*.
48. Ibid., 10.
49. Ramsey, P., *The Patient as Person*. New Haven, CT: Yale University Press, 1970, xi.
50. Ibid., xiv.
51. Ibid., xvi–xv citing Scanlan, J. P., 'The Morality of Deception in Experiments', *Bucknell Review*, 13 (1965) at 26.
52. Ibid., 2.
53. Ibid., 10.
54. Ibid., 2.
55. Fletcher, J., *Morals and Medicine*. Princeton, NJ: Princeton University Press, 1954.
56. Rothman, *Strangers*, 107.
57. Ramsey, *Patient as Person*, 12–13.
58. Ibid., 13.
59. Ibid., 14.
60. Ibid., 14.
61. Ibid., 35 Kant's principle of respect for persons states: 'Act in such a way that you treat humanity, whether in your own person or in the person of another, always at the same time as an end and never simply as a means', Kant, I., *Grounding for the Metaphysics of Morals* (1785) translated by J. W. Ellington. Indianapolis, IN: Hackett Publishing Co., 1981, para. 429.
62. Ramsey, *Patient as Person*, 20.
63. Ibid., 39.

64. Feinberg, J., *Harm to Others: The Moral Limits of the Criminal Law*. New York: Oxford University Press, 1984, 33–5.
65. Ramsey, *Patient as Person*, 13.
66. Alexander, D., 'Foreword: Regulation of Research with Children: The Evolution from Exclusion to Inclusion', *Journal of Health Care Law and Policy*, 6 (2002), 1–13, 2.
67. Ibid., 3 citing Nielsen v. Regents of the University of California *et al.*, No 665–049 Civ. 8–9 (Super Ct. San Francisco, Cal., 23 Aug. 1973).
68. Ibid., 4.
69. Ramsey, P., 'The Enforcement of Morals: Non-Therapeutic Research on Children', *Hastings Center Report*, 6 (August 1976), 21–30, 21 citing Ramsey P., 'Medical Progress and Canons of Loyalty to Experimental Subjects', *Proceedings of Conference on Biological Revolution/Theological Impact* sponsored by the Institute for Theological Encounter with Science and Technology, Fordyce House, St Louis, Missouri (6–8 April 1973), 51–77.
70. The National Commission's discussion can be found in: National Commission for the Protection of Human Subjects of Biomedical and Behavioral Research, *Report and Recommendations: Research Involving Children*. Washington DC: US Government Printing Office, 1977, DHEW Publication No. (OS) 77–0004, 94–121.
71. McCormick, R. A., 'Proxy Consent in the Experimentation Situation', *Perspectives in Biology and Medicine*, 18 (Autumn, 1974), 2–23, 11.
72. Ibid., 9.
73. Ibid., 12.
74. McCormick, R. A., 'Experimentation in Children: Sharing in Sociality', *Hastings Center Report*. 6 (December 1976), 41–6, 43.
75. Ramsey, P., 'Children as Research Subject: A Reply', *Hastings Center Report* 7 (April 1977), 40–1, 40.
76. See McCormick, 'Sharing in Sociality', 42.
77. Veatch, R. M., 'Three Theories of Informed Consent: Philosophical Foundations and Policy Implications' in the National Commission for the Protection of Human Subjects of Biomedical and Behavioral Research, *The Belmont Report: Ethical Principles and Guidelines for the Protection of Human Subjects of Research*, Appendix vol. II. Washington DC: US Government Printing Office, section 26, 26–41.
78. Ibid., 26–41.
79. Ibid., 26–41. Italics in the original.
80. Ibid., 26–42.
81. Ramsey, *Patient as Person*, xvi–xv.
82. Toulmin, S., 'Fetal Experimentation: Moral Issues and Institutional Controls', National Commission for the Protection of Human Subjects of Biomedical and Behavioral Research, *Research on the Fetus*, Appendix. Washington DC: US Government Printing Office, 1976, DHEW Publication No. (OS) 76–128, section 10, 10–7, 10–8.
83. Rawls, J., *A Theory of Justice*. Cambridge MA: Harvard University Press, 1972, 249 as cited by V. Worsfold, 'A Philosophical Justification of Children's Rights', *Harvard Educational Review*, 44 (1974), 142–57, 154–5.

84. National Commission, *Research Involving Children*, 107.
85. Ramsey, *Patient as Person*, 24.
86. Beecher, *Research and the Individual*, 63.
87. Bartholome, W. G., 'Parents, Children, and the Moral Benefits of Research'. *Hastings Center Report*, 6 (December 1976), 44–5.
88. Curran, W. J., and Beecher, H. K., 'Experimentation in Children: A Reexamination of Legal Ethical Principles', *Journal of the American Medical Association*, 210 (1969), 77–83.
89. Bartholome, 'Parents, Children', 44–5.
90. Ackerman, T. F., 'Fooling Ourselves with Child Autonomy and Assent in Nontherapeutic Clinical Research', *Clinical Research*, 27 (1979), 345–8, 345.
91. Ibid., 345.
92. Ibid., 346–7. Ackerman cites two empirical studies that support his arguments: Schwartz, A. H., 'Children's Concepts of Research Hospitalization', *New England Journal of Medicine*, 287 (1972), 589–92; and Abramovitch, R., Freedman, J. L., Thoden, K., and Nikolich, C., 'Children's Capacity to Consent to Participation in Psychological Research: Empirical Findings', *Child Development*, 62 (1991), 1100–9.
93. Ackerman, 'Fooling Ourselves'.
94. Ross, L. F., *Families, Children and Health Care Decision Making*. Oxford: Clarendon Press, 1998, esp. ch. 5. I examine the issue of moral development in this book in Chap. 4, 'Should We Provide Healthy Children with Greater Protection in Medical Research?'
95. Department of Health, Education, and Welfare, National Institutes of Health, 'Protection of Human Subjects: Proposed Policy', *Federal Register* 38 (9 Oct. 1973), 27882–5; and Department of Health, Education, and Welfare, National Institutes of Health, 'Protection of Human Subjects: Policies and Procedures', *Federal Register*, 38 (16 Nov. 1973), 31738–49.
96. Alexander, 'Foreword', 5.
97. National Commission for the Protection of Human Subjects of Biomedical and Behavioral Research, *The Belmont Report: Ethical Principles and Guidelines for the Protection of Human Subjects of Research*. Washington DC: US Government Printing Office, 1978, DHEW Publication No. (OS) 78–12. On the web at: *http://ohsr.od.nih.gov/guidelines/belmont.html*, hereinafter cited as *Belmont Report*.
98. National Commission, *Research Involving Children*.
99. Department of Health, Education, and Welfare (DHEW). (45 CFR Part 46), 'Protection of Human Subjects: Proposed Regulations on Research Involving Children', *Federal Register*, 43 (21 July 1978), 31786–94; and Department of Health, Education and Welfare (DHEW), '(45 CFR Part 46) Notice of Proposed Regulations Amending Basic HEW Policy for Protection of Human Research Subjects', *Federal Register*, 44 (14 Aug. 1979), 47688–729.
100. Department of Health and Human Services (DHHS). (45 CFR Part 46, Subpart A), 'Protection of Human Subjects: Final Regulations Amending Basic HHS Policy for the Protection of Human Research Subjects', *Federal Register*, 46 (26 Jan. 1981), 8366–91; and Department of Health and Human Services, (45 CFR

Part 46, Subpart D), 'Additional Protections for Children Involved as Subjects in Research', *Federal Register*, 48 (8 March 1983), 9814–20.

101. Department of Agriculture, Department of Energy, National Aeronautics and Space Administration, Department of Commerce, Consumer Product Safety, Commission International Development Cooperation Agency, Agency for International Development, Department of Housing and Urban Development, Department of Justice, Department of Defense, Department of Education, Department of Veterans Affairs, Environmental Protection Agency, Department of Health and Human Services, National Science Foundation, and Department of Transportation Agencies: 7 CFR Part 1c; 10 CFR Part 745; 14 CFR Part 1230; 15 CFR Part 27; 16 CFR Part 1028; 22 CFR Part 225; 24 CFR Part 60; 28 CFR Part 46; 32 CFR Part 219; 34 CFR Part 97; 38 CFR Part 16; 40 CFR Part 26; 45 CFR Part 46; 45 CFR Part 690; 49 CFR Part 11. 'Federal Policy for the Protection of Human Subjects, Final Rule', *Federal Register*, 56 (18 June 1991), 28003–18, hereinafter cited as the Common Rule.

102. Department of Health and Human Services (DHHS). (45 CFR 46 Subpart D), 'Additional Protections for Children Involved as Subjects in Research', *Federal Register*, 56 (18 June 1991), 28032, hereinafter cited as Subpart D by CFR number.

103. National Commission, *Research Involving Children*, 2.

104. Ibid., 2–3.

105. Institutional Review Boards (IRBs) serve the primary purpose of protecting the rights and welfare of human research subjects. The first federal document to propose committee review of research procedures was dated 17 November 1953 and applied only to intramural research at the newly opened clinical center at the NIH. See Subcommittee on Health of the Committee on Labor and Public Welfare, United States Senate, *Federal Regulation of Human Experimentation*. Washington DC: US Government Printing Office, 1975, Publication No. 45–273–0 as cited by R. J. Levine, *Ethics and Regulation of Clinical Research, 2nd edn*. New Haven CT: Yale University Press, 1986, 322. The first federal policy was not issued for another decade. On 8 February 1966, the Surgeon General issued a memorandum requiring prior review of all research involving human subjects funded by US Public Health Service Grants. See Steward, W. H., 'Clinical Investigations Using Human Subjects', Memorandum dated 8 February 1966 cited by Levine, *Ethics and Regulation*, 323.

      Initially most IRB committees were composed of scientists and physicians. Revisions in US Public Health Service policy and DHEW and DHHS regulations have evolved to *require* a more diverse composition. The duties of the IRBs have also expanded. The history of IRBs is given in Levine, *Ethics and Regulations*, ch. 14.

106. Gross, C. P., Anderson, G. F., and Powe, N. R., 'The Relation between Funding by the National Institutes of Health and the Burden of Disease', *New England Journal of Medicine*, 340 (1999), 1881–7.

107. American Academy of Pediatrics (AAP) Committee on Drugs, 'Guidelines for the Ethical Conduct of Studies to Evaluate Drugs in Pediatric Populations', *Pediatrics*, 60 (1977), 91–101, 99. This same concern is expressed in the Committee's revised statement in 1995. American Academy of Pediatrics (AAP)

Committee on Drugs, 'Guidelines for the Ethical Conduct of Studies to Evaluate Drugs in Pediatric Populations', *Pediatrics*, 95 (1995), 286–94, 286.

108. Begley, S., Hager, M., and Wilson, L., 'Desperation Drugs. Frustrated AIDS Patients are Spurring the FDA to Relax the Rules of the Game', *Newsweek*, 114 (7 August 1989), 48–9 & 51; Gould, S. J., 'AIDS and FDA Drug-Approval Policy: An Evolving Controversy', *Journal of Health & Social Policy*, 2 (1990), 39–46; and Shilts, R., *And the Band Played On: Politics, People, and the AIDS Epidemic*. New York: St. Martin's Press, 1987.

109. Department of Health and Human Services, Food and Drug Administration, 'New Drug, Antibiotic, and Biological Drug Product Regulations, Accelerated Approval', *Federal Register*, 57 (11 December 1992), 58942–60.

110. The persistent lag time is discussed in the final rule regarding drug testing in children. See Department of Health and Human Services (DHHS) Public Health Service (PHS) Food and Drug Administration (FDA), 21 CFR Parts 201, 312, 314, and 601, 'Regulations Requiring Manufacturers to Assess the Safety and Effectiveness of New Drugs and Biological Products in Pediatric Patients, Part II, Final Rule', *Federal Register*, 63 (2 December 1998), 66632–72, 66632–3.

111. Department of Health and Human Services (DHHS), Public Health Service (PHS), and Food and Drug Administration (FDA), 21 CFR Part 201, 'Specific Requirements on Content and Format of Labeling for Human Prescription Drugs; Revision of "Pediatric Use" Subsection In the Labeling, Part II', *Federal Register*, 59 (13 December 1994): 64240–50.

112. FDA, 'Regulations Requiring Manufacturers', 66632.

113. Department of Health and Human Services (DHHS), Public Health Service (PHS), and Food and Drug Administration (FDA), 'Labeling and Prescription Drug Advertising; Content and Format for Labeling for Human Prescription Drugs', *Federal Register*, 44 (26 June 1979), 37434–67, 37453.

114. Ibid., 37465.

115. FDA, 'Specific Requirements', 64240–1.

116. Ibid., 64242.

117. 'Proceedings of Workshop, Inclusion of Children in Clinical Research' (5 September 1996), unpublished, on file with author, supplied by Mona Rowe, Deputy Director, Office of Science Policy, Analysis and Communication, National Institute of Child Health and Human Development.

118. American Academy of Pediatrics (AAP), Council on Pediatric Research, 'Meeting the Research Needs of Children and Youth: Research along the Life Cycle', unpublished, undated manuscript that served as a background piece for the meeting, on file with author.

119. Shirkey, 'Therapeutic Orphan'.

120. AAP Committee on Drugs (1995), 'Ethical Conduct', 286.

121. Department of Health and Human Services, Food and Drug Administration (FDA), 21 CFR Parts 201, 312, 314, and 601, 'Regulations Requiring Manufacturers to Assess the Safety and Effectiveness of New Drugs and Biological Products in Pediatric Patients, Part V', *Federal Register*, 62 (15 August 1997), 43900–16, 43902.

122. Department of Health and Human Services (DHHS), Public Health Service (PHS), and Food and Drug Administration (FDA), 21 CFR Parts 201, 312, 314, and 601, 'Regulations Requiring Manufacturers to Assess the Safety and Effectiveness of New Drugs and Biological Products in Pediatric Patients, Part II, Final Rule', *Federal Register*, 63 (2 December 1998), 66632–72.

123. Food and Drug Administration Modernization Act (FDAMA) of 1997, Public Law 105–15, 111 Stat. 2296 (1997).

124. Best Pharmaceuticals for Children Act, Public Law 107–9, 115 Stat. 1408 (2002).

125. See Ch. 13, section 9, 'Further Anecdotal Support' where I give an example. In response to a written request from the FDA, GlaxoSmithKline (GSK) performed two clinical trials of Flovent (an anti-inflammatory inhalational medication) for asthma in young children. The data were uninterpretable with respect to both safety and efficacy, and yet GSK was granted six months of additional exclusivity.

126. Department of Health and Human Services (DHHS), and US Food and Drug Administration (FDA), 'The Pediatric Exclusivity Provision, January 2001 Status Report to Congress'. On the web *at* http://www.fda.gov/cder/pediatric/reportcong01.pdf. Note a recent article in *JAMA* discusses the benefits of FDAMA. See Roberts, R., Rodriquez, W., Murphy, D., and Crescenzi, T., 'Pediatric Drug Labeling: Improving the Safety and Efficacy of Pediatric Therapies', *JAMA*, 290 (2003), 905–11.

127. Association of American Physicians & Surgeons, Inc. v. FDA, 226 F.Supp.2d 204 (D.D.C. 2002).

128. Associated Press, 'Reversal on "Pediatric Rule"', *New York Times* (20 April 2002), A13. Two of the bills introduced by Congress were S.2394, which would amend the Federal Food, Drug, and Cosmetic Act to require labeling containing information applicable to pediatric patients, introduced in the Senate 29 April 2002, and H.R. 4730, introduced in the House 14 May 2002.

129. American Physicians and Surgeons, 222.

130. Pediatric Research Equity Act of 2003 (Public Law 108–55).

131. Department of Health and Human Services (DHHS), 'HHS Identifies Drugs for Pediatric Testing and Announces FY 2003 and FY 2004 Funding', Press Release, 21 Jan. 2003. On the web at: http:/ /www.hhs.gov/news/press/2003pres/20030121.html.

132. 'NIH Policy and Guidelines for the Inclusion of Children as Participants in Research Involving Human Subjects', 6 March 1998. On the web at: http:/ / grants1.nih.gov/grants/guide/notice-files/not98–024.html.

133. National Institutes of Health Office of Extramural Research, 'Questions and Answers about the NIH Policy and Guidelines on the Inclusion of Children as Participants in Research involving Human Subjects' (March 1999). On the web at: http:/ /grants.nih.gov/grants/funding/children/pol_children_qa.htm.

134. See, e.g., Hilts, P. J., 'VA [Veteran's Administration] Hospital Is Told to Halt All Research', *New York Times* (29 March 1999), A25; Guerrero, L. M., and Herguth, R. C., 'Human Tests Halted; UIC Projects Suspended after Probe', *Chicago Sun-Times* (28 August 1999), 1; Hilts, P. J., 'US Halts Human Research

at Alabama', *New York Times*, National edition (22 January 2000), A.10; Stolberg, S. G., 'Gene Therapy Ordered Halted at University', *New York Times*, National edition (22 January 2000), A.1; Hilts, P. J., 'Safety Concerns Halts Oklahoma Research', *New York Times*, National edition (11 July 2000), D.10; and Hubler, E., 'FDA Move Halts Local Research; Thousands of Projects Suspended at Six CU [Colorado University]-Affiliated Institutions', *Denver Post* (24 September 1999), A.01; Kolata, G., 'Johns Hopkins Death Brings Halt to US-Financed Human Studies', *New York Times*, National edition (20 July 2001), A1; and Hopper, L., 'Prisoner Enrollment Halted in Studies; Feds Cite Safety Lapses in Projects at UTMB [University of Texas at Medical Branch at Galveston]', *Houston Chronicle* (1 September 2000), A31 (Metfront).

135. Koski, G., 'National Human Research Protections Advisory Commission Transcript, 29 January 2002'. On the web at: http:/ /www.hhs.gov/ohrp/nhrpac/mtg01–02/0129NHR.txt.

136. Subpart D, CFR §46.407.

137. Nelson, R. M., 'A Brief History of Protocol Reviews Under 45 CR §46.407'. Presentation at the American Society of Bioethics and Humanities, Montreal, October 2003; and Office for Human Research Protections (OHRP), 'Children Involved in Research 45 CFR part 46, subpart D', n.d. On the web at: http:/ / ohrp.osophs.dhhs.gov/cpanl.htm. Another panel was convened in September 2004. The process and evolution of 407 panels are discussed in Chs. 14 and 15.

138. Children's Health Act of 2000, Public Law 106–310 (2000).

139. National Association of Children's Hospitals, Press Release: 'Children's Hospitals Herald White House Signing of "Children's Health Act of 2000" ' (18 Oct. 2000), available at http:/ / www.childrenshospitals.net/nach/news/pr_healthact 2000.asp.

140. Children's Health Act, §1003.

141. Department of Health and Human Services (DHHS), and Food and Drug Administration (FDA). 21 CFR Parts 50 and 56, 'Additional Safeguards for Children in Clinical Investigations of FDA-Regulated Products', *Federal Register*, 66 (24 April 2001), 20589–600.

142. Children's Health Act, §1003.

143. Department of Health and Human Services (DHHS), 'Protections for Children in Research: A Report to Congress', May 2001. On the web at: http:// www.hhs.gov/ohrp/reports/ohrp502.pdf

144. Ibid., 18.

145. Ibid., 22.

146. Best Pharmaceuticals for Children Act.

147. Field, M. J., Behrman, R. E. (eds.), Committee on Clinical Research Involving Children, the Institute of Medicine (IOM), *The Ethical Conduct of Clinical Research Involving Children*. Washington DC: National Academies Press, 2004; hereinafter this reference is cited as the IOM, *Ethical Conduct*.

148. Ibid., 13.

149. Committee on Assessing the System for Protecting Human Research Subjects, Board on Health Sciences Policy, Institute of Medicine, *Preserving Public Trust:*

Accreditation and Human Research Participant Protection Programs. Washington DC: National Academy Press, 2001.

150. About the World Medical Association. On the web at: http://www.wma.net/e/about.html.

151. 2nd General Assembly of the World Medical Association (WMA], Declaration of Geneva, Geneva Switzerland 1948 reprinted in Beecher, *Research and the Individual*, 235.

152. 'International Code of Medical Ethics'.

153. 'Draft Code'.

154. 18th WMA Declaration of Helsinki.

155. The WMA, 'Declaration of Helsinki: Ethical Principles for Medical Research Involving Human Subjects' was adopted by the 18th WMA, Helsinki, Finland, 1964; and amended multiple times at WMA meetings: the first revision occurred at the 29th WMA, Tokyo, Japan, 1975. The principle cited is principle III.4. The 1975 version is reprinted in Levine, *Ethics and Regulation*, 427–9.

156. 'Draft Code'.

157. Ibid.

158. 18th WMA Declaration of Helsinki.

159. Principle 24 of the 2000 and 2002 versions of the Declaration of Helsinki. After the 1975 revisions of Tokyo, Japan, the Declaration of Helsinki has been amended at the 35th WMA, Venice, Italy, 1983, the 41st WMA Hong Kong, China, 1989, the 48th WMA Somerset West, Republic of South Africa, 1996, the 52nd WMA, Edinburgh, Scotland, 2000. Note of clarification on para. 29 added by the WMA General Assembly, Washington 2002. The 2002 version can be found on the web at http://www.wma.net/e/policy/17-c_e.html.

160. This guideline was implemented as principle 11 in the 1983 and 1996 versions of the Declaration of Helsinki. It is moved to principle 25 in the 2000 and 2002 versions. The 2002 version can be found on the web as cited in endnote 159.

161. MRC, (1962–3) 'Responsibility'.

162. Ibid.

163. The correspondence is described in Curran and Beecher, 'Experimentation: A Reexamination', 81.

164. Ibid., 83.

165. Royal College of Physicians. *Supervision of the Ethics of Clinical Research Investigations in Institutions.* London, UK: Royal College of Physicians,1973; Department of Health and Social Security, *Supervision of the Ethics of Clinical Research Investigations and Fetal Research.* London: Department of Health and Social Services, HSC (IS) 153, 1975; and British Paediatric Association (BPA), 'Guidelines to Aid Ethical Committees Considering Research Involving Children', *Archives of Diseases of Childhood*, 55 (1980), 75–7.

166. BPA, (1980) 'Guidelines', 77.

167. Nicholson, *Medical Research*.

168. Ibid., 234.

169. MRC (1962–3), 'Responsibility'.

170. Nicholson, *Medical Research*, 231.

171. Ibid., 150–1.
172. Ibid., 151.
173. Ibid., 151.
174. Ibid., 233. Of note, the BPA used the terms negligible, minimal, and more than minimal risk in its 1980 document. See BPA (1980), 'Guidelines'. The working group on ethics recommended that the British guidelines use the same terminology as the American guidelines (Nicholson, *Medical Research*, 105ff.). In 1992, the BPA revised its terminology to read minimal, low, and high risks which is NOT consistent with the American terminology. See British Paediatric Association, *Guidelines for the Ethical Conduct of Medical Research Involving Children*. London: British Paediatric Association, 1992.
175. Medical Research Council (MRC), 'The Ethical Conduct of Research on Children, 1991', reprinted in the *Bulletin of Medical Ethics*, 76 (1992), 8–10.
176. BPA (1992), 'Guidelines'.
177. Royal College of Paediatrics and Child Health (RCPCH), Ethics Advisory Committee, 'Guidelines for the Ethical Conduct of Medical Research Involving Children', *Archives of Disease in Childhood*, 82 (2000), 177–82
178. BPA (1992), 'Guidelines', 3; RCPCH, 'Guidelines', 177.
179. MRC (1992), 'Ethical Conduct' Principle 3.2 at 9. The Medical Health Council of Australia has a similar requirement: 'consent cannot be given for, research that is contrary to the child's or young person's best interests'. See National Health and Medical Research Council Act 1992. http://www.health.gov.au/nhmrc/publications/pdf/e35.pdf.
180. BPA, 'Guidelines', 13; RCPCH, 'Guidelines', 180. Payment is not mentioned in the US federal regulations, although it is supported by the recent IOM report. See also IOM, *Ethical Conduct*. This topic is discussed further in Ch. 8, 'Payment in Pediatric Research'.
181. Alderson, P., 'Did Children Change, or the Guidelines?' *Bulletin of the Institute of Medical Ethics*, 150 (1999), 38–44, 43.
182. DHHS and FDA, 'Pediatric Exclusivity Provision'; and Roberts *et al.*, 'Pediatric Drug Labeling'.
183. Rothman, *Strangers*.
184. *Belmont Report*.
185. This is actually a requirement of all research, not just pediatric research. It is a principle espoused in virtually all national and international guidelines. It is discussed in greater detail in Ch. 10, 'Minimizing Risks: Diabetes Research in Newborns'.
186. Ramsey, *Patient as Person*, 26; Jonas, H., 'Philosophical Reflections on Experimenting with Human Subjects' in P. A. Freund (ed.), *Experimentation with Human Subjects*. New York: Braziller, 1970, 1–31, 28–9.

2

Access versus Protection: Minority Representation in Pediatric Research

1. Introduction

The traditional research subject was an adult white male. In 1994, the NIH announced that all research it funded would need to include women and minorities (or explain their exclusion).[1] In 1998, the NIH added the requirement to include children.[2] The shift in policies reflects a shift in focus. When the National Commission (for the Protection of Human Subjects of Biomedical and Behavioral Research) addressed fairness in subject selection in the *Belmont Report* of 1979, the main concern was to ensure fairness in the distribution of risks.[3] As discussed in Chapter 1, by 1994 the concern was focused on fairness in the distribution of benefits.

There are data to show that despite the initiatives to include women and minorities, both women and minorities remain underrepresented in clinical research.[4] However, little is known as to whether these discrepancies hold in pediatric research. To begin to examine this issue, several students and I conducted several empirical projects to examine (1) the extent to which pediatric researchers are reporting race and ethnicity (hereinafter referred to as R/E) data; (2) the representation of Black, Hispanic, and Asian children and their parents in pediatric medical research; (3) the extent to which language may be a barrier in pediatric research; and (4) how R/E data are collected in pediatric research.

In this chapter, I will focus on four key findings from this project: First, collecting R/E data in medical research is difficult because the data are not presented in a standardized format. Second, we found that Black children and their parents are overrepresented in pediatric research and Hispanic children and their parents are underrepresented in pediatric research compared to their representation in the census. Third, the participation rates of Black subjects were not equivalent in all types of research. Rather, we found greater overrepresentation in clinical trials than in nontherapeutic research, but we also found a greater representation in research that is potentially stigmatizing. Fourth, language barriers exist in pediatric research, and the greatest number of Hispanic and Asian participants are enrolled in research in which translation services are available.

Our empirical data focus on race and ethnicity. Such data are important but not sufficient. Given the growing consensus within the pediatric community that race and ethnicity are not explanatory variables for health care disparities,[5] we attempted to examine whether researchers are reporting other sociodemographic data that might help explain racial and ethnic differences.[6] Before concluding, I share our experience in obtaining such data.

2. *Methods*

All full-length articles published in the paper edition of three general pediatric journals, *Pediatrics, Journal of Pediatrics*, and *Archives of Pediatrics and Adolescent Medicine*, published from July 1999 through June 2000 and from July 2002 through 2003 were collected and reviewed. Articles were excluded for four reasons. First, they were excluded if they did not include at least one US researcher and all subjects from US institutions because R/E classifications differ in other countries. Second, articles were excluded if they did not include some prospective data collection. Our goal was to understand the inclusion of minority children and parents in research in which they and/or their parents had to consent to participate. Retrospective data analysis, often done without consent, reflects the patient population of a particular researcher, but it does not reflect access to, or uptake of, clinical research participation by members of various ethnic communities. Third, articles were excluded if they studied a population other than children and/or their parents (e.g., health care providers). Fourth, articles were excluded if they were case studies with less than 8 or if they had more than 10,000 subjects, studied a population other than children and/or their parents (e.g., health care providers), or were based on national surveys. Our reason for excluding articles with less than 8 subjects was that case studies are neither a systematic investigation nor generalizable and do not qualify as research under the Common Rule.[7] Studies with over 10,000 subjects were excluded because many were based on national datasets such as National Health and Nutrition Examination Survey (NHANES) in which minority families are oversampled in order to ensure adequate sizes for subset analyses. We excluded these studies because (1) the data are collected for use by researchers in many different fields and are not funded by or focused on pediatric health care, and are thus not representative of pediatric research; (2) the same subjects would be counted numerous times; and (3) the practice of oversampling minorities in these large studies would skew the data to show high minority participation.

We recorded whether the articles documented R/E in the methods or results section of the studies [RESULTS], and whether they discussed R/E in the discussion, limitations, or conclusions of the article [DISCUSSION]. We also recorded whether the articles provided race/ethnicity (R/E) data of children- and parent-subjects, and what the R/E breakdown was. When possible, we recorded R/E of subjects analyzed. We recorded whether the studies reported R/E data of children- and parent-subjects, and what the R/E breakdown was. All subjects labeled as Black, African American, or African other are labeled as Black. All subjects labeled as White or White, non-Hispanic are labeled as White. All subjects labeled as Hispanic, Latino, Puerto Rican, White Hispanic, or Black Hispanic are labeled as Hispanic. All subjects labeled as Asian American, Pacific Islander, Chinese, Japanese, Southeast Asian, or Indian are labeled as Asian/PI. All subjects labeled as Native American, American Indian, or Alaskan Native are labeled as Native American/Alaskan Indian. All subjects labeled as non-White, non-Black, mixed, multicultural, or other are labeled as Other. For both data-sets, we assumed that the race of parent and child were the same, unless stated otherwise. In 1999–2000, we did not survey the researchers on how they collected the data (i.e. self-identification, interviewer assessment), but we did in 2002–2003. In 2002–2003, we also asked whether subjects were excluded because of language barriers, and whether any part of the research (e.g., consent form, questionnaire) was translated into other languages.

In 1999–2000 we also documented the type of research that was described in the articles, including whether the articles involved (1) phase III clinical trials (research that compares an experimental drug against an alternative drug, possibly a placebo, to determine the efficacy of the experimental drug) in response to the NIH mandate that specifically addressed the need for subset analyses in such trials; and (2) therapeutic research, which we defined as providing a treatment or service to a child or parent. Phase III clinical trials are a subset of all therapeutic research. We also reviewed all articles that coded for a potentially stigmatizing research topic (topics included were child abuse and neglect, HIV, psychiatric issues, and high-risk behaviors). Other types of research were examined in the larger project and are defined and discussed elsewhere.[8]

Corresponding authors were invited to participate in a voluntary survey that sought to clarify R/E data reported in the articles in both 1999–2000 and 2002–2003. In 2002–2003, the authors were also queried about how R/E data on subjects were ascertained, whether research was translated, and whether language barriers existed.

Approval from the University of Chicago Institutional Review Board for the project and for waived written consent was obtained prior to contacting any of the authors of the articles. Data was analyzed using the computer programs Excel and SPSS for Windows.

3. Results

Five hundred and twenty six studies were examined and 192 studies qualified for further study in 1999–2000; 692 studies were examined and 228 studies qualified for further study in 2002–2003. In 1999–2000, R/E were reported in 114 studies and survey data provided additional or new information on 25 studies such that we have R/E data on 128 (67%) of articles. In total, the articles analyze data from 110,942 subjects for which we have R/E data on 84,323 subjects (76%). This includes 78,736 children-subjects for which we have R/E data on 58,413 subjects (74%). In 2002–2003, R/E were reported in 146 studies, and survey data provided additional or new information on 40 studies such that we have R/E data on 160 (70%) of the studies. Overall, we have R/E data on 98, 416 of 125,360 subjects (79%) and 64, 766 of 73,096 children-subjects (89%).

The data show that collecting R/E data in published medical research is difficult because the data are not presented in a standardized format. In 1999–2000, race and ethnicity of subjects were described by over ten different labels. In Table 1, the number of studies in which some of the more common labels used in the article is provided. Of note is that Hispanic subjects were considered a race in some studies and an ethnicity in others. In studies where Hispanic subjects are classified by their ethnicity ($n=5$), the subjects are also counted by their race, and so 544 children-subjects and 436 adult-subjects are counted twice. In 23 studies, some subjects were classified as non-White or non-Black. When the researchers were asked to clarify their data, they often

Table 1.   Racial and ethnic divisions used by studies

White	88
Black	92
Asian	23
Hispanic (Race)	36
Latino (Ethnicity)	5
Native American	10
Black Asian	1
Mixed race	5
Others	45
Non-Whites	13
Non-Blacks	10

This table is reprinted with permission from Walsh, C. A., and Ross, L. F. 'Are Minority Children Over- or Underrepresented in Pediatric Research?', *Pediatrics*, 112 (2003), 890–5, 891, Table 1.

responded that the 'non-White' subjects were predominantly but not exclusively Black and the 'non-Black' subjects were predominantly but not exclusively White. If the researchers could give an exact breakdown of the racial identity of all of the 'non-White' or 'non-Black' subjects, then the subjects were classified by race; otherwise we classified them as 'Other' (see Table 2). They account for 2,702 (less than 5%) children-subjects and 398 (less than 2%) adult-subjects in 1999–2000. Socio-economic classifications and the data provided are even less standardized.

Table 2 provides an overall account of the study population, breaking it down into children-subjects, adult-(parent) subjects, and all (parent and children)-subjects by R/E using five labels: White, Black, Asian, Hispanic, and Other. Other races represent a conglomeration of subjects labeled in the research as 'Other', Native American, 'Mixed', 'non-White' and 'non-Black'. The table provides a breakdown of the number and percentage of each group's participation in research compared with their percent representation in the census (for all persons living in the US younger than 18 years, 18 years or older, and in aggregate). The census characterizes Hispanics as an ethnicity and all the other groups as a race, so the census total adds up to more than 100%. In contrast we have combined race and ethnicity data such that our data adds up to 100%. Not to lose any possible reporting of Hispanic subjects, we double counted Hispanic ethnicity subjects by categorizing them as Hispanics even though they were also classified as a race by the researchers. This accounted for only 1% of all the subjects and less than 10% of all children-subjects categorized as Hispanics in 1999–2000 and only 42 adult-subjects counted twice (Hispanic used as race and ethnicity) in 2002–2003.

In both data sets, the majority of subjects are White (55%) although their participation is lower than their proportion in the US population (73%). Blacks are overrepresented in the research compared to their proportion in the census; Hispanics are underrepresented. Asian subjects, who account for less than 4% of all subjects, were underrepresented in 1999–2000. In 2002–2003, Asian parents are overrepresented and Asian children are underrepresented. We will explore this finding below.

Table 3 describes R/E data of children-subjects in 1999–2000 for all research and for three subsets of research: clinical trials, therapeutic research more generally, and potential stigmatizing research. In therapeutic research, White children subjects are underrepresented according to the census data, but overrepresented when compared to the percentage of White children subjects in all research. Black children are overrepresented and Hispanic children are underrepresented in all studies and in each subcategory when compared with the census data. When compared with their participation in all research (column 1), Black and Hispanic children are underrepresented in

Table 2. Number and percent of subjects categorized by race and ethnicity compared with 1999–2000 pediatric journal data and 2000 Census data

	Total-subjects			Children-subjects			Adult-subjects		
	2002–2003 journal data (#) %	1999–2000 journal data %	2000 Census data, total population %	2002–2003 journal data (#) %	1999–2000 journal data %	2000 Census data <18 years %	2002–2003 journal data (#) %	1999–2000 journal data %	2000 Census data, >18 years %
White	(54,683) 55	55	73	(35,457) 55	54	69	(19,226) 57	57	75
Black	(22,221) 23	26	13	(16,702) 26	26	15	(5,519) 16	26	12
Hispanic	(9135) 9	9.7	14	(5627) 9	10	17	(3508)* 11	8.7	12
Asian and Pacific Islander	(6,486) 7	1.5	4	(2,804) 4	1.5	4	(3,682) 11	1.3	4
Native American and Alaska Native	(754) 1	0.7	1	(715) 1	0.3	1	(39) 0	1.5	1
Other	(5137) 5	8	8	(3461) 5	8	12	(1676) 5	6	7

* Includes 42 adult-subjects counted twice (Hispanic used as race and ethnicity)

Table 2 is reprinted with permission from Kelly, M. L., Ackerman, P. D., and Ross, L. F., 'The Participation of Minorities in Pediatric Research' (data sources omitted). *Journal of the National Medical Association* 2005; 97 (6): 777–83, 780 Table 2, 2005; 97(6): 777–83, 778, Table 1.

Table 3.   R/E of subjects for whom data are available by type of research

	All studies (*n*=128)	Therapeutic studies (*n*=37)	Clinical trials (*n*=18)	PSR studies (*n*=36)
Total # Children r/e available	58,413	14,099	4,357	17,953
# White (%)	31,362 (54)	8,100 (58)	2,278 (52)	7,989 (45)
# Black (%)	15,259 (26)	3,088 (22)	1,405 (32)	5,323 (30)
# Hispanic (%)	5,894 (10)	1,222 (8.7)	287 (6.6)	3,116 (17)
# Other (%)	5,898 (10)	1,690 (12)	387 (8.9)	1,526 (8.5)

This table is modified and reprinted with permission from Walsh, C. A., and Ross, L. F., 'Are Minority Children Over- or Underrepresented in Pediatric Research?', *Pediatrics*, 112 (2003), 890–5, 893, Table 4.

therapeutic research generally, but in phase III clinical trials, Black children-subjects are overrepresented and White and Hispanic children-subjects are underrepresented. The most significant difference occurs in potentially stigmatizing research (PSR) where White subjects are significantly underrepresented, but Black and Hispanic subjects are significantly overrepresented.

Finally, in 2002–2003, 157 of 228 (69%) of researchers responded to most or all of our survey. Table 4 shows how they responded to our query regarding how R/E data were collected in their research study. Most of the researchers allowed for at least some patient-subject self-reporting (*n*=93 or 59%), although some researchers used more than one methodology.

Most of the articles (82%) did not state whether language proficiency was an inclusion or exclusion criterion. Twenty-two articles (9.6%) specifically stated

Table 4.   Researchers report how they collect race and ethnicity data

METHOD*	Total number of surveys (157)
Patient-subject self-report	93
Researcher determination	28
Third-party determination (from medical records or name or birth certificate)	26
Other	1
Did not answer	31

* Respondents could offer more than one method.
Table 4 is reprinted with permission from Kelly, M. L., Ackerman, P. D., and Ross, L. F., 'The Participation of Minorities in Pediatric Research'. *Journal of the National Medical Association* 2005: 97 (6):777–83, 780 Table 2.

that English language was an inclusion criterion; 17 (7.5%) stated that translation was provided; one study was done exclusively in Spanish and two studies were observational making language irrelevant. With our survey data, we were able to clarify that one of the studies that described itself as 'English language only' included only children who spoke English although the parental consent forms were available in English and Spanish, and we reclassified this study as providing translation. Our survey data also identified an additional 46 studies in which translation into at least one additional language was provided; this resulted in a total of 64 studies (28%) that provided some translation.

Our survey data permitted us to clarify the use of Spanish and Asian/PI translation in pediatric research. Whereas article data alone detected 17 studies involving Spanish translation, our surveys identified an additional 38 studies. Thus, at least 55 studies (24.1%) were accessible to Spanish-speaking only subjects. Article data alone detected two studies translated into at least one Asian/PI language. Our survey data identified an additional five studies. Thus at least seven studies (3.1%) were accessible to subjects speaking only an Asian/PI language.

Of the 160 studies for which we have R/E data, 84 (52.5%) enrolled Hispanic subjects and 56 (35%) enrolled Asian/PI subjects. The relationship between the availability of translation and minority participation in these research protocols are described in Table 5. Studies in which Spanish translation was provided accounted for less than half of the studies in which Hispanic subjects were enrolled, but nearly three-fifths of all Hispanic subjects enrolled in these studies. It is not known whether translation was available for most (29 of 56) studies enrolling Asian/PI subjects. Nevertheless, most Asian/PI subjects were enrolled in studies in which translation was provided. This was particularly important for Asian/PI adult-subjects as one study that provided translation accounted for 3055 adult Asian/PI subjects (83% of all Asian/PI adult-subjects or 47% of all Asian/PI subjects).

4. Discussion

Our research provides data on the proportional representation of minority children in pediatric research. Despite an extensive literature that shows that minority (adults) are underrepresented in medical research,[9] there are scant data regarding minority children. Our data found that Black children are overrepresented in medical research overall. The overrepresentation of Black children in pediatric research stands in acute contrast with their decreased access to pediatric health care services, even when they have the same health care insurance.[10] One possible explanation for the overrepresentation of Black children is the location of many academic medical centers in poor

Table 5. Participation of Hispanic and Asian/PI subjects in studies in which race/ethnicity data are available in relationship to the availability of translation

	Studies enrolling Hispanic subjects # (%) (n=84)	# (%) of Hispanic subjects (n=9,135)	#(%) of Hispanic children (n=5,627)	Studies enrolling Asian/PI subjects # (%) (n=56)	# (%) of Asian/PI subjects (n=6,486)	# (%) of Asian/PI children (n=2,804)
Translation available	38 (45.2)	5,347 (58.5)	3,425 (60.9)	4 (7.1)	3,920 (60.4)	865 (30.8)
Not translated	34 (40.5)	3,240 (35.5)	1,667 (29.6)	23 (41.1)	1,531 (23.6)	1,180 (42.1)
Translation status unknown	12 (14.3)	548 (6.0)	535 (9.5)	29 (51.8)	1,035 (16.0)	759 (27.1)

Table 5 is reprinted with permission from Kelly, M. L., Ackerman, P. D., and Ross, L. F., 'The Participation of Minorities in Pediatric Research', Journal of the National Medical Association 2005, 97 (6): 777–83, 781, Table 3.

urban sites with a large minority population.[11] The majority of subjects for pediatric research are recruited from these catchment areas.

In contrast, Hispanic children and their parents are underrepresented compared to their proportion in the census, although there are many reasons why the data may be inaccurate. First, guidelines for the collection of race/ethnicity data used by the NIH is based on OMB directive 15. Directive 15 allows for Hispanic data to be collected as a race or as an ethnicity,[12] whereas the US census collects Hispanic data as only an ethnicity.[13] If the Hispanic label is used for ethnicity, some researchers may not collect data on Hispanic participation as they may decide only to collect race (often collecting only white or black race without defining the rest of the population, or lumping them in the category of 'Other').[14] R/E data are also complicated by the fact that within the Hispanic and Latino communities there are different attitudes about whether to classify themselves as a race or ethnicity. Hispanic subjects may be undercounted because of the lack of consistency in reporting or because Hispanic individuals may classify themselves as a race or as an ethnicity for different purposes. It is not clear how Hispanic individuals would classify themselves, or how researchers would classify them, in the various research studies published.[15] Hispanic individuals may also be underrepresented because most research excludes those who do not speak English.[16]

To say that minority children are overrepresented, then, is imprecise. Our data confirm that discussing 'minorities' as a group overlooks the fact that some minority children are overrepresented while others are underrepresented. We found that Black children were overrepresented, Hispanic children were underrepresented, and Asian/PI children were proportionally represented in pediatric research (in 2002–2003) but underrepresented in 1999–2000.

Even our data are inadequate. While categorizing populations as 'Black', 'Hispanic', and 'Asian/PI' is preferable to classifying members of these groups as 'non-White' or 'Other', it suggests monolithic Black, Hispanic, and Asian/PI populations.[17] There are persuasive data to show that diversity within each ethnic group can be as significant as intergroup differences which limit the utility of these classifications for research on ethnic disparities.[18]

Various factors may explain the persistent underrepresentation of Hispanic children. First, we found that Hispanic subjects were identified in only 84 of the 160 (52.5%) articles in which R/E were reported. It could be that Hispanic subjects were included in some of the other studies but were not identified by their ethnicity because only race data were collected and reported.[19]

Second, it could be that Hispanic subjects did not identify themselves as Hispanic. Although self-reporting was the most common method for collecting R/E data, there are different attitudes within the Hispanic and Latino communities about whether and when to classify oneself by ethnicity (Hispanic) versus when to describe oneself by race (e.g., Black or White).[20]

Third, Hispanic children and their parents may also be underrepresented because of language barriers.[21] In our study we found that 55 studies were accessible to Spanish-speaking subjects (or their guardians) and these studies accounted for the enrollment of nearly three-fifths of the Hispanic subjects. Of course, it is not clear how many of the subjects actually required Spanish translation within these studies.

The one subset of studies in which Hispanic children were overrepresented was research on potentially stigmatizing subjects. One concern is that the researchers may be using race and ethnicity as proxies for other social factors such as low socioeconomic status and social disempowerment.[22] There are some data to show racial selection bias in child abuse studies,[23] and a tendency to make comparisons between minorities and white patients for diseases and conditions associated with promiscuity, underachievement, and antisocial behavior.[24] Alternatively, it may be that there is (1) some over-representation of minority children in certain conditions categorized as potentially stigmatizing research (e.g., 82% of all reported pediatric AIDS cases are in Black and Hispanic children [25]); and/or (2) that these studies were performed mainly at academic medical centers in which there is a preponderance of minority children [26] such that the overrepresentation of minority children in PSR is epidemiologically proportional to the diseases and conditions and/or to the research locations. Our sample was too small for further analyses.

Whereas our 1999–2000 data found an underrepresentation of Asian/PI children- and adult-subjects, in 2002–2003 we found that Asian/PI adult-subjects were overrepresented and Asian/PI children were proportionately represented; even this may be an underreporting because some researchers only collected data as 'White subjects or Other'.

The increased representation of Asian/PI subjects may be explained by the availability of translation in the research. Although we could only identify four studies in which translation into one or more Asian/PI languages was available, these studies accounted for three-fifths of the Asian/PI subjects who were identified as Asian/PI in the research. Most of the overrepresentation of adult Asian/PI subjects in 2002–2003 can be explained by one study in which the research was translated. This study enrolled 3,055 Asian/PI adult-subjects who account for over 80% of all of the Asian/PI adult-subjects and almost one-half of all of the Asian/PI subjects enrolled, although it is not clear how many of the subjects within any of these studies actually required or utilized translation services. Thus, whether the difference represents a true change, improved reporting, or a limitation of our methodology is not clear.

Another possible explanation for the increased representation of Asian/PI subjects is the smaller percentage of children-subjects and total subjects classified as 'Other' in our current data (5%) versus 8% classified as 'Other' in 1999–2000 (p<.001). The difference may merely represent better reporting of ethnic minorities. Fifty-six of the 160 studies (35%) that reported R/E gave Asian/PI data (compared with 23 of the 128 studies (18%) articles in 1999–2000, p<.01). One possible explanation may be how the subjects' race/ethnicity is determined. We do not know whether there is an increase in subject self-reporting of R/E between our two data sets because we did not collect this data in 1999–2000.

Given the higher participation of minority children and their parents in both data sets, it is important to consider whether their participation is proportionate in all types of research or whether there are types of research in which they are relatively under- or overrepresented compared with their participation in research more generally. Bleyer *et al.* perform such a meta-analysis examining the participation of children by R/E in pediatric clinical cancer trials between 1 January 1991 and 30 June 1994. They found that the Hispanic, Black, and other racial groups accounted for 11.6, 10.4, and 4.7% of the subjects which was comparable to the proportion of the children as cancer patients (9.1, 10.7, and 4.3% respectively).[27] As such, they found that the representation of minority children was equal or greater than expected. Their results of proportional representation, however, was antici-patable because more than 90% of children younger than 15 years of age diagnosed with cancer were enrolled in cancer clinical trials such that research participation mirrored disease prevalence.[28] It would be important to see if this holds in clinical trials in which participation is lower.

In our study, we found that Black children are overrepresented and White and Hispanic children are underrepresented in phase III clinical trials compared both to the census and to the population of research subjects as a whole. It would be more accurate to compare participation of research subjects to the percent of individuals with a particular condition, as was done by Bleyer *et al.* But unless such studies are national in scope, the comparison would also need to correct for the sites in which the research took place. For example, if cancer research were being done in Utah where the minority population is quite low, then one could not expect 10% of the subjects to be Black children. Our data set was too small with regard to any particular condition and thus we were unable to perform such analyses. Still, our data suggest that Black children do have fair access to the potential benefits that may accrue from participation in clinical trials, although Hispanic children may not.

When one considers all therapeutic research, however, Black and Hispanic children are underrepresented relative to their participation in research over-all (p<.01), although Black are overrepresented in this research in comparison with their percentage in the US census. We have no data to explain why Black families do take advantage of clinical trials but not of therapeutic research more generally. The problem may be at the stage of recruitment, enrollment, or retention; additional studies are needed to determine the cause.

Our data is also limited by our methodology. We only examined the R/E of subjects who participated in published research in three pediatric journals. Much pediatric research that is done does not get published, and there are many other journals in which pediatric research is published. It is unclear whether the populations in published research are similar to the populations in unpublished research, and whether our selected journals are representative of other pediatric publications. In addition, we focused on the R/E break-down of those subjects analyzed in the research. One would want to know if high minority participation rates are due to (1) over-recruitment of minorities for research; (2) a greater likelihood of enrolling, if recruited; or (3) a greater likelihood of completing the research once enrolled. Unfortunately, the num-ber and R/E breakdown of subjects recruited and enrolled were rarely and inconsistently reported,[29] despite the recommendations by CONSORT.[30] Other data, however, about minority mistrust of research participation [31] and difficulty in retention once recruited,[32] suggest that the first explanation is most likely. Further empirical data in pediatric research is needed to elucidate the causes for this high degree of minority participation.

Our data are limited by the quality of reporting R/E data. Although there are federal standards meant to standardize data collection and publication among federal agencies (OMB directive 15), there is wide variation in local, state, and national governmental agencies [33] and no standardization for reporting such data in medical journals.[34] Studies examining R/E data for medical and public health uses show that the collection of R/E data is inconsistent, and its accuracy is indeterminate.[35] We also found that dif-ferent articles used different classifications.

5.   How Should One Respond to the Data?

I believe that both those who support greater protection and those who support greater access will find some of our data laudatory and some of it distressing. But one's response should be tempered by the lack of socio-economic context. Although there are serious and significant health care disparities in medicine, including pediatric medicine, based on race and ethnicity, Isaacs and Schroeder correctly note that '[a]t the same time, the wide differences in health between the haves and the have-nots are largely ignored . . . We contend that increased attention should be given to the reality of class and its effect on nation's health.'[36]

We tried to examine sociodemographic factors. We recorded whether the researchers reported on any social markers (e.g., specific SES measurements, public or private insurance, parental marital status, single-parent home, parental/ household income, parental education level, parental employment, welfare recipient (AFDC), community location as inner city or suburban, father involvement, child school status, child out of home placement, or neighborhood income) in the RESULTS, and whether they discussed any social markers in the DISCUSSION. We did not attempt to examine whether other demographic factors like age, gender, or pubertal status were recorded or discussed.

We found that the social marker data reported by researchers varied tremendously. Some articles merely stated that all subjects were on Medicaid, while other articles reported detailed education, job, and income data. The lack of uniformity regarding what socioeconomic and sociodemographic data should be collected and reported confounds the issues even further.[37] Discussion of social markers, like the reporting of social markers, also varied greatly. Some articles merely stated that a potential limitation of their study findings was that all subjects had a Medicaid card; other articles discussed detailed correlations between social markers and their results.

Table 6 shows that the actual reporting of social markers did not vary statistically between the two time periods; 48% reported social markers in 1999–2000 and 51% in 2002–2003. The percent of articles in which social markers were discussed also did not vary.

Table 6. Reporting or discussing race/ethnicity (R/E) and social markers (SMs) in pediatric research in two different time periods

	Reported # (%)		Discussed # (%)	
	1999–2000 (n=192)	2002–2003 (n=228)	1999–2000 (n=192)	2002–2003 (n =228)
R/E and SM	74 (39)	97 (43)	33 (17)	47 (21)
R/E only	40 (21)	59 (26)	11 (6)	28 (12)*
SM only	18 (9)	19 (8)	27 (14)	29 (13)
No R/E no SM	60 (31)	53 (23)	121 (63)	124 (54)

*P <.025

This table is reprinted with permission from Ackerman, P. D., Kelly, M. L., Walsh, C. A., and Ross, L. F. 'Do Peer Guidelines or Editorial Policies Affect the Reporting and Discussion of Race and Ethnicity in Pediatric Research?' 12 (2005), 17–31, 22 Table 1.

Isaacs and Schroeder point out: 'Race and class are both independently associated with health status, although it is often difficult to disentangle the individual effects of the two factors.'[38] Such information would be difficult to tease out in the articles we reviewed as only 39% and 43% reported on both R/E and social markers in 1999–2000 and 2002–2003 respectively, and less than half of those who reported these data discussed their significance.

6.　Conclusion

It is important to understand which children participate in research and why. Without such understanding we cannot know if we are serving all of our children adequately and fairly. As a matter of social justice, we need to ensure that *all* children will benefit from the translation of health care research into health outcomes. Current disparities in health outcomes between minority children and their Caucasian counterparts[39], and between children of lower and higher-family socioeconomic status,[40] suggest that this is not occurring.

References

1. Department of Health and Human Services (DHHS), Public Health Service (PHS), and National Institutes of Health (NIH), 'NIH Guidelines on the Inclusion of Women and Minorities as Subjects in Clinical Research, Part VIII', *Federal Register*, 59 (28 March 1994), 14508–13.
2. National Institutes of Health (NIH), 'Policy and Guidelines on the Inclusion of Children as Participants in Research Involving Human Subjects'. On the web at http:/ /grants.nih.gov/grants/guide/notice-files/not98–024.html.
3. National Commission for the Protection of Human Subjects of Biomedical and Behavioral Research, *Belmont Report: Ethical Principles and Guidelines for the Protection of Human Subjects of Research*. Washington DC: US Government Printing Office, 1978, DHEW Publication No. (OS) 78–12. Found on the web at: http:/ /ohsr.od.nih.gov/guidelines/belmont.html.
4. See, e.g., Vidaver, R. M., Lafleur, B., Tong, C., Bradshaw, R., and Marts, S. A., 'Women Subjects in NIH-Funded Clinical Research Literature: Lack of Progress in Both Representation and Analysis by Sex', *Journal of Women's Health & Gender-Based Medicine*, 9 (2000), 495–504; Harris, D. J., and Douglas, P. S., 'Enrollment of Women in Cardiovascular Clinical Trials Funded by the National Heart, Lung, and Blood Institute', *New England Journal of Medicine*, 343 (2000), 475–80; Heiat, A., Gross, C. P., and Krumholz, H. M., 'Representation of the Elderly, Women, and Minorities in Heart Failure Clinical Trials', *Archives of Internal Medicine*, 162 (2002),1682–8; Haynes, M. A., and Smedley, B. D. (eds.) for the Institute of Medicine (IOM), *The Unequal Burden of Cancer: An Assessment of NIH Research and Programs for Ethnic Minorities and the Medically Underserved*. Washington DC: National Academy Press, 1999, hereinafter cited as IOM, *Unequal Burden*; and Gifford, A. L., Cunningham, W. E., Heslin, K. C.,

Andersen, R. M., Nakazono, T., Lieu, D. K., Shapiro, M. F., and Bozzette, S. A. for the HIV Cost and Services Utilization Study Consortium, 'Participation in Research and Access to Experimental Treatments by HIV-Infected Patients', *New England Journal of Medicine*, 346 (2002), 1373–82.

5. See, e.g., American Academy of Pediatrics (AAP), Committee on Pediatric Research, 'Race/ Ethnicity, Gender, Socioeconomic Status—Research Exploring their Effects on Child Health: A Subject Review', *Pediatrics* 105 (2000), 1349–51; and Rivera, F. P., and Finberg, L., 'Use of the Terms Race and Ethnicity', *Archives of Pediatrics and Adolescent Medicine*, 155 (2001), 119.

6. See, e.g., Olson, L. M., Lara, M., and Pat Frintner, M., 'Measuring Health Status and Quality of Life for US Children: Relationship to Race, Ethnicity, and Income Status', *Ambulatory Pediatrics*, 4 (4 Suppl.) (2004), 377–86.

7. Department of Health and Human Services (HHS). (45 CFR 46 Subpart A), 'Final Regulations Amending Basic HHS Policy for the Protection of Human Research Subjects', *Federal Register*, 46 (26 January 1981), 8366–91; revised *Federal Register*, 56 (18 June 1991), 28003–18. Subpart A is known as the Common Rule because it was adopted by many federal agencies.

8. Walsh, C. A., and Ross, L. F., 'Are Minority Children Over- or Under-represented in Pediatric Research?' *Pediatrics*, 112 (2003), 890–5.

9. See, e.g., IOM, *Unequal Burden*; Heiat *et al.*, 'Representation'; Gifford *et al.*, 'Participation by HIV-Infected Patients'; and Evelyn, B., Toigo, T., Banks, D., Pohl, D., Gray, K., Robins, B., and Ernat, J., 'Participation of Racial/ Ethnic Groups in Clinical Trials and Race-Related Labeling: A Review of New Molecular Entities Approved 1995–1999', *Journal of the National Medical Association*, 93 (2001), 18S–24S; reprinted with permission on the web at: http://www.fda.gov/ cder/reports/ race_ethnicity/race_ethnicity_report.htm.

10. See, e.g., Orr, S. T., Miller, C. A., and James, S. A., 'Differences in Use of Health Services by Children According to Race: Relative Importance of Cultural and System-Related Factors', *Medical Care*, 22 (1984), 848–53; Flores, G., Bauchner, H., Feinstein, A. R., Nguyen, U. S., 'The Impact of Ethnicity, Family Income, and Parental Education on Children's Health and Use of Health Services', *American Journal of Public Health*, 89 (1999), 1066–71; Lillie-Blanton, M., and Hoffman, C., 'Racial and Ethnic Inequities in Access to Medical Care: Introduction', *Medical Care Research & Review*, 57 (Suppl. 1) (2000), 5–10; Weinick, R. M., Zuvekas, S. H., and Cohen, J. W., 'Racial and Ethnic Differences in Access to and Use of Health Care Services, 1977 to 1996', *Medical Care Research & Review*, 57 (Suppl. 1) (2000), 36–54; and Weitzman, M., Byrd, R. S., and Auinger, P., 'Black and White Middle Class Children Who Have Private Health Insurance in the United States', *Pediatrics*, 104 (Suppl. 1) (1999), 151–7.

11. Moy, E., Valente, E. Jr., Levin, R. J., and Griner, P. F., 'Academic Medical Centers and the Care of Underserved Populations', *Academic Medicine*, 71 (1996), 1370–7. One could argue that the location of academic medical centers (AMCs) cannot be an important explanatory factor because minority adults are not overrepresented. Rather, the data show minority adults are underrepresented. See, e.g., IOM, *Unequal Burden*; Gifford *et al.*, 'Participation by HIV-infected

patients'; and Evelyn *et al.*, 'Race-Related Labeling'. There are data that suggest that the role of AMCs differs for pediatric and adult research, particularly in recruitment for clinical trials. Almost 50% of research involving adult-subjects are contracted out to CROs (contracting research organizations) whereas the role of CROs in pediatric trials is much smaller, although growing. See, e.g., Campbell, E. G., Weissman, J. S., Moy, E., and Blumenthal, D., 'Status of Clinical Research in Academic Health Centers: Views from the Research Leadership', *JAMA*, 286 (2001), 800–6; and Heffner, S., 'Beyond the CRO'. On the web at: http:// www.contractpharma.com/ March044.htm.

12. Office of Management and Budget, *Directive No. 15: Race and Ethnic Standards for Federal Statistics and Administrative Reporting*, (1977). A copy of this directive can be found as Appendix 1 to the Executive Office of the President, Office of Management and Budget, Office of Information and Regulatory Affairs, 'Recommendations from the Interagency Committee for the Review of the Racial and Ethnic Standards to the Office of Management and Budget Concerning Changes to the Standards for the Classification of Federal Data on Race and Ethnicity', *Federal Register*, 62 (9 July 1997), 36873–949, 36874, Appendix 1. Directive 15 was revised most recently in 1997. Office of Management and Budget, 'Revisions to the Standards for the Classification of Federal Data on Race and Ethnicity', *Federal Register*, 62 (30 October 1997), 58781–90.

13. US Census Bureau, Population Estimates: Race/ Ethnicity <http://eire.census. gov/popest/data/race.php>.

14. Flores, G., Fuentes-Afflick, E., Barbot, O., Carter-Pokras, O., Claudio, L., Lara, M., McLaurin, J. A., Pachter, L., Ramos-Gomez, F. J., Mendoza, F., Valdez, R. B., Villarruel, A. M., Zambrana, R. E., Greenberg, R., and Weitzman, M., 'The Health of Latino Children: Urgent Priorities, Unanswered Questions, and a Research Agenda', *JAMA*, 288 (2002), 82–90.

15. Ibid.

16. Frayne, S. M., Burns, R. B., Hardt, E. J., Rosen, A. K., and Moskowitz, M. A., 'The Exclusion of Non-English-Speaking Persons from Research', *Journal of General Internal Medicine*, 11 (1996), 39–43.

17. Oppenheimer, G. M., 'Paradigm Lost: Race, Ethnicity, and the Search for a New Population Taxonomy', *American Journal of Public Health*, 91 (2001), 1049–55.

18. See, e.g., Flores *et al.*, 'Health Priorities'; Flores, G., Bauchner, H., Feinstein, A. R., and Nguyen, U-S. D. T., 'The Impact of Ethnicity, Family Income and Parental Education of Children's Health and Use of Health Services', *American Journal of Public Health*, 89 (1999),1066–71; Weinick, R. M., Jacobs, E. A., Stone, L. C., Ortega, A. N., and Burstin, H., 'Hispanic Healthcare Disparities: Challenging the Myth of a Monolithic Hispanic Population', *Medical Care*, 42 (2004), 313–20; Louie, K. B., 'White Paper on the Health Status of Asian Americans and Pacific Islanders and Recommendations for Research', *Nursing Outlook*, 49 (2001), 173–8; and Fang, J., Madhavan, S., and Alderman, M. H., 'Low Birth Weight: Race and Maternal Nativity—Impact of Community Income', *Pediatrics*, 103 (1999), e5. Found on the web at: http://www.pediatrics.org/cgi/ content/full/103/1/e5; and Gimenez, M. E., 'Latino'/'Hispanic'—Who Needs a

Name? The Case Against a Standardized Terminology', *International Journal of Health Services*, 19 (1989), 557–71.

19. Flores *et al.*, 'Health Priorities'.

20. Ibid.

21. See ibid; see also Lange, J. W., 'Methodological Concerns for Non-Hispanic Investigators Conducting Research with Hispanic Americans', *Research in Nursing and Health* 25 (2002), 411–19.

22. See, e.g., Weitzman *et al.*, 'Black and White'; Goodman, A. H., 'Why Genes Don't Count (for Racial Differences in Health)', *American Journal of Public Health*, 90 (2000), 1699–1702; Osborne, N. G., and Feit, M. D., 'The Use of Race in Medical Research', *JAMA*, 267 (1992), 275–9; and Jones, C. P., 'Levels of Racism: A Theoretic Framework and a Gardener's Tale', *American Journal of Public Health*, 90 (2000), 1212–15.

23. Ards, S., Chung, C., and Myers, S. L. Jr., 'The Effects of Sample Selection Bias on Racial Differences in Child Abuse Reporting', *Child Abuse & Neglect*, 22 (1998), 103–15; Lane, W. G., Rubin, D. M., Monteith, R., and Christian, C. W., 'Racial Differences in the Evaluation of Pediatric Fractures for Physical Abuse', *JAMA*, 288 (2002), 1603–9; Kenny, M. C., and McEachern, A. G., 'Racial, Ethnic, and Cultural Factors of Childhood Sexual Abuse: A Selected Review of the Literature', *Clinical Psychology Review*, 20 (2000), 905–22; and Powers, J. L., and Eckenrode, J., 'The Maltreatment of Adolescents', *Child Abuse & Neglect*, 12 (1988), 189–99.

24. Osborne and Feit, 'The Use of Race'.

25. Centers for Disease Control and Prevention. 'HIV/ AIDS Surveillance by Race/ Ethnicity'. Found on the web at: http://www.cdc.gov/hiv/graphics/minority.htm. See specifically slides 3 and 4.

26. Moy *et al.*, 'Academic Medical Centers'.

27. Bleyer, W. A., Tejeda, H., Murphy, S. B., Brawley, O. W., Smith, M. A., and Ungerleider, R. S., 'Equal Participation of Minority Patients in US National Pediatric Cancer Clinical Trials', *Journal of Pediatric Hematology Oncology*, 19 (1997), 423–7.

28. Ibid. at 426.

29. Gross, C. P., Mallory, R., Heiat, A., and Krumholz, H. M., 'Reporting the Recruitment Process in Clinical Trials: Who are These Patients and How Did They Get There?' *Annals of Internal Medicine*, 137 (2002), 10–16.

30. Begg, C., Cho, M., Eastwood, S., Olkin, I., Rennie, D., and Stroup, D. F., 'Improving the Quality of Reporting of Randomized Controlled Trials. The CONSORT Statement', *JAMA*, 276 (1996), 637–9. The CONSORT statement was most recently updated by Moher, D., Schulz, K. F., and Altman, D. G., 'The CONSORT Statement: Revised Recommendations for Improving the Quality of Reports of Parallel-Group Randomised Trials', *Lancet*, 357 (2001), 1191–4.

31. IOM, *Unequal Burden*; Corbie-Smith, G., Thomas, S. B., Williams, M. V., and Moody-Ayers, S., 'Attitudes and Beliefs of African Americans toward Participation in Medical Research', *Journal of General Internal Medicine*, 14 (1999), 537–46; Kressin, N. R., Meterko, M., and Wilson, N. J., 'Racial Disparities in Participation in Biomedical Research', *Journal of the National Medical Association*, 92 (2000),

62–9; Giuliano, A. R., Mokuau, N., Hughes, C., Tortolero-Luna, G., Risendal, B., Ho, R. C. S., Prewitt, T. E., and McCaskill-Stevens, W. J., 'Participation of Minorities in Cancer Research: The Influence of Structural, Cultural, and Linguistic Factors', *Annals of Epidemiology*, 10 (8 Suppl.) (2000), S22–34; and Shavers-Hornaday, V. L., Lynch, C. F., Burmeister, L. F., and Torner, J. C., 'Why are African Americans Under-Represented in Medical Research Studies? Impediments to Participation', *Ethnicity & Health*, 2 (1997), 31–45.

32. IOM, *Unequal Burden;* and Shavers-Hornaday, 'Why Under-Represented?'

33. Westermeyer, J., 'Problems with Surveillance Methods for Alcoholism: Differences in Coding Systems Among Federal, State, and Private Agencies', *American Journal of Public Health*, 78 (1988), 130–3.

34. International Committee of Medical Journal Editors, 'Uniform Requirements for Manuscripts Submitted to Biomedical Journals', *Annals of Internal Medicine*, 126 (1997), 36–47.

35. Evelyn, B. *et al.*, 'Race-Related Labeling'; Centers for Disease Control [CDC], 'Reporting Race and Ethnicity Data—National Electronic Telecommunications System for Surveillance, 1994–1997', *MMWR—Morbidity & Mortality Weekly Report*, 48 (1999), 305–12.

36. Isaacs, S. L., and Schroeder, S. A., 'Class—The Ignored Determinant of the Nation's Health', *New England Journal of Medicine*, 351 (2004), 1137–42, 1137.

37. See, e.g., Flores *et al.*, 'Impact of Ethnicity'; Berkman, L. F., and Macintyre, S., 'The Measurement of Social Class in Health Studies: Old Measures and New Formulations', *IARC Scientific Publications*, 138 (1997), 51–64; Burchard, E. G., Ziv, E., Coyle, N., Gomez, S. L., Tang, H., Karter, A. J., Mountain, J. L., Perez-Stable, E. J., Sheppard, D., and Risch, N., 'The Importance of Race and Ethnic Background in Biomedical Research and Clinical Practice', *New England Journal of Medicine*, 348 (2003), 1170–5; Cooper, R., 'A Note on the Biologic Concept of Race and its Application in Epidemiologic Research', *American Heart Journal*, 108 (3 Part 2) (1984), 715; and Epstein, A. M., and Ayanian, J. Z., 'Racial Disparities in Medical Care', *New England Journal of Medicine*, 344 (2001), 1471–3.

38. Isaacs and Schroeder, 'Class' citing Wong, M. D., Shapiro, M. F., Boscardin, W. J., Ettner, S. L., 'Contribution of Major Diseases to Disparities in Mortality', *New England Journal of Medicine*, 347 (2002), 1585–92.

39. See, e.g., Flores *et al*, 'Impact of Ethnicity'; Weitzman *et al.*, 'Black and White'; Gonzalez, P. C., Gauvreau, K., Demone, J. A., Piercey, G. E., and Jenkins, K. J., 'Regional Racial and Ethnic Differences in Mortality for Congenital Heart Surgery in Children May Reflect Unequal Access to Care', *Pediatric Cardiology*, 24 (2003), 103–8; and Lieu, T. A., Lozano, P., Finkelstein, J. A., Chi, F. W., Jensvold, N. G., Capra, A. M., Quesenberry, C. P., Selby, J. V., and Farber, H. J., 'Racial/Ethnic Variation in Asthma Status and Management Practices among Children in Managed Medicaid', *Pediatrics*, 109 (2002), 857–65.

40. See, e.g., Olson, 'Measuring Health Status'; Erickson, S. R., Munzenberger, P. J., Plante, M. J., Kirking, D. M., Hurwitz, M. E., and Vanuya, R. Z., 'Influence of Sociodemographics on the Health-Related Quality of Life of Pediatric Patients with Asthma and their Caregivers', *Journal of Asthma*, 39 (2002), 107–17.

3

Overview of the Common Rule and Subpart D

1. Introduction

As discussed in Chapter 1, the National Commission (for the Protection of Human Subjects of Biomedical and Behavioral Research) published over 20 reports and appendices in the 1970s, the most often cited of which is *The Belmont Report*.[1] The National Commission's report entitled *Research Involving Children* was published one year earlier.[2] The Code of Federal Regulations (CFR) 45 part 46, Federal Policy for the Protection of Human Subjects, were developed based on these reports. Subpart A of 45 CFR 46 is known as the Common Rule because it has been adopted by sixteen federal agencies and departments of the US government. It was most recently revised in 1991.[3] Subpart D provides additional protections for research involving children; it, too, was revised in 1991.[4] In April 2001, the Food and Drug Administration (FDA) wrote interim rules that adopted most of Subpart D for all research subject to its regulatory authority.[5]

In this chapter, I examine in detail 45 CFR Part 46 as it applies to children-subjects in order to set the foundation for much of my critique. Two decades later, I believe that the regulations to protect human subjects remain quite viable and useful, although a few modifications may be necessary. I also enumerate several issues regarding human subject protections that are not addressed in the federal regulations that will be explored in future chapters.

2. Motivation: The Children's Health Act of 2000

My systematic examination of the regulations of children as research subjects began in 2000 when the Children's Health Act was passed by US Congress.[6] The Act required the Department of Health and Human Services (DHHS) to conduct a review of Subpart D and to consider 'any modifications necessary to ensure the adequate and appropriate protection of children participating in research'.[7] As discussed in Chapter 1, the Best Pharmaceutical for Children Act of 2002 (BPCA) mandated the Institute of Medicine (IOM) to conduct a study of current protections provided to children involved in research.[8] Specifically, the IOM was charged to examine:

(1) the appropriateness of the federal regulations for children of different ages and maturity levels;

(2) the interpretation of regulatory criteria for approving research involving children, including the concept of 'minimal risk';

(3) the processes for securing parent's and children's agreement to a child's participation in research;

(4) the expectations and comprehension of children and parents about what it means to participate in research and how research differs from medical treatment;

(5) the appropriateness of payment to a child, parent, guardian, or legally authorized representative for the child's participation in research;

(6) the compliance with and enforcement of federal regulations; and

(7) the roles and responsibilities of institutional review boards (IRBs) in reviewing research involving children.

The charge to the IOM pointed to some critical issues that are ambiguous or not addressed in the current regulations, many of which will be addressed in this book. The IOM report, *The Ethical Conduct of Clinical Research Involving Children*, was published in 2004.[9] Throughout this book, I will refer to the solutions proposed by the IOM and how it does or does not improve protections for children.

3.   The Common Rule: What is Research and How is it Regulated?

The Common Rule begins with the question: 'To what does this policy apply (CFR §46.101)?' The answer is 'all research involving human subjects conducted, supported or otherwise subject to regulation by any Federal Department or Agency (CFR §46.101(a))'. Most health care institutions that receive any federal funds and engage in research apply for a FWA or federalwide assurance (previously a MPA or multiple project assurance). An FWA asserts that

Institutions conducting federally-supported human subject research and the [Institutional Review Board(s)] IRB(s) designated under the Institution's Assurance will comply with the Federal Policy for the Protection of Human Subjects, known as the Common Rule. All federally supported human subject research will also comply with any additional human subject regulations and policies of the supporting Department or Agency. All human subject research conducted or supported by the Department of Health and Human Services (DHHS) will comply with all Subparts of DHHS regulations at Title 45 Code of Federal Regulations Part 46 (45 CFR 46 and its Subparts A, B, C, and D).[10]

To ensure compliance with the federal regulations, institutions create IRBs that are charged with the review of biomedical and behavioral research conducted at their institutions. The Common Rule is quite clear that the protection of human subjects includes a scientific and ethical review of the research by a 'properly' constituted IRB.[11] Some research is exempt. This includes (1) research conducted in established or commonly accepted education settings, involving normal educational practices[CFR §46.101(b)(1)]; (2) research involving the use of educational tests (cognitive, diagnostic, aptitude, achievement) survey procedures, interview procedures, or observation of public behavior [CFR §46.101(b)(2)]; and (3) research involving the collection or study of existing data, documents, records, pathological specimens or diagnostic specimens, if these sources are publicly available or if the information is recorded by the investigator in such a manner that subjects cannot be identified [CFR §46.101(b) (4)] In Subpart D, exemptions are reviewed to see if they are applicable to children-subjects. While the exemption at CFR §46.101(b)(2) regarding educational tests applies, research involving survey or interview procedures or observation of public behavior does not apply to research with children.

Although some other research can be expedited, most other research must undergo full review by an IRB to ensure that the research meets the following requirements:

(1) Risks to subjects are minimized.[12]
(2) Risks to subjects are reasonable in relation to anticipated benefits if any, to subjects, and the importance of the knowledge that may reasonably by expected to result. In evaluating risks and benefits, the IRB should consider only those risks and benefits that may result from the research as distinguished from risks and benefits of therapies subjects would receive even if not participating in the research. The IRB should not consider possible long-range effects of applying the knowledge gained in the research.
(3) Selection of subjects is equitable. In making this assessment the IRB should take into account the purposes of the research and the setting in which the research will be conducted and should be particularly cognizant of the special problems of research involving vulnerable populations(CFR §46.111(a)(1–3))

The first two criteria, taken together, define the range of permissible research activities. It is necessary but not sufficient that the risk/benefit ratio be favorable to the subject. It is also necessary that the risks are minimized. The issue of whether current research minimizes risks is discussed in Chapter 13 on placebo-controlled asthma trials and in Chapter 10 on newborn screening for type 1 diabetes. The third criterion focuses on questions of justice regarding subject selection. I addressed this in Chapter 2 regarding the overrepresentation of minority children in pediatric research. Subject selection is also addressed in terms of 'captive populations' (see Chapters 9 and 10) and in terms of minimizing risks (Chapters 10, 11, 12, and 14).

The BPCA charged the IOM to look at the role and responsibilities of institutional review boards in reviewing research involving children. The IOM report offers several important recommendations including (1) that all research involving children should be conducted under the oversight of a formal program for protecting human participants in research;[13] (2) that there is a need for pediatric expertise on IRBs reviewing protocols that seek to enroll children;[14] and (3) that there is a need to test and evaluate means to improve the efficiency as well as the quality and consistency of reviews of multicenter studies, including those involving infants, children, and adolescents.[15] In Chapter 7, I include data I collected with colleagues on the current state of oversight in pediatric research. We found that most research does undergo IRB review and that adequate consent mechanisms are included. However, we did find some inconsistencies involving what research ought to be classified as exempt that indicates that further guidance and consensus development are necessary. Again, I hope this book will serve as a catalyst for these overdue developments.

4. Subpart D: Risks and Benefits

In Subpart D, research is distinguished by level of risk and whether the research presents the prospect of direct benefit. The categorization of the research affects whose consent is necessary, whether the child's dissent is binding, and whether national review is necessary.

The first category, CFR §46.404 or research not involving greater than minimal risk, can be approved by an IRB and requires only one parent's permission and the child's assent. To understand what such research might entail, one must have a sense of what is considered minimal risk research. In its report, *Research Involving Children*, the National Commission defined 'minimal risk' as: 'the probability and magnitude of physical or psychological harm that is normally encountered in the daily lives, or in the routine medical or psychological examination, of healthy children.'[16]

The definition of minimal risk in the federal regulations, however, is not found in Subpart D but in Subpart A, and it applies to research involving child and adult subjects. In Subpart A, minimal risk is defined as: 'the probability and magnitude of harm or discomfort anticipated in the research are not greater in and of themselves than those ordinarily encountered in daily life or during the performance of routine physical or psychological examinations or tests (CFR §46.102 (i)).' Most noticeable, then, is that the definition leaves out the final phrase 'of healthy children', or even 'of healthy subjects'. The significance of this omission is examined in Chapter 5.

CFR §46.405 involves research involving greater than minimal risk but presenting the prospect of direct benefit to the individual subjects. Research in this category can be approved by an IRB provided that (a) the risk is justified by the anticipated benefit to the subjects; and (b) the relation of the anticipated benefit to the risk is at least as favorable to the subjects as that presented by available alternative approaches. Such research can be approved with one parent's permission and the child's assent, although the child's dissent can be overridden.

In its report, *Research Involving Children*, the National Commission did not define 'direct benefit' or what degree of probability is required for research to offer 'the prospect of direct benefit'. The report by Congress in 2001 noted that further clarification was needed to define what counts as 'the prospect of direct benefit for the individual subject'.[17] The IOM report defined 'direct benefit' as 'a tangible positive outcome (e.g., cure of disease, relief of pain, and increased mobility) that may be experienced by an individual'.[18] It also distinguished between 'direct benefit' and 'collateral' or indirect benefit.[19] It then argued that direct benefits could be understood 'relationally';[20] that is, compared with the subjects' other options. Consider, then, children with terminal cancer whose only options are palliative care or enrollment in a Phase I oncology research protocol. Phase I oncology trials are designed to determine toxicity, although a small number of subjects (less than 5%) receive an unintended direct benefit defined as some degree of tumor response. According to the IOM report, these studies can be classified as offering the prospect of a direct benefit. This is significant because it allows children to be exposed to greater risks than otherwise would be permissible with local IRB review and because it means that the child's refusal is not necessarily dispositive. I disagree with the classification of Phase I oncology trials as offering the prospect of direct benefit and argue it perpetuates the therapeutic misconception of this type of research.[21] I discuss the concept of direct benefit and how Phase I oncology trials should be evaluated in Chapter 6.

CFR §46.406 addresses research involving greater than minimal risk and no prospect of direct benefit to individual subjects, but likely to yield generalizable knowledge about the subject's disorder or condition. Such research can be approved by an IRB if (1) the risk represents a minor increase over minimal risk; (2) the intervention or procedure presents experiences to subjects that are reasonably commensurate with those inherent in the actual or expected medical, dental, psychological, social, or educational situations; and (3) the intervention is likely to yield generalizable knowledge about the subject's disorder or condition which is of vital importance for the understanding or amelioration of the subjects' disorder or condition. For research classified under 45.406, permission from both parents and the child's assent are required.

In its report, *Research Involving Children*, the National Commission did not offer a working definition for a 'minor increase over minimal loss' but rather, offered vague guidelines based on an IRB's determination of degree of risk and harm.[22]. It also did not define what is meant by a 'disorder or condition'. The 2002 Report to Congress found that clarification of the terms 'minor increase over minimal risk' and 'disorder or condition' were needed.[23] The IOM committee noted that 'disorder or condition' could be interpreted so narrowly as to only permit the participation of those with 'an illness, disease, injury or defect' or so broadly as to allow children with social and economic disadvantages to participate in much more research than their more privileged counterparts.[24] The IOM committee took a middle ground allowing some children 'at risk' for a disorder or condition to be included within the concept of 'disorder or condition' in CFR §46.406:

If a characteristic of a group of children is to be designated as a condition that allows children to be exposed to a higher level of risk without prospect of benefit, the link between the characteristic and a deficit in health or well-being should be supported by scientific evidence of clinical knowledge.[25]

The definition of 'disorder or condition' in the IOM report is somewhat more conservative than the definition provided by the National Human Research Protections Advisory Committee (NHRPAC). NHRPAC defined the concept of disorder or condition as 'relating to a specific characteristic which describes a group of children, a physical, social, psychological, or neuro-developmental condition affecting children, or the risk of certain children developing a disease in the future based on diagnostic testing or physical examination.'[26] NHRPAC elaborated that there are certain conditions including poverty or having a genetic predisposition that can 'under appropriate circumstances, warrant permissible research that presents levels of risk that are a minor increase over minimal without the prospect of direct benefit'.[27]

Through case studies, I attempt to develop some guidelines as to when, if ever, 'at risk' children should be included within the concept of having a disorder or condition under CFR §46.406. First, in Chapters 10 and 11, I discuss what it means to be 'at risk' for type 1 diabetes. I conclude that a positive family history can define one as 'at risk' although high risk genetic alleles without a family history does not. This is important for determining which children should be enrolled in diabetes research. Second, in Chapter 12, I argue that children at environmental risk for lead poisoning (plumbism) should also be included in the concept of having a 'disorder or condition'.

Third, in Chapter 14, I consider whether ethnicity is relevant for classifying children to be 'at risk' for type 2 diabetes. The American Diabetes Association states that ethnicity is a risk factor *in combination with* other risk factors.[28] In this chapter, I argue that a child of Asian ancestry without other risk factors should not be classified as 'at risk'.

The distinction of whether a child has a disorder or condition is important under the current regulations because only children with a 'disorder or condition' can participate in research that poses a minor increase over minimal risk and does not offer the prospect of direct benefit (CFR §46.406). By contrast, healthy children can only be exposed to minimal risk (CFR §46.404). In Chapter 4, I argue that permitting children with a 'disorder or condition' to be exposed to greater risk than healthy children is unethical. Rather, I argue that the appropriate standard to which a researcher may expose all children is 'one in which the probability of physical and psychological harm is no more than that to which it is appropriate to intentionally expose a child for educational purposes in family life situations'.[29]

Much of the diabetes research in Chapters 10, 11, and 14 could be ethical under this revised risk standard if the studies sought to enroll only those who are 'at risk'. I argue that whether a child has a 'disorder or condition', or is 'at risk' for a 'disorder or condition' is relevant for how risk is perceived by the child and parent, and this perception should influence the child's suitability as a research subject.

CFR §46.407 addresses research not otherwise approvable which presents an opportunity to understand, prevent, or alleviate a serious problem affecting the health or welfare of children. Such research cannot be approved by a local IRB but must be reviewed by a panel of experts convened by the secretary of the Department of Health and Human Services (DHHS). The panel must determine that the research (b)(i) presents a reasonable opportunity to understand, prevent, or alleviate a serious problem affecting the health or welfare of children; (b)(ii) will be conducted in accordance with sound ethical principles; and (b)(iii) provides for the processes to obtain parental permission and the child's assent.

The National Commission did not define what is meant by 'more than a minor increase over minimal risk' nor did it define what is a 'reasonable opportunity'. It has been noted by others that research under CFR §46.406 is required to yield generalizable knowledge about the subject's disorder or condition which is of vital importance; whereas the research under CFR §46.407 is only required to yield information that will 'further the understanding, prevention or alleviation of a serious problem'.[30] An explanation is needed to explain why there is a lower threshold of scientific importance for research under CFR §46.407 and whether this lower threshold should be revised given that the research needs federal and not local review. I concur with the IOM that 407 process should be reserved for 'exceptional situations' and research of 'major significance'.[31] Although I do not address the terminology in detail, I do discuss the 407 review process in Chapters 14 and 15.

5.   *Informed Consent Requirements*

Each of the research categories in Subpart D requires that adequate provisions are made for soliciting consent which includes both parental permission and the child's assent. The regulations provide guidance as to what this entails in section CFR §46.408. While IRBs determine when children are capable of providing assent (CFR §46.408(a)), the regulations require that the IRB take into account the ages, maturity, and psychological state of the children involved (CFR §46.408(c)). This judgment can be made for all children involved in research under a particular protocol, or for each child, as the IRB deems appropriate (CFR §46.408(c)). The child's assent can also be waived for certain research approvable under CFR §46.116 of Subpart A (CFR §46.116(c) (1–2)).

Under CFR §46.408, some research requires permission from only one parent (CFR §46.404 and CFR §46.405) and other research requires permission from both parents unless one parent is deceased, unknown, incompetent, or not reasonably available, or when only one parent has legal responsibility for the care and custody of the child (CFR §46.406 and CFR §46.407). Parental permission can also be waived, but under very limited circumstances. When parental permission is waived, an appropriate mechanism to protect the children must be substituted (CFR §46.408(c)).

I will examine several controversies with the current consent requirements in Chapter 5. For example, I question whether the requirement to procure permission from both parents provides any additional protection; whether parental waivers should be expanded or restricted; and whether the child him- or herself can serve as an appropriate substitute mechanism if parental permission is waived.

6.   *Pediatric Sub-populations*

The National Commission was particularly aware that some populations are more vulnerable than others. In both the Belmont Report and in the report, *Research Involving Children*, the National Commission considered the vulnerability of children.[32] The National Commission believed that younger children were more vulnerable than older children and recommended research begin with animals, then adults, followed by older children. I concur with this position as can be seen in Chapter 10 where I argue to restrict research on newborns when older populations can substitute because newborns are more vulnerable.

Another vulnerable sub-population are members of minority racial and ethnic groups as well as those of lower socio-economic standing. These concerns are raised in the *Belmont Report*,[33] although not specifically considered in relationship to children and not addressed in the report focused on children. The data I present in Chapter 2 show that minority children are overrepresented in pediatric research. This is true despite the fact that they have less access to health care generally.

The National Commission addressed three additional vulnerable pediatric sub-populations: wards of the state, institutionalized children, and children confined to correctional institutions.[34] Their recommendations for children who are wards can be found in Subpart D. CFR §46.409 permits research on children who are wards of the state related to their status as wards; or if the research is 'being conducted in schools, camps, hospitals, institutions, or similar settings in which the majority of children involved as subjects are not wards'. Children who reside in institutions or who are confined in correctional facilities are also particularly vulnerable. The National Commission argued that they should only participate in research 'only if the conditions regarding research on the institutionalized mentally infirm or on prisoners (as applicable) are fulfilled in addition to the criterion set forth herein'.[35] The ethical and policy issues raised by children who are not members of intimate families or who do not reside within a family structure are unique and incredibly complex. I do not address these issues in this book.[36]

7. Issues Not Addressed in Current Federal Regulations

There are several issues that are not addressed in either Subpart A or Subpart D of the federal regulations to protect human subjects. Two such issues are payment to subjects and compensation for injuries. The IOM committee was charged to look at payment for participation, not for compensation. I too will focus on payment and not compensation and will concur with the IOM report that it is morally permissible to pay children, but I will argue for this position using very different arguments than those offered by the IOM report. The IOM committee argued to permit payment to reimburse for reasonable expenses and 'as gestures of appreciation'.[37] In Chapter 8, I will argue that in a system in which the permissible level of risks to which children can be exposed in research is restricted, payment beyond a gesture of appreciation is morally permissible.

Another issue not addressed in Subpart D is the issue of children who may be at increased risk for non-voluntary consent because of the setting in which the research is undertaken. Consider, for example, primary and secondary schools. In schools, children are accustomed to follow orders and to do what the teacher assigns. School children may also agree to participate in research because they do not understand their right to refuse or because they feel compelled to accede to peer pressure. Even their parents may not understand that the research being done in the school setting is truly voluntary. In Chapter 9, I discuss what additional protections should be offered when research is planned for the school venue. I use Subpart C of the federal regulations,[38] the regulations designed to protect prisoners as a guide for research involving children in schools. The concern regarding prisoners is that they are vulnerable because of constraints on their freedom.[39] I believe that similar concerns hold regarding school children asked to participate in research in the school setting.

A second research venue that may hamper voluntary consent is the hospital newborn nursery. In Chapter 10, I consider whether post-partum mothers are giving voluntary consent for their infants in the hospital nursery. I argue that newborns captive in the hospital nursery are more vulnerable than other infants and children and suggest that research be done, when possible, beyond the nursery stay.

8.   Concluding Thoughts

Current regulations regarding research subjects provide a wonderful stepping stone from which to examine the promises and pitfalls of balancing access and protection. My goals are: (1) to affirm those regulations that provide necessary protection; (2) to reject or propose modifications to those regulations that either fail to protect or provide unnecessary and burdensome protections; and (3) to recommend additional guidelines when necessary to ensure that human subject protections simultaneously provide appropriate protection and adequate opportunities for researchers and subjects to promote the health of current and future populations.

References

1. National Commission for the Protection of Human Subjects of Biomedical and Behavioral Research, *The Belmont Report: Ethical Principles and Guidelines for the Protection of Human Subjects of Research*. Washington DC: US Government Printing Office, 1978, DHEW Publication No. (OS) 78–12. On the web at: *http:// ohsr.od.nih.gov/guidelines/belmont.html*; hereinafter cited as *Belmont Report*.
2. National Commission for the Protection of Human Subjects, *Report and Recommendations: Research Involving Children*. Washington DC: US Printing Office,

1977, DHEW Publication No. (OS) 77–0004; hereinafter cited as National Commission, *Research Involving Children*.

3. Department of Health and Human Services (DHHS). (45 CFR Part 46 Subpart A), 'Final Regulations Amending Basic HHS Policy for the Protection of Human Research Subjects', *Federal Register*, 46 (26 January 1981), 8366–91; revised *Federal Register*, 56 (18 June 1991), 28003–18; hereinafter cited by its CFR number in endnotes and in the text.

4. Department of Health and Human Services (DHHS). (45 CFR Part 46, Subpart D), 'Protections for Children Involved as Subjects in Research', *Federal Register*, 48 (8 March 1983), 9814–20; revised *Federal Register*, 56 (18 June 1991), 28032; hereinafter cited by its CFR number in endnotes and in the text.

5. Department of Health and Human Services (DHHS), Food and Drug Administration (FDA). (21 CFR Parts 50 and 56), 'Additional Safeguards for Children in Clinical Investigations of FDA-Regulated Products', *Federal Register* 66 (24 April 2001), 20589–600; hereinafter cited by CFR number in notes and in the text.

6. Children's Health Act of 2000, Public Law 106–310 (2000).

7. Ibid., §1003.

8. Best Pharmaceuticals for Children Act (BPCA), Public Law 107–9, 115 Statute 1408 (2002).

9. Field, M. J., and Behrman, R. E. (eds.), Committee on Clinical Research Involving Children, the Institute of Medicine (IOM), *The Ethical Conduct of Clinical Research Involving Children*. Washington DC: National Academies Press, 2004; hereinafter this reference is cited as IOM, *Ethical Conduct*.

10. Department of Health and Human Services (DHHS), Office for Human Research Protections, 'Federalwide Assurance of Protection for Human Subjects'. On the web at *http://www.hhs.gov/ohrp/humansubjects/assurance/filasurt.htm* (version date 3/20/2002).

11. A properly constituted IRB consists of at least 5 members with varying backgrounds (CFR §46.107(a)); at least one member whose primary concerns are in nonscientific areas (CFR §46.107(c)); and at least one member who is not affiliated with the institution (CFR §46.107(d)).

12. The requirement to minimize risk is found in the Common Rule at CFR §46.111(a) (1). It was discussed in the National Commission's report, *Research Involving Children* (National Commission, *Research Involving Children*, 2 [Recommendation 2 C]). One of the National Commission's suggestions for minimizing risks to children was to do the research on animals first, followed by adults and only then by older children (ibid., 2–3). This guideline, however, is no longer strictly followed. For example, in 1998, NIH promulgated guidelines that require researchers to include children or justify their exclusion 'NIH Policy and Guidelines for the Inclusion of Children as Participants in Research Involving Human Subjects', 6 March 1998. On the web at: *http://grants1.nih.gov/grants/guide/notice-files/not98–024.html*. I believe that the spirit of this policy change, to ensure that accurate information is obtained regarding medical treatments for children, is being violated in many studies in which children are enrolled but there are no plans for subset analysis. See the asthma case study in Ch. 12. When the Food and

Drug Administration adopted Subpart D in light of the Children's Health Act of 2000, it reaffirmed the need to minimize risk (CFR § 56.111).

13. IOM, *Ethical Conduct*, 248 [Recommendation 8–1].
14. Ibid., 253 [Recommendation 8–3].
15. Ibid., 266 [Recommendation 8–5].
16. National Commission, *Research Involving Children*, xx.
17. Department of Health and Human Services, Office for Human Research Protections, 'Protections for Children in Research: A Report to Congress in Accord with Section 1003 of P.L. 106–310, *Children's Health Act of 2000*. May 2001'. Found on the web at: *http://www.hhs.gov/ohrp/reports/ohrp502.pdf*,18; hereinafter cited as 'Report to Congress'.
18. IOM, *Ethical Conduct*, 132.
19. IOM, *Ethical Conduct*, 132 citing Churchill, L. R., Nelson, D. K., Henderson, N. M. P., Davis, A. M., Leahey, E., and Wilfond, B. S., 'Assessing Benefits in Clinical Research: Why Diversity in Benefit Assessment Can Be Risky', *IRB: A Review of Human Subjects Research*, 25 (May/June 2003), 1–8.
20. IOM, *Ethical Conduct*, 133 citing Kodish, E., 'Pediatric Ethics and Early-Phase Childhood Cancer Research: Conflicted Goals and the Prospect of Benefit', *Accountability in Research*, 10 (2003), 17–25.
21. Appelbaum, P. S., Roth, L. H., Lidz, C. W., Benson, P., and Winslade, W., 'False Hopes and Best Data: Consent to Research and the Therapeutic Misconception', *Hastings Center Report*, 17 (April 1987), 20–4.
22. National Commission, *Research Involving Children*, xx.
23. 'Report to Congress', 18.
24. IOM, *Ethical Conduct*, 129.
25. Ibid., 130.
26. National Human Research Protections Advisory Committee (NHRPAC), 'Clarifying Specific Portion of 45 CFR 46 Subpart D that Governs Children's Research', undated. Found on the web at: *http://www.hhs.gov/ohrp/nhrpac/documents/nhrpac16.pdf*, 3.
27. Ibid., 3.
28. American Diabetes Association, 'Type 2 Diabetes in Children and Adolescents', *Pediatrics*, 105 (2000), 671–80.
29. Ackerman, T., 'Moral Duties of Parents and Non-Therapeutic Research Procedures Involving Children', *Bioethics Quarterly*, 2 (1980), 94–111 as cited in S. L. Leiken, 'An Ethical Issue in Biomedical Research: The Involvement of Minors in Informed and Third Party Consent', *Clinical Research*, 31 (1983), 34–40, 38.
30. IOM, *Ethical Conduct*, 134.
31. Ibid., 134.
32. In the *Belmont Report*, the concern is between children and adults (see 'Belmont Report'). In *Research Involving Children*, the concern is between older and younger children (see National Commission, *Research Involving Children*, 4).
33. *Belmont Report*.
34. National Commission, *Research Involving Children*, 19–20.
35. Ibid., 20.

36. My work in pediatric ethics has focused on children who are members of intimate families (see Ross, L. F., *Children, Families, and Health Care Decision-Making*. Oxford UK: Clarendon Press, 1998). The ethical issues raised by children and adolescents who are not members of intimate families require a separate analysis.

37. Ibid., 225–6.

38. US Department of Health, Education, and Welfare (DHEW), 'Additional Protections Pertaining to Biomedical and Behavioral Research Involving Prisoners as Subjects', *Federal Register*, 43 (16 November 1978), 53652–6.

39. National Commission for the Protection of Human Subjects of Biomedical and Behavioral Research, *Research on Prisoners: Report and Recommendations*. Washington DC: US Department of Health, Education and Welfare, 1976.

4

Should We Provide Healthy Children with Greater Protection in Medical Research?

1. Introduction

In this chapter, I examine whether Subpart D of the federal regulations on human subject protections provides appropriate protection for all children when research offers no prospect of direct benefit (also known as 'nontherapeutic research'). I show that Subpart D provides greater protection for healthy children and allows children who have a disorder or condition to be exposed to greater risk of harm. I argue that this double standard is unjust because the distribution of burdens falls disproportionately on children with a disorder or condition. I propose suggestions for revising the federal regulations.

2. Minimal Risk Research (CFR §46.404)[1]

When research does not offer the prospect of direct benefit, the National Commission (for the Protection of Human Subjects of Biomedical and Behavioral Research) classifies risks into three categories: minimal risk, a minor increase over minimal risk, and more than a minor increase over minimal risk.[2] As discussed in Chapter 3, minimal risk was defined by the National Commission as: 'the probability and magnitude of physical or psychological harm that is normally encountered in the daily lives, or in the routine medical or psychological examination, of healthy children.'[3]

The definition of minimal risk that is used in Subpart D is the definition of minimal risk found in the Common Rule (Subpart A), and applies to research involving child- and adult-subjects. Minimal risk is defined as: 'the probability and magnitude of harm or discomfort anticipated in the research are not greater in and of themselves than those ordinarily encountered in daily life or during the performance of routine physical or psychological examinations or tests.'[4, (CFR §46.102i)] All children can participate in research that poses minimal risks.

Consider how the definition of minimal risk in the federal regulations differs from the National Commission's definition. The definition in the federal regulations leaves out the final phrase 'of healthy children' (or since it is found only in Subpart A, 'of healthy subjects'). Although some ignore this omission and interpret the minimal risk standard as an absolute standard,[5] others have argued that this omission means that the concept of minimal risk is relative to the risks ordinarily encountered by the particular subject.[6]

Those who believe that the minimal risk standard is an absolute standard argue that it applies a standard degree of risk to all children regardless of their health status or previous life experiences. This interpretation is supported by the examples of minimal risk offered by the National Commission in its report, *Research Involving Children*. The examples include routine immunizations, modest changes in diet or schedule, physical examinations, obtaining blood and urine specimens, and developmental assessments.[7] The problem with this interpretation is that it begs the question by assuming what it needs to prove. The examples provided by the National Commission are offered in a report in which minimal risk is defined relative to the healthy child, but the definition of minimal risk in the federal regulations is not. Proponents of an absolute standard further argue that minimal risk must be absolute, otherwise it would be unnecessary to have a standard that allows only children with a disorder or condition to participate in nontherapeutic research that poses a minor increase over minimal risk (CFR §46.406).

Those who argue that minimal risk is relative argue that the omission of the phrase 'of healthy children' was deliberate and that it means that minimal risk is not to be interpreted as what is 'ordinarily encountered' for a healthy individual, but what is 'ordinarily encountered' for the subject at hand. For example, it suggests that it is more acceptable to enroll a child who has been treated for cancer in a study that requires multiple blood draws over a short period of time than a healthy child because the cancer survivor has experienced multiple blood draws. This means that the cancer survivor can be exposed to greater risks than the healthy child.

Freedman *et al.* argue that the concept of minimal risk is appropriately relational and context-dependent, and represents a categorical judgment that compares the proposed research experiences with experiences that are typical in the everyday life of children.[8] A commensurate risk standard means that children with previous medical experiences, (i.e. children with a disorder or condition), would be permitted to be exposed to greater risks than their healthy counterparts.[9] One problem with a commensurate risk standard is that it does not accommodate those children who have had an adverse experience with a particular procedure and who may be even more fearful of undergoing the procedure than a healthy (procedure-naïve) child. For example, a child who has had a prior bad experience with venipuncture may have an exaggerated fear of it.

Regardless of whether one adopts an absolute or relative interpretation of minimal risk, it is not clear what the 'risks of ordinary life' entail. Kopelman has shown that this is a vague standard as it can mean (1) all the risks ordinary people encounter; (2) the risks all people ordinarily encounter; or (3) the minimal risks all ordinary people ordinarily encounter.[10] The first option would allow very risky procedures to be classified as minimal risk because some ordinary people pursue risky activities (e.g., parachuting). The second option is much more restrictive, constituting a least common denominator of risk. It has problems because it assumes that 'we know the kind of risks we all encounter and their probability and magnitude'.[11] Surveys of pediatric researchers, pediatric chairpersons, and IRB chairpersons show otherwise as there are wide differences regarding what different researchers would classify as minimal risk.[12] The third option is not illuminating because it converts the first part of the minimal risk definition into a useless tautology.[13]

A second problem with the 'risks of ordinary life' is that it assumes that what a child ordinarily encounters is acceptable. The risks ordinarily encountered in 'a routine physical or psychological examination or test' are classified as minimal, but as Kopelman points out, these tests are a source of anxiety for many.[14] Thompson also notes that children commonly encounter experiences at school that threaten their self-image, but that this should not justify similar threats in the research setting.[15] Rather, Thompson argues, investigators should be hesitant to violate basic ethics principles regardless of whether these principles may be violated regularly by others in everyday life.[16] As such, the current definition of minimal risk does not provide adequate nor appropriate guidance as to the appropriate risk threshold for research involving children.

3. Minor Increase Over Minimal Risk (CFR §46.406)

When research involves more than minimal risk and does not offer the prospect of direct benefit, an IRB can approve the project in two situations. First, if the increment is no more than a minor increase over minimal risk; the research project can be permitted if (a) the research activity is commensurate with procedures that those who have this disorder or condition ordinarily experience; and (b) the research must hold out the promise of significant benefit in the future to children suffering from or at risk for the disorder or condition (CFR §46.406). Second, if the research involves more than a minor increase over minimal risk, then it can be permitted if (a) it presents 'a reasonable opportunity to further the understanding, prevention, or alleviation of a serious problem affecting the health or welfare of children'; and (b) is approved by National Review (CFR §46.407). Although rarely used before the year 2000, the Office for Human Research Protections (OHRP) has recently been asked to review over a dozen cases. In this chapter I focus on research that entails no more than a minor increase over minimal risk (CFR §46.406).

Is it ethical to allow children to participate in research that poses a minor increase over minimal risk? Freedman *et al.* argue that the threshold of a minor increase over minimal risk is the appropriate threshold for permissible research with children.[17] Freedman *et al.* compare asking a parent to agree to the child's participation in research that entails a minor increase over minimal risk with asking a parent to allow a child to participate in a new situation with its attendant risks. For example, they compare a child's research participation with his participation in an overnight camping trip for the first time: 'the parental decision to permit exposure to new risks is not itself governed by, but rather anchored to, the risks of everyday life. . . . A prohibition on such research involvement would be to the long-term detriment of this child and other children, just as a prohibition on new experiences is harmful to children over the long term.'[18]

There are two problems with Freedman *et al.*'s interpretation. First, while a prohibition of such research would be harmful to children as a class, it is not harmful to a particular child. Those who do not participate in nontherapeutic research often reap its rewards as free riders. Second, Freedman *et al.* fail to address that the threshold of a minor increase over minimal risk in the regulations only applies to children with a disorder or condition. Even if one denies that minimal risk is relative, the federal regulations clearly permit children with a disorder or condition to be exposed to greater risks than healthy children under CFR §46.406. Only children with a disorder or condition can participate in nontherapeutic research that poses a minor increase over minimal risk.

Why should only children with a disorder or condition be allowed to participate in nontherapeutic research that exposes them to a minor increase over minimal risk? Those who support the distinction argue it is appropriate because the research must be related to the disorder and therefore cannot be conducted on healthy subjects. The argument, however, is pragmatic, and not necessarily true. For example, pharmacokinetic studies of new antihypertensive agents could be done in healthy children from a physiologic perspective. However, since testing of experimental drugs involves more than minimal risk, researchers are only permitted to enroll children with high blood pressure (a disorder or condition) even though they will not gain any direct benefit from participating.

A second reason given to permit children with a disorder or condition to participate in research that poses a minor increase over minimal risk is that these children may have benefited from research done on similarly situated children in the past. Thus, these children may have an obligation to promote such research to benefit future children with the same disorder or condition. The problem with this argument is that it if there is a moral duty to help future generations, it is at best imperfect and no particular child has a strict obligation to participate.[19] The problem is exacerbated by the fact that only a non-random subset of parents will consent to their child's participation. Silverman argues that failures in the informed consent process lead to serious inequities in research as the process serves as a social filter: better educated and wealthier individuals are more likely to refuse to participate and are underrepresented in most research.[20] The data to support this claim are equivocal. Some researchers have found that parents who volunteer their children are more likely to be in the lower socioeconomic categories than those who refuse to volunteer,[21] although others have not.[22] At minimum, these studies suggest that we need to be wary regarding justice in the allocation of risks and benefits.

The recommendation only to allow children with a disorder or condition to participate in research that entails more than minimal risk was controversial when it was first suggested by the National Commission. Two commissioners dissented in the original report. Commissioner Cooke was concerned by its vague nature and its purely utilitarian justification;[23] Commissioner Tuttle argued that sick children cannot be deemed to be a morally relevant separate class for purposes of relaxing protective measures and mechanisms.[24] Rather, Commissioner Tuttle emphasized that if sick children could be deemed a morally relevant class, surely they would deserve special protections given their vulnerable state.[25]

One reason that children with a disorder or condition are more vulnerable as potential research subjects than healthy children is that they and their parents often have a prior relationship with the physicians who now seek their participation as research subjects.[26] Some parents and children may believe that they have an obligation to support their physicians' research;[27] others may fear that refusing to participate could adversely impact the care their child needs.[28] Thus, one moral argument against permitting children with a disorder or condition to be exposed to greater risks is based on the questionable voluntariness of their participation. There are also data to show that patients and healthy volunteers have different motivations for participating in research,[29] and despite the consent process, it is unclear whether patients (or their parents) understand that nontherapeutic studies are not designed to advance their medical well-being.[30] As such, the parents of children with a disorder or condition are, or at least may perceive themselves to be, less free to refuse such research.

A second moral argument against exposing children with a disorder or condition to greater risk can be made on the basis of justice in the selection of research subjects. In the *Belmont Report*, the National Commission discussed the inappropriateness of placing further burdens on already burdened persons.[31] A policy that allows those who have a disorder or condition (i.e., who are medically burdened) to be exposed to greater risks in nontherapeutic research does just that and is unjust.

Should the guidelines be revised, then, to permit only healthy subjects to participate in research that poses a minor increase over minimal risk rather than children with a disorder or condition? The strongest argument to support this revision is that healthy children have no previous relationship with the researchers so that their participation may be more voluntary.[32] However, the limited research data that exist suggest that the main reason healthy subjects volunteer for research is the monetary incentive.[33] Financial incentives raise questions of decreased autonomy due to undue financial influence as well as questions of justice because the financial inducements are stronger for those from lower socioeconomic backgrounds. The monetary incentive is additionally problematic for research on children because it may lead to the exploitation of some children by financially desperate parents or the enrollment of some children by well-meaning but less educated parents who do not understand the purpose of the activity. Healthy children, then, like children with a disorder or condition, are vulnerable in the research setting. Given that the risks and benefits should be distributed fairly throughout the population, it is unjust to single out one vulnerable class (healthy children) for research that offers no direct benefit in preference to another vulnerable class (children with a disorder or condition).

4. Revising the Federal Regulations

If the federal regulations regarding children in research should not permit children with a disorder or condition to be exposed to greater risks than healthy children, then the regulations need to be revised. Consider, first, the concept of minimal risk and the phrase 'risks normally encountered by a child'. If children are to be treated fairly as research subjects, then the standard must be interpreted as an absolute (and not a relative) standard. But just because minimal risk is interpreted the same for all subjects does not ensure that the risks are appropriate for each subject. As discussed, risks that a child normally encounters may cause excessive anxiety or threaten a child's self-image.

Ackerman suggests reinterpreting activities which are 'normally encountered by a child' not to mean any activity which a child may have previously experienced, but rather an activity with which the child is familiar and with which he is able to cope well: The fact that a child with cancer has undergone a particular procedure during treatment, e.g., a lumbar puncture, does not guarantee that he or she will not be subjected to considerable stress or anxiety if asked to undergo another one for research.[34] Ackerman has offered the following standard of minimal risk as an alternative: 'A research procedure involving minimal risk is one in which the probability of physical and psychological harm is no more than that to which it is appropriate to intentionally expose a child for educational purposes in family life situations.'[35]

Such a definition of minimal risk would allow for different children to be exposed to different degrees of risk, but the classification of such children would not necessarily break down along the lines of one's health status or previous experience with particular medical procedures.

There is also a need to revise the guidelines concerning the appropriate subjects for nontherapeutic research that poses a minor increase over minimal risk (CFR §46.406). Currently this regulation only applies to children with a disorder or condition. Two options need to be considered: (1) to permit such research on *all* children; or (2) to prohibit such research on *all* children.

The first option would be to permit all children to participate in this type of research. Freedman *et al.* have argued that a minor increase over minimal risk is the appropriate threshold for research on all children.[36] Their argument in support of this option is that it provides adequate protection to the children-subjects while respecting parental responsibility and authority regarding what risks the child may be exposed to at each developmental stage.[37] In contrast, the second option would prohibit all nontherapeutic research that entails more than minimal risk. The argument here is based on the vulnerability of children as a class, and by their inability to consent to their own 'sacrifice' for the common good.

Both options treat all children equally. However, whether both options are morally permissible requires a clearer articulation of what is meant by minimal risk and a minor increase over minimal risk. For example, the moral permissibility of the participation of all children in research that poses a minor increase over minimal risk is questioned by those who believe that parents, as fiduciaries, should not authorize their child's participation when it does not serve the child's best interest.[38] This claim has been challenged by several ethicists. For example, Beecher and Bartholome argue that this position fails to acknowledge the full responsibility that parents have as fiduciaries.[39] They argue that parents as fiduciaries may choose to authorize their child's participation in order to promote her moral development. Alternatively, I have argued that holding parents to a fiduciary role is too restrictive on parental autonomy, and that parental authority should be respected even when it does not serve the child's best interest, provided that the decision does not sacrifice the child's basic needs.[40] As such, it is permissible to participate in research. It is also permissible to prohibit the participation of children on the grounds that the state, in its role as *parens patriae*, can restrict their participation.

If one accepts the moral permissibility of both options, then option one is preferable because it allows children to participate in novel experiences compatible with their development; and it provides the greatest parental latitude that is consistent with a liberal community's respect for parental autonomy.[41] Alternatively, it may be that it is not necessary to choose between the two options. It may be that one can merge the standards of minimal risk and a minor increase over minimal risk using Ackerman's definition of minimal risk. Under this definition, some research currently classified as minimal risk and as a minor increase over minimal risk would be permissible, and some in both classifications would not. Its permissibility will depend on whether the probability of harm is no more than that to which it is appropriate to intentionally expose a child for education purposes in family life situations.

5. *Conclusion*

Recently, an editor of the *New England Journal of Medicine* claimed that '[m]any argue that [research involving healthy persons] requires a higher standard for minimizing risks than research involving people who are sick and who may die from their underlying disease.'[42] Although he made this statement in an article about the death of a healthy adult volunteer in an asthma trial, I have shown that this position is entrenched in Subpart D of the regulations and is the prevailing norm regarding children in research.

We need to be wary of exposing any child to risks when there is no prospect of direct benefit for the child. If children are to participate in such research, and there are strong utilitarian reasons to permit it, then the double standard found in the federal regulations must be revised. I propose that the Department of Health and Human Services reevaluate current pediatric research standards and consider defining minimal risk for children in Subpart D independently from the definition of minimal risk provided in the Common Rule (Subpart A). I would propose the adoption of Ackerman's definition of minimal risk, a definition that focuses on risks and harms to which it is appropriate to intentionally expose a child, and not on whether or not the child is healthy or has a disorder or condition. Using this definition of minimal risk, I do not believe that we need to distinguish between minimal risk and a minor increase over minimal risk, and I would propose merging the two standards.

References

1. Department of Health and Human Services (DHHS). (45 CFR Part 46, Subpart D), 'Protections for Children Involved as Subjects in Research', *Federal Register*

48 (8 March 1983), 9814–20; revised *Federal Register*, 56 (18 June 1991), 28032 at CFR §46.406; hereinafter cited by its CFR number in the text.

2. National Commission for the Protection of Human Subjects of Biomedical and Behavioral Research, *Report and Recommendations: Research Involving Children.* Washington DC: US Printing Office, 1977, DHEW Publication NO. (OS) 77–0004; hereinafter cited as National Commission, *Research Involving Children.*

3. Ibid., xx.

4. Department of Health and Human Services (DHSS). (45 CFR 46 Subpart A), 'Final Regulations Amending Basic HHS Policy for the Protection of Human Research Subjects', *Federal Register*, 46 (26 January 1981), 8366–91; revised *Federal Register*, 56 (18 June 1991), 28003–18 at CFR §46.102i; hereinafter cited in text and endnote by CFR number.

5. See, e.g., Levine, R. J., *Ethics and Regulation of Clinical Research*, 2nd edn. New Haven CT: Yale University Press, 1986; Robinson, W. M., 'Ethical Issues in Pediatric Research', *Journal of Clinical Ethics*, 11 (2000), 145–50; and Children's Workgroup of the National Human Research Protections Advisory Committee (NHRPAC), 'Report to NHRPAC from Children's Workgroup', 1 May 2002. On the web at: http://www.hhs.gov/ohrp/nhrpac/documents/nhrpac16.pdf.

6. Kauffman, R. E., 'Clinical Trials in Children: Problems and Pitfalls', *Paediatric Drugs*, 2 (2000), 411–8; Kenny, N., and Miller, P., 'Comment: Research Involving Children: Clarifying Roles and Authority', *Journal of Clinical Ethics*, 11 (2000), 151–6; Koocher, G. P., and Keith-Spiegel, P., 'Scientific Issues in Psychosocial and Educational Research with Children' in M. A. Grodin, and L. H. Glantz, (eds.), *Children as Research Subjects: Science, Ethics, and Law.* New York: Oxford University Press, 1994, 47–80; and Freedman, B., Fuks, A., and Weijer, C., '*In Loco Parentis:* Minimal Risk as an Ethical Threshold for Research upon Children', *Hastings Center Report*, 23 (March/April 1993), 13–19; and Kopelman, L. M., 'When is the Risk Minimal Enough for Children to be Research Subjects?' in L. M. Kopelman, and J. C. Moskop (eds.), *Children and Health Care: Moral and Social Issues.* Dordrecht, The Netherlands: Kluwer Academic Publishers, 1989, 89–99.

7. National Commission, *Research Involving Children*, xx–xxi.

8. Freedman *et al.*, '*In Loco Parentis*', 15.

9. Ibid., 17.

10. Kopelman, 'When is the Risk', 95.

11. Ibid., 96.

12. Janofsky, J., and Starfield, B., 'Assessment of Risk in Research on Children', *Journal of Pediatrics*, 98 (1981), 842–6; and Shah, S., Whittle, A., Wilfond, B., Gensler, G., and Wendler, D., 'How Do Institutional Review Boards Apply the Federal Risk and Benefit Standards for Pediatric Research?' *JAMA*, 291 (2004), 476–82.

13. Kopelman, 'When is the Risk', 96.

14. Ibid., 97.

15. Thompson, R., 'Vulnerability in Research: A Developmental Perspective on Research Risk', *Child Development*, 61 (1990), 1–16, 7.

16. Ibid., 7.
17. Freedman *et al.*, *'In Loco Parentis'*.
18. Ibid., 17.
19. Jonas, H., 'Philosophical Reflections on Human Experimenting with Human Subjects' in P. A. Freund (ed.), *Experimentation with Human Subjects*. New York: George Braziller, 1970, 1–31; and Kant, I., *Groundwork of the Metaphysic of Morals*, translated by H. J. Paton. New York: Harper & Row, 1964.
20. Silverman, W. A., 'The Myth of Informed Consent in Daily Practice and in Clinical Trials', *Journal of Medical Ethics*, 15 (1989), 6–11.
21. See, e.g., Harth, S. C., Johnstone, R. R., Thong, Y. H., 'The Psychological Profile of Parents Who Volunteer Their Children for Clinical Research: A Controlled Study', *Journal of Medical Ethics*, 18 (1992), 86–93; and Wiley, F. M., Ruccione, K., Moore, I. M. M., McGuire-Cullen, P., Fergusson, J., Waskerwitz, M. J., Perin, G., Ge, J., and Sather, H. N. for the Children's Cancer Group, 'Parents' Perceptions of Randomization in Pediatric Clinical Trials', *Cancer Practice*, 7 (1999), 248–56.
22. Zupancic, J. A. F., Gillie, P., Streiner, D. L., Watts, J. L., and Schmidt, B., 'Determinants of Parental Authorization for Involvement of Newborn Infants in Clinical Trials', *Pediatrics*, 99 (1997), e6. Found on the web at http://www. pediatrics.org/cgi/content/full/99/1/e6; and Koren, G., and Pastuszak, A. 'Medical Research in Infants and Children in the Eighties; Analysis of Rejected Protocols', *Pediatric Research*, 27 (1990), 423–35.
23. Dr Cooke's dissent can be found in National Commission, *Research Involving Children*, 145–6.
24. Dr Turtle's dissent can be found in National Commission, *Research Involving Children*, 146–53.
25. Ibid.
26. Katz, J., *The Silent World of Doctor and Patient*. New York: The Free Press. 1986; and van Stuijvenberg, M., Suur, M. H., de Vos, S., Tjiang, G. C. H., Steyerberg, E. W., Dersen-Lubsen, G., and Moll, H. A., 'Informed Consent, Parental Awareness, and Reasons for Participating in a Randomized Controlled Study', *Archives of Diseases in Childhood*, 79 (1998), 120–5.
27. Zupancic *et al.*, 'Determinants'; Royal College of Physicians, 'Research Involving Patients: Summary and Recommendations of a Report of the Royal College of Physicians', *Journal of the Royal College of Physicians of London*, 24 (1990), 10–14; and van Stuijvenberg *et al.*, 'Informed Consent'.
28. See, e.g., Zupancic *et al.*, 'Determinants'; Royal College of Physicians, 'Research Involving Patients'; Lemmens, T., and Elliott, C., 'Guinea Pigs on the Payroll: The Ethics of Paying Research Subjects', *Accountability in Research*, 7 (1999), 3–20; and Katz, J., *Experimentation with Human Beings*. New York: Russell Sage Foundation, 1972.
29. See, e.g., Lemmens and Elliott, 'Guinea Pigs'; Royal College of Physicians, 'Research Involving Patients'; Royal College of Physicians, 'Research on Healthy Volunteers: A Report of the Royal College of Physicians', *Journal of the Royal College of Physicians of London*, 20 (1986), 243–57; McCarthy, A. M., Richman,

L. C., Hoffman, R. P., and Rubenstein, L., 'Psychological Screening of Children for Participation in Nontherapeutic Invasive Research', *Archives of Pediatrics and Adolescent Medicine*, 155 (2001), 1197–1203; Lasagna, L., 'Special Subjects in Human Experimentation' in P. A. Freund (ed.), *Experimentation with Human Subjects*. New York: George Braziller, 1970, 262–75; Daugherty, C., Ratain, M. J., Grochowski, E., Stocking, C., Kodish, E., Mick, R., and Siegler, M., 'Perceptions of Cancer Patients and Their Physicians Involved in Phase I Trials', *Journal of Clinical Oncology*, 13 (1995), 1062–72; and Schutta, K. M., and Burnett, C. B., 'Factors that Influence a Patient's Decision to Participate in a Phase I Cancer Clinical Trial', *Oncology Nursing Forum*, 27 (2000), 1435–8.

30. See Daugherty *et al.*, 'Perceptions of Cancer Patients'; Schutta and Burnett, 'Factors'; and Appelbaum, P. S., Rother, L. H., Lidz, C. W., Benson, P., and Winslade, W., 'False Hopes and Best Data: Consent to Research and the Therapeutic Misconception', *Hastings Center Report*, 17 (April 1987), 20–4.

31. The National Commission for the Protection of Human Subjects of Biomedical and Behavioral Research, *The Belmont Report: Ethical Principles and Guidelines for the Protection of Human Subjects of Research*. Washington DC: US Government Printing Office, 1978, DHEW Publication No. (OS) 78–12. On the web at: http://ohsr.od.nih.gov/guidelines/belmont.html.

32. Freund, P. A., 'Introduction' in P. A. Freund (ed.), *Experimentation with Human Subjects*. New York: George Braziller, 1970, xii–xviii.

33. See, e.g., Lemmens and Elliott, 'Guinea Pigs'; Royal College of Physicians, 'Research on Healthy Volunteers'; McCarthy *et al.*, 'Psychological Screening'; Lasagna, 'Special Subjects'.

34. Ackerman, T. F., 'Moral Duties of Investigators towards Sick Children', *IRB: A Review of Human Subjects Research*, 3 (June/ July 1981), 1–5, 4.

35. Ackerman, T., 'Moral Duties of Parents and Nontherapeutic Research Procedures Involving Children', *Bioethics Quarterly*, 2 (1980), 94–111 as cited in S. L. Leiken, 'An Ethical Issue in Biomedical Research: The Involvement of Minors in Informed and Third Party Consent', *Clinical Research*, 31 (1983), 34–40, 38.

36. Freedman *et al.*, '*In Loco Parentis*'.

37. Ibid.

38. Ramsey, P., *The Patient as Person*. New Haven CT: Yale University Press, 1970.

39. Beecher, H. K., *Research and the Individual*. Boston MA: Little, Brown & Co., 1970; Bartholome, W. G., 'Parents, Children, and the Moral Benefits of Research', *Hastings Center Report*, 6 (December 1976), 44–5.

40. Ross, L. F., *Children Families and Health Care Decision-Making*. Oxford: Clarendon Press, 1998.

41. See, e.g., Ross, *Children*, ch. 3, 'Constrained Parental Autonomy'; and Buchanan, A. E., and Brock, D. W., *Deciding for Others: The Ethics of Surrogate Decision-Making*. Cambridge: Cambridge University Press, 1989, 233–4.

42. Steinbrook, R., 'Protecting Research Subjects—The Crisis at Johns Hopkins'. *New England Journal of Medicine*, 346 (2002), 716–20.

5

Informed Consent in Pediatric Research

1. Introduction

The first principle of the Nuremberg Code (1946) requires the informed consent of the subject.[1] Proxy consent or proxy permission* was not addressed until the Declaration of Helsinki (1964).[2] US policies regarding consent for the participation of children in research would not be finalized for almost two more decades (1983).[3] As discussed in Chapter 3, CFR §46.408 of Subpart D of the federal regulations stipulates provisions for parental permission and the child's assent in research involving children. In this chapter, I provide a brief overview of the informed consent requirements and waivers in pediatric research under current federal regulations. These consent policies were adopted by the Food and Drug Administration (FDA) in April 2001 with the exception of parental waivers under CFR §46.408(c).[4] I also examine the moral bases for these requirements, whether the current policies are consistent with these moral foundations, and, if not, how the policies ought to be modified.

2. Current Policy

For most research involving children, parental permission is necessary. The elements necessary for a parent to make an informed decision (including risks, benefits, alternatives, and costs) are spelled out in the Common Rule.[5] Subpart D specifies whether one or both parents need to provide permission. If the research involves minimal risk or offers the prospect of direct benefit, an institutional review board (IRB) is empowered to determine that the permission of one parent is sufficient. However, if the research is nontherapeutic and entails more than minimal risk, then 'both parents must

---

* 'Proxy consent' and 'proxy permission' are morally equivalent. The latter is more accurate because consent signifies agreement to participate for oneself whereas permission refers to agreement to participate for a third-party. In general, I use the term 'informed consent' to refer to the process of obtaining agreement to participate in research. In pediatric research, informed consent includes two components: parental permission and the child's assent.

give their permission unless one parent is deceased, unknown, incompetent, or not reasonably available, or when only one parent has legal responsibility for the care and custody of the child (CFR §46.408(b))'.

The regulations also require that adequate provisions are made for soliciting the assent of the children. Assent refers to an affirmative agreement to participate and not mere failure to object (CFR §46.402(b)). Neither the federal regulations nor the National Commission (for the Protection of Human Subjects of Biomedical and Behavioral Research) specified what elements are required for a child's assent.[6] The regulations also do not specify an age at which the child's assent should be procured, although the National Commission recommended seven years.[7]

Parental permission and/or the child's assent can be waived for minimal risk research provided that the research meets the following criteria: (1) it involves no more than minimal risk to the subjects; (2) the waiver or alteration will not adversely affect the rights and welfare of the subjects; (3) the research could not practicably be carried out without the waiver or alteration; and (4) whenever appropriate, the subjects will be provided with additional pertinent information after participation (CFR §46.116(d)). Parental permission can also be waived under Subpart D 'if it is not a reasonable requirement to protect the subjects (CFR §46.408(c))'. However, CFR §46.408(c) requires that an appropriate mechanism for protecting the children is substituted. As mentioned above, the FDA did not adopt the parental consent waivers in its interim rules.[8]

As noted above, the child's assent can be waived or overridden under the provisions of CFR §46.116 of Subpart A, even if the children are capable of assenting, provided that the other criteria (minimal risk, not practical otherwise, and debriefing) are fulfilled. Under Subpart D, an IRB can determine that the assent of the child is not a necessary condition for proceeding with the research '[i]f the IRB determines that the capability of some or all of the children is so limited that they cannot reasonably be consulted' (CFR §46.408(a)). An IRB can also waive or override assent 'if the intervention or procedure involved in the research holds out a prospect of direct benefit that is ... available only in the context of the research' (CFR §46.408(a)).

3.   *Parental Permission*

The primary justification for requiring parental permission for a child's participation in research is to protect the child's best interest. Respecting parental decision-making authority usually accomplishes this because parents 'both care deeply about the welfare of their children and know them and their needs better than others do' and 'bear the consequences' of their decisions.[9]

While both of the above reasons focus on parental autonomy to serve the child's best interest, some modern philosophers on the family argue that parental authority is not solely duty-based.[10] Rather, parental authority is also justified, at least within limits, on the grounds that parents have the right 'to raise their children according to the parents' own standards and values and to seek to transmit those standards and values to their children'.[11] Parental authority is also justified to promote family privacy and this requires significant freedom, including the freedom 'to make important decisions about the welfare of its incompetent members'.[12] Thus, requiring parental permission not only serves to promote the child's best interest but also serves to respect a legitimate parental interest in making decisions for their child.

What is the justification for requiring two-parent consent for research that involves more than minimal risk? Such participation entails more risk and a worse risk/benefit ratio than research for which the IRB may find that the permission of one parent is sufficient (minimal risk research and therapeutic research). This implies that two parents provide greater protection than one parent in deciding about a child's research participation. There are no data to support or refute this position. The fact that children growing up in single-family homes are more likely to grow up in poverty [13] suggests that these children may be more vulnerable and that they and their parent (usually the mother) may agree to participate in research because of disempowerment in relationship to the medical community or because of the financial incentives. To the extent that the second-parent requirement serves as a deterrent to the enrollment of these children, it may provide additional protection.

A problem with the two-parent rule, however, is that it entrenches one way of family decision-making: that parents discuss all of a child's activities and that they both agree to the child's participation. Contrast the participation of a child in research that entails a minor increase over minimal risk, then, with that same child's participation in high school football which only requires one parent's authorization despite the fact that a dozen children will die and more will become paralyzed each year.[14] In some families, one parent makes all of the daily childrearing decisions: why, then, should participation in medical research be an exception?

The requirement goes further: Not only must both parents consider the risks and benefits of the child's participation, but they both must be able and willing to sign for his or her participation. This may require that both parents take time off from work, and as such may be a deterrent due to inconvenience rather than serving as a form of protection or respect for a legitimate parental interest.

There are two situations in which nontherapeutic research that entails more than minimal risk does not require the second parent's permission:

(1) 'when one parent is ... not reasonably available'; and (2) when only one parent has legal responsibility for the care and custody of the child' (CFR §46.408(b)). The first exception is quite vague: is it adequate if the parent says 'dad has not visited in 6 months'? Or does it require that the parent say 'dad is unlocatable ... he is behind in child support and the courts also cannot locate him'. The second exception will depend on state laws and whether and how they promote joint custody between divorcing parents,[15] the extent to which they provide out-of-wedlock fathers with presumed parental rights,[16] and the extent to which individuals must seek judicial rulings to attain or maintain these rights.[17] Whether these legal holdings reflect the actual experience of the child is less clear. Empirical data show decreased involvement of the non-custodial parent over time.[18] It is expensive and inconvenient to get courts involved to legalize de facto custody patterns given that it will make little difference in the daily life of the child but would be required for the child to be involved in medical research.

Does a rule requiring two-parent permission provide additional protection or does it merely serve as an unnecessary obstacle? Two facts suggest that the need for two-parent permission may be obsolete. First, the percentage of unmarried women giving birth to children increased from 5.3% in 1960 to 32.4% in 1996.[19] Second, most American children spend part of their childhood in a single-parent family whether through birth to an unmarried woman, after the death of a parent, or because of divorce.[20] The percentage of children being reared by two parents in an uninterrupted marriage fell from 73% in 1972 to 48% in 1996.[21] These facts do not deny that a second parent may be involved in raising a child outside of marriage, but they do increase the likelihood that (1) the second parent is not involved in the day-to-day care of the child; and (2) in cases of divorce, that parental discord may express itself in disagreement regarding childrearing. Thus, many custodial parents may not find it reasonable or desirable to contact the second parent and may avoid research participation even when they believe the research to be useful, important, or in the child's best interest. They may fear that the second parent will refuse to consent not because of child-centered concerns but because of interpersonal antagonism.

It is also unclear how researchers should explain the need for two-parent permission and its exceptions, and how they should respond when a parent says 'my signature is adequate'. Should the researchers accept the parent's word that the second parent's permission is not needed or will the researcher be required to document the exception and require the parent to provide documentation of sole custody or the other parent's disappearance? Alternatively, how hard must the parent or researcher try to contact the other parent?

To require parental permission for a child to participate in research serves to protect the child and to respect a parent's interest in making decisions about his or her child. To require both parents to consent may add some protection and may promote some respect for parental autonomy, particularly for a non-custodial but involved parent; however, it does so at potentially great cost to family privacy and requires more external intervention into the family than the potential benefits warrant.

4. Parental Waivers

As noted above, parental permission can be waived in two circumstances: (1) if the research qualifies for a waiver of consent under Subpart A of the regulations; and (2) if it is not a reasonable requirement to protect the subjects under Subpart D. The exemption in Subpart A is justified on the grounds that the risks are minimal. It is noteworthy, however, that the regulations seek greater protection for children by applying minimal risk differently for children than for adults. Adult surveys are exempt from IRB review (CFR §46.101(b)(2)) whereas pediatric surveys are not (CFR §46.401(b)) What may appear to be an innocuous question when asked to an adult may be very troubling to a child or adolescent. The exemption in Subpart D is designed to provide protection to those children whose parents are unable to protect them. If parents have failed to protect their child's interests, then a 'mechanism for protecting the children ... is substituted' (CFR §46.408(c)).

In its review of the FDA's interim rule that adopts most of Subpart D, the National Human Research Protections Advisory Committee (NHRPAC) wrote a comment urging the FDA to adopt the parental waivers found in CFR §46.408(c) in order to permit some FDA-related research to be performed without parental permission.[22] NHRPAC noted that some IRBs use §46.408(c) 'to permit waiver of parental permission in research involving mature adolescents in certain circumstances in which it is not in the adolescent's interests to inform his/her parents about the specific illness or behavior that is under study'.[23] NHRPAC went on to say how every state has recognized exceptions from the need for parental consent.[24]

NHRPAC is correct that parental permission can be waived for the treatment of certain diseases and conditions under the specialized consent statutes (e.g., treatment of sexually transmitted diseases, treatment for alcohol and drug dependence). Parental permission can also be waived under the mature minor doctrine, a doctrine that has developed mainly under common law because only a few states have codified it.[25] These policies empower adolescents to consent for medical care.

NHRPAC extrapolates from the clinical domain to the research setting and concludes that mature adolescents should be able to participate in clinical trials involving different experimental treatment protocols related to sexually transmitted diseases (STD), particularly for HIV/AIDS, and/or pregnancy.[26] Whether either the specialized consent statutes or the mature minor statutes should apply to research, however, is not evident. Although the National Commission envisioned parental waivers for cases in which the parents were abusive or neglectful and for cases involving adolescents for conditions covered by the specialized consent statutes,[27] only the abuse and neglect example was cited for parental waivers in the federal regulations (CFR §46.408(c)). In addition, when parental permission is waived, CFR §46.408(c) requires a substitute mechanism to protect the child-subjects. Although NHRPAC suggests that mature adolescents can serve as their own substitute mechanism because they are capable of giving their own consent,[28] the regulations do not address whether the child's own consent is a legitimate substitute mechanism.[29]

What is the justification to interpret CFR §46.408(c) to allow mature adolescents to consent for themselves? Supporters argue that the adolescents are mature and can protect themselves.[30] This argument is based on respect for the child's autonomy. The problem is that this may be too narrow an interpretation of respect for a child's autonomy. Elsewhere, I have argued that respect for children entails some respect for their current autonomy, but also respect for the persons they are becoming.[31] Who they are becoming is dynamic and depends a great deal on how and who are rearing them. If respect for children must accommodate both respect for a child's current autonomy and respect for a child's lifetime autonomy, then Ackerman is correct that 'we fool ourselves if we argue that we have fulfilled our moral duty by standing aside and asking the child to decide'.[32] Rather, parents and researchers show respect by deciding what activities are appropriate for a child. The parents' judgment should take into consideration issues beyond the research protocol: the impact of the child's decision to participate on her short-term and long-term autonomy, as well as the impact of the child's decision to participate on the trajectory of her current life plan and their legitimate attempts to modify it. They may not succeed in modifying it, but that does not invalidate their attempt.

The problem with NHRPAC's argument is that it extrapolates from policies regulating clinical treatments to the research setting, a common practice of academic adolescent medicine researchers.[33] But it is inappropriate to extrapolate from the specialized consent statutes because these statutes were not written to accommodate the competency of mature adolescents.[34] In fact, the statutes do not discuss decision-making capacity nor the requirement of the providing physician to ensure that the minor seeking treatment has such capacity.[35] Rather these statutes were designed as a pragmatic public health response to current adolescent health needs. They were designed to encourage adolescents to seek health care for problems which they might deny, ignore, or delay if they had to inform their parents and/or get parental permission.

Alternatively, NHRPAC may have been justifying adolescent authority using the mature minor doctrine, given NHRPAC's focus on the maturity of the adolescents and its assumption that most of the adolescents will be at least 14 years of age. However, the mature minor doctrine is usually restricted to interventions that are being done for the individual's benefit and are not of a serious nature.[36] There is no legal precedent to extrapolate this concept into the research setting, and there is good justification not to. Even if adolescents are mature and have the decision-making ability to consent to treatment for particular diseases, this does not mean that they have the ability to consent to experimental treatment for particular diseases, given that the risk/benefit ratio of the latter is not as clear-cut as the former. Thus, to empower adolescents to consent for themselves in research may not adequately protect their long-term interests even if it respects their current interests. In addition, extrapolation of the mature minor doctrine to research decisions denies that parents have a legitimate interest in what types of nontherapeutic research their children participate, despite the fact that the parents will bear the consequences if anything were to go wrong.

There are scant empirical data about whether parents and children support waiving the requirement for parental permission. In one study of 100 adolescent–parent pairs, many parents accepted their child's ability to consent to participate in minimal risk non-invasive research.[37] A majority of parents and adolescents did perceive a need for parental consent if the research involved blood or urine testing, suggesting that the FDA's decision not to waive the requirement for parental permission has wide public support despite the position of NHRPAC and the academic adolescent medicine community.

In *The Ethical Conduct of Clinical Research Involving Children*, the Institute of Medicine (IOM) concluded that overall 'it is advisable for parents to be involved in decision making about research participation for adolescents'.[38] The IOM additionally argued that an '[a]dolescent's capacity to make informed decisions should not, however, be dismissed out of hand, especially when requiring parental permission would endanger adolescents or preclude their participation in research with important potential to benefit them or other adolescents in the future.'[39] The problem with this argument is that we are not discussing clinical care but research. Some could argue that, in hindsight, those who were excluded from AIDS clinical drug trials were excluded from research with significant benefits, but there are also many clinical trials in which patient-subjects who receive the experimental drug do not benefit and are even made worse off. The argument that foregoing research endangers the adolescent is a classic example of the 'therapeutic misconception'.[40]

The more serious error in the IOM report is to conflate benefiting the adolescent-subject versus benefiting future adolescents. Research that offers the prospect of direct benefit (CFR §46.405) is quite different from research that offers no prospect of direct benefit but is focused on benefiting future adolescents (CFR §46.404, CFR §46.406). The reason to participate in the former is primarily the prospect of direct benefit, although some subjects or their guardians do enroll them for additional motives including altruism.[41] The reason to participate in nontherapeutic research is to benefit others (or for payment, a topic that I address in Chapter 8). The reasons to participate in nontherapeutic research do not justify overriding parental involvement or at least forgoing some other substitute mechanism.

The IOM committee recommended that IRBs 'should consider granting waivers of parental permission for adolescent participation in research' in four situations. First, if the research is important to the health and well-being of adolescents generally and could not be done without a waiver. Second, if the research involves treatments that state laws permit adolescents to receive without parental permission. Third, if the investigator has presented evidence that the adolescents are capable of understanding the research and their rights as participants. Fourth, if the research protocol includes appropriate safeguards.[42]

The first waiver is already permitted under CFR §46.116(d) when the risks are minimal. In general, this waiver is used for survey research. Nevertheless, because the subjects are minors, the research needs to undergo IRB review (CFR §46.101(b)(2)). The IRB decides if the risks are minimal and if a waiver is appropriate. Surveys that ask questions about sexuality or illegal substance usage may entail emotional or psychological risks to children, particularly if the surveys are administered in a school setting where the children's privacy and right to refuse to participate may be (or at least appear to be) comprom-ised.[43]

The second and third waivers do not pass ethical scrutiny. The second waiver fails because the IOM is making the same erroneous extrapolation made by NHRPAC. The third waiver assumes that a researcher ethically can test an adolescent's capacity to understand a research protocol and then enroll only those who pass the test. It fails to acknowledge that parents often want to decide how and when their children will be approached regarding research and that parents often want this negotiated with the researchers in advance.[44] It also assumes that the researchers' methodology to assess decision-making capacity is valid. Currently there are no validated tests of adolescent decision-making capacity.[45]

Whether or not the fourth waiver is valid depends upon what the IOM committee meant by 'appropriate safeguards'. I contend that a substitute mechanism, as required in CFR §46.408(c), is appropriate when parents have failed to protect their children. That is, substitute mechanisms should only be used as a last resort, and not used merely to sidestep engaged but difficult parents.

In summary, there is no moral justification for IRBs to permit adolescents to consent to research without parental permission, unless (1) there is a substitute mechanism (CFR §46.408(c)); or (2) the research can be done without any consent, that is, without the permission of the parent and without the assent of the child (CFR §46.116(d)).

5. Child's Assent and Dissent

Dr Bill Bartholome, one of the most outspoken advocates for requiring a child's assent, argued that the assent requirement was necessary to show respect for the child.[46] This is a controversial interpretation of what respect for a child entails. According to the National Commission's *Belmont Report*, the principle of respect for persons entails (1) respect for the choices of an autonomous person; and (2) special protection for those not capable of autonomous choice (including children).[47] In this light, Bartholome's position that respect for children requires respect for their choices is a radical departure from the National Commission's use of this term. More consistent with the *Belmont Report*, Denham and Nelson interpret the principle of respect for persons to require parental permission and a child's assent for very different purposes. Parental permission shows respect to the extent that it serves to protect the child. The assent requirement shows respect to the extent that it represents 'an affirmative agreement to be used as a means to another person's ends'[48] and is understood as a statement of preference.[49]

I agree with Denham and Nelson that the principle of respect as it applies to children should not focus on self-determination nor on the ability to make an informed voluntary decision. A richer understanding of this principle, as it applies to children, is needed. I have argued elsewhere that respect for children entails some respect for their current choices, but also respect for the person they are becoming.[50] A parent may choose to restrain a child's short-term autonomy (current choices) in order to promote her lifetime autonomy. As such, it may be respectful of parents to prohibit their child's participation in nontherapeutic research despite the child's desire to do so.

Consider the case of a 10-year-old child who wants a computer game that costs $50. He sees an advertisement for a pharmacokinetics study by his physician. It involves ingestion of an experimental drug and 12 hourly blood draws through an indwelling catheter. The parents refuse to permit their child to participate because they are concerned about the safety of taking an experimental drug. The child is not concerned because he trusts his pediatrician—conflating the pediatrician's role as clinician and scientist. The parents are concerned about a serious, albeit unlikely, adverse event. Acker-man states that parents show respect for the children when they decide whether his well-being is served or not violated by participation.[51] If the parents believe that the child is placed at unacceptable risk by his participa-tion, then their refusal expresses respect for his current and future person-hood. Their discretion is also consistent with the autonomy accorded to parents in our society to make decisions for their children.[52]

If a parent overrides a child's assent and prohibits the child from partici-pating in an activity, the parent fails to respect the child's current autonomy. This is true whether the activity is participation in nontherapeutic research, a school sporting event, or a community choir. The prohibition of discretion-ary or elective activities is neither neglectful nor abusive. The parent may override the child's interest in participation because he or she believes that the activity is too risky, is not worth the time and expense, or does not cohere with the values the parent wants to instill. The parent also may override the child's current autonomy to promote the child's lifetime autonomy.[53]

There is however a moral asymmetry between assent and dissent. Whereas overriding the child's assent prohibits her from participating in a discretion-ary activity that she wants to pursue, overriding the child's dissent means that the parents compel the child's participation in an activity that she does not want to pursue. The primary justification for overriding the child's assent is that the research offers the prospect of direct benefit; i.e. that participation will promote the child's medical best interest. While the competent person's right to refuse is considered primary, even when the refusal is contrary to the individual's 'best interest', the federal regulations specify that the child's dissent can be overridden when the research offers the prospect of direct benefit. (CFR §46.408(b)). Parents can override their child because it is assumed that they know what is in their child's medical interest and will act to promote this, even if it requires that they override the child's other interests, including her interest in autonomous decision-making. Respect for a child refers respect for the child's current interests, beliefs, and goals as well as her future interests, beliefs, and goals—including the goal of survival. The parents may be misguided in their deliberations about the therapeutic value of the protocol, but respect for parental autonomy means respecting parental discretion unless it is abusive or harmful.

While parents are allowed to compel the child's participation when the research offers the prospect of direct benefit, their authority should be more limited when the research does not. Currently a child's dissent can NEVER be overridden if the treatment is nontherapeutic, even if it involves no more than minimal risk. Will Gaylin, a psychiatrist and co-founder of the Hastings Center, a Bioethics think-tank, described a case over 20 years ago that questioned this policy.[54] A physician-researcher asked a father and his son if he could procure a small blood sample from the child for some research. The researcher explained that the research was not for the child's benefit, and that it would hurt a small amount but would cause no long-lasting harm. The father gave his permission, the son refused, and the physician-researcher put away the phlebotomy needle. The father demanded that the researcher take the sample. The father's rationale was: 'This is my child. I was less concerned about the research involved than with the kind of boy I was raising. I'll be damned if I was going to allow my child, because of some idiotic concept of children's rights, to assume he was entitled to be a selfish, narcissistic little bastard.'[55]

This case infuriated Bartholome who argued that the father was not teaching altruism but merely that physical force can dominate.[56] He argued that the child's dissent should be respected because it teaches the child that he does have some control over his environment. The current regulations would support Bartholome in that a child's dissent to minimal research is binding (unless the IRB has waived it). I disagree. While empowering a child to be able to veto minimal risk research may teach the child that he has some control over his environment, it also teaches the child that strangers can restrain his parents' authority, even when it is not abusive or neglectful. It ignores how important it is for children to view their parents as autonomous agents.[57] This does not mean that the child cannot try to change his parents' mind, and in fact, many parents would choose to honor their child's refusal. The same parent can force his child to attend a particular school, to receive specific religious instruction, or to stay home and miss a friend's get-together to share a family meal. The purpose of each of these activities is to inculcate particular values that the parents affirm. Parents may justify their decision on the grounds that it is in the child's best interest. Alternatively, they may justify their decision on the grounds that it will best promote the child's development into the type of person his parents hope he will become. Requiring a child to participate in minimal risk research is no different.

Nevertheless, there may be cases that are classified as minimal risk, particularly cases that involve invasive procedures (e.g. venipuncture) in which respect for a child does require that we respect his dissent. For example, Ackerman agrees with Bartholome that we should respect 'an intractable objection by the child particularly if it is based upon anxiety or fear which cannot be allayed regarding an experimental procedure' because respect for the child requires us 'to decide whether his well-being is served or not violated by participation'.[58]

Bartholome also argued that respecting a child's dissent offers the child a degree of protection in that parents might consent for a procedure that they perceived as 'harmless' but that the child perceives quite negatively.[59] Randall Clark, on the other hand, argues that using the child's dissent as a protective mechanism represents a failure of many different adults from protecting the child.[60] It also inappropriately gives children final authority when they still need guidance and protection.[61] In addition, Clark argues that if the assent/ dissent guidelines are meant to protect the child, then they must be strengthened because currently the IRB has many ways to waive the assent requirement.[62]

I agree that it is inappropriate to depend on children to protect themselves. The value of the assent clause is to ensure that the child is treated respectfully, that the procedures are explained and the child's concerns are addressed, but the assent clause should not be interpreted as permission to abandon a child to his or her autonomy.

This does not mean that the child's dissent can always be ignored. As the risks increase, respect for the child's developing personhood may require that we respect his dissent. For example, an adolescent who does not want to play interscholastic American football should not be forced to take the risks involved. Likewise, an adolescent who does not want to participate in research that entails a minor increase over minimal risk should not be forced to do so.

As the risks increase and the risk/benefit ratio becomes less favorable, parents should not be able to decide unilaterally whether or not their child will participate in research because respect for parental autonomy is not absolute. When the research entails more than minimal risk (that is when the research that would be classified under CFR §46.406 and CFR §46.407), failure to respect the child's dissent fails to respect the child's developing personhood and the child's interest in not being treated solely as a means. If, however, the child assents to being used as a means to advance science, then he or she is being treated both as a means and as an ends (an individual who can pursue other-regarding goals), and the child's participation is moral.[63] Parents need to be aware that nontherapeutic research that entails more than minimal risk, does and should require the voluntary authorization by both the parent and the child.

Clark suggests that requiring the child's assent should be understood to serve mainly as a pedagogical tool.[64] It involves explaining all proposed research to the potential children-subjects in an age-appropriate fashion, even if the child's decisions will not be determinative. It involves exploring when the child's dissent will and will not be dispositive.

6. Concluding Remarks

Informed consent is integral to ethical medical research, although it is neither necessary nor sufficient. In pediatric research, informed consent generally entails procuring parental permission and the child's assent. The process of seeking parental permission serves to protect the child and to respect familial autonomy. It can and should be waived in very limited circumstances. The process of seeking the child's assent serves to affirm respect for the child's developing autonomy without abandoning him or her to it. I have argued that parents should be allowed to waive or override their child's assent only if the research offers the prospect of direct benefit or if the research entails at most minimal risk. This is consistent with respect for wide parental discretion while ensuring that the parents' decisions are neither neglectful nor abusive.

References

1. Nuremberg Code. See Trials of War Criminals before the Nuremberg Military Tribunals under Control Council Law No. 10, vol. II. Washington DC: US Government Printing Office, 1948. On the web at: http://www.ushmm.org/research/ doctors/ codeptx.htm.
2. World Medical Association, 'Declaration of Helsinki: Ethical Principles for Medical Research Involving Human Subjects', Adopted by the 18th World Medical Association (WMA) General Assembly Helsinki, Finland, June 1964 and amended by the 29th WMA General Assembly, Tokyo, Japan, October 1975; 35th WMA General Assembly, Venice, Italy, October 1983; 41st WMA General Assembly, Hong Kong, September 1989; 48th WMA General Assembly, Somerset West, Republic of South Africa, October 1996; and the 52nd WMA General Assembly, Edinburgh, Scotland, October 2000; Note of Clarification on Paragraph 29 added by the WMA General Assembly, Washington 2002; and Note of Clarification on Paragraph 30 added by the WMA General Assembly, Tokyo 2004. On the web at: http://www.wma.net/e/policy/b3.htm.
3. The main guidelines for research involving children are found in Subpart D. Department of Health and Human Services (DHHS). (45 CFR Part 46, Subpart D), 'Protections for Children Involved as Subjects in Research', *Federal Register*, 48 (8 March 1983), 9814–20; revised *Federal Register*, 56 (18 June 1991), 28032; hereinafter cited by its CFR number in the text.
4. Department of Health and Human Services (DHHS), Food and Drug Administration (FDA), 21 CFR Parts 50 and 56, 'Additional Safeguards for Children in Clinical Investigations of FDA-Regulated Products', *Federal Register* 66 (24 April 2001), 20589–600; hereinafter cited by CFR number in the endnotes and text.
5. Subpart A of the federal regulations for the protection of human subject, is known as the Common Rule. The elements of consent delineated in the Common Rule were not written specifically for parents, but hold for 'all subjects or the subjects' legally authorized representative' (CFR §46.116). They include, but are not limited to, the need to be informed about relevant risks, possible benefits, alternatives, and costs, whom to contact with questions, and the right to withdraw (CFR §46.116(a)&(b)). Department of Health and Human Services (DHHS). (45 CFR 46 Subpart A), 'Final Regulations Amending Basic HHS Policy for the Protection of Human Research Subjects', *Federal Register*, 46 (26

January 1981), 8366–91; revised *Federal Register*, 56 (18 June 1991), 28003–18; hereinafter cited by its CFR number in the text.

6. The National Commission did consider what elements are necessary for assent in the context of the 'mentally infirm'. In that report, the National Commission enumerated four criteria as essential. The person must (1) know that procedures will be performed; (2) choose freely to undergo the procedures; (3) communicate this choice unambiguously; and (4) be aware of the option to withdraw. See National Commission for the Protection of Human Subjects of Biomedical and Behavioral Research, *Research Involving those Institutionalized as Mentally Infirm*. Washington DC: US Government Printing Office, 1978. I thank Skip Nelson for pointing out the National Commission's discussion of assent.

7. National Commission for the Protection of Human Subjects, *Report and Recommendations: Research Involving Children*. Washington DC: US Printing Office, 1977, DHEW Publication NO. (OS) 77–0004, 13; hereinafter cited as National Commission, *Research Involving Children*.

8. FDA, 'Additional Safeguards', 20594, [II.H] and codified as CFR §50.55e.

9. Buchanan, A. E., and Brock, D. W., *Deciding for Others: The Ethics of Surrogate Decision-Making*. New York: Cambridge University Press, 1989, 233.

10. See, e.g., Ross, L. F. *Children Families and Health Care Decision-Making*. Oxford: Clarendon Press, 1998; Houlgate, L., *Family and State: The Philosophy of Family Law*. Totowa, NJ: Rowman & Littlefield, 1988; and Schoeman, F., 'Parental Discretion and Children's Rights: Background and Implications for Medical Decision-Making', *Journal of Medicine and Philosophy*, 10 (1985), 45–62.

11. Buchanan and Brock, *Deciding for Others*, 233.

12. Ibid., 234.

13. Hamburg, D. A., *Today's CHILDREN: Creating a Future for a Generation in Crisis*. New York: Times Books, 1994, 194–5.

14. The number of deaths attributed to football includes both direct fatalities (fatalities that result directly from participation in the fundamental skills of football) and indirect fatalities which are caused by systemic failure as a result of exertion while participating in football or by a complication which was secondary to a non-fatal injury. See Mueller, F. O. and Diehl, J. L. for the National Center for Catastrophic Sports Injury Research, 'Annual Survey of Football Injury Research, 1931–2004'. On the web at: http://www.unc.edu/depts/nccsi/SurveyofFootballInjuries.htm.

15. See, e.g., Charlow, A., 'Awarding Custody: The Best Interests of the Child and Other Fictions', in S. R. Humm, B. A. Ort, M. M. Anbari, W. S. Lader, and W. S. Biel (eds.), *Child, Parent, and State*. Philadelphia PA: Temple University Press, 1994, 3–26; and Altman, S., 'Should Child Custody Rules be Fair?' *University of Louisville Journal of Family Law*, 35 (Spring 1996/1997), 325–54.

16. See, e.g., Cashman, T., 'When is a Biological Father Really a Dad?' *Pepperdine Law Review*, 24 (1997), 959–90; and Burns, J. E., 'Note: Should Marriage Matter? Evaluating the Rights of Legal Absentee Fathers', *Fordham Law Review*, 68 (2000), 2299–349.

17. See, e.g., Charlow, 'Awarding Custody'; Cashman, 'Biological Father'; and Burns, 'Should Marriage Matter?'

18. Hamburg, *Today's CHILDREN*, 179.
19. Smith, T. W., 'The Emerging 21st Century American Family. General Social Survey project (GSS) Social Change Report No. 42.' National Opinion Research Center (NORC), University of Chicago, 24 November 1999. On the web at http:// www.norc.uchicago.edu/online/emerge.pdf, 26 [Table 4].
20. Hamburg, *Today's CHILDREN*, 33.
21. Smith, 'Emerging', 29, [Table 6]. Of note, in 1998, there was a slight increase back to 51.7%.
22. Marshall, M. F., Chairperson NHRPAC, 'Comment on: Docket #00N-0074 (24 April 2001), Interim Rule: "Additional Safeguards for Children in Clinical Investigations of FDA-Regulated Products."' On the web at: http://www.hhs.gov/ ohrp/nhrpac/documents/fda.pdf, 1.
23. Ibid., 2.
24. Ibid., 3.
25. Sigman, G. S., and O'Connor, C., 'Explorations for Physicians of the Mature Minor Doctrine', *Journal of Pediatrics*, 119 (1991), 520–5, 521.
26. Marshall, 'Comment', 3.
27. National Commission, *Research Involving Children*, 18–19.
28. Marshall, 'Comment', 2.
29. Veatch, R. M., 'Commentary: Beyond Consent to Treatment', *IRB: A Review of Human Subjects Research*, 3 (February 1981), 7–8.
30. See, e.g., Marshall, 'Comment'; Consensus Conference on Guidelines for Adolescent Health Research, 'Conference Proceedings: Guidelines for Adolescent Health Research, Alexandria VA, 19–20 May 1994', *Journal of Adolescent Health*, 17 (1995), 264–9; and Santelli, J., Rosenfeld, W., DuRant, R., Rosenfeld, W., and Dubler, N., 'Guidelines for Adolescent Health Research: A Position Paper on the Society for Adolescent Medicine', *Journal of Adolescent Health*, 17 (1995), 270–6.
31. Ross, *Children*, esp. ch. 4, 'Respect for the Competent Child'.
32. Ackerman, T. F., 'Fooling Ourselves with Child Autonomy and Assent in Nontherapeutic Clinical Research', *Clinical Research*, 27 (1979), 345–8, 346.
33. See, e.g., Consensus Conference, 'Guidelines'; and Santelli *et al.*, 'Guidelines'
34. See Ross, *Children*, 152–64; and Veatch, 'Beyond Consent'.
35. Veatch, 'Beyond Consent'.
36. Sigman and O'Connor, 'Explorations', 523.
37. Sikand, A., Schubiner, H., and Simpson, P. M., 'Parent and Adolescent Perceived Need for Parental Consent involving Research with Minors', *Archives of Pediatrics and Adolescent Medicine*, 151 (1997), 603–7.
38. Field, M. J., and Behrman, R. E. (eds.), Committee on Clinical Research Involving Children, the Institute of Medicine (IOM), *The Ethical Conduct of Clinical Research Involving Children*. Washington DC: National Academies Press, 2004, 186; hereinafter cited as IOM, *Ethical Conduct*.
39. Ibid., 186.
40. Appelbaum, P., Roth, L., Lidz, C., Benson, P., and Winslade, W., 'False Hopes and Best Data: Consent to Research and the Therapeutic Misconception', *Hastings Center Report*, 17 (April 1987), 20–4.

41. IOM, *Ethical Conduct*, 169.
42. Ibid., 201.
43. I discuss the issues of surveys administered in schools in Ch. 9, section 4, 'Consent for School-Based Research'.
44. Kodish, E., 'Assent and Informed Parental Permission: Insights from the PIC', presentation to the Committee on Clinical Research Involving Children, Washington DC, Institute of Medicine 2003. Cited in IOM, *Ethical Conduct*, 172. Later in the same chapter, the IOM committee stated that 'in the committee's experience and as indicated in some of the research reviewed above, parents often want to decide whether their child will be approached about research participation'. IOM, *Ethical Conduct*, 203.
45. The *MacArthur Competence Assessment Tool for Clinical Research (MACCAT-CR)*, Sarasota Florida: Professional Resource Press 2001 developed by P. S. Appelbaum and T. Grisso has never been validated in adolescents. (Personal communication with Dr Paul Appelbaum, November 2002.)
46. Bartholome, W. G., 'Ethical Issues in Pediatric Research', in H. Y. Vanderpool (ed.), *The Ethics of Research Involving Human Subjects: Facing the 21st century*. Frederick MD: University Publishing Group, Inc, 1996, 339–70, 356–61.
47. National Commission for the Protection of Human Subjects of Biomedical and Behavioral Research, *The Belmont Report: Ethical Principles and Guidelines for the Protection of Human Subjects of Research*. Washington DC: US Government Printing Office, 1978, DHEW Publication No. (OS) 78–12. Found on the web at: http://ohsr.od.nih.gov/guidelines/belmont.html, *hereinafter cited as Belmont Report*.
48. Denham, E. J., and Nelson, R. M., 'Self-Determination is Not an Appropriate Model for Understanding Parental Permission and Child Assent', *Anesthesia and Analgesia* 94 (2002), 1049–51, 1051.
49. Ibid.,1050.
50. Ross, *Children*, esp. ch. 4, 'The Competent Child'.
51. Ackerman, 'Fooling Ourselves', 348.
52. This point has been argued by several ethicists. See e.g., Ross, *Children*; Schoeman, 'Parental Discretion'; and Goldstein, J., Freud, A., Solnit, A. J., *Before the Best Interests of the Child*. New York: Free Press, 1979.
53. Ross, *Children*, 'The Child as Research Subject'.
54. Gaylin, W., 'Competence: No Longer All or None' in W. Gaylin, and R.Macklin, (eds.), *Who Speaks for the Child: The Problems of Proxy Consent*. New York: Plenum Press, 1982, 27–54, 49.
55. Ibid., 49.
56. Bartholome, 'Ethical Issues', 352–3.
57. Goldstein *et al.*, *Before the Best*.
58. Ackerman, 'Fooling Ourselves', 348.
59. Bartholome, 'Ethical Issues'.
60. Clark, R. B., 'Speed, Safety and Dignity: Pediatric Pharmaceutical Development in an Age of Optimism', *University of Chicago Law School Roundtable*, 9 (2002), 1–44.

61. Ibid., 38.
62. Ibid., 23, 31–2.
63. Kant, I., *Grounding for the Metaphysics of Moral* (1785) translated by J. W. Ellington. Indianapolis, IN: Hackett Publishing, 1981.
64. Clark, 'Speed', 38.

6

Phase I Research and the Meaning of 'Prospect of Direct Benefit'

1. Introduction

As described in Chapter 3, Subpart D of the Code of Federal Regulations (CFR) 45 part 46 distinguishes between research that offers and research that does not offer the prospect of direct benefit.[1] If research offers the prospect of direct benefit, then the research is permissible provided that (1) the risk is justified by the anticipated benefit to the subjects; and (2) the relation of the anticipated benefit to the risk is at least as favorable to the subjects as that presented by available alternatives (CFR §46.405). If research does not offer the prospect of direct benefit, then the research is permissible if (1) the risks are no more than minimal (CFR §46.404); (2) the risks are no more than a minor increase over minimal risk and (a) the research is likely to yield generalizable knowledge about the subject's disorder or condition; and (b) the intervention or procedure presents experiences to subjects that are reasonably commensurate with those inherent in their actual or expected medical, dental, psychological, social, or educational situations (CFR §46.406); or (3) the research is not otherwise approvable but presents an opportunity to understand, prevent, or alleviate a serious problem affecting the health or welfare of children and it is approved by a committee convened by the Secretary of the Department of Health and Human Services (DHHS). (CFR §46.407).

In this chapter I examine the issue of whether phase I pediatric oncology trials offer the prospect of direct benefit, the implications of classifying the research as offering or not offering direct benefit, why the current classification schema is inadequate, and an alternative approach to the issue.

2. Phase I Oncology Studies

Following extensive preclinical testing, new drugs must be tested on human beings. Phase I studies are the first time a new entity is introduced into a human subject. Most phase I studies are done on healthy adult volunteers, except in oncology where the toxicities of new entities are potentially significant and phase I testing is conducted in patients with refractory cancer.[2] In phase I oncology testing, the drugs often have a narrow therapeutic window meaning that there is a direct relationship between dose and toxicity and between dose and efficacy.[3] Most phase I oncology studies are cohort studies in which patient-subjects (usually $n=3$) are treated at increasing doses to determine the maximal tolerated dose (MTD), the pharmacokinetics, and drug toxicities to allow researchers to plan for phase II studies of efficacy.

In traditional adult oncology phase I trials, there is an attempt to minimize the toxicity of the new agent by beginning at a very low dose. Given the relationship between dose and efficacy, this means that those who are enrolled earliest in the trial are unlikely to get any therapeutic effect. Because of this, some have argued that the major ethical problem with phase I cancer research is not the risks of toxicity, but the problem of underdosing.[4] As the trial advances, dose-limiting toxicities develop which define the endpoint of the trial. Meta-analyses of adult phase I trials of anticancer drugs show an overall therapeutic response rate of about 5%.[5] The majority of these are partial responses with less than 1% of subjects experiencing a complete response. Death from toxic effects is rare, at 0.5%.[6]

Because of the small number of pediatric oncology patients and the practice that drugs are tested first on animals and adults before children,[7] pediatric oncology phase I trials often begin at 80% of the adult MTD.[8] Starting at such a high dose means that even the earliest enrolled children may receive a dose that has therapeutic benefit. An objective response in pediatric phase I oncology trials is defined as a partial or complete tumor remission, and it occurs in 5–10% of all subjects.[9] The definition of objective response does not include children whose cancer remains stable while on phase I experimental protocols nor improvements in pain control and quality of life. These responses are meaningful to the children and their families, suggesting that the studies may offer even greater potential for therapeutic benefit.[10] Death from toxic effects is rare in pediatric phase I trials at 0.5%,[11] although one pediatric meta-analysis found it to be as high as 2.5%[12] As many as one-fifth of the children experience dose-limiting toxicity (DLT).[13] Other side-effects are common, but their overall frequency, severity, and impact on quality of life have been poorly documented.[14]

3. Do Phase I Studies Offer the Prospect of Direct Benefit

The federal regulations do not define 'direct benefits' or explain how they differ from indirect benefits or other types of benefit. Nancy King proposes that we distinguish between three types of research benefits: direct benefit, collateral benefit, and aspirational benefit.[15] Direct benefit is defined as 'benefit arising from receiving the intervention being studied'; that is, a therapeutic benefit.[16] Collateral benefit (or indirect benefit) is 'benefit that arises from being a subject, even if one does not receive the experimental intervention', e.g. a free medical exam. Collateral benefits can be medical or psychological and include what is known as the 'inclusion benefit', the benefit gained from participation itself.[17] Aspirational benefit is benefit to society. King notes that these benefits are often combined and confused.[18] Subpart D focuses on direct or therapeutic benefit, but researchers often combine direct and collateral benefits and discuss the 'benefit from participating in this research' which includes both the possible therapeutic benefit of receiving the intervention as well as other therapeutic and non-therapeutic benefits including access to skilled clinicians, improvement in symptom management, and psychological benefits.[19]

The medical literature is divided as to whether phase I studies in adults offer a direct or therapeutic benefit. The American Society of Clinical Oncology [ASCO] clearly says that they do: '[p]hase I cancer trials can represent a real therapeutic option for some patients who have failed to respond to other treatment or for whom no other therapies exist.'[20] In contrast, ethicists argue that they are nontherapeutic. Moreno, Caplan, and Wolpe argue that '[a]ll phase I consent forms should include the phrase, prominently displayed in bold type on the first page, "This medical research project is not expected to benefit you,".'[21] Brody also argues that phase I trials, as traditionally designed, must be treated as 'nontherapeutic research'.[22] He argues for newer designs such as the continual reassessment method (CRM) where subjects are treated from the beginning at the dosage anticipated to be recommended for study in a phase II trial.[23]

Most consent forms state that phase I studies are nontherapeutic.[24] In an examination of the 'Benefit Section' of phase I consent forms, Horng *et al.* found that only one in 272 consent forms stated that the subjects were expected to benefit, 11 forms (4%) stated with certainty that subjects would not benefit, 255 (94%) communicated uncertainty about benefit, and 5 forms (2%) said nothing about the chance of benefit. Interestingly 139 forms (51%) alluded to the possibility of benefit in a section other than the designated benefit section.[25]

Whether phase I studies offer the prospect of direct benefit is not critical in adult oncology because under the Common Rule,[26] research is permissible provided that the (1) risks are minimized (CFR §46.111(a)(1)); and (2) the risks are reasonable in relation to the anticipated benefits, if any, to subjects, and the importance of the knowledge that may reasonably be expected to result (CFR §46.111(a)(2)). Phase 1 studies are designed to meet both of these criteria. In pediatric oncology, however, whether the research does or does not offer the prospect of direct benefit is a critical distinction that influences the level of risk to which the subjects can be exposed, the consent mechanisms that are necessary, and whether the study requires local or national review for approval.

There is division within the medical and bioethical pediatric communities as to whether phase I studies provide the prospect of direct benefit. Kodish, a pediatric oncologist-ethicist supports viewing phase I oncology trials as offering the prospect of direct benefit, arguing for a 'relativistic understanding of prospect of benefit'.[27] The phase I trials offer a small chance of controlling the progression of the disease if not reducing the cancer burden compared to non-participation and the receipt of palliative care.[28] Ackerman, a philosopher-medical ethicist, also argues that phase I pediatric oncology trials should be treated as therapeutic research.[29] One concern with stating that phase I trials offer the prospect of direct benefit is the concern of the therapeutic misconception.[30] Many studies have shown that most subjects enroll in phase I trials hoping for personal benefit, despite knowing that the study is designed to determine toxicity and despite what is written on the consent form.[31] In pediatrics, this may result in parental delay in accepting their child's terminal prognosis and may make it harder for parents to acknowledge their child's suffering if they decide to pursue cure at all cost,[32] even though this may not be in either the child's[33] or the family's interest.[34] Using this line of reasoning, Oberman, a lawyer-medical ethicist, and Frader, a pediatric hospice specialist-ethicist, state that phase I tests are explicitly nontherapeutic in nature and that it is an error to think they are therapeutic.[35]

4. *If Phase I studies are Classified as Offering the Prospect of Direct Benefit*

If phase I studies are classified as offering the prospect of direct benefit, then a research protocol can be approved by an IRB provided that (1) the risk is justified by the anticipated benefit to the subjects; (2) the relation of the anticipated benefit to the risk is at least as favorable to the subjects as that presented by available alternative approaches; and (3) consent requirements are met (CFR §46.405). Even in studies that are interpreted as offering the prospect of direct benefit, the IRB must still examine whether the risk/benefit ratio is favorable and whether it is as favorable as the available alternatives.

Is the risk/benefit ratio favorable to the subjects? While the potential for direct benefit for complete or partial remission is about 10%, possibly an additional 5–10% of children experience stability of disease for a period of time. There are also potential collateral benefits. Many discuss the positive side benefits of phase I participation including the inclusion benefit, the reduction of symptoms, enhanced attention in the hospital, and the maintenance of hope.[36] Agrawal and Emanuel examined the literature and found data to document that participating in phase I oncology studies may actually improve patients' quality of life,[37] or provide some psychological benefit.[38] However, Cox points out that quality of life questionnaires often used in oncology interviews may not adequately capture the burdens that trial participation entail including 'an investment of time, emotional and physical energy ... that meant other aspects of their lives were effectively put on hold for the duration of their trial involvement'.[39] Nevertheless, even Cox found that most subjects 'would make the same decision to participate in a similar trial if it was offered to them'.[40] This implies that the subjects interpret the risk/benefit ratio favorably.

Is the risk/benefit ratio to the subjects as favorable as the alternatives? The only alternative for most children with cancer that is not responsive to curative modalities is palliative care. Palliative care ensures comfort measures are managed appropriately, but the treatment offers no chance of cure such that the risk/benefit ratio of phase I trials will often be viewed as 'relatively' favorable.[41] These modalities, however, need not be viewed as diametrically opposed. Providing palliative care services to children enrolled in phase I trials would offer the best of both worlds for the child and future children.[42] The palliative services can minimize side-effects of the phase I drug and thus improve the risk/benefit ratio while enabling the child to participate in the advancement of medical science for future patients.

Research approvable under CFR §46.405 requires one parent permission and the child's assent. The child's dissent can be overridden if 'the intervention or procedure involved in the research holds out a prospect of direct benefit that is important to the health or well-being of the child and is available only in the context of the research' (CFR §46.408(a)). A child's dissent can be overridden in therapeutic research in order to promote the child's medical best interest because it is assumed that the parents know what is in their child's medical interest and will act to promote this. To allow parents to compel their children to participate in phase I trials, however, overstates the potential medical benefit of these trials. Research that may provide unintended (collateral) benefits should not qualify as research that offers the prospect* of direct benefit. To classify phase I research as offering the prospect of direct benefit ignores the fact that the research is NOT designed to provide direct benefit. Ignoring the intent of the research

---

* Even if one were to hold that phase I trials provide a 'possible direct benefit', one would still need to argue that phase I trials, as currently designed, offer the 'prospect' of direct benefit and not the mere possibility of direct benefit. Although the phrase 'prospect of direct benefit' is not defined in the National Commission reports nor in the federal regulations, the phrase 'prospect of direct benefit' connotes a certain expectation of success. I thank Walter Glannon for this clarification.

promotes the therapeutic misconception, and thereby inappropriately empowers parents to compel their children to participate in these trials over their children's dissent.

While phase I pediatric oncology trials may offer a possible direct benefit and may be the best medical alternative for particular children with cancer, I reject classifying such studies under CFR §46.405 because doing so ignores the fact that the researchers' intent is focused on showing safety not efficacy.

5. If Phase I Trials are Classified as NOT Offering the Prospect of Direct Benefit

If phase I studies are classified as NOT offering the prospect of direct benefit, then the research protocol may still be approved under categories CFR §46.404, CFR §46.4.06, or CFR §46.407. In contrast with research approved under CFR §46.405, all these categories focus on aspirational benefits.

CFR §46.404 are the regulations that address minimalrisk research. By definition, a phase I trial of an experimental drug entails more than minimal risk because the new drug entails potentially unknown but significant risks, regardless of pre-clinical data.

To qualify under CFR §46.406, the research must (1) entail no more than a minor increase over minimal risk; (2) be commensurate with the lived experiences of those with a disorder or condition; and (3) be likely to yield generalizable information. Phase I trials are commensurate with the experience of the children to whom it is offered, as many will have been through at least one course of chemotherapy (2). The requirement that it is likely to yield generalizable knowledge (3) places the onus on the oncology community to design trials that will provide scientifically useful data. The advances of the past two decades in pediatric oncology suggest that drug testing in pediatric oncology is well designed.[43] The central issue for approval, then is whether the risks are at most a minor increase over minimal risk (1). Recall that the primary endpoint of these trials is to define MTD. These agents are often known to entail serious and anticipated toxicities, and the trials are an attempt to quantify the risks and to uncover additional unanticipated side-effects. Death is rare, at 0.5%, although one meta-analysis found it to be as high as 2.5%.[44] As such, it is probably correct to say that the research entails more than a minor increase over minimal risk and the research cannot be classified under CFR § 46.406.

Even though the research is not approvable under CFR §46.404 or CFR §46.406, it could be approved under CFR §46.407 if adequate pre-clinical testing is done, the studies are well designed and offer the opportunity to understand, prevent, or alleviate a serious problem affecting the health or welfare of children, and the research is reviewed and approved by a panel convened by the secretary of DHHS. This would mean, however, that all phase I oncology trials would have to undergo national review in addition to local IRB review.

While many phase I oncology trials would easily be approved by a 407 panel, the question is whether this is necessary or desirable. Those who advocate for greater access will be frustrated by this additional obstacle. Even those who are wary of the movement towards increased participation of children in research, may not support the need for 407 panel review because it is not clear what additional protections, if any, the 407 panels would offer. Phase I oncology drugs are only studied in children after they pass phase I and II testing in adults; that is, after safety and efficacy have been established in adults. This does not mean the drug is safe or effective in children; it only confirms that all pre-pediatric testing has been done successfully; i.e., that phase I and II testing in animals and adults have been completed and there is some reason to believe that the drug will be effective in pediatric cancer. Because safety and efficacy of the new drugs have not been established in children, phase I and II testing in children are necessary and the risks must be classified as more than a minor increase over minimal risk for children.

If the 407 process would not provide any additional protection, then the logistical costs in terms of time and effort make 407 review ethically and pragmatically undesirable. However, to approve the research under the current federal regulations without resorting to a 407 panel would mean that IRBs have to approve phase I pediatric oncology trials under CFR §46.405 by claiming that there is sufficient prospect of direct subject benefit. This is problematic for three reasons. First, and most importantly, such a claim ignores the fact that the research is not intended to provide direct benefit. Second, classifying this research under CFR §46.405 overstates the potential medical benefit of most of these trials. Third, consent for research classified as CFR §46.405 allows parental authorization over the children's dissent CFR §46.408(a).

6. An Additional Category for Review in which Intent Matters

Phase I research is done to determine toxicity; the possibility of direct benefit is secondary to the objectives of the study. In an analysis of risk and benefit for the National Bioethics Advisory Commission, Weijer points out that research administered with a therapeutic intent differs in morally relevant ways from research without a therapeutic intent.[45] Focusing exclusively on whether phase I trials could be interpreted as offering the prospect of direct benefit fails to acknowledge the moral relevance of the researchers' intent.

If intentions matter, then phase I studies cannot be said to offer the prospect of direct benefit. This would mean that phase I studies could only be permissible if approved by a 407 panel review. But as discussed above, it is not clear that the 407 review process provides any additional protections in this scenario. Rather, a new category is needed in Subpart D for research that offers the potential* for what I call 'secondary direct benefit' that would not require national review.[46] A secondary direct benefit is a benefit that arises from receiving an experimental intervention when the research is not being done to achieve individual benefit. That is, the experimental intervention offers a potential therapeutic or direct benefit even though the trial lacks therapeutic intent. This contrasts with research in which the experimental intervention offers the prospect of direct benefit and whose study design is therapeutic (e.g. phase III trials comparing an experimental drug against standard therapy). Secondary direct benefits are obtained from receiving the experimental intervention even though the study was not designed to promote this benefit in contrast with the indirect (or collateral) benefits that may accrue from being in the experiment, regardless of whether one receives the experimental intervention. Secondary direct benefits are therapeutic; indirect (or collateral) benefits may or may not be.

Research that has the potential for secondary direct benefits, like phase I pediatric oncology trials, should have its own classification. Research that is likely to yield generalizable knowledge about the subject's disorder or condition, entails more than a minor increase over minimal risk, and provides the potential for secondary direct benefit. This category requires that (1) the risks are justified by the likelihood that the research will yield generalizable knowledge; (2) the research is commensurate with the lived experience of those with the disease or condition; (3) the research offers the potential for a secondary direct benefit, a benefit that is not otherwise available; and (4) consent requirements are met. I have already shown that the first three conditions are met in phase I pediatric oncology trials.

The consent mechanisms for research in this new category should be similar to the mechanisms required for research classified as CFR §46.406. Currently, nontherapeutic research beyond minimal risk requires two-parent consent and the child's assent. In Chapter 5, I argued that two-parent consent probably does not offer additional protections, particularly in an era where more than half of children will spend at least part of their childhood in

---

* To claim that the research offers the 'potential' for secondary direct benefit requires a lower standard than the anticipated probability of success needed to claim that the research offers the 'prospect of direct benefit' but a higher standard than is required for research that offers only a mere 'possibility of benefit'. To distinguish these probabilities, I refer to three categories: (1) research that offers the prospect of direct benefit (therapeutic research currently classified under CFR §46.405); (2) research that offers the potential for secondary direct benefit (secondary therapeutic benefit that would be classified under a new category); and (3) research that offers the possibility of direct benefit (or collateral benefit provided usually in nontherapeutic research). I thank Walter Glannon for this point.

a single-parent household.[47] While one-parent consent would suffice, I adopt the two-parent requirement for consistency with current federal regulations. What is important about the consent requirements for research classified as CFR §46.406, (and CFR §46.407), however, is not the number of parents, but rather, that the child's dissent is always dispositive (CFR §46.408(a)).[48] As the risks increase and the risk benefit ratio becomes less favorable, parents should not be able to decide unilaterally whether or not their child will participate. Parents should be authorized to override a child's objection for research involving more than minimal risk that is *intended* to promote his or her medical best interest, but not authorized to compel their children to participate in phase I research because the research is NOT intended to provide direct benefit. Research in this new category, then, should require parental permission and the child's affirmative assent.[49]

Creating this new category may be overstating a difference and opening a loophole to allow research that does not offer the prospect of direct benefit to be approved locally when it should be reviewed by 407 panels. However, most phase I pediatric oncology trials are presently being approved by local IRBs on the grounds that they offer the prospect of direct benefit (CFR §46.405)[50] despite the low likelihood of benefit and the lack of therapeutic intent. I believe that the new category improves the protection of children as human subjects while ensuring that children are not left as 'therapeutic orphans'. It also incorporates intentions into the classification system of Subpart D, the absence of which is a serious flaw in our current regulatory schema.

References

1. Department of Health and Human Services (DHHS). (45 CFR Part 46, Subpart D), 'Protections for Children Involved as Subjects in Research', *Federal Register,* 48 (8 March 1983), 9814–20; revised *Federal Register,* 56 (18 June 1991), 28032; hereinafter cited by its CFR number in the endnotes and in the text.
2. American Society of Clinical Oncology (ASCO), 'Critical Role of Phase I Clinical Trials in Cancer Treatment', *Journal of Clinical Oncology,* 15 (1997), 853–9.
3. Kodish, E., 'Pediatric Ethics and Early-Phase Childhood Cancer Research: Conflicted Goals and the Prospect of Benefit', *Accountability in Research* 10 (2003), 17–25, 17.
4. Ratain, M. J., Mick, R., Schilsky, R. L., and Siegler, M., 'Statistical and Ethical Issues in the Design and Conduct of Phase I and Phase II Clinical Trials of New Anticancer Agents', *Journal of the National Cancer Institute,* 85 (1993), 1637–43.
5. See, e.g., Estey, E., Hoth, D., Simon, R., Marsoni, S., Leyland-Jones, B., and Wittes, R., 'Therapeutic Response in Phase I Trials of Antineoplastic Agents', *Cancer Treatment Reports,* 70 (1986), 1105–15; Decoster, G., Stein, G., and Holdner, E., 'Responses and Toxic Deaths in Phase I Clinical Trials', *Annals of Oncology,* 1 (1990), 175–81; Von Hoff, D. D., and Turner, J., 'Response Rates,

Duration of Response, and Dose Response Effects in Phase I Studies of Anti-neoplastics', *Investigational New Drugs,* 9 (1991), 115–22.

6. See Decoster *et al.,* 'Responses and Toxic Deaths'.
7. Although there are some circumstances where testing in animals and adults is not possible such as in diseases for which there are no good animal models or in diseases that only present in children (e.g., prematurity), the general practice of testing first in animals and adults was recommended by the National Commission. See National Commission for the Protection of Human Subjects, *Report and Recommendations: Research Involving Children.* Washington DC: US Printing Office, 1977, DHEW Publication NO. (OS) 77–0004, 2 [recommendation 2(b)], hereinafter cited as National Commission, *Research Involving Children.* Of note, however, the recommendation is not written into the federal regulations, and there is some movement to promote the participation of children earlier in the process. See Alexander, D., 'Foreword: Regulation of Research with Children: The Evolution from Exclusion to Inclusion', *Journal of Health Care Law and Policy,* 6 (2002), 1–13. As I discussed in the Introduction, I do not support such a change in practice.
8. Smith, M., Bernstein, M., Bleyer, W., Borsi, J., Ho, P., Lewis, I. J., Pearson, A., Pein, F., Pratt, C., Reaman, G., Riccardi, R., Seibel, N., Trueworthy, R., Unger-leider, R., Vassal, G., and Vietti, T., 'Conduct of Phase I Trials in Children with Cancer', *Journal of Clinical Oncology,* 16 (1998), 966–78.
9. See, e.g., Shah, S., Weitman, S., Langevin, A. M., Bernstein, M., Furman, W., and Pratt, C., 'Phase I Therapy Trials in Children with Cancer', *Journal of Pediatric Hematology/Oncology,* 20 (1998), 431–8; Furman, W. L., Pratt, C. B., and Rivera, G. K., 'Mortality in Pediatric Phase I Clinical Trials', *Journal of the National Cancer Institute,* 81 (1989), 1193–4; Estlin, E. J., Cotterill, S., Pratt, C. B., Pearson, A. D. J., and Bernstein, M., 'Phase I Trials in Pediatric Oncology: Perceptions of Pediatricians from the United Kingdom Children's Cancer Study Group and the Pediatric Oncology Group', *Journal of Clinical Oncology,* 18 (2000), 1900–5.
10. See Shah *et al.,* 'Phase I'; and Agrawal, M., and Emanuel, E. J., 'Ethics of Phase 1 Oncology Studies: Reexamining the Arguments and Data', *JAMA,* 290 (2003), 1075–82.
11. See Decoster *et al.,* 'Responses and Toxic Deaths'; Estlin *et al.,* 'Perceptions'.
12. See Furman *et al.,* 'Mortality'.
13. See Estlin *et al.,* 'Perceptions'.
14. Agrawal and Emanuel, 'Ethics of Phase I'.
15. King, N. M. P., 'Defining and Describing Benefit Appropriately in Clinical Trials', *Journal of Law, Medicine, and Ethics,* 28 (2000), 332–43.
16. King, 'Defining', 333.
17. Lantos, J. D., 'The "Inclusion Benefit" in Clinical Trials', *Journal of Pediatrics,* 134 (1999), 130–1.
18. King, 'Defining', 333.
19. Ibid.
20. ASCO, 'Critical Role', 853.

21. Moreno, J., Caplan, A. L., and Wolpe, P. R., 'Updating Protections for Human Subjects Involved in Research', *JAMA,* 280 (1998), 1951–8, 1954.

22. Brody, B. A., *The Ethics of Biomedical Research: An International Perspective.* New York: Oxford University Press, 1998, 169–75, 174.

23. Ibid., 172. This methodology may be less relevant in pediatric phase I testing because dosing often begins at a much higher level.

24. Horng, S., Emanuel, E., Wilfond, B., Rackoff, J., Martz, K., and Grady, C., 'Descriptions of Benefits and Risks in Consent Forms for Phase 1 Oncology Trials', *New England Journal of Medicine* 347 (2002), 2134–40. The authors examined 90 consent forms for phase I trials enrolling adults, 7 enrolling children, and 3 enrolling children and adults. Ibid., 2136.

25. Ibid.

26. Department of Health and Human Services (DHHS). (45 CFR 46 Subpart A), 'Final Regulations Amending Basic HHS Policy for the Protection of Human Research Subjects', *Federal Register,* 46 (26 January 1981), 8366–91; revised *Federal Register,* 56 (18 June 1991), 28003–18; hereinafter cited by its CFR number in the text. This is known as the Common Rule.

27. Kodish, 'Pediatric Ethics', 19.

28. Ibid. This is not to say that palliative care does not offer a clinical benefit. Palliative care offers an important clinical value in minimizing pain and suffering. I thank Rick Kodish, M.D., for bringing this to my attention.

29. Ackerman, T. F., 'Phase I Pediatric Oncology Trials', *Journal of Pediatric Oncology Nursing,* 12 (1995), 143–5.

30. Appelbaum, P. S., Roth, L. H., Lidz, C. W., Benson, P., and Winslade, W., 'False Hopes and Best Data: Consent to Research and the Therapeutic Misconception', *Hastings Center Report,* 17 (April 1987), 20–4.

31. See, e.g., Daugherty, C., Ratain, M. J., Grochowski, E., Stocking, C., Kodish, E., Mick, R., and Siegler, M., 'Perceptions of Cancer Patients and Their Physicians Involved in Phase I Trials', *Journal of Clinical Oncology,* 13 (1995), 1062–72; Agrawal and Emanuel, 'Ethics of Phase I'; and Hutchison, C., 'Phase I Trials in Cancer Patients: Participants' Perceptions', *European Journal of Cancer Care,* 7 (1998), 15–22.

32. Ulrich, C., Grady, C., and Wendler, D., 'Palliative Care: A Supportive Adjunct to Pediatric Phase I Clinical Trials for Anticancer Agents', *Pediatrics,* 114 (2004), 852–5; Levetown, M., 'Ethical Aspects of Pediatric Palliative Care', *Journal of Palliative Care,* 12 (1996), 35–9.

33. See, e.g., Ulrich *et al.* 'Palliative Care'; Levetown, 'Ethical Aspects'; and Ackerman, T. F., 'The Ethics of Phase I Pediatric Oncology Trials', *IRB: A Review of Human Subjects Research,* 17 (January/February 1995), 1–5.

34. Kreicbergs, U., Valdimarsdottir, U., Onelov, E., Henter, J-I., and Steineck, G., 'Talking about Death with Children Who Have Severe Malignant Disease', *New England Journal of Medicine,* 351 (2004), 1175–86.

35. Oberman, M., and Frader, J., 'Dying Children and Medical Research: Access to Clinical Trials as Benefit and Burden', *American Journal of Law and Medicine,* 29 (2003), 301–17.

36. See, e.g., Kodish, 'Pediatric Ethics'; and Ackerman, 'Phase I'.

37. See, e.g., Agrawal and Emanuel, 'Ethics of Phase I'; and Shah *et al.*, 'Phase I'.
38. See, e.g., Daugherty *et al.*, 'Perceptions'; Hutchison, 'Phase I'; and Moore S., 'A Need to Try Everything: Patient Participation in Phase 1 Trials', *Journal of Advanced Nursing,* 33 (2001), 738–47.
39. Cox, K., 'Assessing the Quality of Life of Patients in Phase I and II Anti-Cancer Drug Trials: Interviews versus Questionnaires', *Social Science & Medicine,* 56 (2003), 921–34, 924.
40. Ibid., 924–5.
41. See Kodish, 'Pediatric Ethics', 19.
42. Ulrich *et al.*, 'Palliative Care'.
43. Bernstein, M. L., Reaman, G. H., and Hirschfeld, S., 'Developmental Therapeutics in Childhood Cancer: A Perspective from the Children's Oncology Group and the US Food and Drug Administration', *Hematology/Oncology Clinics of North America,* 15 (2001), 631–55.
44. See Decoster *et al.*, 'Responses and Toxic Deaths'; Estlin *et al.*, 'Perceptions'; and Furman *et al.*, 'Mortality'.
45. Weijer, C., 'The Ethical Analysis of Risks and Potential Benefits in Human Subjects Research: History, Theory, and Implications for US Regulation', in National Bioethics Advisory Commission (NBAC), *Ethical and Policy Issues in Research Involving Human Participants,* vol. 2, Commissioned Papers, August, 2001. Found on the web at: http://www.georgetown.edu/research/nrcbl/nbac/humen/overvol 2.pdf, P-1-P–29.
46. In 1997, I proposed the inclusion of another category in Subpart D to accommodate phase I tests which would have to offer the prospect of 'indirect benefit'. See Ross, L. F., 'Children as Research Subjects: A Proposal to Revise the *Federal Regulations* using a Moral Framework', *Stanford Law and Policy Review,* 8 (1997), 159–76. Given that collateral benefits are referred to as 'indirect benefit' by NBAC, I now use the terminology of 'secondary direct benefit'. See National Bioethics Advisory Commission, *Research Involving Persons with Mental Disorders that may Affect Decisionmaking Capacity, Report and Recommendations.* Washington DC: US Government Printing Office, 1998.
47. Hamburg, D. A., *Today's CHILDREN: Creating a Future for a Generation in Crisis.* New York: Times Books, 1994, 33.
48. The only exception is if the IRB judges the children as too immature (CFR §46.408(a)).
49. In Ross, 'Children as Research Subjects', I argued that the older child's dissent should be definitive in phase I trials, but I was willing to allow parents to authorize the participation of younger children. While I still support parental authority to enroll their young children in phase I trials, I now argue that the dissent of all children capable of giving assent should be determinative.
50. Kodish, 'Pediatric Ethics'.

7

Human Subject Protections in Pediatric Research

1. Introduction

The first US federal requirements for institutional review of research and for the development of institutional review boards (IRBs) were announced by the Surgeon General in 1966 in a federal policy statement requiring IRB review for all research performed with Public Health Service grants.[1] IRB review is currently required for all US research involving human subjects that is federally funded, regulated by the Food and Drug Administration (FDA), or is performed at an institution that accepts federal funds.[2] IRBs are charged with ensuring that the research is scientifically and ethically sound and that appropriate informed consent is obtained.[3] When the subjects are children, informed consent often includes obtaining parental permission and the child's assent.[4]

The requirement to *document* IRB review and the procurement of consent in published research reports is more recent. The International Committee of Medical Journal Editors (ICMJE), formerly the Vancouver Group, is a group of medical journal editors who in 1978 established guidelines for manuscript submission to their journals.[5] These guidelines have been revised numerous times. The 1981 edition of these guidelines first required researchers to document that the research had IRB review.[6] In 1991, the ICMJE added that when 'informed consent has been obtained by authors, this should be clearly stated in the article'.[7] These guidelines for manuscript submission have been adopted by over 500 journals, often as part of their primary instructions for manuscript preparation.

Previous studies have shown that documentation of IRB review and informed consent (IC) is not universal, even in journals that state it as a requirement,[8] even true in research focused on pediatric health.[9] With two colleagues, Eric Weil and Robert 'Skip' Nelson, I sought to determine (1) to what extent research published in three peer-reviewed pediatric journals documented IRB approval and IC; and (2) to what extent the researchers who failed to document IRB and IC stated that they had obtained appropriate IRB review and consent from subjects. My hypothesis was that research in pediatric journals, particularly research using children as subjects, would be meticulous about the procurement and documentation of IRB approval and informed consent.

2. Methods

All full-length articles published in the paper edition of three pediatric journals (*Pediatrics, Journal of Pediatrics*, and *Archives of Pediatrics & Adolescent Medicine*) between January and December 2000 were examined. These three peer-reviewed pediatric journals are current signatories of the ICMJE guidelines. They all have required proper documentation of IRB approval since at least 1983 and informed consent since 1991. We excluded articles if they did not include empirical data, were case studies or meta-analyses, or did not include at least one US researcher or enroll US subjects, in order to focus on research done in settings that require the researchers to conform to the Common Rule. The articles included in the study were reviewed to see if they mentioned IRB approval and informed consent. If either or both of these features were missing from the article, corresponding authors were asked to voluntarily participate in a follow-up survey either via e-mail or by telephone.

We examined the rate of IRB approval/waiver and the procurement of informed consent. We classified IRB approval/waiver into three categories. 'Presence of IRB review in article' refers to those articles in which IRB approval or exempt status was documented in the article. 'Presence of IRB review in survey' consists of those articles in which the researchers responded to the survey stating that they had IRB approval or that they had obtained an IRB-exemption. 'Waiver of IRB Review' consists of those articles in which the researchers responded to the survey stating that (1) they thought their research was exempt; (2) they did not believe their research needed to go through the IRB because their research used publicly available data; and (3) 'No, I did not get IRB approval' without explanation.[10] In other words, no survey response was recorded as not having IRB approval or waiver; we assumed that researchers failed to seek IRB approval because they believed that their research was exempt.

Similarly, we classified IC (informed consent) into three categories. 'Presence of IC in article' refers to those articles which documented that informed consent mechanisms had been approved or waived. 'Presence of IC in survey' consists of those articles in which the researchers responded to the survey stating that their IC mechanisms (including waiver) had been reviewed by an IRB. 'Waiver of IC' consists of those articles in which the researchers stated that (1) they had not discussed the issue of informed consent with their IRB and did not obtain informed consent because they thought it met the criteria to be waived; or (2) they failed to obtain informed consent and offered no reason. In other words, no survey response was recorded as not having IC mechanisms or waiver; we assumed that researchers who failed to get informed consent believed that IC was waived for their research.

All of the studies were classified into one of three types of research based on how the data were collected: (1) clinical trials/other medical studies included both randomized controlled studies as well as other medical interventions such as blood tests, anthropomorphic measurements, and modified feedings; (2) behavioral studies included studies that obtained information through written or oral surveys, interviews, standard educational tests, quality assurance projects, and observational studies; and (3) pre-existing data or tissue studies included the use of publicly available databases, chart reviews, and the use of pre-existing tissue collections. All the studies may involve subjects who are or are not identified, a distinction that will be important for determining if the research is or is not exempt. We then examined whether the rate of IRB approval/waiver and the procurement of IC varied depending on the type of study being reported.

We also divided the research into those studies that included children-subjects and those studies using only adult-subjects (either parents, medical professionals, or other third parties) to determine if this influenced whether the researchers documented IRB review and consent procedures. Data were analyzed using the computer program STATA. In addition to this survey, we also examined all exempt articles. Articles were classified as exempt if (1) the researchers obtained exempt status from the IRB [IRB-exempt]; (2) the researchers stated the research was exempt according to their understanding of the research regulations; or (3) the researchers stated they did not seek IRB review.

The validity of an exemption was determined using the criteria stated in the federal regulations (CFR §46.101(b) and CFR §46.401 (b)) by both myself and Nelson. Articles were classified as 'Exempt' (met the federal regulation requirements], 'Not Exempt' (failed to meet the federal regulations requirements) or 'Probably Exempt' (cases where the research would be exempt or not exempt depending on whether the data were linked to identifiers or not). While all of the research classified as 'probably exempt' could use linked or unlinked data, the research methodology as described in the article did not give enough information to determine this. Differences in classification between myself and Nelson were resolved through discussion with eventual agreement on all classifications.

We then examined the validity of both IRB and researcher-exempt research. This was to determine (1) what research was classified as exempt; and (2) whether research that sought IRB exemption was more likely to be in accordance with the federal regulations' exemption criteria than research that did not receive IRB review but was presumed to be exempted by the researcher.

This research was approved by both the University of Chicago Institutional Review Board and the Children's Hospital of Philadelphia's Committees for the Protection of Human Subjects. The University of Chicago waived the requirement for documenting the written informed consent of the subjects [the journal articles' authors] under CFR §46.116.

3. Results

Five-hundred and seventy-five original articles published in the three journals in the year 2000 were reviewed. One hundred and ninety-six were excluded for lacking original data, for not having at least one US researcher or any US subjects, or for being a case study. Of the remaining 379 articles, 197 (52.0%) documented IRB review, 164 (43.3%) documented IC, and 131 (34.6%) properly documented the presence of both IRB review and IC (see Figure 1). Two hundred and fifty one surveys were sent out (249 to those lacking documentation of one or both ethical criteria and two to those with proper documentation for clarification purposes). Of those that received surveys, 14 declined to participate, 23

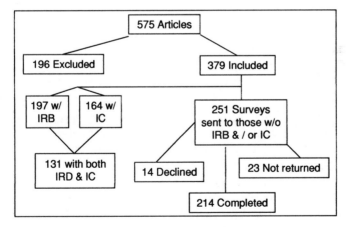

Figure 1. *Articles Documenting IRB Review Only, Informed consent (IC) only, and both IRB review and IC. This figure is reprinted with permission from Weil, E., Nelson, R. M., and Ross, L. F., Are research ethics standards satisfied in pediatric journal publications?' Pediatrics, 110 2002, 364 – 370, 366 fig. 2.*

were not returned, and 214 were completed for a 90.8% survey response rate. We have IRB data on 92.1% of these articles, informed consent data on 90.8% of the articles; and both IRB and informed consent documentation on 90.2% of the articles.

We examined whether the rate of IRB approval and the procurement of informed consent varied depending on the type of study reported. The results are reported in Table 7. IRB approval was highest in clinical/medical studies and lowest in studies using pre-existing data. Similarly, the highest percentage of IC documentation was found in clinical/medical studies and the lowest in studies using pre-existing data. The last column shows the number of studies where we have no data. This takes into account those who did not document IRB or IC review in the article and who either did not respond or declined to participate in our survey.

We then examined the validity of the exemptions granted by the IRB or determined by the researcher. The results are found in Tables 8 through 11. The highest percentage of exemption claims were made for pre-existing data (47.6%), and the least number of claims were made for medical/clinical research (7.0%). However, the highest 'error' rate for exemptions was seen in medical/clinical studies where nine of 11 research projects were mistakenly classified as exempt (Table 8). No significant difference was seen between exemption claims made by institutions (Hospital or University IRBs or private organizations) or researchers. Both groups incorrectly categorized the research as exempt in approximately one-fourth of the cases (Table 9). With respect to the type of study, there were no significant differences between when a researcher sought IRB exemption or self-exemption (Table 10).

In Table 11, we give the reasons why we classify the 'Exempt' research as either 'Exempt', 'Probably Exempt', or 'Not Exempt', based on the federal regulations criteria. Two-thirds of the studies that were 'Exempt' used publicly available databases. Another 21.4% were surveys of adults. All the studies that were 'Probably Exempt' could have been done without linked data, but the methodology in the articles did not specify whether the researchers anonymized the data. The most frequently used reason for determining that a study was 'Not Exempt' was that the study could be done only with identifiable data.

Of the 379 studies examined, 16.9% involved adult-subjects such as parents, health care providers, and health policy analysts. The level of documentation in these articles for both IRB approval and waiver and informed consent methodology did not differ significantly from the rest of the studies. Several studies categorized themselves as quality assurance or quality improvement studies.

Table 7.   IRB approval and informed consent

Type of Study		Presence of IRB Review and IC			Waiver of IRB Review and IC	Unknown
		Article n (%)	Survey n (%)	Article plus survey n (%)	n (%)	n (%)
Medical/Clinical (n=157)	IRB Review	109 (69.4)	34 (21.7)	143 (91.1)	6 (3.8)	8 (5.1)
	IC	114 (72.6)	30 (19.1)	144 (91.7)	4 (2.5)	9 (5.7)
Behavioral (n=98)	IRB Review	56 (57.1)	24 (24.5)	80 (81.6)	11 (11.2)	7 (7.1)
	IC	41(41.8)	38 (38.8)	79 (80.6)	11 (11.2)	8 (8.2)
Pre-existing Data (n=124)	IRB Review	32 (25.8)	42 (33.9)	74 (59.7)	35 (28.2)	15 (12.1)
	IC	9 (7.3)	64 (51.6)	73 (58.9)	32 (25.8)	19 (15.3)
All (n=379)	IRB Review	197 (52.0)	100 (26.4)	297 (78.4)	52 (13.7)	30 (8.0)
	IC	164 (43.3)	132 (34.8)	296 (78.1)	47 (12.4)	36 (9.5)

Legend: 'Presence of IRB Review and IC': refers to those articles in which IRB review (or exemption) and/or IC mechanisms (or waiver) were either documented in the article (Article) or confirmed by the researchers in the survey (Survey) or in either (Article plus Survey). 'Waiver of IRB Review and IC' refers to those articles about which the researchers stated in the survey either that IRB review was not necessary or that IC could be waived without IRB review. 'Unknown' refers to those articles in which the data were missing in the article and the authors did not respond to our surveys and telephone calls. This table is reprinted, with modifications, with permission from E. Weil, R. Nelson, and L. F. Ross, 'Are research ethics standards satisfied in pediatric journal publications?' *Pediatrics*, 110 (2002), 364–70, 367 Table 1.

Table 8.   Validity of exempt status

Type of study	Claimed exempt	Clearly exempt	Probably exempt	Not exempt	Error rate of studies claimed to be exempt
Medical/Clinical (n=157)	11 (7.0%)	1	1	9	81.8–90.9%
Behavioral (n=98)	23 (23.5 %)	18	0	5	21.7%
Pre-existing data (n=124)	59 (47.6%)	37	11	11	18.6–37.3%
All (n=379)	93 (24.5%)	56	12	25	26.9–39.8%

This table is reprinted with permission from E. Weil, R. M. Nelson, and L. F. Ross, 'Are research ethics standards satisfied in pediatric journal publications?' *Pediatrics,* 110 (2002), 364–70, 367 Table 2.

4. Discussion

Our data show the procurement and documentation of IRB approval and informed consent in all articles reporting the results of research involving human subjects published in three pediatric journals that have required both such procedures since at least 1991 (*Journal of Pediatrics* has had this requirement since the early 1980s). This requirement is not required by all medical journals. In 1997, Amdur and Biddle found that about one-quarter of the 102 English-language biomedical research journals listed in the 1995 Abridged Index Medicus did not 'present or refer the author to any information related to human research ethics'.[11]

Table 9.   Validity of exemption: researcher vs. institution claims

	Claimed exempt (researcher) n= 52	(%)	Claimed exempt (institution) n= 41	(%)	All exempt n = 93	(%)
Clearly exempt	32	(61.5)	24	(58.5)	56	(60.2)
Probably exempt	6	(11.5)	6	(14.6)	12	(12.9)
Not Exempt	14	(26.9)	11	(26.8)	25	(26.9)

This table is reprinted with permission from E. Weil, R. M. Nelson, and L. F. Ross, 'Are research ethics standards satisfied in pediatric journal publications?' Pediatrics,110 (2002), 364–70, 367 Table 3.

Table 10. Validity of exemption determination by researchers or IRB for different types of research

Type of Study	Whose exemption?	'Clearly Exempt'	'Probably Exempt'	'NOT Exempt'
Medical/Clinical (n= 11)	Researcher exempted ($n = 6$)	1 (16.7%)	0 (0.0%)	5 (83.3%)
	IRB exempted ($n = 5$)	0 (0.0%)	1 (20.0%)	4 (80.0%)
Behavioral (n= 23)	Researcher exempted ($n = 12$)	10 (83.3%)	0 (0.0%)	2 (16.7%)
	IRB exempted ($n = 11$)	8 (72.7%)	0 (0.0%)	3 (27.3%)
Pre-existing data (n=59)	Researcher exempted ($n = 34$)	21 (61.8%)	6 (17.6%)	7 (20.6%)
	IRB exempted ($n = 25$)	16 (64.0%)	5 (20.0%)	4 (16.0%)
All (n=93)	Researcher exempted ($n = 52$)	32 (61.5%)	6 (11.5%)	14 (27.0%)
	IRB exempted ($n = 41$)	24 (58.5%)	6 (14.6%)	11 (26.8%)

This table is reprinted and revised with permission from E. Weil, R. M. Nelson, and L. F. Ross, 'Are research ethics standards satisfied in pediatric journal publications?' *Pediatrics*, 110 (2002), 364–70, 367 Table 4.

Drummond and Yank examined 53 articles in five major general medicine research journals that involved prospective research on humans to determine how often informed consent and IRB approval were recorded.[12] Although the focus of this editorial article was to argue that reporting IRB approval and consent was the responsibility of both the editor and the researchers, the article revealed the magnitude of the 'gap' between manuscript requirements and actual manuscript content. Only 53% of the articles stated informed consent was obtained, and only 42% recorded IRB approval. Informed consent and IRB approval were both mentioned in 32% of the articles.[13] These data are consistent with what Rikkert *et al.* found in their study of geriatric journals a year earlier.[14]

Ruiz-Canela *et al.* advanced the debate by contacting authors to inquire about whether or not informed consent and IRB approval were obtained when one or both were not mentioned in the article.[15] They reviewed 767 clinical trials published between 1993 to 1995 and found that 64% of the articles documented both IRB approval and consent. They sent follow-up surveys to the remaining authors and were able to document that 22.4% failed to get IRB approval and 20.6% failed to have a means to procure consent. These numbers may be low because 7.7% and 5.6% of data were missing for IRB review and IC respectively.

Table 11.   Reasons for exempt classifications

Reasons for exempt classification	Number of studies
Clearly exempt	($N = 56$)
1. Survey of adults	12 (21.4%)
2. Pre-existing tissue/data	2 (3.6%)
3. Publicly available databases	37 (66.1%)
4. Educational setting	1 (1.8%)
5. Observed public behavior	3 (5.4%)
6. Epidemiology	1 (1.8%)
Probably exempt	($N = 12$)
1. Could be done w/ or w/o linked data	12 (100.0%)
Not exempt	($N=25$)
1. Identifiable data	17 (68.0%)
2. Prospective tissue/data collection	7 (28.0%)
3. Non-educational pediatric surveys	1 (4.0%)

This table is reprinted with permission from E. Weil, R. M. Nelson, and L. F. Ross, 'Are research ethics standards satisfied in pediatric journal publications?' *Pediatrics*, 110 (2002), 364–70, 368 Table 5.

We hypothesized that research published in peer-reviewed pediatric journals would conform to research ethics standards because of the increased vulnerability of children as research subjects. Two recent studies found this was not the case. Bauchner and Sharfstein asked whether researchers in child health documented IRB review and consent mechanisms. They examined 561 articles related to child health published in five peer-reviewed journals in 1999. Although the pediatric population is considered to be one of the most vulnerable in research, the authors found that only 61% of publications had proper ethics documentation.[16] Sifers *et al.* examined all empirical studies published in four major journals in child psychology in 1997 and found that parental consent and the child's assent were documented in only 41.5% and 18.8% of the articles respectively.[17] Roggin *et al.* examined 149 pediatric surgical studies and found that slightly less than one-fourth of the studies documented IRB approval.[18] The documentation of IRB review in child health research is nearly identical to the findings in the literature generally.[19]

Our results are within the same range. Of the 379 articles included in our study, 52.0% documented IRB review and 43.3% documented IC methods explicitly in the article, and only 34.6% properly documented both. What was notable, however, was the variation in documentation depending on the type of research. Better documentation is expected in clinical trials where physical risks to subjects are most obvious. This is what we found (see Table 7) when we divided the research into three categories (medical/clinical studies, behavioral studies, and pre-existing data studies). Better documentation might also be expected in research that only included children-subjects although this was previously refuted at least for subjects in pediatric surgery, [20] and was not confirmed by our data. The research ethics standards of the ICJME do not make these distinctions. IRB review/waiver and IC are required for most research published in these journals, but we found documentation of both of these practices in only one-third of the articles.

Despite the lack of documentation, we found that, according to author reports, most research is properly getting IRB review (297/379 studies or 78.4%). Furthermore, we found that research that traditionally requires IRB approval and consent (medical studies and clinical trials) are the most likely to document it in the article or state that they had obtained it in response to questioning (91.1%). Least attention is given to obtaining IRB approval in pre-existing data studies (60.6%). Such a hierarchy is problematic: although the likely types of harm differ depending on the research category, the effects of the harms can be just as significant regardless of the category. Our data suggest that researchers may not consider the potential harm from a breach of confidentiality of identifiable information in both clinical and non-clinical research (i.e. surveys, medical records reviews, database analyses).[21]

Twenty-four percent of the articles in our study claimed IRB-exempt status. As can be seen in Table 8, the majority of these exempt claims were made for studies involving pre-existing data. We found that between 26.9% and 39.8% of research classified as exempt needed greater IRB review, depending respectively on whether the data in the 'Probably Exempt' category was collected without or with identifiers. These numbers could be even higher, depending on the results of those studies that were not included because of missing data. Furthermore, the IRBs did not perform any better in determining when research was exempt than the researchers (Table 9). The relative performance of the researchers and the IRBs were similar for each study category (Table 10). Both groups incorrectly categorized the research as exempt in approximately one-fourth of the cases. This number may be an underestimate depending on whether the studies in the 'Probably Exempt' category were performed with or without data linked to patient identifiers.

We also found that most of the researchers had methods for procuring consent. If we assume that all exempt research may waive consent, then 90.5% had consent mechanisms (Table 7). This overestimates the actual number of proper consent procedures because a significant number of exempt studies, both IRB and researcher-determined, were inappropriately exempt. The standards for waiving consent are currently in flux because new HIPAA (Health Information Portability and Accountability Act) regulations grant patients greater right to know when their health data are being used.[22]

One limitation to our study is that our results are based on researchers' answers. We did not confirm their IRB review with their institutional IRB and we did not confirm their claims to procuring informed consent from subjects. It is possible that the respondents erred in their survey responses. A second limitation is that not all may agree on our inclusion and exclusion criteria. For example, we did not include case studies or reports that described a small number of cases. Although publication of case studies raises important ethical issues,[23] they are neither a systematic investigation nor generalizable and thus do not qualify as research under the federal regulations. In contrast, we did include all studies that described quality improvement and quality assurance projects, although it is often uncertain whether quality improvement studies are research.[24] A third limitation is that we may have misclassified some research such that our determination of what research gets reviewed and what research includes appropriate consent mechanisms may be misleading. Finally, we may have misunderstood the methodology described in the articles and thereby misclassified research as not exempt when it could be exempt.

Although some institutions already require all research to be submitted to the IRB with the IRB having final authority whether or not to exempt a research project, this is not currently true of all institutions. Despite our findings that IRBs and researchers do equally well in determining when research can be exempt, we believe that all research judged to be exempt by researchers should be submitted to IRBs because of the actual or perceived conflicts of interests and biases that researchers have in making decisions about research risk [25] and because IRB review provides an additional layer of human subject protection.

We also realize that while IRB approval and informed consent are necessary, they are not sufficient to guarantee that the research is ethical. Much work needs to be done to improve the IRB process [26] and to educate researchers regarding the responsible conduct of research, including the purpose of IRB review and of informed consent. The new federal requirements that all researchers receiving federal funding be certified in research ethics will serve to alert some researchers to the need for IRB approval and what is required for research to be exempt.[27] In this regard, institutions should also have a mechanism for continued education of IRB members regarding current research ethics standards. We found that the misunderstanding about federal policies governing research exemption affects IRB members and researchers alike.

The journal peer-review process can motivate researchers to pay more attention to research ethics standards, too. Medical journal editors should be more consistent about their own requirements, and should reaffirm the importance of the guidelines established by the ICMJE. The documentation of IRB approval and informed consent should appear in all journal articles reporting research involving human subjects. Journals should require more extensive documentation at the time of submission, and refuse to review articles that fail to conform to these practices. All articles involving research with human subjects should document in the methods section (1) IRB review and approval; (2) the classification by the IRB of the research and the reasons for that classification; (3) the IRB requirements for informed consent (i.e., waiver, waiver of written documentation, full informed consent), and (4) the IRB reasons for the consent requirements. Such a publication requirement would affirm the editors' commitment to the ethical principles regarding human subject protection. In pediatric research, the publication of the criterion under which the research was approved (e.g., minimal risk CFR §46.404) could lead to greater discussion about how to interpret the guidelines (e.g., concepts of risk, prospect of direct benefit) detailed in Subpart D.

5. Conclusion

Our research found that a small but non-trivial number of pediatric research protocols do not obtain IRB approval or a waiver. However, we also found that the lack of documentation of IRB approval and/or informed consent in three pediatric journals does not necessarily indicate that they were not obtained. Most research that did not go through an IRB would have been exempt under current guidelines. Despite our findings that IRBs erred as frequently as researchers when classifying research as exempt, I support a policy that would require all research to go through IRB review because it provides an independent assessment of human subject protections. Furthermore I support a policy requiring published pediatric researchers to document under what classification the research was approved in order to encourage community discussion and consensus.[28]

References

1. Surgeon General Memorandum referred to in Levine, R. J., *Ethics and Regulation of Clinical Research,* 2nd edn. New Haven CT: Yale University Press, 1986, 323.
2. Department of Health and Human Services, Office for Human Research Protections (OHRP), 'Federalwide Assurance of Protection for Human Subjects (ver-

sion date 3/20/2002)'. On the web at http://www.hhs.gov/ohrp/humansubjects/ assurance/filasurt.htm.

3. Department of Health and Human Services (DHHS). (45 CFR 46 Subpart A), 'Final Regulations Amending Basic HHS Policy for the Protection of Human Research Subjects', *Federal Register,* 46 (26 January 1981), 8366–91; revised *Federal Register,* 56 (18 June 1991), 28003–18; hereinafter cited by its CFR number in the text.

4. Department of Health and Human Services (45 CFR Part 46, Subpart D), 'Protections for Children Involved as Subjects in Research', *Federal Register* 48 (8 March 1983): 9814–20; revised *Federal Register* 56 (18 June 1991): 28032 at CFR 46.408; hereinafter cited by its CFR number in the text.

5. International Committee of Medical Journal Editors, 'Uniform Requirements for Manuscripts Submitted to Biomedical Journals', *JAMA,* 269 (1993), 2282–6.

6. International Committee of Medical Journal Editors. 'Uniform Requirements for Manuscripts Submitted to Biomedical Journals', *Annals of Internal Medicine,* 96 (1982), 766–71.

7. International Committee of Medical Journal Editors, 'Statement from the International Committee of Medical Journal Editors', *JAMA,* 265 (1991), 2697–8.

8. See, e.g., Drummond, R., and Yank, V., 'Disclosure to the Reader of Institutional Review Board Approval and Informed Consent', *JAMA,* 277(1997), 922–3; Rikkert, M., ten Have, H., and Hoefnagels, W., 'Informed Consent in Biomedical Studies on Aging: Survey of Four Journals', *BMJ,* 313 (1996), 1117–22; Ruiz-Canela, M., Martinez-Gonzalez, M. A., Gomez-Gracia, E., and Fernandez-Crehuet, J., 'Informed Consent and Approval by Institutional Review Boards in Published Reports on Clinical Trials', *New England Journal of Medicine,* 340 (1999), 1114–15; Bauchner, H., and Sharfstein, J., 'Failure to Report Ethical Approval in Child Health Research: Review of Published Papers', *BMJ,* 323 (2001), 318–19; Karlawish, J. H. T., Hougham, G. W., Stocking, C. B., and Sachs, G. A., 'What is the Quality of the Reporting of Research Ethics in Publications of Nursing Home Research?' *Journal of the American Geriatrics Society',* 47 (1999), 76–81; and Roggin, K. K., Chwals, W. J., and Tracy, T. F., 'Institutional Review Board Approval for Prospective Experimental Studies on Infants and Children', *Journal of Pediatric Surgery,* 36 (2001), 205–8.

9. See, e.g., Bauchner and Sharfstein, 'Failure'; Roggin *et al.,* 'Institutional Review Board'; and Sifers, S. K., Puddy, R. W., Warren, J. S., and Roberts, M. C., 'Reporting of Demographics, Methodology, and Ethical Procedures in Journals in Pediatric and Child Psychology', *Journal of Pediatric Psychology,* 27 (2002), 19–25.

10. Eric Weil, personal communications, June–September 2001.

11. Amdur, R. J., and Biddle, C., 'Institutional Review Board Approval and Publication of Human Research Results', *JAMA,* 277 (1997), 909–14.

12. Drummond, and Yank, 'Disclosure'.

13. Ibid.

14. Rikkert *et al.,* 'Informed Consent'.

15. Ruiz-Canela *et al.,* 'Informed Consent and Approval'.

16. Bauchner and Sharfstein, 'Failure'.

17. Sifers *et al.*, 'Reporting', 9.
18. Roggin *et al.*, 'Institutional Review Board'.
19. See citations in reference 8.
20. Roggin *et al.*, 'Institutional Review Board'.
21. Ruiz-Canela *et al.*, 'Informed Consent and Approval'.
22. Health Information Portability and Accountability Act (HIPAA) Public. Law No. 104–91, 110 Stat. 1936 (1996). The law that was passed in 1996 gave Congress three years to write legislation for health care privacy or the responsibility would be given to the Department of Health and Human Services. The deadline passed without legislation and in December 2000 guidelines were published in the *Federal Register*. See Department of Health and Human Services (DHHS) Office of the Secretary Office of the Assistant Secretary for Planning and Evaluation. 45 CFR Parts 160 and 164, 'Standards for Privacy of Individually Identifiable Health Information, Part II', *Federal Register* 65 (28 December 2000), 82462–829. Final rules were published in the *Federal Register* in 2002. See Office for Civil Rights, HHS, 'Standards for Privacy of Individually Identifiable Health Information. Final Rule', *Federal Register* 67 (14 August 2002), 53181–273.
23. See, e.g., Fost, N., and Cohen, S., 'Ethical Issues Regarding Case Reports: To Publish or Perish the Thought', *Clinical Research,* 24 (1976), 269–73; and Murray, J. C., and Pagon, R. A., 'Informed Consent for Research Publication of Patient-Related Data', *Clinical Research,* 32 (1984), 404–8.
24. Casarett, D., Karlawish, J., H., and Sugarman, J., 'Determining When Quality Improvement Initiatives Should Be Considered Research: Proposed Criteria and Potential Implications', *JAMA,* 283 (2000), 2275–80.
25. See, e.g., Janofsky, J., and Starfield, B., 'Assessment of Risk in Research on Children', *Journal of Pediatrics* 98 (1981), 842–6; Thompson, D. F., 'Understanding Financial Conflicts of Interest', *New England Journal of Medicine,* 329 (1993), 573–6; Merz, J. F., 'IRB Review: Necessary, Nice, or Needless', *Annals of Epidemiology,* 8 (1998), 479–81; and Koski, G., 'Risks, Benefits, and Conflicts of Interest in Human Research: Ethical Evolution in the Changing World of Science', *Journal of Law, Medicine and Ethics,* 28 (2000), 330–1.
26. See, e.g., National Bioethics Advisory Commission, *Ethical and Policy Issues in Research Involving Human Participants. Vol. I: Report and Recommendations of the National Bioethics Advisory Commission,* August 2001. Located at http://www.georgetown.edu/research/nrcbl/nbac/human/overvol1.pdf; and Advisory Committee on Human Radiation Experimentation, *Final Report: Advisory Committee on Human Radiation Experiments.* Washington DC: US Government Printing Office, 1995, 816–28.
27. National Institutes of Health (NIH), 'Required Education in the Protection of Human Research Participants. Notice OD-00–039' (5 June 2000, revised 25 August 2000). Located at http://grants.nih.gov/grants/guide/notice-files/NOT-OD-00–039.html.
28. The value of documenting under what classification the research was approved is also relevant in research sent to DHHS for 407 review. See Chs. 14 and 15.

8

Payment in Pediatric Research

1. Introduction

Ideally, research subjects would be motivated by idealism and altruism by which I mean that they would share in, support, and be motivated by the goals of the researchers. In addition, all research ideally would require the participation only of competent adults who could affirm their support of the research by providing their own informed and voluntary consent to participate as subjects. This is particularly desirable for research that does not offer the prospect of direct benefit because it provides moral justification for exposing the subjects to the risk of harm. The researcher legitimately can expose research participants to risk of harm on the grounds that competent individuals can choose life goals that are other-regarding. If the research subject is altruistic, there is reason to believe that his or her consent is voluntary and informed. Pragmatically, payment may also offer a bonus to the researchers: when research subjects share in the goals of the research, they may be more compliant with the protocol and its requirements.[1]

To participate as a research subject for altruistic reasons, even if it does not serve one's own medical interests, need not be irrational. It can be rational to serve as a research subject because it results in better health care for society as a whole, and potentially improves the health care of the individual subject, even if only indirectly. It is rational for an individual to be a free-rider and reap the benefits of research without exposing oneself to any risks, if enough other individuals are willing to serve as research subjects. However, if too many people seek to free-ride and not enough people are willing to serve as research subjects, then we are all worse off because the research necessary to improve health care cannot be done.

One solution is to exhort altruistic behavior; an alternative solution is to offer payment. Although payment could lead to very motivated subjects, the concern is that some people will then choose to be research subjects not because they believe in or support the research cause, but solely or at least primarily for the money. This approach also may cause practical problems, particularly if subjects lie about their medical status in order to meet eligibility criterion.[2]

Although researchers have been paying healthy research subjects for years, the ethical issues surrounding paid research subjects remain unresolved. Governmental regulations and guidelines, both in the US and abroad, provide little guidance. These ethical issues are even more controversial when the research subjects are children. In this chapter, I examine the ethics of payment in pediatric research that does not offer the prospect of direct benefit (a.k.a nontherapeutic research). I consider the ethical objection that payment perverts motivation. This can have two adverse consequences: (1) it may distort the voluntariness of the parent's permission and the child's assent; and (2) it may lead to an unjust recruitment or selection of subjects. I find the arguments not compelling and argue that it is morally permissible, although not morally obligatory, to provide payment for participation in pediatric research. I then consider related issues that need to be resolved to decide what is a fair price for the participation of children in nontherapeutic research.

2. Current Policies and Guidelines

The reports by the National Commission (for the Protection of Human Subjects of Biomedical and Behavioral Research) and the federal regulations derived from these reports provide little guidance with respect to payment. In the *Belmont Report*, the National Commission declared that 'informed consent requires conditions free of coercion and undue influence'.[3] It defined the latter as occurring 'through an offer of an excessive, unwarranted, inappropriate, or improper reward or other overture in order to obtain compliance'.[4] It noted that inducements 'that would ordinarily be acceptable may become undue influences if the subject is especially vulnerable'.[5] The federal regulations governing the protection of research subjects state that no 'undue inducement' be offered to encourage people into volunteering.[6] Macklin argues this means that '*some* inducement is acceptable to promote adequate numbers to serve as research subjects'.[7]

International guidelines reflect the same concern regarding 'undue inducements'. The Tri-Council Policy of Canada (1998 revised in 2000 and 2002) included issues of payment in their chapter on consent.[8] The authors explained:

Item 7 is intended to prevent the development of a payment structure for research participation that might place undue pressure on research subjects either to join or remain within a research project. It does not imply that subjects should be paid for their participation in research. In research projects where subjects will be compensated, REBs [Research Ethics Boards] should be sensitive to the possibility of undue inducement for participation, such as payments that would lead subjects to undertake actions that they would not ordinarily accept. REBs should pay attention to issues such as the economic circumstances of those in the pool of prospective subjects, and to the magnitude and probability of harms.[9]

The Royal College of Physicians (UK) has addressed the issue of payment in two documents, one on research involving healthy volunteers[10] and the other on research involving patients.[11] With respect to healthy volunteers, the Royal College argued that volunteers should be paid for inconvenience and discomfort, but never for undergoing risk.[12] The Royal College's position was that payment should not function to persuade individuals to volunteer against their better judgment nor to induce them to volunteer more frequently. With respect to patients, the Royal College stated that payments to patients are generally undesirable but are occasionally acceptable in studies that are lengthy and tedious.[13] The Royal College also argued that payments to patients should not be provided for undergoing risk and should not be used to persuade patients to volunteer against their better judgment.[14]

The universal theme is that payment to adult research subjects is suspect because it may unduly influence individuals, particularly individuals from vulnerable populations. Payment is justifiable to compensate for time and discomfort, but not to induce individuals to take risks.

US guidelines provide even less guidance with regard to paying children-subjects. Payment is not mentioned in the National Commission's report, *Research Involving Children* (1977),[15] nor in Subpart D of the federal regulations that offers additional protections to children.[16] The American Academy of Pediatrics [AAP] Committee on Drugs addressed this issue in 1977:

It is in accord with the traditions and ethics of our society to reward people who do something for us or who participate and cooperate with us in achieving our goals. However, serious ethical questions arise when payment is offered to adults acting on behalf of minors in return for allowing minors to participate as research subjects. Although there are altruistic and other incentives inherent in offering to become a research subject, external incentives must be avoided and payment or other material benefits should not be large enough or of a nature to induce responsible persons to agree to allow a dependent to participate in a study or to subject them to painful or invasive procedures.[17]

The AAP supported the decision of the investigators to make funds and facilities available to reimburse the child (or the family) for any costs incurred because of the child's involvement in the study. However, payment beyond token gestures of appreciation should be avoided.[18] It recommended that the institutional review boards [IRBs] review compensation proposals to determine whether they may function as an 'undue influence'. The AAP retained this position when the statement was revised in 1995 and went further by suggesting: ' The remuneration should not be beyond a token gesture. If remuneration is to be provided to the child, it is best if it is not discussed before the study's completion. This will help assure that the remuneration is not part of the reasons that a child volunteered or is volunteered for a study'.[19]

Most recently, the Institute of Medicine (IOM) Committee on Clinical Research Involving Children published a report in which it encouraged that IRBs, research institutions, and sponsors of research to devise 'explicit written policies on acceptable and unacceptable types of payments'.[20] In contrast to the AAP, the IOM committee recommended that payment be part of the consent process, although it should not be emphasized as a benefit of participating.[21] While most have argued against payments that might be undue inducements, the IOM justified permitting payments 'to reduce certain barriers to research participation'[22] reflecting the change in focus from protecting children from research risks to promoting greater access to research participation. It rejected payments to parents beyond direct reimbursement (e.g. parking), but supported the provision of reasonable age-appropriate compensation for children based on time involved when the research does not offer the prospect of direct benefit.[23]

The IOM's conclusion is exceptional internationally. The National Council on Bioethics in Human Research (NCBHR) (Canada) published recommendations for research involving children in 1992 and revised its recommendations in 1993. These recommendations permit payment for out-of-pocket expenses. The NCBHR recommendations permitted 'token rewards' but suggested that '[the] reward not be mentioned prior to conclusion of the child's participation in the research and not be contingent on the child's completion of participation in the research'.[24]

The Working Group (UK) of the Institute of Medical Ethics specifically addressed payment in pediatric research in its 1986 document and concluded that 'appropriate expenses be paid'.[25] It then stated that 'it is important, however, that any payments should be only to cover expenses or loss of income and should not be large enough to act as an inducement to parents to enter their children into a research project.'[26] The Working Group argued that whether these same payments would be an inducement for an adult to participate is not relevant because the adult who consents is the same person as the adult who is exposed to the research risks. The Working Group argued that it would be unethical to offer the parents any substantial reward to induce them to authorize their children's participation and exposure to risks.[27] It is problematic both because of the separation between who consents and who is exposed to risk, and because parents are expected to act in their child's medical best interest. Nevertheless, the Working Group conceded that a small present to the children may be appropriate (e.g., a badge).[28]

The British Paediatric Society took a stronger stance in 1992 and stated that for consent to be voluntary, researchers must 'offer families no financial inducement although expenses should be paid'.[29] This was reaffirmed in 2000 by the renamed Royal College of Paediatrics and Child Health.[30] Directive 2001/20/EC of the European Parliament and of the Council of 4 April 2001 also concluded that 'in clinical trials on minors, no incentives or financial inducements should be given except costs'.[31]

Payment to children, then, is viewed with even greater suspicion than payment to adults. Most of the guidelines suggest that researchers should only reimburse expenses incurred by the child-subject and family. A 'token gesture of appreciation' such as a badge or sticker may also be given directly to the children, but nothing beyond that. The recent IOM report is the sole exception. If the IOM recommendations are adopted, then only in the US would children involved in nontherapeutic research be eligible for an incentive payment beyond a token gesture.

3.   *Motivation*

One objection to payment is that it would pervert subject motivation. Paul Ramsey argued that nontherapeutic research is ethical if and only if the subject is a co-adventurer with the researcher; that is, if the subject shares in, and is motivated by, the goals of the research.[32] If research subjects are not co-adventurers, then they are the mere objects of the researchers and are not being treated with the respect owed to all persons.[33] The concern is that payment could encourage the recruitment of individuals who are not invested in the research. While this is possible, it is also possible to support the goals of research while being paid for it. The researcher is in this position. For some subjects, particularly those for whom the time requirements may be burdensome, payment may allow them to share in the goals and values of medical research that they otherwise could not afford to do.

Because Ramsey held that research subjects must be co-adventurers for the research to be ethical, he rejected the participation of children in all nontherapeutic research. He rejected their participation because even if the child's parents supported the goals of research, most children would not be able to do so.[34] One could argue, however, that motivation does not need to be as pure as Ramsey suggests in order to be respectful of the subjects as persons. Rather, one could argue that the subject does not need to share in the researcher's goal (the partnership or co-adventurer model), but rather that respect for the subject only requires that one respect the subject's autonomy to decide what activities and risks he or she is willing to undertake. The subject can then take into consideration the opportunity costs of participating as a research subject as opposed to engaging in other activities. The research subjects then are being treated as means [for the researcher's goals], but also simultaneously as ends [autonomous agents who choose to participate for their own goals]. That is, the principle of respect for persons as applied to research subjects does not require that the subject be a co-adventurer, but only that the subject believes that the medical research is good (or at least useful), decides that the risks are acceptable in relationship to the benefits, and consents voluntarily. In pediatric research, consent is construed broadly to include parental permission and the child's assent.

If the parent and child do not need to be co-adventurers, what are morally justifiable motivations for parents to authorize their child's participation in nontherapeutic research? At minimum, the motives should be morally acceptable if provided by parents for the authorization of their child's participation in the myriad of other scholastic and extra-scholastic activities in which the child might participate. Parents have wide discretion in deciding what is in their child's interests and third-party intervention is limited to decisions that are abusive or neglectful. This is because parental motives are generally presumed to promote the child's best interest.[35] This presumption allows parents to authorize their child's participation in activities based on many different reasons, and to allow their child to be exposed to some risks in the pursuit of certain benefits, values, beliefs, or even for entertainment (e.g., skateboarding).

Consider, for example, parents who value participation in social projects, such as community service. These parents may try to inculcate similar values into their child, and require that their child spend one weekend day with them in a soup kitchen. Even if the child never shares in these values and goals, they are values which responsible parents may try to inculcate. The activity is not without risk; for example, the child may get burned ladling out the soup or the child may be emotionally upset meeting children his own age who are homeless.

What if these same parents decide to enroll their child into a minimal-risk nontherapeutic research project to help advance science. Again, the activity is not without risk. The child may develop a fear of hospitals and physicians or he may be upset by a survey question. Nevertheless, responsible parents can decide to encourage their child's participation in order to help others and advance science despite the risks of harm.

If some parents are willing to expose their children to some risks and harms to instill values, why should they not be allowed to enroll their child in order for their child to both serve science and earn money? In fact, the latter lesson may be more generalizable: to teach the child that one can be rewarded for doing the right thing.

What then is known about subject motivation? The empirical data show that healthy adult volunteers enroll in research for many different and often overlapping reasons.[36] Some volunteer for altruistic reasons; some for the privileges that may accrue; and some for the money. Empirical data also show that parents enroll their healthy children for many different and often overlapping reasons.[37] These reasons include: (1) the parents' own altruistic beliefs, (2) therapeutic misconception; (3) the parents feel obligated to help the researchers; (4) incentives such as more frequent medical care or free medications; and (5) compensation payments—even payments meant merely to compensate for out-of-pocket expenses.

Motives matter. We do not want parents to authorize their children's participation in research that fails to respect the child; i.e., that they authorize participation in research against their children's interests solely for the monetary inducements. But motives need not be as pure as the co-adventurer model requires.

4.   Consent

The principle of consent is a cornerstone of ethical medical research.[38] Consent is complicated in pediatric research because it (usually) requires both the assent of the subject and permission from one or both of her guardians. One concern regarding payment's impact on motivation is that it will distort the subject or guardian's voluntary and informed consent.

Ramsey, a leading critic of participation of children in nontherapeutic research, argued that parents, as their child's fiduciary, could not consent to the child's participation if the research posed any risks and did not offer the prospect of direct benefit.[39] Elsewhere, I have refuted the claim that parents must act as their child's fiduciary agent, because it holds parents to an inappropriate standard.[40] If parents were required to serve as a fiduciary for a child's health care, then the parent would be required to focus exclusively on the child's medical best interest and would not be allowed to consider the child's non-medical interests, nor the parent's own interests. But parents do, and should, consider the child's non-medical interests, their own needs and interests, and the needs and interests of other family members. Compromises need to be made within families, and they are permissible provided that the parents do not sacrifice the needs or interests of any particular family member. Parents morally can authorize their child to serve as a research subject to serve non-medical goals such as teaching the child that it is good to help others.[41]

This is not to suggest that parents can authorize their child's participation in any research. Parents cannot authorize their child's participation if such participation would be abusive or neglectful. The state, in its role as parens patriae, has an obligation to protect its children-citizens, and it does this by restricting the amount of risk to which children subjects can be exposed.

Current regulations in the US require nontherapeutic research involving healthy children to entail at most minimal risk(CFR §46.404). If the children are patients, i.e., they have a disease or condition related to the research, then the child can participate in nontherapeutic research in which the risks entail a minor increase over minimal risk (CFR §46.406).[42] The only pediatric research, then, that should be approved by an institutional review board [IRB] is research in which the risks are within the moral limits defined by the regulations. This is not to deny that a research project that is IRB-approved may be more harmful than expected due to unanticipated or unknown risks, or that a research project may be more harmful than expected to a particular child because of idiosyncratic factors such as an exaggerated fear of nail clipping. The requirement for parental permission and the child's assent can help in this regard.

For Ramsey, consent serves as an affirmation that the subject shares in the researcher's goals (i.e., that the subject is a partner or co-adventurer). Again, I believe this is too demanding. Rather, I believe that consent is valid if it voluntarily affirms the subject's authority to decide what activities and risks he or she is willing to undertake. In pediatric research, as discussed in Chapter 5, consent includes both parental permission and the child's assent. Parental permission serves two important goals. The primary reason for seeking parental authorization is to protect the child. Parents are presumed to have greatest interest in the health and well-being of their child, and they will be responsible if the child is harmed. Parents may also authorize their child's participation in research because they want to inculcate particular values into their child. Their permission implies that they believe that the child's participation is an appropriate undertaking, from both the perspective of risks and of benefits. The child's assent affirms his willingness to participate and that he does not perceive his participation as contrary to his interests.

If parents can authorize the participation of their children in at least some medical research, then the question remains whether payment will distort their decision-making or invalidate their authorization. The concern is that payment will induce them to ignore their obligations to protect their child, and expose their child to activities and risks that they would not otherwise accept. This is compounded by a concern that payment will be a greater inducement for those of lower socioeconomic status [SES].[43]

It is worth noting that there is an inherent assumption that money negatively influences decision-making. It is possible that parents and children motivated by money give a more voluntary and informed consent than the co-adventurer because they are not blinded by the lofty research goals that the co-adventurer embraces, goals that are often unrealized. This is particularly true if the subjects are also patients, because patient-subjects or their parents often believe that the research must offer the prospect of direct benefit, even when it is not designed to do so.[44] In addition, if one accepts the premise that parents know what is best for their child and for themselves, a financial incentive to enroll their child as a research subject may be the impetus to encourage or enable them to do the right thing. The offer of money does not necessarily invalidate the parent's permission or the child's assent. The offer only becomes morally objectionable if it encourages the parent and/or the child an incentive to take a risk that either one would not otherwise accept.

5.   *Recruitment and Selection of Subjects*

A second concern regarding payment's impact on motivation is that it will lead to unfair subject recruitment and selection. The National Commission expressed concern that payment could have 'undue influence' on an individual's decision whether or not to participate, particularly in a vulnerable population such as children. In an article on the various vulnerabilities of pediatric research subjects, Ken Kipnis points out that children may be particularly vulnerable to research payments because they often lack disposable funds and the opportunities to be of significant service to others that earn them tangible rewards.[45] Kipnis refers to this as allocational vulnerability, one of numerous vulnerabilities that may adversely affect the protection of human subjects in pediatric research. Nevertheless, Kipnis does not reject payment to children; rather, he recommends that compensation policies sensitively address the underlying vulnerabilities.[46]

The current position of many pediatricians and pediatric ethicists in favor of increased participation of children in research[47] would harmonize with a policy that permits payment to pediatric subjects because payment is expected to increase participation. But there remains a moral discomfort or moral intuition that offering payment is exploitative.[48]

One particular concern is that payment is exploitative because it will lead to the over-recruitment of pediatric research subjects from families of low SES and minority ethnicity. As discussed in Chapter 2, our data demonstrated that minority children are already overrepresented in research. Of note, however, is that we found that this overrepresentation occurred in both therapeutic and nontherapeutic research. Black children were serving as 'guinea pigs' but they also had greatest access to clinical trials. In fact, the overrepresentation of Black children in clinical trials was statistically greater than their overrepresentation in pediatric research generally (32% versus 26%, $p<.05$).

The current empirical data regarding allocational vulnerability are more ambiguous than one might predict. While some studies have found overrepresentation of pediatric research subjects from lower SES;[49] other studies have found overrepresentation of pediatric research subjects from higher SES,[50] and still others have found no correlation.[51] The mixed motives provided by parents and children to explain why they agree to participate in research suggest that subject selection in current research is not overly distorted by SES. Our data were inadequate to show whether or not there was a correlation between sociodemographic factors and participation in research.[52]

This is not to deny that large payments could have perverse influence in that they could encourage individuals to take risks they otherwise would not accept. In pediatrics, large payments could encourage parents to expose their children to activities that they would otherwise not authorize or encourage children to take risks they would otherwise avoid, but whether financial remuneration will have a differential impact requires close scrutiny. Whether the sociodemographic or ethnic representation of children will change based on financial incentives is unknown. The potential for financial remuneration to have a differential effect merits close scrutiny.

Another concern in subject selection is that payment will lead some subjects and their parents to provide inaccurate personal information to ensure that they meet subject eligibility criteria.[53] Inaccurate screening information may increase the risk of harm to the subject or threaten the scientific validity of the data. At minimum, the potential for increased risk of harm to ineligible subjects should be explained clearly in the consent process. The threat to the data validity means that researchers may need to impose stricter screening protocols which may make recruitment both more difficult and more expensive, obviating the benefit of subject payment to the accrual process. The possibility that ineligible subjects might enroll and be exposed to an increased risk of harm could also change the IRB's assessment of the risk/benefit ratio of the research which in turn could make the research proposal impermissible under current federal guidelines. Payment in research will place greater onus on the research community to identify and assess the degree and amount of risks that a research project poses if false information regarding eligibility is provided, whether intentionally or not.

While the possibility that payment will adversely effect the validity of subject eligibility is serious, there is no evidence demonstrating whether or how often it occurs in pediatric research. The concern merits further scrutiny. It also suggests that additional precautions and procedures should be established to confirm eligibility for research protocols in which inaccurate information could place subjects at greater risk, but it does not yet justify an absolute prohibition on payment.

A third concern is that payment may lead to professional research subjects.[54] There are some reasons, however, to believe that this is unlikely to occur in children. First, the National Commission recommended that vulnerable populations, like children, should only be selected as research subjects after adequate research is done on animals and adults.[55] Although this requirement is not stipulated in the federal regulations, it traditionally applies in practice. The result is that there are fewer opportunities for children to serve repeatedly in research. Second, there are additional protections for research enrolling children that makes it less desirable and more cumbersome to enroll children.

6. *Paying Subjects*

If payment does not distort motivation, subject selection, or the voluntariness of consent, then it is morally appropriate to discuss what is a fair price for research participation. Two recent papers by research ethicists from the Department of Clinical Bioethics of the National Institutes of Health [NIH] addressed paying adult[56] and child research subjects[57] respectively. I will consider each in turn.

In 1999, Dickert and Grady examined three different models of payment for the adult-subject: the free-market model, wage payment model, and reimbursement model.[58] The free-market model[59] allows supply and demand to determine the price for participating in a given study at a given site. It permits investigators to increase pay to complete studies quickly. The danger of such a model is that it may lead to 'undue inducements' encouraging subjects who would otherwise be unwilling. In fact, some subjects may be so eager to participate that they will provide unreliable medical histories to avoid being excluded, placing the subject at greater risk (including death) and making the findings less reliable.[60]

At the other extreme is the reimbursement model[61] in which payment is only provided to cover subjects' expenses. It is based on the view that subjects should not have to make financial sacrifices to participate. To achieve complete revenue neutrality, however, might mean the need to reimburse subjects for their time away from work making this model inegalitarian as physicians would be reimbursed at a higher amount than their secretaries for the same activity. In general, reimbursement is understood only to cover expenditures such as travel, meals, and parking and not to cover non-financial expenses such as effort or discomfort. The expense reimbursement model does not preferentially induce vulnerable populations to participate; in fact, it may make them less likely to participate (e.g., if they cannot afford to take time off from work). The problem is that it may not yield sufficient incentive to get an adequate number of subjects.

The wage-payment model[62] involves paying subjects on a scale commensurate with that of other unskilled jobs. It differs from the market model in that the payment is standardized according to the unskilled labor market rather than the supply of eligible persons; it differs from the reimbursement model in that the payment may make studies attractive to people with low income potentials without being an undue inducement as most subjects will have other options for earning an unskilled labor wage. Dickert and Grady support this model because it adheres to a basic assumption of the principle of justice: that similar people should be treated similarly.[63]

Other payment models exist. For example, Saunders and Sugar propose a fair share model in which study participants are partners in the research process and are paid a percentage of the per patient compensation to the investigator or institution.[64] Dickert and Grady reject this proposal on grounds similar to the market model.[65] The concern again is that the amount of money may be an undue influence. McGee suggested a proportional reward model in which payment is proportional to time and inconvenience.[66] The problem is that it leads to differential pricing depending on one's salary or hourly wage outside of the research context. Menikoff, on the other hand, suggested a proportional reward model based on risk.[67] The danger with this model is its potential for undue inducement; that is, that subjects may accept risks they otherwise would not.

The debate in the adult literature stands in stark contrast with the pediatric literature on paying subjects. Although paying for children's participation in medical research has become relatively common in the US,[68] the justifications and rationales differ dramatically from those offered for adults. In 2001, Grady with Wendler and other NIH colleagues examined the issue of paying children-subjects.[69] In contrast with the earlier paper, this paper did not focus on how research subjects should be remunerated; that is, whether the appropriate payment scheme is the market, the wage-earner, or the remuneration model. Rather, this paper focused on the different types of research-related payments and whether they distort the decision-making process.

Wendler *et al.* describe four types of research-related payments: (1) reimbursement (for direct research-related expenses); (2) compensation (for time and inconvenience); (3) appreciation (bonuses given after participation to say thanks); and (4) incentive payments (to encourage the child's enrollment).[70] They unconditionally approve of the first two types of payments but are reluctant to permit the latter two. I will show, however, that these distinctions are less clear-cut than the authors believe.

Wendler *et al.* argue in favor of reimbursement payments because they do not distort decision-making since they are 'revenue neutral'.[71] They support this form of payment as it minimizes the costs of participation of the families. In some ways, this form of payment is most important to those of low socio-economic status who otherwise may not be able to afford to participate in research. As such, reimbursement payments ensure equitable access to all. These payments do not distort decision-making because they merely negate the inability of some to participate but do not give financial incentive to participate.

Wendler *et al.* also support compensation payments which they describe as remuneration for time and inconvenience. This form of payment acknowledges that there is an opportunity cost to research participation and that payment could 'zero out' the level of burden that families experience for a given amount of time and inconvenience.[72] Wendler *et al.* distinguish these payments from incentive payments which are payments given to encourage the child's enrollment. However, as they acknowledge, it is difficult to determine the point at which compensation payments zero out the level of burden. This means that compensation payments will sometimes 'inadvertently exceed families actual burden, providing an incentive for them to enroll in research'.[73] They also acknowledge that 'the potential for compensation payments to act as inadvertent incentives is increased by the fact that a protocol's level of burden will vary from family to family.'[74]

To minimize the potential of compensation payments serving as incentive payments, the authors suggest that compensation payments should be directed to the person who bears the burdens (usually the child). When parents contribute their own time, their compensation should be calibrated to the economic resources of the least well-off families. They suggest that parental time be compensated by minimum-wage levels.[75]

Wendler *et al.* support reimbursement and compensation payments for all research to minimize the costs and burdens of research participation on the families, and they recommend that institutions specify standards for reimbursement and compensation.[76] They are more reluctant to support appreciation and incentive payments because they fear these payments may distort decision-making. They recommend banning post-facto appreciation payments on the grounds that they may offer undue inducements because participants will become aware of them before participation.[77] They also argue that incentive payments can directly distort decision-making, and highlight the vulnerability of those families who may enroll for the money. As such, they recommend that IRBs should approve incentives in limited cases only,[78] and that payments should be kept small in order to negate, or at least to minimize, the distortion. Given these concerns, why do they tolerate incentive payments? The argument appears to be pragmatic: there is a need to ensure adequate enrollment.[79]

Wendler *et al.* need to reconsider their support of compensation payments given their attitude about incentive payments. Compensating parents for their time at the minimum-wage level acknowledges that parents can choose among many activities for their children, and compensation payments offset the opportunity costs of research participation. But compensation also functions as a monetary incentive, particularly for parents of lower socio-economic status with limited work opportunities. Parents are rarely compensated for the activities in which they enroll their children. To the contrary, such participation often requires a participation fee and the parent's presence means that the parent is forgoing work opportunities. Dickert and Grady's argument that adult-subjects should be paid minimum wage because it is fair to pay people for work that is valuable to society holds when the adults are the subjects of the research.[80] To pay parents so that their children can perform work that is valuable to society is not compensation, but a monetary incentive for the parents. As such, the distinction between compensation payments and incentive payments is unclear: paying individuals for their time may serve as an incentive, whether wittingly or unwittingly.

7.   Is the Distinction between Paying Adult-Subjects versus Children-Subjects Morally Legitimate?

The two NIH papers on paying research subjects highlight contradictory attitudes about payment depending on the age of the subjects. Wendler et al. argue that payment beyond cost should be the exception rather than the norm in pediatric research, whereas Dickert and Grady support wage payments for all adult research participants. The difference reflects conflicting attitudes about the meaning of research participation for adults and children. Dickert and Grady argue in favor of wage payment for adults mainly for pragmatic reasons; i.e., to ensure adequate and rapid enrollment. They also offer a moral argument: payment is fair because it allows 'people to be paid for work that is valuable to society.'[81] In the latter article, by contrast, the reasons offered to remunerate children are purely pragmatic: 'Although banning all incentive payments beyond reimbursement and compensation is ethically defensible, doing so runs the risk of impeding socially valuable pediatric research. To avoid this cost, small incentive payments may be acceptable when needed to ensure sufficient enrollment in important research.'[82]

It is noteworthy that the authors did not argue, on moral grounds, that children could be compensated for performing work useful to society. But they could have. Consider extrapolating Dickert and Grady's argument that the ethical model for paying research subjects is the wage-earner model, and apply this model to children research subjects. Such a model has some tradition in that children have been in the workforce for hundreds of years. Current child labor laws allow children aged 16 and 17 years to perform any non-hazardous job, and allow children 14 and 15 years old to work outside school hours in various non-manufacturing, non-mining, non-hazardous jobs. Fourteen is the minimum age for most non-agricultural work.

However, children of any age may deliver newspapers, perform in radio, television, movie, or theatrical productions, work in businesses owned by their parents (except in mining, manufacturing, or hazardous jobs), perform babysitting or perform minor chores around a private home. Also, children at any age may be employed as homeworkers to gather evergreens and make evergreen wreaths.[83]

If research participation is viewed as just another means of earning money, adolescents at least age 14 years old, like adults, can choose to participate in research or can seek other ways to earn money. In fact, most adolescents have worked before they graduate from high school.[84] Although the Fair Labor Standards Act restricts the jobs that adolescents may hold based on risk, more than 70 teenage workers are estimated to die from work-related injuries each year,[85] and over 64,000 teens receive care in an emergency department each year from work-related injuries.[86] This number is believed to undercount significantly actual injuries.[87] Participating in minimal risk nontherapeutic research would seem to be relatively safe, given current federal regulations regarding the amount of risk a child can be exposed to in such research.[88]

One way to determine how much to pay adolescents to serve as research subjects is to ask how to compensate them for the opportunity costs of not working. In this vein, paying minimum wage makes research participation an economically viable alternative, and it involves less risk and a greater service to society. However, adolescents who view participation as just a means to earn money will probably choose alternative opportunities because research opportunities are erratic. Those who do participate, then, will probably do so out of mixed motives including an interest in advancing science or helping others. Unlike Ramsey, I have argued that this can be morally acceptable.

Although children younger than 14 years can also work to earn money, their opportunities are much more restricted.[89] This raises the concern that they may be unduly influenced by the promise of minimum-wage payments for research participation because they have relatively few opportunities to earn money otherwise. One solution, then, is to restrict the types of research in which they are allowed to participate, how much money they can earn, and what form their payment can take. For example, procedures that are considered minimal risk in older adolescents may be judged as more than minimal risk in younger children, making them ineligible to participate according to current regulations. In addition, younger children can be restricted to a specific number of research projects over a specific time-span, and payments can be restricted to educational gift certificates or savings bonds that do not mature until the children are adults. These restrictions may make the payments less attractive, but given societal unease regarding payment and employment for this age group, this is also morally acceptable.

Some readers may be offended by my arguments. While they concede the need to do nontherapeutic research on children, and they may even concede the need to pay children to get adequate enrollment, they may object to the conceptualization of the child's research participation using an economic analysis of opportunity costs. Grant and Sugarman claim that using an economic paradigm obscures the ethical issues.[90] They argue that incentives must be understood in the context of power, that they are 'one of the various ways in which people can get other people to do what they want them to do'.[91] They do not argue against all incentives, only incentives that become problematic because they are conjoined with one or more factors such as subject dependency, high risk, or where the incentive is being used to overcome a principled objection to participate.[92]

I do not disagree. Throughout this chapter I have argued that we do not want payment in research to encourage an individual to do something he would not otherwise do. Nevertheless, even if a subject were to choose to participate in research for altruistic reasons, it is rational to at least consider the opportunities foregone. Donating oneself and one's time to medical research precludes one from other opportunities: whether other opportunities to act charitably; to earn money, or to indulge in leisure activities.

Let me add four clarifications. First, none of this is meant to imply that children-subjects must be paid, although the data show that a significant number of pediatric research subjects are being paid.[93] Ideally research subjects would share the goals of the researchers and would be motivated by the desire to see the research succeed (Ramsey's co-adventurer). But even if they are motivated by idealism, payment does not necessarily taint their motivation or distort their consent. In many cases, then, payment of pediatric research subjects can be morally permissible.

Second, it is important to remember that the debate regarding paying children-subjects takes place in a system in which the degree of risk to which a child-subject can be exposed is constrained by federal regulations, and IRBs are entrusted to ensure that these limits are obeyed. Whether payment to children in a more open research market [94] could be justified raises additional issues regarding the proper moral limits of surrogate decision-making, the potential for 'undue influence' of those of lower economic standing, and the meaning of altruism when the participant is a child with developing capacities for moral reasoning and decision-making. The reader should not extrapolate from these arguments.

Third, I do not mean to imply that medical researchers should encourage or even permit children to participate in numerous studies and thereby become professional research subjects.[95] All I have argued is that if one believes it is moral for children to participate in research that offers them no prospect of direct benefit, then the moral arguments precluding payment for this service are not compelling. The wage-earner model could be modified to provide fair compensation for children-subjects. It can be modified both in the amount of money (a minimum wage for a child-subject can be less than that for an adult-subject); and in the form the payment is made (one may decide to restrict the form to saving bonds that do not mature for years; or gift certificates).

Fourth, parents should NOT be offered any payment beyond their direct costs (e.g., bus fare, parking). Any additional payment (e.g. compensation for time) should not be offered unless the parents are subjects too (e.g., asked to fill out a survey), and then payment should be provided as appropriate for their participation. By directing the money to the child, parental temptation is reduced, permitting parents to focus on their primary duty to protect their child. One may object because payment to the child could be transferred within the family unit; e.g., if parents are aware that their daughter earned $X, they may reduce her allowance or require her to pay for necessary school supplies. Clearly we cannot and do not want to monitor how families negotiate their finances. However, one would imagine that if a child is forced to transfer her payment to her parents that her willingness to participate in future research would decrease, particularly if the research involves painful or potentially embarrassing procedures. The federal guidelines that require limits on pediatric research risks protect the child to a large degree. The assent requirement provides children with some bargaining power against their parents.

8. *Healthy Subjects versus Patient Subjects*

The issues of whether and how much to pay human subjects is less commonly discussed in the context of patients as research subjects,[96] although there are some data that show that payment is occurring.[97] The distinction between patient-subjects and healthy volunteer-subjects is not meaningful in the nontherapeutic research context. One could even argue that patient-subjects are more vulnerable in the nontherapeutic research context because (1) of the therapeutic misconception,[98] (2) the subjects and parents may feel some degree of obligation to the clinician-researcher; and (3) the researchers may place pressure to participate on subjects and their parents, even if unwittingly.

Dickert and Grady argue that adult patient subjects, like their healthy adult counterparts, should be allowed to receive remuneration according to a minimum wage-earner model.[99] I propose that pediatric patient-subjects should also be eligible for payment for nontherapeutic research. I offer two reasons. First, justice requires that equals be treated equally. If the research offers no prospect of direct therapeutic benefit, then patient-subjects and healthy subjects are equals. Second, payment to children-patients for their participation in nontherapeutic research may help parents to distinguish between therapeutic and nontherapeutic research objectives. When possible, recruitment should be done by a researcher other than the clinician to further distinguish the research activity from clinical care. Again, the minimum wage-earner model and child labor laws can be useful guidance in devising non-coercive pay scales.

9. *Conclusion*

There is general suspicion about paying research subjects, particularly children-subjects, in US and international policies and guidelines, the recent IOM report being an exception. I support the position of the IOM. I have rejected the main moral objection that payment perverts motivation such as to undermine consent and fair subject selection. Rather, I have argued for a lower motivation standard that only requires that the payment does not undermine an individual's authority to decide in what activities and risks he or she is willing to participate. It is morally permissible to pay children research subjects, although the amount and form of payment may need to be modified in comparison to adult research subjects.

Greater public discourse and transparency are needed with regard to institutional, sponsor, and researcher policies and practices regarding the payment of children and parents in pediatric research. Clearer guidelines need to be developed and disseminated in order to ensure that particular research communities do not seek unduly to influence the recruitment or consent of vulnerable subjects. The recommendations in this chapter could serve as a starting point.

References

1. Giuffrida, A., and Torgeerson, D. J., 'Should We Pay the Patient? Review of Financial Incentives to Enhance Patient Compliance', *BMJ,* 315 (1997), 703–7.
2. See, e.g., Hermann, R., Heger-Mahn, D., Mahler, M., Seibert-Grafe, M., Klipping, C., Breithaupt-Grogler, K., and de Mey, C., 'Adverse Events and Discomfort in Studies on Healthy Subjects: The Volunteer's Perspective. A Survey Conducted by the German Association for Applied Human Pharmacology', *European Journal of Clinical Pharmacology,* 53 (1997), 207–21; Apseloff, G., Swayne, J. K., and Gerber, N., 'Medical Histories May Be Unreliable in Screening Volunteers for Clinical Trials', *Clinical Pharmacology and Therapeutics,* 60 (1996), 353–6; and Risch, S. C., Levine, R. J., Jeward, R. D., Eccard, M. B.,

McDaniel, J. S., and Risby, E. D., 'Ensuring the Normalcy of "Normal" Volunteers', *American Journal of Psychiatry*, 147 (1990), 682–3.

3. National Commission for the Protection of Human Subjects of Biomedical and Behavioral Research, *The Belmont Report: Ethical Principles and Guidelines for the Protection of Human Subjects of Research*. Washington DC: US Government Printing Office, 1978, DHEW Publication No. (OS) 78–12. On the web at: http://ohsr.od.nih.gov/guidelines/belmont.html; hereinafter cited as *Belmont Report*.

4. Ibid.

5. Ibid.

6. Department of Health and Human Services (DHHS). (45 CFR 46 Subpart A), 'Final Regulations Amending Basic HHS Policy for the Protection of Human Research Subjects', *Federal Register*, 46 (26 January 1981), 8366–91; revised *Federal Register*, 56 (18 June 1991), 28003–18 at CFR §46.103; hereinafter known as the Common Rule, cited by CFR number in the text.

7. Macklin, R., ' "Due" and "Undue" Inducements: On Paying Money to Research Subjects', *IRB: A Review of Human Subjects Research*, 3 (May 1981), 1–6, 1.

8. Medical Research Council of Canada, Natural Science and Engineering Research Council of Canada, and the Social Science and Humanities Research Council of Canada, *Tri-Council Policy Statement. Ethical Conduct for Research Involving Humans*. August 1998 with 2000 and 2002 updates. On the web http://www.pre.ethics.gc.ca/english/pdf/TCPS%20June2003_E.pdf, 2.7 [Table 1, item 7].

9. Ibid., 2.8.

10. Royal College of Physicians, 'Research on Healthy Volunteers: A Report of the Royal College of Physicians', *Journal of the Royal College of Physicians of London*, 20 (1986), 243–57.

11. Royal College of Physicians, 'Research Involving Patients: Summary and Recommendations of a Report of the Royal College of Physicians', *Journal of the Royal College of Physicians of London*, 24 (1990), 10–14

12. Royal College of Physicians, 'Healthy Volunteers', 248.

13. Royal College of Physicians, 'Research Involving Patients', 13. Of note, the concern that research may be lengthy and tedious was also a justification for payment of healthy volunteers. See Royal College of Physicians, 'Healthy Volunteers', 248.

14. Royal College of Physicians, 'Research Involving Patients', 13.

15. National Commission for the Protection of Human Subjects, *Report and Recommendations: Research Involving Children*. Washington DC: US Government Printing Office, 1977, DHEW Publication NO. (OS) 77–0004; hereinafter cited as National Commission, *Research Involving Children*.

16. Department of Health and Human Services (DHHS). (45 CFR Part 46, Subpart D), 'Protections for Children Involved as Subjects in Research', *Federal Register*, 48 (8 March 1983), 9814–20; revised *Federal Register*, 56 (18 June 1991), 28032; hereinafter cited by its CFR number in the text.

17. American Academy of Pediatrics (AAP) Committee on Drugs, 'Guidelines for the Ethical Conduct of Studies to Evaluate Drugs in Pediatric Populations', *Pediatrics*, 60 (1977), 91–101, 96.

18. Ibid.

19. American Academy of Pediatrics (AAP] Committee on Drugs, 'Guidelines for the Ethical Conduct of Studies to Evaluate Drugs in Pediatric Populations', *Pediatrics*, 95 (1995), 286–94, 293.

20. Field, M. J., and Behrman, R. E. (eds.), Committee on Clinical Research Involving Children, the Institute of Medicine (IOM), *The Ethical Conduct of Clinical Research Involving Children*. Washington DC: National Academies Press, 2004, 225; hereinafter this reference is cited as the IOM, *Ethical Conduct*.

21. Ibid.

22. Ibid., 226.

23. Ibid., 226.

24. National Council on Bioethics in Human Research (NCBHR)/Conseil national de la bioethique en recherché chez les sujets humains (CNBRH), 'Revised Recommendations of the NCBHR Report on Research Involving Children', *NCBHR/CNBRH Communique* 4 (1993), 8–11,10 [point 13 b].

25. Nicholson, R. H. (ed.), *Medical Research with Children: Ethics, Law and Practice*. Oxford: Oxford University Press, 1986, 204.

26. Ibid.

27. Ibid.

28. Ibid., 204–5.

29. British Paediatric Association, Ethics Advisory Committee, *Guidelines for the Ethical Conduct of Medical Research Involving Children*. London: British Paediatric Association, 1992, 13.

30. Royal College of Paediatrics and Child Health, Ethics Advisory Committee, 'Guidelines for the Ethical Conduct of Medical Research Involving Children', *Archives of Disease in Childhood*, 82 (2000), 177–82, 180.

31. The European Parliament and the Council of the European Union, 'Directive 2001/20/EC of the European Parliament and of the Council of 4 April 2001 on the Approximation of the Laws, Regulations and Administrative Provisions of the Member States Relating to the Implementation of Good Clinical Practice in the Conduct of Clinical Trials on Medicinal Products for Human Use', *Official Journal of the European Communities 1.5.2001 L 121/34*. Found on the web at: http://europa.eu.int/eur-lex/pri/en/oj/dat/2001/l_121/l_12120010501en00340044. pdf, 20 [Article 4D].

32. Ramsey, P., *The Patient as Person*. New Haven CT: Yale University Press, 1970, 5–7.

33. Ibid., 6–7, esp. endnote 5 where Ramsey quotes Immanuel Kant. Ramsey's notion of respect is based on Kant's work. See Kant, I., *Grounding for the Metaphysics of Morals* (1785) translated by J. W. Ellington. Indianapolis, IN: Hackett Publishing Co., 1981, para. 429.

34. Ramsey, *Patient as Person*, 6–7.

35. See, e.g., Buchanan, A. E., Brock, D. W., *Deciding for Others: The Ethics of Surrogate Decision Making*. New York: Cambridge University Press, 1989, 232–4. There are problems with the concept that parents should be held to a best interest standard; and some have argued that parents should only be held to a 'good enough' standard or a 'least detrimental alternative' standard. For an

argument supporting a 'good enough' standard, see, Ross, L. F., *Children, Families and Health Care Decision-Making*. Oxford: Clarendon Press, 1998, 42–4. For an argument supporting a 'least detrimental alternative' standard, see Goldstein, J., Freud, A., and Solnit, A., *Before the Best Interests of the Child*. New York, Free Press, 1979, 24–5.

36. See Hermann *et al.*, 'Adverse Events'; Novak, E., Seckman, C. E., and Stewart, R. D., 'Motivations for Volunteering as Research Subjects', *Journal of Clinical Pharmacology & New Drugs* 17 (1977), 365–71; Lemmens, T., and Elliott, C., 'Guinea Pigs on the Payroll: The Ethics of Paying Research Subjects', *Accountability in Research*, 7 (1999), 3–20; Bigorra, J., and Banos, J. E., 'Weight of Financial Reward in the Decision by Medical Students and Experienced Healthy Volunteers to Participate in Clinical Trials', *European Journal of Clinical Pharmacology*, 38 (1990), 443–6; Tishler, C. L., and Bartholomae, S., 'The Recruitment of Normal Healthy Volunteers: A Review of the Literature on the Use of Financial Incentives', *Journal of Clinical Pharmacology*, 42 (2002), 363–73; and Ayd, F. J. Jr., 'Motivations and Rewards for Volunteering to be an Experimental Subject', *Clinical Pharmacology and Therapeutics*, 13 (1972), 771–8.

37. See, e.g., Hayman, R. M., Taylor, B. J., Peart, N. S., Galland, B. C., and Sayers, R. M., 'Participation in Research: Informed Consent, Motivation and Influence', *Journal of Paediatrics & Child Health*, 37 (2001), 51–4; Autret, E., Dutertre, J. P., Barbier, P., Jonville, A. P., Pierre, F., and Berger, C., 'Parental Opinions about Biomedical Research in Children in Tours, France', *Developmental Pharmacology and Therapeutics*, 20 (1993), 64–71; van Stuijvenberg, M., Suur, M. H., de Vos, S., Tjiang, G. C., Steyerberg, E. W., Derksen-Lubsen, G., and Moll, H. A., 'Informed Consent, Parental Awareness, and Reasons for Participating in a Randomized Controlled Study', *Archives of Diseases in Childhood*, 79 (1998), 120–5; and McCarthy, A. M., Richman, L. C., Hoffman, R. P., and Rubenstein, L., 'Psychological Screening of Children for Participation in Nontherapeutic Invasive Research', *Archives of Pediatrics and Adolescent Medicine*, 155 (2001), 1197–203.

38. See *Belmont Report*; and Ramsey, *Patient as Person*, 2.

39. Ramsey, *Patient as Person*, 11–19.

40. Ross, *Children*, 77–80 & 90–5.

41. Ibid.

42. As I argued in Ch. 4, 'Should We Provide Healthy Children with Greater Protection in Medical Research?', I do not believe that there should be a double-standard. I proposed that all children should be allowed to participate in research 'in which the probability of physical and psychological harm is no more than that to which it is appropriate to intentionally expose a child for educational purposes in family life situations'. Ackerman, T., 'Moral Duties of Parents and Non-Therapeutic Research Procedures Involving Children', *Bioethics Quarterly*, 2 (1980), 94–111 as cited in S. L. Leiken, 'An Ethical Issue in Biomedical Research: The Involvement of Minors in Informed and Third Party Consent', *Clinical Research*, 31 (1983), 34–40, 38.

43. Silverman, W. A., 'The Myth of Informed Consent in Daily Practice and in Clinical Trials', *Journal of Medical Ethics,* 15 (1989), 6–11; and Thong, Y. H., and Harth, S. C., 'The Social Filter Effect of Informed Consent in Clinical Research', *Pediatrics,* 87 (1991), 568–9.
44. Appelbaum, P. S., Rother, L. H., Lidz, C. W., Benson, P., and Winslade, W., 'False Hopes and Best Data: Consent to Research and the Therapeutic Misconception', *Hastings Center Report,* 17 (April 1987), 20–4; and Horng, S., and Grady, C., 'Misunderstanding in Clinical Research: Distinguishing Therapeutic Misconception, Therapeutic Misestimation, and Therapeutic Optimism', *IRB: a Review of Human Subjects Research,* 25 (January/February 2003), 11–16.
45. Kipnis, K., 'Seven Vulnerabilities in the Pediatric Research Subject', *Theoretical Medicine and Biology,* 24 (2003), 107–20, 117–19.
46. Ibid., 118.
47. IOM, *Ethical Conduct;* Steinbrook, R., 'Testing Medications in Children', *New England Journal of Medicine,* 347 (2002), 1462–70; Gleason, C. on behalf of the Society for Pediatric Research/American Pediatric Society and endorsed by the Ambulatory Pediatric Association, 'Statement before the Institute of Medicine Committee on Clinical Research Involving Children Participation and Protection of Children in Clinical Research', 9 July 2003. On the web at: http://www.aps-spr.org/Public_Policy/2003_Docs/IOM0709.htm; and American Academy of Pediatrics, Press Release, 'Pediatricians Celebrate Passage of Pediatric Rule Legislation: Medicines Prescribed to Children Will Be Tested', 19 November 2003. On the web at: http://www.aap.org/advocacy/washing/ped_rule_passes.htm.
48. Nicholson, *Medical Research with Children; Belmont Report;* British Paediatric Association, *Guidelines;* Tishler, C. L., and Bartholomae, S., 'Repeat Participation among Normal Healthy Research Volunteers: Professional Guinea Pigs in Clinical Trials?' *Perspectives in Biology and Medicine,* 46 (2003), 508–20; and Fernhoff, P. M., 'Paying for Children to Participate in Research: A Slippery Slope or an Enlightened Stairway?' *Journal of Pediatrics,* 141 (2002), 153–4.
49. Harth, S. C., Johnstone, R. R., and Thong, Y. H., 'The Psychological Profile of Parents Who Volunteer Their Children for Clinical Research: A Controlled Study', *Journal of Medical Ethics,* 18 (1992), 86–93; and Harth, S. C., and Thong, Y. H., 'Parental Perceptions and Attitudes About Informed Consent in Clinical Research Involving Children', *Social Science & Medicine,* 41 (1995), 1647–651.
50. See, e.g., Hayman *et al.,* 'Participation'; Autret *et al.,* 'Parental Opinions'.
51. Bassett, M., Dunn, C., Battese, K., and Peek, M., 'Acceptance of Neonatal Genetic Screening for Hereditary Hemochromatosis by Informed Parents', *Genetic Testing,* 5 (2001), 317–20; van Stuijvenberg *et al.,* 'Informed Consent'.
52. Kelly, M. L., Ackerman, P. D., and Ross, L. F., 'The Participation of Minorities in Pediatric Research'. In review, 2005, See also Ch. 2, 'Access versus Protection: Minority Representation in Pediatric Research'.
53. See, e.g., Hermann *et al.,* 'Adverse Events'; Apseloff *et al.,* 'Medical Histories'; and Risch *et al.,* 'Ensuring the Normalcy'.

54. See Lemmens and Elliott, 'Guinea Pigs'; and Tishler and Bartholomae, 'Repeat'.
55. *Belmont Report,* 2 & 3.
56. Dickert, N., and Grady, C., 'What's the Price of a Research Subject? Approaches to Payment for Research Participation', *New England Journal of Medicine,* 341 (1999), 198–203.
57. Wendler, D., Rackoff, J. E., Emanuel, E. J., and Grady, C., 'The Ethics of Paying for Children's Participation in Research', *Journal of Pediatrics,* 141 (2002), 166–71.
58. Dickert, and Grady, 'What's the Price'.
59. Ibid., 199, 200–1.
60. Ibid., 200–1; see also Hermann *et al.,* 'Adverse Events'; Apseloff *et al.,* 'Medical Histories'.
61. Dickert and Grady, 'What's the Price', 200, 201.
62. Ibid., 199–200, 201.
63. Ibid., 201.
64. Saunders, C. A., and Sugar, A. M., 'What's the Price of a Research Subject? Letter to Editor', *New England Journal of Medicine,* 341 (1999), 1550–1.
65. Dickert, N., and Grady, C., 'What's the Price of a Research Subject? In reply', *New England Journal of Medicine,* 341 (1999), 1552.
66. McGee, G., 'Subject to Payment?' *JAMA,* 278 (1997), 199–200.
67. Menikoff, J., 'Just Compensation: Paying Research Subjects Relative to the Risks They Bear', *American Journal of Bioethics,* 1 (2001), 56–8.
68. Weise, K. L., Smith, M. L., Maschke, K. J., and Copeland, H. L., 'National Practices Regarding Payment to Research Subjects for Participating in Pediatric Research', *Pediatrics,* 110 (2002), 577–82.
69. Wendler *et al.,* 'Ethics of Paying'.
70. Ibid., 167.
71. Ibid., 167.
72. Ibid., 167.
73. Ibid., 167.
74. Ibid., 167.
75. Ibid., 167.
76. Ibid., 169.
77. Ibid., 169.
78. Ibid., 169.
79. Ibid., 170.
80. Dickert, and Grady, 'What's the Price', 201.
81. Ibid., 201.
82. Wendler *et al.,* 'Ethics of Paying', 170.
83. US Department of Labor, Youth and Labor, 'Compliance Assistance—The Fair Labor Standards Act/Child Labor (29 USC 201 et seq.)'. On the web at http://www.dol.gov/dol/compliance/comp-flsa-childlabor.htm.
84. Runyan, C. W., and Zakocs, R. C., 'Epidemiology and Prevention of Injuries among Adolescent Workers in the United States', *Annual Review of Public Health,* 21 (2000), 247–69, 247.

85. Ibid., 247.

86. Ibid., 247.

87. Ibid., 247.

88. Research involving children would remain much safer than many work opportunities available to children with my proposal to revise the risks to which it is permissible to expose children that was described in Ch. 4, 'Should We Provide Healthy Children with Greater Protection in Medical Research?'

89. US Department of Labor, 'Compliance'.

90. Grant, R. W., and Sugarman, J., 'Ethics in Human Subjects Research: Do Incentives Matter?' *Journal of Medicine and Philosophy,* 29 (2004), 717–38, 721.

91. Ibid., 721.

92. Ibid,. 717.

93. See Wendler *et al.,* 'Ethics of Paying', 166 citing data from Center Watch. Center Watch can be found on the web at: http://www.centerwatch.com. See also, Borzekowski, D. L. G., Rickert, V. I., Fortenberry, J. D., 'At What Price? The Current State of Subject Payment in Adolescent Research', *Journal of Adolescent Health,* 33 (2003), 378–84.

94. Research approved under 407 panels could be a test case. This is discussed in Ch. 15, 'Evolution of the 407 Process', endnote 48.

95. Lemmens and Elliott, 'Guinea Pigs'; Tishler and Bartholomae, 'Repeat'.

96. Royal College of Physicians, 'Research Involving Patients'; Lemmens and Elliott, 'Guinea Pigs'; and Dickert, N., Emanuel, E., and Grady, C., 'Paying Research Subjects: An Analysis of Current Policies', *Annals of Internal Medicine,* 136 (2002), 368–73.

97. Wendler *et al.,* 'Ethics of Paying', 166; Borzekowski, 'At What Price?'

98. Appelbaum *et al.,* 'False Hopes'; Horng and Grady, 'Misunderstanding'.

99. Dickert and Grady, 'What's the Price', 199.

9

Research in Schools

1. Introduction

Most research on children is done in the clinical setting. Schools are a tempting venue, however, because they include all children and not just those who have access and seek medical care. Schools are also a source of a large study population at one time in one place.

There are no data about how much research is done in schools. In 1985, an article discussed the growth of funding by the National Institutes of Health (NIH) for school-based research.[1] Funding for health promotion and disease prevention research initiatives in school-based settings began in the mid-1970s. By 1985, the National Heart Lung and Blood Institute (NHLBI) of the NIH was funding fifteen cardiovascular school-based research studies, and several other Institutes were also funding studies.[2] Personal communication with administrators in several Chicago public and private schools revealed that over one dozen biomedical and behavioral projects are currently underway and that most schools do not have a written policy about what biomedical and behavioral research is permissible and what protections are or should be in place.[3]

Research at schools can be classified either as pedagogical research or biomedical and behavioral research. Pedagogical research includes evaluation of teaching methodologies and subject content; academic success and its correlation with ethnicity, gender, absenteeism, and the like. Biomedical and behavioral research includes traditional medical research such as studies to determine the prevalence of asthma or hypertension in a peer cohort or the efficacy of school-based health clinics, and survey research such as large-scale epidemiological surveys on health and nutritional attitudes and behaviors of children or adolescents and surveys on risk-taking behaviors.

There are very few articles that examine the practices and policies that govern (or ought to govern) school-based research. Rather, the majority of articles are written by researchers who are interested in how to gain access,[4] and they discuss recruitment,[5] incentives,[6] consent,[7] and school politics.[8] In this chapter, I examine (1) the arguments for and against doing biomedical and behavioral research in schools; (2) whether additional human subject protections are necessary; and (3) whose consent is necessary and how it should be procured. Although the third question was answered legislatively for survey research done in schools under the Protection of Pupils Rights Amendment (PPRA) to require written parental consent [9], the debate by researchers prior to its passage is instructive. It shows how the federal regulations governing consent in pediatric research were interpreted by some researchers and IRBs, despite clear guidance that such interpretations were contrary to the spirit of the regulations. Whether the regulations permit parental consent waivers for some other biomedical and behavioral research is still being debated, and this could impact what research is done at schools and whose consent is necessary.

2. Arguments for and against Biomedical and Behavioral Research in the School Setting

While it is easy to understand why pediatric researchers want to do research in the schools, it is not so obvious why school officials agree to allow medical research. For some research, the answer is that it may promote the school's educational mission: a researcher who seeks to implement an HIV curriculum and wants to do pre- and post-test evaluations may be encouraged by officials at inner city schools that do not have the resources to develop new curriculum, or by teachers who may not have the expertise to teach the new material. For other research such as surveys of health risks behavior, nutrition, or the state of adolescent mental health, the benefit to any particular school is less clear-cut, and the results, even if useful to the schools, may be years in coming.

Although there are no data as to why school officials permit medical researchers in their schools, one could postulate at least four reasons: (1) the opportunity to create links within the community between schools, families, and health centers; (2) the indirect and intangible benefits from research participation; (3) altruism and community service; and (4) to promote understanding of youth behaviors and attitudes.

Are these reasons persuasive? The value and effectiveness of creating community links and of indirect school benefit from research participation are difficult to assess without empirical data, but could justify participation for at least some research. The decision to allow the students to participate, however, may backfire. Researchers may not fulfill their end of the agreement (e.g., provide feedback, thank the teachers who provided time and space) or the researchers may publicize the results in such a way as to reflect negatively on the school and its local community. In addition, the school may incur indirect costs. To respect student privacy, the schools cannot just give researchers the list of students, but rather, school personnel may have to be involved in recruitment and procurement of consent. School personnel may be asked to mail out consent forms; teachers may be asked to collect forms and to remind students to bring back the signed consents and refusals; the surveys may be administered during class time, interrupting academic plans and requiring alternative activities for those who do not agree to participate. Even if the researchers offer incentives for students and teachers, the real costs to the schools, in terms of personnel time and opportunity costs, may exceed the benefits.

The third reason that school officials offer is based on a sense of altruism. The concept of altruism, however, is complicated because the officials are agreeing to the participation of their students not of themselves. That is, the altruistic decision to help others is made by one party whereas the activity is done by others. At minimum, this implies that decisions or policies about participation should not be made solely at the administrative level but should seek input from teachers, school boards, parents and students.

On the other hand, understanding youth behaviors and attitudes may be a compelling reason. Educators need to know the values, beliefs, and practices of children and adolescents in order to design appropriate curricula that support positive habits and other curricula to effect behavioral changes, particularly given the increasing role of schools in health promotion and disease prevention. However, the time from research participation to data interpretation and validation may be several years and be outdated by the time feedback is provided. At minimum, this means that the students who participate do not benefit but rather, that the benefits accrue to some future cohort of students.

Although school officials may refuse to participate because of the research topic, the indirect costs in terms of personnel and/or curriculum time, and/or previous bad experiences; the most compelling objection is that the research hinders or does not promote the school's educational mandate. This is a serious issue that can justify a school official's decision to refuse the school's participation. The objection can also be made by parents who are critical of the school's decision to participate in the research, particularly parents who may not approve of their children's participation because of the topic or parents who are critical of how previous research was publicized or used. Even if the data collected may directly benefit the children by suggesting health curricular reform, school officials may seek to avoid the indirect costs by acting as a free-rider and using the data derived from the participation of children in other schools.

In summary, research that does not directly promote the educational mission of the school needs to be justifiable to the numerous parties affected by participation: the students, their parents, the teachers, school administrators, and the school board. While school officials may decide to participate on a case-by-case basis, such decision-making runs the risk of idiosyncratic decision-making by individual school officials. School reform efforts have led to greater awareness of the importance of involving parents in decisions both about how school time is used and what activities are appropriate for their children's education.[10] It may be more appropriate for schools to develop written policy about whether and when to permit biomedical or behavioral research; and if so, what types of biomedical and behavioral research and under what terms. Involving the larger school community in the policy development could promote trust and cooperation and ensure that research activities are consistent with the goals and values of the community.

3. Human Subject Protections

Although most research must be reviewed and approved by an institutional review board (IRB), most educational research done in schools is exempt (CFR §46.101(b) and CFR §46.401(b)). In contrast, most medical and social science research in schools require IRB review (CFR §46.101). This includes survey procedures that may be exempt from IRB review when the subjects are adults (CFR §46.101b(3)), but are specifically NOT exempt in children (CFR §46.401(b)). IRB review is one mechanism to determine that the questions are not so sensitive that they increase the risk level of the survey participation beyond minimal risk, the level of risk to which it is permissible to expose healthy children (CFR §46.404).

Most schools do not have IRBs of their own, unless they do federally funded research and are then required to have a federal-wide assurance (FWA) which formalizes the institution's commitment to protect human subjects, and requires the school to have an IRB or a contractual affiliation with an IRB that will review its research for both its scientific validity and its protection of human subjects. Most schools do not need an IRB because medical research is generally reviewed and approved by the IRB at the researchers' institution (which also has an FWA). Even if a school does not have its own IRB, school officials should play an active role in human subject protection when the subjects are their students. When research is performed in schools, school officials have an obligation to ensure that the rights of their students are respected and to protect the students from harm. To ensure that the students' rights are respected, school officials should examine the consent process which often includes the requirement for both parental permission and the child's assent. To protect children as human subjects, school officials ought to review the content of the research and evaluate it in light of the environment in which it will be undertaken, particularly since peer pressure may inhibit voluntariness or raise concerns that certain 'answers' are not peer-acceptable. Finally, school personnel who will be involved in the research at any level should have some training in the protection of human subjects as they relate to children.

Currently most schools do not have a specific review process to evaluate research proposals that involve students in schools. Rather, most schools accept the review of the researchers' IRB. If one believes that the venue may make children more vulnerable, then specific policies should be designed to ensure that the research is respectful and does not cause harm. An analogy may be helpful. Prisoners, like schoolchildren, are a captive population. During World War II, large numbers of prisoners voluntarily participated in research to develop treatment for infectious disease, and after the war, they continued to participate in research not related to their health and well-being.[12] This raised questions regarding voluntariness and coercion. It also raised concerns that the prisoners might believe that either punitive action would result from non-participation, or that secondary benefits, like earlier parole, might be contingent on participation. There were also serious justice concerns: why should one population be asked to take risks when the benefits would accrue to another? The National Commission wrote a report in 1976 arguing that prisoners were a vulnerable population that needed additional protection,[13] and additional regulations were written to protect them (Subpart C).[14]

Subpart C provides recommendations about what type of research can be done with prisoners and how IRBs should review such research. Although the National Commission concluded that children were also a vulnerable population and provided specific recommendations regarding risk, risk-benefit, and consent for research involving children,[15] these recommendations did not address the ethical concerns of doing research in a captive setting such as schools. I believe that the recommendations for the protection of prisoners as human subjects is a useful starting point for the protection of students in schools as human subjects.

What type of research can involve prisoners? First, research that is focused on issues of particular concern to prisoners (CFR §46.306 (a)(2)). Second, research involving prisoners is permitted when it focuses on 'practices, both innovative and accepted, which have the intent and reasonable probability of improving the health or well-being of the subject' (CFR §46.306 (a)(2)(iv)). If there were restrictions on the type of research that could be done on children in the school setting, one would permit research focused on issues of particular concern to children qua schoolchildren. This would support research focused on curricular content, student performance, and the like. In fact, such research is permitted and is exempt from IRB review because such research is considered essential to the academic mission. Likewise, research on the efficacy of school-based health programs would also be permissible.

Other research on prisoners, however, requires additional protections. For example, 'research on social and psychological problems, such as alcoholism, drug addiction and sexual assaults,' which is also more prevalent in prisons than elsewhere can be approved only 'after the Secretary has consulted with appropriate experts, including experts in penology medicine and ethics, and published notice, in the *Federal Register*, of his intent to approve such research' (CFR §46.306 (a)(2)(iv)). That is, when the research does not directly relate to prisoners as prisoners, the research needs greater justification and greater public scrutiny. One could make a similar argument that research performed in schools that does not directly relate to children as students deserves closer scrutiny. At minimum, the researchers should provide a justification for why the research needs to be done in the school setting. The case of surveys that examine social, behavioral, and psychological attitudes and practices will be discussed below.

Subpart C requires that research involving prisoners is reviewed and that 'At least one member of the Board shall be a prisoner, or a prisoner representative with appropriate background and experience to serve in that capacity'(CFR §46.304(b)). While the Common Rule requires that IRBs have appropriate expertise in pediatrics if the research will involve children (CFR §46.107(b)), there is no requirement in Subpart D to have a representative for schoolchildren. By analogy with Subpart C, one could imagine that a parent, an educator, a school board member, or other school official may have special insight into the particular issues that research may raise for student-subjects, their parents, and their community. The school official could play a critical role in the IRB's discussion of the protection of students as human subjects. The school official could provide insight from his or her expertise in pedagogy and child-development, and could evaluate the topics and questions for their potential sensitivity to their particular students in their particular community. A member of the school board or parent-volunteer might also want to attend as a representative of parents.

Subpart C addresses several issues regarding prisoner research that is germane to research on children in schools.* First, research done in schools should be focused on topics relevant to schoolchildren. Second, the researchers should provide a justification for why the research needs to be done in the school setting. Third, the research be reviewed at an IRB meeting

---

* This is not to suggest that schoolchildren and adult prisoners are similarly situated. First, enrollment in an educational institution is a benefit that is provided free to US children whereas incarceration in an US penal institution is a burden imposed on those who violate US law. Second, schoolchildren are presumed to be incompetent and special consent requirements are imposed whereas adults, even incarcerated adults, are presumed competent to consent for themselves regarding research participation. The consent issues for research in schools is discussed in section 4 below.

in which at least one school official is in attendance. The attendance of a school board member or parent-volunteer may also be useful.

4.   *Consent for School-Based Research*

A major part of IRB review is to examine the consent mechanisms of proposed research protocols. In research involving pediatric subjects, this entails both the permission of the parents or guardians and the assent of the child, and when, if ever, either can be waived.

Most of the literature on consent in school-based research focuses on survey research. These surveys often ask about the adolescent's use of alcohol and illicit drugs, sexual activities, experiences of abuse, and the like. They are controversial both in the content (whether it is appropriate to administer surveys on such topics in schools) and in the process (whose consent is necessary and how the consent should be procured). The process debate has focused on the question of whether parental consent must be 'active' or whether 'passive consent' is adequate.[16] Active parental consent means that parents are given consent forms that they must read and sign. If the parents fail to fill it out or fail to send it back, it is interpreted to mean that parental consent was not given and the child is not permitted to participate. Passive consent means that barring parental refusal either by calling the school or by signing a form that expressly denies permission, the parents are presumed to have agreed to their child's participation. Passive consent assumes that no response means that the parents are in agreement with their child's participation. It is justified on the ground that parents who fail to give active consent do not necessarily disapprove of their child's participation, but may fail to sign an informed consent form because of apathy, other priorities, or illiteracy. While it is correct that some parents who do not consent are not against participation, this is NOT true of all. Whereas passive consent approaches often get less than 1–2% parental refusals, aggressive active consent procedures often get a minimum of 10% refusals.[17] O'Donnell and colleagues conclude:

The assumption that permission has been given unless parents take the initiative to indicate otherwise may be comforting to researchers and school administrators, but the assumption that lack of parental response equals consent may be incorrect or at least overstated, given the discrepancy between the parental refusal rates we obtained and those reported for studies relying on waivers of consent.[18]

The major moral objection to passive consent procedures is that there is no proof that the parents are even aware that a research opportunity exists because the research may be described in a letter that the child fails to bring home, or is written in a language that the parent cannot read. Thus, it is not truly passive parental consent but presumed parental consent.

The phrase 'passive consent' is not used in the federal regulations and is in fact not consistent with the federal regulations. It was specifically rejected by the Office for Protection for Research Risks (OPRR now the Office for Human Subjects Protections or OHRP): 'mere non-objection should not be considered as the equivalent of consent.'[19] Rather, the federal regulations require researchers to obtain written informed consent from the research subject and parent or what the school literature refers to as 'active' consent, another phrase not used in the federal regulations.

One way to circumvent the need for 'active' parental consent that is consistent with the federal regulations is for the researcher and the IRB to conclude that the research fulfills the criteria to waive written consent as delineated in Subpart A. To qualify for a waiver, the research must fulfill four criteria: (1) the research involves no more than minimal risk to the research; (2) the waiver or alteration will not adversely affect the rights and welfare of the subjects; (3) the research could not practicably be carried out without the waiver or alteration; and (4) whenever appropriate, the subjects will be provided with additional pertinent information after participation (CFR §46.116 (d)).

Let us consider whether survey research could fall under this exemption and whether the informed consent of the parents could be waived. The claim that the research entails at most minimal risk (criterion 1) is controversial.[20] There is great variability between individuals regarding what questions and types of information are perceived as sensitive. Researchers may not be sensitive to the concerns of some parents and children within the communities in which their research will take place. Some survey questions that the researchers perceive to be benign may involve more than minimal risk to some children. This is why the federal regulations seek third-party review (by IRBs) and review and consent by the children's parents who are presumed to be best-situated to know how their children may react to certain probing questions.

The researchers also argue that written parental consent is unnecessary since it provides no additional protection to the adolescents such that the waiver or alteration will not adversely affect the rights and welfare of the subjects (criterion 2). Consider, then, a case described in the literature in which the researchers were seeking to understand sexual experience and safe sexual practices in a community where a condom availability program had been implemented. A pre-survey used passive parental consent, but a group of parents took the researchers to court. The parents 'contended that specific questions about students' sexual activities were inappropriate and threatened the welfare of students'.[21] The court ruled that active consent was required and the post-intervention survey employed active consent procedures.[22] Interestingly, the focus of the article was not about whether 'active' or 'passive' parental consent was morally appropriate, but only on how the consent method adversely affected subject accrual.

Researchers have also argued that adolescents should be allowed to consent for themselves because 'more safeguards do not need to be introduced to protect children from questions about subject matter they regularly confront in school, in the media at home and in their peer groups'.[23] As I argued in Chapter 4, familiarity does not necessarily mean that the adolescent copes well with the subject matter. Medical researchers have justified exposing sick children to more invasive procedures and greater risks than their healthy peers based on their previous experiences. Ackerman explains why the argument morally fails: 'The fact that a sick child has undergone a particular procedure, such as a lumbar puncture, during treatment does not guarantee that he or she will not be subjected to considerable stress or anxiety.'[24] Similarly, we should not focus on whether a child may have previous experience with a subject, but rather whether the child is able to cope well with the subject matter or whether it is appropriate to intentionally expose a child to the subject for educational purposes.[25] Thus it is not clear that survey research fulfills criterion 2.

The third criterion requires that the research cannot practicably be carried out without the waiver or alteration. Researchers contend that surveys should not require parental consent because it biases the research study population. The evidence supports the concerns about bias. For example, Severson and Ary found that seventh-grade students who did not have written parental consent reported significantly higher rates of cigarette and marijuana usage than did students who obtained parental consent.[26] Kearney found that written parental consent produced a sample that overrepresented White students and underrepresented Black and Asian Americans.[27] Anderman *et al.* found that children who obtained parental consent were more likely to be White, live in two-parent households, have a B or better grades, and be involved in extracurricular activities.[28] While there is abundant evidence that seeking parental consent biases the research,[29] this is true of all research that seeks consent. Only those who want to be studied agree to participate. Respect for persons means that some data will not be collected. To argue that the bias justifies overriding an individual's or his or her surrogate's right to refuse to participate fails because it promotes expedience over respect. Further justification is necessary to fulfill this criterion.

Survey research in schools do not clearly meet the necessary criteria to waive written informed consent, although one could imagine that different IRBs would make different determinations.[30] Nevertheless, the question about whether parental consent for survey research administered in schools can be waived was resolved legislatively. The Protection of Pupils Rights

Amendment (PPRA) also known as the Hatch Amendment was passed in 1994. The Hatch Amendment required that surveys funded by Department of Education have written parental consent.[31] The PPRA was revised in 2001 in the No Child Left Behind Act[32] which expanded the requirement for parental consent to any survey research done in institutions that receive funds from any program of the Department of Education including all public primary and secondary schools. By establishing a right of parents to be informed and give consent for survey research administered in schools, the question of whether the waiver under Subpart A could apply is moot, although it is still relevant for surveys administered in other venues.

Under the revised PPRA, schools are required to develop and adopt policies, in conjunction with parents, regarding the following: (1) the right of parents to inspect upon request a survey created by a third party before the survey is administered or distributed by a school to students; and (2) arrangements to protect student privacy in the event of the administration of a survey to students, including the right of parent to inspect, upon request, the survey, if the survey contains questions about 'sensitive topics' including: (a) political affiliations or beliefs of the student or student's parent; (b) mental or psychological problems of the student or student's family; (c) sex behavior or attitudes; (d) illegal, anti-social, self-incriminating, or demeaning behavior; (e) critical appraisals of others with whom respondents have close family relationships; (f) legally recognized privileged relationships, such as with lawyers, doctors, or ministers; (g) religious practices, affiliations, or beliefs of the student or parents; or (h) income, other than as required by law to determine program eligibility.[33]

In accordance with the PPRA, most survey research administered in the school setting requires written parental consent. It may be more costly and cumbersome, but the expense can be justified to ensure the protection of children as human subjects in research performed in schools.

The PPRA, however, does not resolve the issue of whether parental consent can be waived for other biomedical and behavioral research performed in the schools. The Society for Adolescent Medicine (SAM), the National Human Research Protections Advisory Committee (NHRPAC), and the Institute of Medicine (IOM) have argued that parental permission should be waived for research on conditions for which adolescents can seek medical care without parental permission.[34] As discussed in Chapter 5, SAM, NHRPAC, and IOM all note that the National Commission's report, *Research Involving Children*, suggested that parental permission be waived for this type of research,[35] but the example was not included in the federal regulations. Even if the omission from the regulations was mere oversight, one must remember that the regulations do not allow children to consent for themselves but require a substitute mechanism for protecting children-subjects. Although these advisory groups suggest that mature adolescents can serve as their own substitute mechanism because they are capable of giving their own consent (at least for these conditions), the regulations do not address whether the child's own consent is a legitimate substitute mechanism.[36]

The main problem with the position of SAM, NHRPAC, and the IOM is that it extrapolates from policies regulating clinical treatments to the research setting, but extrapolation is inappropriate because these statutes were not written to accommodate the competency of mature adolescents.[37] In fact, the statutes do not discuss decision-making capacity nor the requirement of the providing physician to ensure that the minor seeking treatment has such capacity.[38] These statutes were instead designed as a pragmatic public health response to current adolescent health needs. They were designed to encourage adolescents to seek health care for problems which they might deny, ignore, or delay if they had to inform their parents and/or get parental permission.

There is good reason not to extrapolate. Even if adolescents are mature and have the decision-making ability to consent to treatment for particular diseases, this does not mean that they have the ability to consent to research about these particular diseases, because the risk/benefit ratio of the latter is not as clear cut as the former.[39] In addition, as I will discuss below, doing this research in the school setting may increase the adolescent's vulnerability to understand that participation is voluntary, that he or she may withdraw at any time, and that the adolescent has the rights to confidentiality and privacy regarding medical information. Thus, biomedical and behavioral research, if appropriate to be undertaken in the schools, must require parental permission and the child's assent.

5.   Child and Youth Assent

The federal regulations are clear that the child's dissent is dispositive, particularly for nontherapeutic research such as surveys (CFR §46.408). The concern is the extent to which children, particularly children in schools understand this. While the National Commission considered children to be vulnerable, I would add that children are even more vulnerable in certain settings.[40] In school, children are at increased vulnerability because their ability to understand their right to refuse may be compromised because children at school are generally expected to follow their teachers' instructions.[41] Whether students understand their rights in school-based research has not been examined. Whether teachers who may serve as the proctors of the research understand the students' rights and whether they need to be trained in human subject protections are also unexamined. For example, empirical data are lacking as to whether students understand that they can refuse to participate in the school setting, even if the rest of the class does participate; and that they can refuse to answer certain questions or stop mid-survey, even if they consented initially. The limited data about children's understanding about their rights in research suggest that many children do not understand these rights.[42] Simple steps can be taken to help children such as telling them that the researchers will not be upset if they want to stop and reminding them that they can choose not to answer questions or perform specific tasks that make them feel uncomfortable.

It is also questionable whether children can give voluntary consent in the classroom setting. The environment may interfere with the children's ability to refuse because children and adolescents tend to defer to peer pressure. That is, some students may grudgingly agree to participate because their peers are participating and they do not want to appear different, rather than consenting to participate because they value the research or their participation. The school is also an ethically troublesome venue because it may make it difficult for the child to keep their answers confidential. Peer pressure may compel them to share their answers with classmates both during the research and afterwards when classmates may demand that they divulge their answers.

Steps should be taken by schools to ensure human subject protections. First, just as all research personnel in medical centers are required to have some training in human subject protections, all school personnel who are involved in any aspect of biomedical or behavioral research should undergo some training in the protection of human subjects with special emphasis on children as research subjects. Second, when research surveys are being conducted, measures must be taken within the school to ensure that students' answers are kept confidential such as separating desks more than might be typical in classroom academic setting, not having teacher-or researcher-proctors walk between the desks, and providing the students with a separate paper to cover their answers. Third, steps should be taken after the research is completed to educate and remind children that their responses were confidential and that individuals need not discuss their research participation with their peers.

Concerns of voluntariness and confidentiality also hold for other non-survey medical and behavioral research performed in schools. Recently, the Office for Human Research Protections (OHRP) suspended an NIH-funded IRB-approved study with the acronym SATURN (Student Athletic Testing Using Random Notification). The SATURN project required student-athletes to participate in research as a requirement for participating in interscholastic athletics.[43] Athletic participation was contingent upon signing the consent form, and then the student-athletes were tested randomly for drug use. The student-athletes who tested positive for drugs twice could be suspended from sports participation which threatened the student's right to confidentiality with respect to the results of his or her research participation.[44] If children and adolescents will participate in biomedical and behavioral research in schools, they need to understand and have the opportunity to exercise their research rights which include the right to confidentiality of study results, the right not to participate, and the right to withdraw at any time.

Despite IRB review and the requirement for parental permission and the child's assent, some children may be disturbed by their participation in medical or behavioral research, including survey research, either immediately or some time after participation. Programs or services should be in place for children to seek support. This should be part of the research design and children should be given information about these services both before and after the research is performed.

6.   *Recommendations*

While schools are an enticing venue in which to do biomedical and behavioral research, parents, students, teachers, school officials, researchers, and IRBs need to be sensitive to the unique problems that such research may raise. Schools should have written policies that address the need to protect human subjects when research is done in the school setting. At minimum, these guidelines should require that:

(1) The research topic be relevant to schoolchildren;
(2) The researchers provide a justification for why the research needs to be done in the school setting;
(3) The research be reviewed at an IRB meeting in which at least one school official is in attendance. The attendance of a school board member or parent-volunteer may also be useful;
(4) Written parental consent be required for all medical and behavioral research performed in schools;
(5) All school personnel involved in any aspect of biomedical or behavioral research should undergo some training in human subject protections with emphasis on children;
(6) Children and adolescents be given the opportunity to understand and exercise their research rights. These include: the right to confidentiality, the right to refuse to participate, and the right to withdraw even if they agreed to participate; and
(7) Programs or services should be in place after research participation to address follow-up concerns.

References

1. Stone, E. J., 'School-Based Health Research Funded by the National Heart, Lung, and Blood Institute', *Journal of School Health,* 55 (1985), 16–174.
2. Ibid.
3. Ross personal communications, June–August 2004.
4. Harrell, J. S., Bradley, C., Dennis, J., Frauman, A. C., and Criswell, E. S., 'School-Based Research: Problems of Access and Consent', *Journal of Pediatric Nursing,* 15 (2000), 14–21; and Esbensen, F-A., Deschenes, E. P., Vogel, R. E., West, J., Arboit, K., and Harris, L., 'Active Parental Consent in School-Based Research: An Examination of Ethical and Methodological Issues', *Evaluation Review,* 20 (1996), 737–53.
5. Harrington, K. F., Bilkley, D., Reynolds, K. D., Duvall, R. C., Copeland, J. R., Franklin, F., and Raczynski, J., 'Recruitment Issues in School-Based Research: Lessons Learned from the High 5 Alabama Project', *Journal of School Health,* 67 (1997), 415–21.
6. See Harrell *et al.,* 'School-Based Research'; and Ross, J. G., Sundberg, E. C., and Flint, K. H., 'Informed Consent in School Health Research: Why, How and Making It Easy', *Journal of School Health,* 69 (1999), 171–6.
7. See Ross *et al.,* 'Informed Consent'; and Gans, J. E., and Brindis, C. D., 'Choice of Research Setting in Understanding Adolescent Health Problems', *Journal of Adolescent Health,* 17 (1995), 306–13.
8. See Harrell *et al.,* 'School-Based Research'; Gans and Brindis, 'Choice'; and Peterson, A. V. Jr., Mann, S. L., Kealey, K. A., and Marek, P. M., 'Experimental Design and Methods for School-Based Randomized Trials: Experience from the Hutchinson Smoking Prevention Project (HSPP)', *Controlled Clinical Trials,* 21 (2000), 144–65.
9. The Protection of Pupil Rights Amendment (PPRA) was originally passed in 1994. PPRA, 20 U.S.C. 1232h (1994) 34 CFR Part 98. Found on the web at: http://www.ed.gov/policy/gen/guid/fpco/ppra/index.html. It was revised under the No Child Left Behind Act of 2001, 20 U.S.C. 6301 et seq. (2002).
10. Consent policies for pediatric research are found in both Subpart A and Subpart D. See Department of Health and Human Services (DHHS). (45 CFR 46 Subpart A), 'Final Regulations Amending Basic HHS Policy for the Protection of Human Research Subjects', *Federal Register,* 46 (26 January 1981), 8366–91; revised *Federal Register,* 56 (18 June 1991), 28003–18, CFR §46.101(b); hereinafter referred to as the Common Rule and cited by its CFR number in the text; and Department of Health and Human Services (DHHS). (45 CFR Part 46, Subpart D), 'Protections for Children Involved as Subjects in Research', *Federal Register,* 48 (8 March 1983), 9814–20; revised *Federal Register,* 56 (18 June 1991), 28032, CFR §46.401(b); hereinafter referred to as Subpart D and cited by its CFR number in the text.
11. See Esbensen *et al.,* 'Active Parental'.
12. National Commission for the Protection of Human Subjects of Biomedical and Behavioral Research, *Research on Prisoners: Report and Recommendations.*

Washington DC: US Department of Health, Education and Welfare, 1976, 1; hereinafter cited as National Commission, 'Prisoners'.

13. Ibid.

14. Department of Health, Education, and Welfare (DHEW), 'Additional Protections Pertaining to Biomedical and Behavioral Research Involving Prisoners as Subjects', *Federal Register,* 43 (16 November 1978), 53652–6 hereinafter cited by CFR number in text.

15. National Commission for the Protection of Human Subjects. *Report and Recommendations: Research Involving Children.* Washington DC: US Printing Office, 1977, DHEW Publication NO. (OS) 77–0004, hereinafter cited as National Commission, *Research Involving Children.*

16. See, e.g., Severson, H., and Biglan, A., 'Rationale for the Use of Passive Consent in Smoking Prevention Research: Politics, Policy and Pragmatics', *Preventive Medicine,* 18 (1989), 267–79; O'Donnell, L. N., Duran, R. H., Doval, A. S., Breslin, M. J., Juhn, G. M., and Stueve, A., 'Obtaining Written Parent Permission for School-Based Health Surveys of Urban Young Adolescents', *Journal of Adolescent Health,* 21 (1997), 376–83; Pokorny, S. B., Jason, L. A., Schoeny, M. E., Townsend, S. M., and Curie, C. J., 'Do Participation Rates Change When Active Consent Procedures Replace Passive Consent?' *Evaluation Review,* 25 (2001), 567–80; Beck, S., Collins, L., Overkolser, J., and Terry, K., 'A Comparison of Child Who Receive and Who Do Not Receive Permission to Participate in Research', *Journal of Abnormal Child Psychology,* 12 (1984), 573–80; Dent, C. W., Galaif, J., Sussman, S., Stacy, A., Burtun, D., and Flay, B. R., 'Demographic, Psychosocial and Behavioral Differences in Samples of Actively and Passively Consented Adolescents', *Addictive Behaviors,* 18 (1993), 51–6; Noll, R. B., Zeller, M. H., and Vannatta, K., 'Potential Bias in Classroom Research: Comparison of Children with Permission and Those Who Do Not Receive Permission to Participate', *Journal of Clinical Child Psychology,* 26 (1997), 36–42; Kearney, K. A., Hopkins, R. H., Mauss, A. L., and Weisheit, R. A., 'Sample Bias Resulting from a Requirement for Written Parental Consent', *Public Opinion Quarterly,* 47 (1983), 96–102; Baker, J. R., Yardley, J. K., and McCaul, K., 'Characteristics of Responding-, Nonresponding-, and Refusing-Parents in an Adolescent Lifestyle Choice Study', *Evaluation Review,* 25 (2001), 605–18; and Unger, J. B., Gallaher, P., Palmer, P. H., Baezconde-Barbanati, L., Trinidad, D. R., Cen, S., and Johnson, C. A., 'NO NEWS IS BAD NEWS: Characteristics of Adolescents Who Provide Neither Parental Consent Nor Refusal for Participation in School-Based Survey Research', *Evaluation Review,* 28 (2004), 52–63.

17. See, e.g., O'Donnell *et al.,* 'Obtaining'; Pokorny *et al.,* 'Do Participation Rates'; and Schuster, M. A., Bell, R. M., Berry, S. H., and Kanouse, D. E., 'Impact of a High School Condom Availability Program on Sexual Attitudes and Behaviors', *Family Planning Perspectives* 30 (1998), 67–72.

18. O'Donnell *et al.,* 'Obtaining'.

19. Ibid., 'Obtaining' citing personal communication with Diane Aiken of OPRR, 381.

20. Severson and Biglan, 'Rationale'; and O'Donnell *et al.,* 'Obtaining'.

21. Schuster *et al.,* 'Impact'.

22. Ibid.

23. Esbensen *et al.* 'Active Parental', 752.

24. Ackerman, T. F., 'Moral Duties of Investigators toward Sick Children', *IRB: A Review of Human Subjects Research,* 3 (June/July 1981), 1–5, 4.

25. Ackerman, T., 'Moral Duties of Parents and Non-Therapeutic Research Procedures Involving Children', *Bioethics Quarterly,* 2 (1980), 94–111. The issue of whether healthy children should be given greater protection in research is discussed in detail in Chapter 4, 'Should We Provide Healthy Children with Greater Protection in Medical Research?'

26. Severson, H., and Ary, D. V., 'Sampling Bias Due to Consent Procedures with Adolescents', *Addictive Behaviors,* 8 (1983), 433–7.

27. Kearney *et al.,* 'Sample Bias'.

28. Anderman, C., Cheadle, A., Curry, S., Diehr, P., Schultz, L., and Wagner, E., 'Selection Bias Related to Parental Consent in School-Based Survey Research', *Evaluation Review,* 19 (1995), 663–74.

29. See, e.g., Dent *et al.,* 'Demographic'; Baker *et al.,* 'Characteristics'; Severson and Ary, 'Sampling Bias'; Kearney *et al.,* 'Sample Bias'; and Anderman *et al.* 'Selection Bias'.

30. See, e.g., Janofsky, J., and Starfield, B., 'Assessment of Risk in Research on Children', *Journal of Pediatrics*, 98 (1981), 842–6; and Shah, S., Whittle, A., Wilfond, B., Gensler, G., and Wendler, D., 'How Do Institutional Review Boards Apply the Federal Risk and Benefit Standards for Pediatric Research?' *JAMA*, 291 (2004), 476–82.

31. Protection of Pupil Rights Amendment (PPRA) (1994).

32. No Child Left Behind Act of 2001.

33. Ibid.

34. Adolescents can seek medical care for health care relating to sexuality, mental health, and drug abuse under the specialized consent statutes. The arguments to waive parental permission for research in these areas have been made by numerous groups. See Santelli, J. S., Rosenfeld, W. D., DuRant, R. H., Dubler, N., Morreale, M., English, A., and Rogers, A. S., 'Guidelines for Adolescent Health Research: A Position Paper of the Society for Adolescent Medicine', *Journal of Adolescent Health,* 17 (1995), 270–6, hereinafter cited as SAM position paper; Consensus Conference on Guidelines for Adolescent Health Research, 'Conference Proceedings: Guidelines for Adolescent Health Research', Alexandria VA, 19–20 May 1994, *Journal of Adolescent Health,* 17 (1995), 264–9; Final Report to NHRPAC from Children's Workgroup (undated). On the web at: http://www.hhs.gov/ohrp/nhrpac/documents/nhrpac16.pdf; and Field, M. J., Behrman, R. E. (eds.), for the Committee on Clinical Research Involving Children, *The Ethical Conduct of Clinical Research Involving Children.* Washington DC: National Academy Press, 2004, hereinafter cited as the IOM, *Ethical Conduct.* See also discussion in Chapter 5, esp. text corresponding to endnotes 22–38.

35. See National Commission, *Research Involving Children*, 18. The example is omitted from CFR §46.408(c).

36. Veatch, R. M., 'Commentary: Beyond Consent to Treatment', *IRB: A Review of Human Subjects Research,* 3 (February 1981), 7–8.
37. See Veatch, 'Beyond Consent'; and Ross, L. F., *Children Families and Health Care Decision-Making.* Oxford: Clarendon Press, 1998.
38. See Veatch, 'Beyond Consent'; and Ross, *Children.*
39. See Ross, *Children.*
40. Kipnis K., 'Seven Vulnerabilities in the Pediatric Research Subject', *Theoretical Medicine & Bioethics,* 24 (2003), 107–20; and Weithorn, L. A., and Scherer, D. G., 'Children's Involvement in Research Participation Decisions: Psychological Considerations' in M. A. Grodin, and L. H. Glantz, *Children as Research Subjects: Science, Ethics, and Law.* New York: Oxford University Press, 1994, 131–79.
41. See Kipnis. 'Seven'; and Weithorn and Scherer, 'Children's Involvement'.
42. See Weithorn and Scherer, 'Children's Involvement'; Hurley, J. C., and Underwood, M. K., 'Children's Understanding of Their Research Rights Before and After Debriefing: Informed Assent, Confidentiality, and Stopping Participation', *Child Development,* 73 (2002), 132–43; Ondrusek, N., Abramovitch, R., Pencharz, P., and Koren, G., 'Empirical Examination of the Ability of Children to Consent to Clinical Research', *Journal of Medical Ethics,* 24 (1998), 158–65; Melton, G. B., Koocher, G. P., and Saks, M. J. (eds.), *Children's Competence to Consent.* New York: Plenum Press, 1983; and Abramovitch, R., Freedman, J. L, Henry, K., and Van Brunschot, M., 'Children's Capacity to Agree to Psychological Research: Knowledge of Risks and Benefits and Voluntariness', *Ethics & Behavior* 5 (1995), 25–48.
43. Shamoo, A. E., and Moreno, J. D., 'Ethics of Research Involving Mandatory Drug Testing of High School Athletes in Oregon', *American Journal of Bioethics,* 4 (2004), 25–31.
44. Ibid.

10

Minimizing Risks: Diabetes Research in Newborns

1. Introduction

In January 2002, a Florida newspaper proclaimed that 'Florida had taken a progressive step in becoming the first state offering to screen newborns for the risk of developing juvenile diabetes'.[1] The newborn screening involves identifying children with a genetic predisposition to type 1 diabetes. It is offered as a voluntary test in conjunction with the mandatory newborn metabolic screening. Infants discovered to be at increased risk are recruited for follow-up studies to determine if and when the child develops autoantibodies (pre-clinical disease) or overt diabetes. No therapies to prevent or retard the development of type 1 diabetes exist, and no experimental therapies are part of the research proposal.

Newborn screening for diabetes raises ethical issues at two levels. At the primary level, one asks whether an informed parent should give permission for her child's participation. This type of ethical inquiry focuses on what information is needed for informed consent, who is the proper person to grant permission for enrollment, and whether subjects are being recruited fairly. At the secondary or meta-ethical level, one asks whether parents should be asked to enroll their newborns. This type of ethical inquiry focuses on whether healthy newborns are the appropriate population for predictive genetic screening for conditions in which testing only leads to knowledge of increased susceptibility and for which no therapies or prevention exist.

If the meta-ethical question is answered affirmatively, one must examine the primary-level concerns. However, if the meta-ethical question is answered in the negative, then the first level concerns become moot. If the research protocol does not pass ethical research standards, then parental permission should not be sought. This is true regardless of how many parents might consent. In this chapter I will focus on the meta-ethical question regarding subject selection. Although I answer it negatively, and therefore do not need to address the consent issues, I will address them because there are data to show that over 90% of parents give permission for diabetes screening of their newborns in the US and abroad.[2]

2.   Diabetes Prediction Studies in Newborns

In the US, type 1 diabetes has an annual incidence of 15 per 100,000 under age 18 years, making it the most common metabolic disease of childhood.[3] Of major concern is that type 1 diabetes is increasing at a yearly rate of 2.5% throughout the world.[4] As such, Florida's interest in diabetes prediction research in newborns is not unique. The BABY-DIAB studies in Germany and Australia are prospective studies from birth of children with at least one parent with insulin-dependent diabetes mellitus (IDDM). The studies are designed to perform serial blood tests on the children for evidence of auto-antibody development[5] and its relationship with environmental triggers.[6]

Although newborns with an affected first-degree relative have a tenfold higher incidence of developing type 1 diabetes,[7] most newborn studies do not focus on these children because they only account for 10% of type 1 diabetes cases.[8] The DIPP (Diabetes Prediction and Prevention study) in Finland seeks to identify all newborns with HLA-DQB1 genotypes that confer a high ($\sim$8%), or moderate risk (1.7–2.6%) of developing type 1 diabetes (compared with a national average risk of 0.7%).[9] Approximately 94.4% of parents consent to genetic screening and 14.8% of the children are found to be at some degree of increased risk.[10] The Norwegian Babies against Diabetes (NOBADIA) seeks to identify the 4% of newborns in the general population with the highest genetic risk (12%) for developing diabetes.[11] Begun in 1998, these infants will be followed for 15 years. In Colorado, the Diabetes Autoimmunity Study in the Young (DAISY) seeks to identify newborns with the highest risk genotypes ($\sim$2.3%) to participate in serial antibody screening:[12] 94% of mothers consent.[13] The Florida newspaper report[14] refers to the Prospective Assessment in New-borns for Diabetic Autoimmunity (PANDA) study in which infants at in-creased genetic risk will be followed for antibody development to uncover possible environmental triggers such as breast feeding, immunizations, and viral infections.[15]

To date, the only combined primary prediction and prevention study in newborns is the Trial to Reduce IDDM in the Genetically at Risk (TRIGR) in Finland. Following encouraging results of a pilot study in 1992–3,[16] the second TRIGR pilot study was launched in 1995 to examine whether avoiding cow's milk protein for the first 6–8 months of life prevents diabetes in infants with an affected first-degree relative.[17] The diet was effective in NOD mice[18], although there are some preliminary data to suggest it is ineffective in humans.[19]. After weaning from breast milk, infants enrolled in TRIGR were randomized to receive either Nutramigen exclusively (a casein-hydrolysate formula that lacks intact cow's milk) or Enfamil (with 20% Nutramigen to control for taste and smell).[20] No results are available yet.

It is noteworthy that all of the studies described above include disclosure of the child's genetic risk to the parents. Contrast such disclosure with the general consensus in the medical and medical ethics communities against clinical predictive genetic-testing of children when no treatment exists.[21] And yet, despite the medical and ethical consensus against clinical predictive testing of children, over 90% of parents consent to research that involves predictive screening of their newborns for diabetes. In the next three sections, I address (1) What are the risks and benefits of such newborn research screening?; (2) What is required for newborn research screening to be ethical?; and (3) Do current newborn diabetes research screening projects fulfill these ethical requirements? I then consider whether the high rate of parental permission successfully challenges the ethical problems raised by this screening research.

3. The Risks and Benefits of Diabetes Susceptibility Research in Newborns

The expert consensus against isolated predictive identification of newborns and children for increased genetic susceptibilities when no preventive measures are available is based on the lack of therapeutic benefit.[22] It is presumed that the psychosocial risks outweigh the psychosocial benefits,[23] although there are scant empirical data regarding the psychosocial risks and benefits of predictive screening with disclosure of results of children generally,[24] let alone for newborn screening for a specific condition like type 1 diabetes. Although NOBADIA plans to do extensive psychological follow-up,[25] there are very few data on the psychosocial risks associated with identifying newborns for a genetic predisposition to diabetes.[26] The data that do exist regarding predictive diabetes identification were generated from studies that identified children (beyond infancy) or adults who had islet cell antibodies (a marker of beta cell destruction).[27] These studies found that families were initially quite anxious about the results, but most of the anxiety dissipated by four months.[28] However, anxiety persisted in some subgroups (e.g., those who relied on self-blame and wishful thinking as coping strategies [29]), such that the researchers concluded that some participants may experience greater distress than others.[30]

In addition, whether the anxiety will remain low needs to be determined. Psychological follow-up from other newborn screening programs suggests that harms can accrue over a much longer period, and that they can wax and wane. Consider, for example, alpha-1 antitrypsin deficiency (alpha-1) screening begun in Sweden in the early 1970s.[31] Alpha-1 is an autosomal recessive predisposition to chronic lung disease in young adulthood with variable penetrance and expressivity. Parents of at-risk children were counseled that smoking and smoky environments could hasten or worsen their children's pulmonary symptoms. Psychological data were procured for 20 years on a subset of families with a child who screened positive.[32] The data showed that parents initially had strong negative emotional reactions to the diagnosis;[33] and yet, despite negative attitudes, the majority of parents had a positive attitude about the screening program that had identified their child's risk.[34]

The alpha-1 screening program did not screen additional children after the pilot project, in part because of the psychological stress it had caused in some families who had tested positive.[35] Follow-up data however continue to this day. Short-term follow-up found increased smoking by fathers of affected children[36], and negative long-term effects in the mental and physical health of the mother;[37] in mother–child but not father–child interactions;[38] in parents' long-term emotional adjustment to their children's alpha-1 status;[39] and in the parents' view of their children's health,[40] although this improved over time.[41] However, the children, as young adults, were aware of the dangers of smoking and smoky environments and had a positive attitude about alpha-1 screening.[42] In 1997, the World Health Organization (WHO) reviewed the data and published a memorandum in support of implementing alpha-1 newborn screening.[43] Although Sweden remains somewhat ambivalent,[44] Oregon had a similar program in the 1970s,[45] and supports reimplementation.[46]

Alpha-1 and type 1 diabetes are not completely analogous. First, as noted by the alpha-1 researchers, some of the psychological stress might have been avoided if the parents had been informed about the testing and given the opportunity to consent to or refuse testing, which was not the case when alpha-1 testing was incorporated into universal screening programs in the 1970s.[47] All of the predictive diabetes newborn screening programs described above include a separate informed consent process. And yet, even if a separate informed consent is required, it may not be enough in part because 'the pressure of the hospital setting, the parents' physician and emotional condition immediately after birth, and the cultural belief that "medical testing is good for you" will lead most parents to consent'.[48] A second dissimilarity between the two conditions is that there are preventive measures that can be taken for alpha-1 which improve the benefit/harm ratio for alpha-1 screening. One would hypothesize greater harm in predictive information about type 1 diabetes when subjects and their families have no control over the development of diabetes.[49]

What, then, are the risks and benefits of predictive identification of newborns at increased risk for type 1 diabetes? One potential clinical benefit is that parents can be taught the signs and symptoms of clinical disease so that their children are diagnosed early, and avoid being diagnosed in the emergency setting of diabetic ketoacidosis. The risk, however, is that parents may overreact and interpret a child's normal urination habits as a sign of polyuria. A second potential clinical benefit is that the parents will be familiar with a diabetes center and will make the transition to clinical care easier. However, a high-risk allele does not confer certainty of disease, and parents may become very anxious and make life plans based on an increased susceptibility, a susceptibility that materializes in less than 20% of individuals. A low-risk allele may give parents false reassurance of their child's health because some children with low-risk genetic alleles develop diabetes.

The most serious clinical risk, however, is that parents will conflate the experimental and nontherapeutic nature of diabetes screening with the established public health newborn screening programs geared to detect metabolic and endocrine disorders that require immediate treatment. Parents may decide that all newborn screening is experimental and refuse PKU and diabetes screening, despite the high medical benefit of the former. Alternatively, parents may conflate the experimental and established public health screening programs and consent to both without understanding that the former is nontherapeutic. This will leave them unprepared for a positive test result. Data show that the receipt of a positive test result has more negative effects than anticipated in population-based screening (versus less negative effects than anticipated in testing of high-risk families).[50]

There are also potential psychosocial benefits and risks raised by experimental screening of newborns for diabetes. One potential psychosocial benefit is that the parent can prepare. And yet, given the high rate of false positives (the highest-risk allele confers less than a 20% risk of developing diabetes), many parents will prepare unnecessarily, and the danger is that they may begin treating their child as ill, when the child has at most an increased risk of becoming ill in the future.[51] This is particularly true when the genetic factor is but one contributor to a higher relative risk of an illness that also depends on unknown individual or environmental co-factors.[52] It may also adversely affect the parent–child relationship.[53] This risk may be exaggerated in the newborn period which is a particularly vulnerable time in parent–child relationships.[54] Even families who have received a positive screening test that is quickly confirmed to be negative (e.g., false positive hypothyroid screen), report greater strain on marriage and difficulties in their relationships with their children.[55] Imagine then a positive screening test that only reflects increased susceptibility over a lifetime! These children may spend their childhood as neither healthy nor ill but 'at risk.'[56] Such labeling may cause familial stress,[57] and may be stigmatizing for the family reflected in difficulty procuring health insurance.[58]

The concerns about genetic discrimination in health insurance are serious. Several studies have documented that genetic information leads to discrimination in health insurance,[59] although the magnitude of the problem is not clear. The Institutional Review Board (IRB) guidebook prepared by the Office of Human Research Protections (OHRP) specifically states that subjects in genetic research must be made aware of the potential for discrimination in health and life insurance.[60]

In summary, given the low sensitivity and specificity of predictive genetic screening for type 1 diabetes in newborns, the current potential medical benefits of such information for the child and family are minimal. They must be judged in light of the possible medical and psychosocial risks, and the possibility that such experimental screening programs will be confused with established public health screening programs. If the risks of identifying newborns as being at risk for type 1 diabetes are judged as more than minimal, then the federal regulations do not allow such research to be done on healthy children.[61]

4. Subject Selection

Even if researchers could successfully argue that the risks are no more than minimal, the research may still not pass muster because the regulations also require that the study design minimizes risks.[62] To minimize risks in a vulnerable population like children, the National Commission recommended that research should be conducted when possible on animals, then adults, and then older children.[63] Unfortunately, the demographics of type 1 diabetes,[64] and the increasing number of new cases in children under 4 years of age,[65] mean that such research must be done on young children.

One ethical issue with regard to subject selection is whether it matters if the research is done on newborns versus older infants. Newborns are attractive for population genetic screening research because (1) virtually all newborns in developed countries are born in hospitals; (2) virtually all undergo screening for PKU and hypothyroidism making screening already accepted; and (3) large amounts of blood can be obtained from the placenta at delivery without any physical risk to the baby. A delay of three months would not interfere with predictive research as autoantibodies and overt disease rarely develop before then.[66] One argument to support the delay is that it would distinguish this research study from current metabolic newborn screening. The major drawback of such a study design would be lower participation. Attempting to enroll children at primary care clinics is much less efficient than enrollment in the hospital. It requires the active recruitment by many primary care physicians who may not have a vested interest in the project, and may not be willing to spend the time to get consent from the parent. It would also require a separate blood sample which both increases the physical riskiness of the study (albeit minimally), but could result in lower parental consent. This raises the counter-argument that delaying the research will lead to inequities in access because not all children obtain pediatric preventive services. While inequities in access is important for newborn conditions like PKU and hypothyroidism for which early treatment is known to be effective, inequity in newborn research opportunity, particularly for nontherapeutic research opportunities, is not a compelling moral concern.

A second argument to support the delay is based on the increased vulnerability of newborns and the newborn–parent relationship.[67] The validity of this argument depends upon whether this vulnerability is significantly reduced by three months. The vulnerability is magnified by the fact that newborns in hospital nurseries are a captive population. As I argued in the previous chapter, research using captive populations should be limited to research that directly affects the captive population. In this case, the predictive diabetes research cannot be justified because there is no intervention that needs to be implemented early.

In the last chapter, I argued for institutional changes in the review of research involving captive populations like schoolchildren. I proposed that research protocols intended to be performed at schools should be reviewed at an institutional review board (IRB) meeting in which school officials are present and prepared to participate. Likewise, one could similarly propose that a professional advocate such as a doula or other health care professional knowledgeable about parents and newborns (e.g., health visitors in the UK) participate in the IRB review process. The doula or health visitor could also play a critical role in ensuring a robust consent process for research that is appropriately performed in this venue.

5. The Meaning of 'At Risk'

Another way to reduce risk in genetic susceptibility research is to design studies that do not require disclosure of individual results because non-disclosure eliminates the psychosocial harms of classifying an individual as 'at risk'. In such a study, one would request parental permission (1) to procure a blood sample of the infant; and (2) to track whether or not the infant develops diabetes by annual contact with local hospitals, pediatric endocrinologists, diabetes registries, or the families themselves. In Sweden, long-term studies have been done in this way.[68] Such a study design would minimize risk, an ethical requirement enumerated in the federal regulations (CFR §46.111(a)(1))

Critics might object to this study design requirement for two reasons. First, they may object on the grounds that parents will not consent to genetic testing of their newborns under these conditions because the empirical data show that individuals want genetic research results,[69] and that parents want genetic information about their children.[70] Still, whether the parents will consent is an empirical question for which there are no data. Second, critics might also object because a policy of non-disclosure in the general population means that follow-up autoantibody screening studies will be more expensive because the researchers cannot target those at high-risk. This concern is valid, and will require innovative study designs. At minimum, consent should not only be sought for procuring the initial blood sample, but also for permission to be recontacted to obtain follow-up data without disclosure of genetic results.

If one assumes that the research has scientific merit, and that it is unrealistic to assume that it can be done without identifying those individuals 'at risk', the question of the appropriate subject population remains. Given the demographics of the disease, it will require the participation of young children. The question is whether the young children should be recruited from the general population, or only from high-risk families (i.e., a family with an affected first-degree relative). The scientific advantage of screening the low-yield general population is that it will increase the number of infants identified. The advantage of selectively screening the high-risk community is that one will identify a larger proportion of individuals 'at risk' with a smaller sample. The major disadvantages of only recruiting from high-risk families are that the total number identified may be too small for some research and there is fear that this sample population may be biased. For example, most studies have concluded that islet cell antibodies (ICAs) are less predictive in the general population than in high-risk families [71] with the exception of Schatz *et al.* in the US.[72]

The difference between screening the general population versus testing the high-risk community should not be seen as a value-neutral design choice. While type 1 diabetes is a serious public health problem for which population screening of infants would be appropriate if and when preventive measures are developed, the questions remain regarding how and with which infants should the early stages of nontherapeutic research proceed, given the increased vulnerability of infants? Again, the answer becomes clearer if one uses the criteria that research must be designed to minimize risks, including psychosocial risks. There is some empirical evidence to support restricting the identification of risk to children in high-risk families. Children in these families are often viewed as 'at risk' even before genetic markers are discovered, and are often labeled as such by their families even if they do not undergo genetic testing.[73] The parents' behavior is not without merit: siblings have a fifteen-fold increased chance of developing type 1 diabetes than an individual from the general population. In addition, although the data are anecdotal, parents in families in which either a parent or child has diabetes frequently do monitor their other children for signs of glycosuria (spilling sugar in the urine) or hyperglycemia (high blood sugar).[74] The exact percentage of parents who test their children and how often they do so is unknown because this information is rarely shared with physicians.[75]. Given the baseline anxiety that already exists within these families, genetic and immunological testing do not induce the anxiety,[76] but rather either confirm or refute these concerns, albeit only probabilistically.

Even if one focuses on infants from high-risk families, the ethical requirement to minimize risk would support designing predictive studies that do not require disclosure of the results. Virtually all of the German and Australian BABYDIAB data could have been procured without disclosing results (except for thirteen children from whom the German researchers requested more frequent testing because they had more than one positive antibody.[77] While this additional information may have been valuable, it greatly increased the potential psychosocial harms of the research and could have been omitted.[78])

Finally, one must consider prediction research that is coupled with prevention. Clearly the children need to be identified in order to employ the prevention strategy. Both the concern of introducing the 'at risk' status into the healthy population and the high false positivity rate have led many ethicists to conclude that initial studies should be restricted to children from high-risk families, despite their therapeutic potential.[79] Appropriately, TRIGR was designed in this manner.[80]

6. *Parental Permission*

Given my arguments that newborn population screening for diabetes is unethical at this time, the issue of parental permission is moot. However, critics may argue that my ethical analysis must be wrong given that over 90% of parents permit their newborns' participation; or if not wrong, at least overly paternalistic.

The critics' argument is this: If the benefits do not clearly outweigh the risks, how do I explain that 94% of parents consent to screening for type 1 diabetes? In part, the high uptake can be explained by our culture's unequivocal support of testing generally.[81] The low frequency of positive results in the general population makes it attractive to individuals who seek reassurance.[82] The high uptake may also be explainable, in part, because of how the test is offered. Data show that uptake is highest when requested in person and when testing can be done immediately.[83] In the case of newborn screening for type 1 diabetes, the blood may have already been procured (DAISY) or will be procured for traditional newborn screening.

One solution, then, may be to require more active parental involvement. A voluntary newborn screening program for Duchenne Muscular Dystrophy (DMD), a progressive neuromuscular disorder for which no treatment exists, has been offered in Wales for the last decade and it also has a 94% uptake rate.[84] Clarke, one of the principal investigators, has suggested requiring parents to mail the blood spot for the DMD screening in order to yield a lower 'more appropriate' uptake rate. As Clarke explains: 'To suggest that a lower uptake rate for a screening test would be preferable, that we should set a threshold of motivation so that infants are not screened unless their parents actively choose it, is certainly unusual but is perfectly appropriate in the context of an untreatable disease.'[85] To this end, the researchers implemented a pilot project to determine the feasibility of providing newborn screening for DMD in a way that made the optional nature of the text explicit. The result was an uptake of 78%, significantly lower than the current methodology.[86]

The analogy is not perfect. DMD is uniformly fatal whereas type 1 diabetes is treatable, although currently there does not exist a treatment for either condition that can be provided presymptomatically that will prevent or delay the onset of the disease.[87] DMD is also virtually 100% penetrant (the likelihood of developing the disease if one has the gene) in contrast with the genetic markers for type 1 diabetes that only result in an increased susceptibility. This means that there are many newborns identified as being at increased risk for type 1 diabetes who will not develop the disease. There are many dangers with creating awareness and labeling individuals 'at risk' in a low-risk population:[88] leading to vulnerable child syndrome, inappropriately treating the child as 'ill' even before symptoms develop, or trying unproven and potentially dangerous preventive measures.[89] Because the genetic markers for type 1 diabetes only offer predispositional information and no preventive measures are available, one could make an argument, similar to Clarke's, that infants should not be screened unless the parents actively choose it: 94% uptake seems too high.

Even if the uptake is higher than it would be if (1) parents truly understood the risks and benefits of such research; or (2) active parental involvement were required, the critics' cry of paternalism must be addressed. Paternalism is 'the intentional overriding of one's person's known preferences or actions by another person, where the person who overrides justifies the action by the goal of benefiting or avoiding harm to the person whose will is overridden.'[90] But the situation at hand is not about interfering with an individual's decision about whether or not to participate in research, but whether to interfere with a parent's autonomy about whether or not to enroll *her child* in research. The issue, then, is not about whether or not to respect individual autonomy, but parental autonomy. Proxy decision-making can be more restrained than individual autonomy because individuals may take risks that they cannot authorize others to take.[91]

My argument to restrict proxy decision-makers seems to contradict my position that parental decisions should be respected unless the decisions are abusive or neglectful.[92] The fallacy with this objection is that it assumes no restrictions on parental autonomy. Parental autonomy is not absolute and others have responsibility to protect children.[93] Constraints on parental autonomy stem from both the developing autonomy of the child as well as community evaluation of the appropriate risks to which it is appropriate to expose children. In the realm of medical research, institutional review boards (IRBs) have an obligation to ensure that the research risks are minimized CFR §46.111(a)(1); and there are limits to the risks to which children can be exposed in nontherapeutic research (CFR §46.404 and CFR §46.406) without national review). It is only within the restricted boundaries of ethical research that parental autonomy ought to be respected. As such, it is morally justifiable to require either that risk status is not disclosed or that only children of high-risk families be eligible for participation.

7. Conclusion

Type 1 diabetes is a significant health problem in children, and accurate prediction in infancy will be necessary to prevent or delay its onset. However, prediction research in the newborn period has potentially serious psycho-social implications, particularly when it is being introduced into the unsuspecting general population, and research designs must account for them. To minimize harm to infants and their families I propose three recommendations that balance the need for research access with protection:

1. If the research is solely predictive, that is, it does not incorporate a prevention strategy, then the sample should be collected outside of the nursery because newborns are vulnerable, particularly newborns in the hospital nursery. By requiring a separate sample to be collected at a future time, parents can make a more informed and voluntary decision about the risks and benefits of their child's participation in nontherapeutic research.

2. If the research is solely predictive, then studies should be designed, when possible, to avoid disclosure of increased susceptibility results.

3. If disclosure is necessary, then the research should be restricted to children with an affected first-degree relative, and this would hold even for prediction–prevention protocols.

References

1. (Editorial) 'Infant Diabetes Test is Good Start', *St Petersburg Times* (8, January 2002), 8A, hereinafter cited as Editorial, 'Infant Diabetes'.
2. See, e.g., Flanders, G., Graves, P., and Rewers, M., 'Review: Prevention of Type 1 Diabetes from Laboratory to Public Health', *Autoimmunity,* 29 (1999), 235–46; and

Kimpimaki, T., Kupila, A., Hamalainen, A. M., Kukko, M., Kulmala, P., Savola, K., Simell, T., Keskinen, P., Ilonen, J., Simell, O., and Knip, M., 'The First Signs of B-Cell Autoimmunity Appear in Infancy in Genetically Susceptible Children from the General Population: The Finnish Type I Diabetes Prediction and Prevention Study', *Journal of Clinical Endocrinology and Metabolism*, 86 (2001), 4782–6.

3. 'Prevention of Type 1 Diabetes Mellitus', Conference Summary from American Diabetes Association. On the web at Diabetes Forum: http://www.diabetesforum. net/cgi-bin/display_engine.pl?category_id=15&content_id=230 hereinafter cited as Conference Summary.

4. Heine, R. J., 'Diabetes in the Next Century: Challenges and Opportunities', *Netherlands Journal of Medicine*, 55 (1999), 265–70.

5. See, e.g., Ziegler, A-G., Hummel, M., Schenker, M., and Bonifacio, E., 'Autoantibody Appearance and Risk for Development of Childhood Diabetes in Offspring of Parents with Type 1 Diabetes: The 2-year Analysis of the German BABYDIAB Study', *Diabetes*, 48 (1999), 460–8; Hummel, M., Fuchtenbusch, M., Schenker, M., and Ziegler, A-G., 'No Major Association of Breast-Feeding, Vaccinations, and Childhood Viral Diseases with Early Islet Autoimmunity in the German BABY-DIAB Study', *Diabetes Care*, 23 (2000), 969–74; Roll, U., Christie, M. R., Fuchtenbusch, M., Payton, M. A., Hawkes, C. J., Ziegler, A-G., 'Perinatal Autoimmunity in Offspring of Diabetic Parents: The German Multicenter BABY-DIAB Study: Detection of Humoral Immune Responses to Islet Antigens in Early Childhood', *Diabetes*, 45 (1996), 967–73; Colman, P. G., Steele, C., Couper, J. J., Beresford, S. J., Powell, T., Kewming, K., Pollard, A., Gellert, S., Tait, B., Honeyman, M., and Harrison, L. C., 'Islet Autoimmunity in Infants with a Type 1 Diabetic Relative is Common but is Frequently Restricted to One Autoantibody', *Diabetologia*, 43 (2000), 203–9; and Couper, J. J., 'Annotation: Environmental Triggers of Type 1 Diabetes', *Journal of Paediatrics and Child Health*, 37 (2001), 218–20.

6. See Roll *et al.*, 'Perinatal'; and Cooper, 'Environmental Triggers'.

7. Buzzetti, R., Quattrocchi, C. C., and Nistico, L., 'Dissecting the Genetics of Type 1 Diabetes: Relevance for Familial Clustering and Differences in Incidence', *Diabetes/Metabolism Review*, 14 (1998), 111–28.

8. See Flanders *et al.*, 'Prevention'; and Dahlquist, G. G., 'Primary and Secondary Prevention Strategies of Pre-Type 1 Diabetes: Potentials and Pitfalls', *Diabetes Care*, 22 (2S Supplement) (1999), 4B–6B.

9. See Kimpimaki *et al.*, 'First Signs'. The DIPP study is actually a prediction and prevention study. Infants who are identified by genotype are followed for autoantibody development. Older infants and children who consistently test positive for these autoantibodies are offered enrollment in a prevention trial that uses intranasal insulin. Because the prevention component does not begin until months to years of age, the prevention component is not discussed in this chapter, but rather, in the context of childhood prevention trials in Chapter 11. For the purpose of this chapter, DIPP functions as a newborn prediction study.

10. Ronningen, K. S., 'Genetics in the Prediction of Insulin-Dependent Diabetes Mellitus: From Theory to Practice', *Annals of Medicine*, 29 (1997) 387–92.

11. See Kimpimaki *et al.*, 'First Signs'.

12. See Flanders *et al.*, 'Prevention'.

13. Ibid.
14. See Editorial, 'Infant Diabetes'.
15. Greener, M., 'PANDA Identifies Babies At Risk of Developing Type 1 Diabetes', *Molecular Medicine Today,* 6 (2000), 3.
16. 'Conference Summary'.
17. Paronen, J., Knip, M., Savilahti, E., Virtanen, S. M., Ilonen, J., Akerblom, H. K., and Vaarala, O., 'Effect of Cow's Milk Exposure and Maternal Type 1 Diabetes on Cellular and Humoral Immunization to Dietary Insulin in Infants at Genetic Risk for Type 1 Diabetes', *Diabetes,* 49 (2000), 1657–65.
18. Karges, W., Hammond-McKibben, D., Cheung, R. K., Visconti, M., Shibuya, N., Kemp, D., and Dosch, H-M., 'Immunological Aspects of Nutritional Diabetes Prevention in NOD Mice: A Pilot Study for the Cow's Milk Based IDDM Prevent Trial', *Diabetes,* 46 (1997), 557–64.
19. See, e.g., Norris, J. M., Beaty, B., Klingensmith, G., Yu, L., Hoffman, M., Chase, H. P., Erlich, H. A., Hamman, R. F., Eisenbarth, G. S., and Rewers, M., 'Lack of Association Between Early Exposure to Cow's Milk Protein and Beta-Cell Autoimmunity: Diabetes Autoimmunity Study in the Young (DAISY)', *JAMA,* 276 (1996), 609–14; and Couper, J. J., Steele, C., Beresford, S. D., Powell, T., McCaul, K., Pollard, A., Gellert, S., Tait, B., Harrison, L. C., and Colman, P. G., 'Lack of Association between Duration of Breast Feeding or Introduction of Cow's Milk and Development of Islet Autoimmunity', *Diabetes,* 48 (1999), 2145–9.
20. See Paronen *et al.,* 'Effect of Cow's Milk'.
21. See, e.g., Institute of Medicine (IOM), *Assessing Genetic Risks: Implications for Health and Social Policy.* Washington DC: National Academy Press, 1994; Working Party of the Clinical Genetics Society (UK), 'The Genetic Testing of Children', *Journal of Medical Genetics,* 31 (1994), 785–97; American Society of Human Genetics (ASHG)/American College of Medical Genetics (ACMG), 'Points to Consider: Ethical, Legal, and Psychosocial Implications of Genetic Testing in Children and Adolescents', *American Journal of Human Genetics,* 57 (1995), 1233–41; and American Academy of Pediatrics (AAP), Committee on Bioethics, 'Ethical Issues with Genetic Testing in Pediatrics', *Pediatrics,* 107 (2001), 1451–5.
22. See IOM, *Assessing Genetic Risks*; Working Party, 'Genetic Testing'; ASHG/ACMG, 'Points to Consider'; AAP, 'Ethical Issues'; Kodish, E., 'Testing Children for Cancer Genes: The Rule of Earliest Onset', *Journal of Pediatrics,* 135 (1999), 390–5; Siegler, M., Amiel, S., and Lantos, J., 'Scientific and Ethical Consequences of Disease Prediction', *Diabetologia,* 35 (Suppl. 2) (1992), S60–S68; and Nordenfelt, L., 'Prevention and Ethics in Medicine: The Case of Diabetes Prevention', *Journal of Pediatric Endocrinology & Metabolism,* 9 (1996), 381–6.
23. See, e.g., IOM, *Assessing Genetic Risks*; ASHG/ACMG, 'Points to Consider'; and Michie, S., 'Predictive Genetic Testing in Children: Paternalism or Empiricism' in T. Marteau and M. Richards (eds.), *The Troubled Helix: Social and Psychological Implications of the New Genetics.* Cambridge: Cambridge University Press, 1996, 177–83.

24. See, e.g., Michie, 'Paternalism or Empiricism'; and Broadstock, M., Michie, S., and Marteau, T. M., 'The Psychological Consequences of Predictive Genetic Testing: A Systematic Review', *European Journal of Human Genetics,* 8 (2000), 731–8.
25. See Ronningen, 'Genetics'.
26. See, e.g., Yu, M. S., Norris, J. M., Mitchell, C. M., Butler-Simon, N., Groshek, M., Follansbee, D., Erlich, H., Rewers, M., and Klingensmith, G. J., 'Impact on Maternal Parenting Stress of Receipt of Genetic Information Regarding Risk of Diabetes in Newborn Infants', *American Journal of Medical Genetics,* 86 (1999), 219–26; and Hummel, M., Ziegler, A. G., and Roth, R., 'Psychological Impact of Childhood Islet Autoantibody Testing in Families Participating in the BABY-DIAB Study', *Diabetic Medicine,* 21 (2004), 324–8.
27. See, e.g., Johnson, S. B., Riley, W. J., Hansen, C. A., and Nurick, M. A., 'Psychological Impact of Islet Cell-Antibody Screening: Preliminary Results', *Diabetes Care,* 13 (1990), 93–7; Johnson, S. B., and Tercyak, K. P., 'Psychological Impact of Islet Cell-Antibody Screening for IDDM on Children, Adults and Their Family Members', *Diabetes Care,* 18 (1995), 1370–2; Carmichael, S. L., Johnson, S. B., Weiss, A., Fuller, K. G., She, J. X., and Schatz, D. A., 'Psychological Impact of Screening Programs in Mothers of Children At-Risk for Type 1 Diabetes', *Diabetes,* 49 (Suppl. 1) (2000), A317; Johnson, S. B., 'Screening Programs to Identify Children at risk for Diabetes Mellitus: Psychological Impact on Children and Parents', *Journal of Pediatric Endocrinology & Metabolism,* 14 (2001), 653–9; and Weber, B., and Roth, R., 'Psychological Aspects in Diabetes Prevention Trials', *Annals of Medicine,* 29 (1997), 461–7.
28. Ibid.
29. See, e.g., Carmichael *et al.*, 'Psychological Impact'; Johnson, 'Screening Programs'; and Weber and Roth, 'Psychological Aspects'.
30. See, e.g., Johnson, 'Screening Programs'; and Weber and Roth, 'Psychological Aspects'.
31. Thelin, T., McNeil, T. F., Aspegren-Jansson, E., and Sveger, T., 'Psychological Consequences of Neonatal Screening for Alpha-1-Antitrypsin Deficiency. Parental Reactions to the First News of Their Infants' Deficiency', *Acta Paediatrica Scandinavica,* 74 (1985), 787–93; and Heyerdahl, S., 'Psychological Problems in Relation to Neonatal Screening Programmes', *Acta Paediatrica Scandinavica,* 77 (1988), 239–41.
32. See Thelin *et al.*, 'Psychological Consequences: Parental Reactions'; Heyerdahl, 'Psychological Problems'; Thelin, T., McNeil, T. F., Aspegren-Jansson, E., and Sveger, T., 'Identifying Children At High Somatic Risk: Parents' Long-Term Emotional Adjustment to Their Children's Alpha-Antitrypsin Deficiency', *Acta Psychiatrica Scandinavica,* 72 (1985), 323–30; Thelin, T., McNeil, T. F., Aspegren-Jansson, E., and Sveger, T., 'Psychological Consequences of Neonatal Screening for Alpha-1-Antitrypsin Deficiency. Parental Attitudes Toward "ATD-Check-Ups" and Parental Recommendations Regarding Future Screening', *Acta Paediatrica Scandinavica,* 74 (1985), 841–7; McNeil, T. F., Thelin, T., Aspegren-Jansson, E., Sveger, T., and Harty, B., 'Psychological Factors in Cost-Benefit Analysis of Somatic Prevention. A Study of the Psychological Effects of

Neonatal Screening for Alpha 1-Antitrypsin Deficiency', *Acta Paediatrica Scandinavica*, 74 (1985), 427–32; Thelin,T., McNeil, T. F., Aspegren-Jansson, E., and Sveger, T., 'Identifying Children at High Somatic Risk: Possible Long-Term Effects on the Parents' View of Their Own Health and Current Life Situation', *Acta Psychiatrica Scandinavica*, 71 (1985), 644–53; McNeil, T. F., Thelin, T., Aspegren-Jansson, E., and Sveger, T., 'Identifying Children At High Somatic Risk: Possible Effects on the Parents' Views of the Child's Health and Parents' Relationship to the Pediatric Health Services', *Acta Psychiatrica Scandinavica*, 72 (1985), 491–7; and McNeil, T. F., Harty, B., Thelin, T., Aspegren-Jansson, E., and Sveger, T., 'Identifying Children At High Somatic Risk: Long-Term Effects on Mother-Child Interaction', *Acta Psychiatrica Scandinavica*, 74 (1986), 555–62.
33. See Thelin *et al.*, 'Psychological Consequences: Parental Reactions'.
34. Ibid.
35. McNeil *et al.*, 'Psychological Factors'.
36. See Thelin *et al.*, 'Psychological Consequences: Parental Reactions'.
37. See Thelin *et al.*, 'Identifying Children: Possible Long-term Effects'; McNeil *et al.*, 'Identifying Children: Long-Term Effects'; and Sveger, T., Thelin, T., and McNeil, T. F., 'Neonatal Alpha-1-Antitrypsin Screening: Parents' Views and Reactions 20 Years After the Identification of the Deficiency State', *Acta Paediatrica*, 88 (1999), 315–18.
38. See McNeil *et al.*, 'Identifying Children: Long-Term Effects'.
39. See McNeil *et al.*, 'Identifying Children: Possible Effects'.
40. Ibid.
41. Thelin *et al.*, 'Identifying Children: Parents' Long-Term Emotional'.
42. Sveger, T., Thelin, T., and McNeil, T. F., 'Young Adults with Alpha-1-Antitrypsin Deficiency Identified Neonatally: Their Health Knowledge About and Adaptation to the High-Risk Condition', *Acta Paediatrica*, 86 (1997), 37–40.
43. 'Memoranda: Alpha$_1$-Antitrypsin Deficiency: Memorandum from a WHO meeting', *Bulletin of the World Health Organization*, 75 (1997), 397–415.
44. Sveger, T., and Thelin, T., 'A Future for Neonatal Alpha-1-Antitrypsin Screening?' *Acta Paediatrica*, 89 (2000), 628–31.
45. O'Brien, M. L., Buist, N. R. M., and Murphey, W. H., 'Neonatal Screening for Alpha-1-Antitrypsin Deficiency', *Journal of Pediatrics*, 92 (1978), 1006–10.
46. Wall, M., Moe, E., Eisenberg, J., Powers, M., Buist, N., and Buist, A. S., 'Long-Term Follow-Up of a Cohort of Children with Alpha-1-Antitrypsin Deficiency', *Journal of Pediatrics*, 116 (1990), 248–51.
47. Sveger and Thelin, 'A Future'.
48. Wertz, D., 'Testing Children and Adolescents' in J. Burley, and J. Harris (eds.), *A Companion to Genethics*. Oxford: Blackwell Publishers, 2002, 92–113, 107.
49. See, e.g., Senior, V., Marteau, T. M., and Peters, T. J., 'Will Genetic Testing for Predisposition for Disease Result in Fatalism? A Qualitative Study of Parents Responses to Neonatal Screening for Familial Hypercholesterolaemia', *Social Science and Medicine*, 48 (1999), 1857–60; and Lefcourt, H. M., *Locus of Control: Current Trends in Theory and Research*, 2nd edn. New York: Halstead, 1982.

50. Michie, S., and Marteau, T. M., 'Predictive Genetic Testing in Children: The Need for Psychological Research' in A. J. Clarke (ed.), *The Genetic Testing of Children*. Oxford: Bios Scientific Publishers, 1998, 169–81.
51. See McNeil *et al.*, 'Identifying Children: Possible Effects'.
52. Croyle, R. T., and Lerman, C., 'Psychological Impact of Genetic Testing' in R. T. Croyle (ed.), *Psychosocial Effects of Screening for Disease Prevention and Detection*. New York: Oxford University Press, 1995, 11–38.
53. See McNeil *et al.*, 'Identifying Children: Long-Term Effects'; Headings, V. E., 'Counselling in a Hospital-Based Newborn Screening Service', *Patient Counselling & Health Education*, 2 (1980), 80–3; and Clayton, E. W., 'What Should Be the Role of Public Health in Newborn Screening and Prenatal Diagnosis?' *American Journal of Preventive Medicine*, 16 (1999), 111–15.
54. See Clayton, 'Role of Public Health'; and Fyro, K. 'Neonatal Screening: Life-Stress Scores in Families Given a False-Positive Result', *Acta Paediatrica Scandinavica*, 77 (1988), 232–8.
55. Tymstra, T., 'False Positive Results in Screening Test: Experience of Parents of Children Screened for Congenital Hypothyroidism', *Family Practice*, 3 (1986), 92–6.
56. Davison, C., Macintyre, S., and Smith, G. D., 'The Potential Social Impact of Predictive Genetic Testing for Susceptibility to Common Chronic Disease: A Review and Proposed Research Agenda', *Sociology of Health & Illness*, 16 (1994), 340–71.
57. Thelin *et al.*, 'Identifying Children: Parents' Long-Term Emotional'; Headings, 'Counselling'; and Clayton, 'Role of Public Health'.
58. Croyle and Lerman, 'Psychological Impact'; Clayton, 'Role of Public Health'; and Reilly, P. R., Boshar, M. F., and Holtzman, S. H., 'Ethical Issues in Genetic Research: Disclosure and Informed Consent', *Nature Genetics*, 5 (1997), 16–20.
59. Billings, P. R., Kohn, M. A., de Cuevas, M., Beckwith, J., Alper, J. S., and Natowicz, M. R., 'Discrimination as a Consequence of Genetic Testing', *American Journal of Human Genetics*, 50 (1992), 476–82; and Geller, L. N., Alper, J. S., Billings, P. R., Barash, C. I., Beckwith, J., and Natowicz, M. R., 'Individual, Family, and Societal Dimensions of Genetic Discrimination: A Case Study Analysis', *Science and Engineering Ethics*, 2 (1996), 71–88.
60. Office for Human Research Protections 'Institutional Review Board Guidebook', Chap. 5, Part H: Human Genetic Research. On the web at: http://www.hhs.gov/ohrp/irb/irb_chapter5ii.htm#h12.
61. Department of Health and Human Services (DHHS) (45 CFR Part 46, Subpart D), 'Protections for Children Involved as Subjects in Research', *Federal Register*, 48 (8 March 1983), 9814–20; revised *Federal Register*, 56 (18 June 1991), 28032, CFR § 45.404, hereinafter cited by its CFR number in the endnotes and in the text.
62. The requirement to minimize risk is found in the Common Rule, Department of Health and Human Services (DHHS). (45 CFR 46 Subpart A), 'Final Regulations Amending Basic HHS Policy for the Protection of Human Research Subjects', *Federal Register*, 46 (26 January 1981), 8366–91; revised *Federal Register*, 56 (18 June 1991), 28003–18, CFR §46.111, hereinafter cited by its CFR number

in endnotes and in the text. This requirement is enumerated by various reports on what is required for research to be ethical in general. See, e.g., National Commission for the Protection of Human Subjects of Biomedical and Behavioral Research, *Belmont Report: Ethical Principles and Guidelines for the Protection of Human Subjects of Research* (Washington DC: US Government Printing Office, 1979); Nuremberg Code, see Trials of War Criminals before the Nuremberg Military Tribunals under Control Council Law No. 10, vol. II. Washington DC: US Government Printing Office, 1948. On the web at: http:// www.ushmm.org/research/doctors/codeptx.htm; World Medical Association Declaration of Helsinki, 'Ethical Principles for Medical Research Involving Human Subjects', adopted by the 18th World Medical Association (WMA) General Assembly Helsinki, Finland, June 1964 and amended by the 29th WMA General Assembly, Tokyo, Japan, October 1975; 35th WMA General Assembly, Venice, Italy, October 1983; 41st WMA General Assembly, Hong Kong, September 1989; 48th WMA General Assembly, Somerset West, Republic of South Africa, October 1996; and the 52nd WMA General Assembly, Edinburgh, Scotland, October 2000; Note of Clarification on Paragraph 29 added by the WMA General Assembly, Washington 2002; and Note of Clarification on Paragraph 30 added by the WMA General Assembly, Tokyo 2004. On the web at: http://www.wma.net/e/policy/b3.htm; and Medical Research Council of Canada, Natural Science and Engineering Research Council of Canada, Social Science and Humanities Research Council of Canada. Tri-Council Policy Statement. Ethical Conduct for Research Involving Humans. August 1998 with 2000 and 2002 updates. On the web http://www.pre.ethics.gc.ca/english/pdf/TCPS./ .20 June 2003_E.pdf. The requirement to minimize risks is not found in Subpart D of the federal regulations, but is recommended in many reports on research with children. See, e.g., National Commission for the Protection of Human Subjects of Biomedical and Behavioral Research, *Report and Recommendations: Research Involving Children.* Washington DC: US Printing Office, 1977, DHEW Publication NO. (OS) 77–0004; and R. H. Nicholson (ed.)., *Medical Research with Children: Ethics, Law and Practice.* Oxford: Oxford University Press, 1986.

63. National Commission, *Research Involving Children*, 2 & 3.
64. See Conference Summary; Heine, 'Diabetes'; and EURODIAB ACE Study Group. 'Variation and Trends in Incidence of Childhood Diabetes in Europe', *Lancet*, 355 (2000), 873–6.
65. See EURODIAB ACE Study Group, 'Variations and Trends'; and Feltbower, R. G., McKinney, P. A., and Bodansky, H. J., 'Rising Incidence of Childhood Diabetes is Seen at All Ages and in Urban and Rural Settings in Yorkshire, United Kingdom', *Diabetologia*, 43 (2000), 682–4.
66. See Kimpimaki *et al.*, 'First Signs'.
67. See Headings, 'Counselling'; and Clayton, 'Role of Public Health'.
68. Samuelsson, U., Sundkvist, G., Borg, H., Fernlund, P., and Ludvigsson, J., 'Islet Autoantibodies in the Prediction of Diabetes in School Children', *Diabetes Research and Clinical Practice*, 51 (2001), 51–7.

69. See, e.g., Applebaum-Shapiro, S. E., Peters, J. A., O'Connell, J. A., Aston, C. E., and Whitcomb, D. C., 'Motivations and Concerns of Patients with Access to Genetic Testing for Hereditary Pancreatitis', *American Journal of Gastroenterology*, 96 (2001), 1610–7; Terry, S. F., and Terry, P. F., 'A Consumer Perspective on Informed Consent and Third-Party Issues', *Journal of Continuing Education in the Health Professions*, 21 (2001), 256–64; Merz, J. F., Magnus, D., Cho, M. K., and Caplan, A. L., 'Protecting Subjects' Interests in Genetics Research', *American Journal of Human Genetics*, 70 (2002), 965–71; Richards, M. P. M., Ponder, M., Pharoah, P., Everest, S., and Mackay, J., 'Issues of Consent and Feedback in a Genetic Epidemiological Study of Women with Breast Cancer', *Journal of Medical Ethics*, 29 (2003), 93–6; and Banks, T. M., 'Misusing Informed Consent: A Critique of Limitations on Research Subjects' Access to Genetic Research Results', *Saskatchewan Law Review*, 63 (2000), 539–80.

70. Malkin, D., Austalie, K., Shuman, C., Barrera, M., and Weksberg, R., 'Parental Attitudes to Genetic Counseling and Predictive Testing for Childhood Cancer', *American Journal of Human Genetics*, 59 (1996), A7; Patenaude, A. F., Basili, L., Fairclough, D. L., and Li, F. P., 'Attitudes of 47 Mothers of Pediatric Oncology Patients toward Genetic Testing for Cancer Predisposition', *Journal of Clinical Oncology*, 14 (1996), 415–21; Geller, G., Bernhardt, B. A., Doksum, T., Helzlsouer, K. J., Wilcox, P., and Holtzman, N. A., 'Decision-Making about Breast Cancer Susceptibility Testing: How Similar are the Attitudes of Physicians, Nurse Practitioners, and At-Risk Women', *Journal of Clinical Oncology*, 16 (1998), 2868–76; Berkendorf, J. L., Teutenauer, J. E., Hughes, C. A., Eads, N., Willison, J., Powers, M., and Lerman, C., 'Patients' Attitudes about Autonomy and Confidentiality in Genetic Testing for Breast-Ovarian Cancer Susceptibility', *American Journal of Medical Genetics*, 73 (1997), 296–303; and Campbell, E. and Ross, L. F., 'Health Care Professional and Parental Attitudes Regarding Genetic Testing for Violent Traits in Childhood', *Journal of Medical Ethics*, 30 (2004), 580–6.

71. See, e.g., Veijola, R., Reijonen, H., Vahasalo, P., Sabbah, E., Kulmala, P., Ilonen, J., Akerblom, H. K., and Knip, M., 'HLA-DQB1-Defined Genetic Susceptibility, Beta Cell Autoimmunity, and Metabolic Characteristics in Familial and Non-familial Insulin-Dependent Diabetes Mellitus', *Journal of Clinical Investigation*, 98 (1996), 2489–95; Bingley, P. J., Bonifacio, E., Shattock, M., Gillmor, H. A., Sawtell, P. A., Dunger, D. B., Scott, R. D., Bottazzo, G. F., and Gale, E. A., 'Can Islet Cell Antibodies Predict IDDM in the General Population?' *Diabetes Care* 16 (1993), 45–50; and Landin-Olsson, M., Palmer, J. P., Lernmark, A., Blom, L., Sundkvist, G., Nystrom, L., and Dahlquist, G., 'Predictive Value of Islet Cell and Insulin Autoantibodies for Type 1 (Insulin-Dependent) Diabetes Mellitus in a Population-Based Study of Newly-Diagnosed Diabetic and Matched Control Children', *Diabetologia*, 35 (1992), 1068–73.

72. Schatz, D., Krischer, J., Horne, G., Riley, W., Spillar, R., Silverstein, J., Winter, W., Muir, A., Derovanesian, D., Shah, S., Malone, J., and Maclaren, N., 'Islet Cell Antibodies Predict Insulin-dependent Diabetes in United States School Age Children as Powerfully as in Unaffected Relatives', *Journal of Clinical Investigation*, 93 (1994), 2403–7.

73. See, e.g., Marteau, T. M., 'Psychology and Screening, Narrowing the Gap Between Efficacy and Effectiveness', *British Journal of Clinical Psychology*, 1994; 33: 1–10; and Wagner, A., Tibben, A., Bruining, G. J., Aanstoot, H. J., Tiems, I., Blondeau, M. J. C. E., and Niermeijer, M. F., 'Preliminary Experience with Predictive Testing for Insulin-Dependent Diabetes Mellitus', *Lancet*, 346 (1995), 380–1.

74. See, e.g., Wagner *et al.*, 'Preliminary'; Lucidarme, N., Donmingues-Muriel, E., Castro, D., Czernichow, P., and Levy-Marchal, C., 'Appraisal and Implications of Predictive Testing for Insulin-Dependent Diabetes Mellitus', *Diabetes & Metabolism*, 23 (1998), 550–3; and Shepherd, M., Hattersley, A. T., and Sparkes, A. C., 'Predictive Genetic Testing in Diabetes: A Case Study of Multiple Perspectives', *Qualitative Health Research*, 10 (2000), 242–59.

75. See, e.g., Lucidarme *et al.*, 'Appraisal'.

76. See e.g., Ziegler *et al.*, 'Autoantibody Appearance'; Nordenfelt, 'Prevention and Ethics'; Hummel *et al.*, 'Psychological Impact'; and Lucidarme *et al.*, 'Appraisal'

77. See Roll *et al.*, 'Perinatal'.

78. The researchers of the BABYDIAB study disagree. They found that most parents in high-risk families want to know the autoantibody status and genetic risks of their children. See Hummel *et al.*, 'Psychological Impact'. They state that their data found that disclosure of autoantibody status reduced anxiety in the family, although not surprisingly anxiety was greater in those whose children were autoantibody-positive compared to those who were antibody-negative (ibid.). The researchers acknowledge some limitations to their study. They sampled parental anxiety when the children were 5 years of age. Therefore their data do not address the level of anxiety that these parents may experience during their children's infancy, which is a more vulnerable period than later in childhood. Nevertheless, even if the BABYDIAB data regarding reduced anxiety is validated throughout childhood, the data can only be generalized to children who are members of high-risk families (at least one parent with type 1 diabetes), and not to the general public.

79. See, e.g., Siegler *et al.*, 'Scientific and Ethical'; Nordenfelt, 'Prevention and Ethics'; and Roth, R., 'Psychological and Ethical Aspects of Prevention Trials', *Journal of Pediatric Endocrinology and Metabolism*, 14 (2001), 669–74.

80. Disturbingly, DIPP is seeking to enroll children from the general population. This is discussed further in the next chapter.

81. See Wertz, 'Testing Children'; and Nelkin, D., and Tancredi, L., *Dangerous Diagnostics: The Social Power of Biological Information*. New York: Basic Books, 1989.

82. See, e.g., Andrykowski, M. A., Lightner, R., Studts, J. L., and Munn, R. K., 'Hereditary Cancer Risk Notification and Testing: How Interested is the General Population?' *Journal of Clinical Oncology*, 15 (1997), 2139–48; and Marteau, T. M., and Croyle, R. T., 'The New Genetics: Psychological Responses to Genetic Testing', *BMJ*, 316 (1998), 693–6.

83. See Marteau and Croyle, 'The New Genetics'.

84. Clarke, A. J., 'Newborn Screening' in P. S. Harper and A. J. Clarke, *Genetics, Society and Clinical Practice*. Oxford: Bios Scientific Publishers. 1997, 107–17.

85. Ibid., 115.

86. Parsons, E. P., Clarke, A. J., Hood, K., and Bradley, D. M., 'Feasibility of a Change in Service Delivery: The Case of Optional Newborn Screening for Duchenne Muscular Dystrophy', *Community Genetics*, 3 (2000), 17–23.

87. Escolar, D. M., and Scacheri, C. G., 'Pharmacologic and Genetic Therapy for Childhood Muscular Dystrophies', *Current Neurology & Neuroscience Reports*, 1 (2001), 168–74; and Diabetes Prevention Trial—Type 1 Diabetes Study Group, 'Effects of Insulin in Relatives of Patients with Type 1 Diabetes Mellitus', *New England Journal of Medicine*, 346 (2002), 1685–91.

88. See Clarke, 'Newborn Screening'; and Davison *et al.*, 'Potential Social Impact'.

89. Johnson and Tercyak, 'Psychological Impact'; Davison *et al.*, 'Potential Social Impact'; Burris, S., and Gostin, L. O., 'Genetic Screening from a Public Health Perspective: Three "Ethical" Principles' in J. Burley, and J. Harris (eds.), *A Companion to Genethics*. Oxford: Blackwell Publishers, 2002, 455–64; and Clarke, A. J., 'The Genetic Dissection of Multifactorial Disease: The Implications of Susceptibility Screening', in P. S. Harper and A. J. Clarke, *Genetics, Society and Clinical Practice*. Oxford: Bios Scientific Publishers. 1997, 93–106.

90. Beauchamp, T. L., and Childress, J. F., *Principles of Biomedical Ethics, 4th edn.* New York: Oxford University Press, 1994, 274.

91. Buchanan, A. E., and Brock, D. W., *Deciding for Others: The Ethics of Surrogate Decision Making*. New York: Cambridge University Press, 1989; and Ross, L. F., *Children, Families, and Health Care Decision-Making*. Oxford: Clarendon Press, 1998.

92. Ross, *Children*. I thank Ellen Wright Clayton, MD, JD. for asking me to address this.

93. Ross, *Children*.

11

Diabetes Prediction and Prevention Research in Childhood

1. Introduction

As mentioned in the previous chapter, type 1 diabetes is the most common metabolic disease of childhood and its incidence is increasing worldwide.[1] Approximately two-thirds of individuals who develop diabetes will do so before the age of 20,[2] and children under age 4 are the fastest-growing population of individuals diagnosed with type 1 diabetes in many countries.[3] Hence, prediction and prevention research will need to focus on children. In this chapter, I provide an overview of recent diabetes prediction and prediction/prevention studies beyond the newborn period. I examine whether these studies are permissible under current federal regulations, and whether the modifications I propose improve human subject protections. In the process, I further clarify whether and when children 'at risk' for 'a disorder or condition' should qualify for having 'a disorder or condition'.[4]

2. Epidemiology

There are two distinct populations at risk for developing type 1 diabetes. One population includes first-degree relatives of an individual with type 1 diabetes who have a tenfold greater risk than the general population (members of high-risk families).[5] However, these cases only account for 10% of individuals who will develop type 1 diabetes. The second population, then, includes the 90% of all new cases that present sporadically in the general population.[6]

In both the high-risk and general populations, genetic screening alone is a poor predictor. It is also a poor predictor in high-incidence countries.[7] Immune markers have better specificity as they signify on-going disease process. At clinical onset, 80–90% of newly diagnosed patients are positive for one or more beta-cell autoantibody.[8] However, it appears unlikely that any single marker will have sufficient sensitivity and specificity to be used in isolation for effective disease prediction.

A third tool for identifying children presymptomatic for type 1 diabetes is a metabolic test of the first-phase insulin response (FPIR) in response to an intravenous glucose tolerance test (IVGTT). In combination with genetic and immune markers it can help to classify the risk most accurately,[9] but it is a sign of significant beta cell destruction or a late pre-clinical stage. It is also the most invasive requiring the insertion of an intravenous line and several venipunctures.

3.   *Prediction and Prediction and Prevention Studies in Children*

Many prediction studies focus on individuals from high-risk families (e.g. BABY-DIAB in Germany and Australia[10] and DiMe in Finland[11]). The BABY-DIAB are prospective studies from birth of evolving autoantibody status among children with at least one parent with diabetes mellitus; DiMe involves the recruitment of families with a child with new-onset diabetes younger than 15 years to study the genetic, immunological, and environmental factors that contribute to the development of type 1 diabetes. A concern with these studies, however, is whether they are generalizable to the general population. For example, most studies have concluded that islet cell antibodies (ICAs), an immune marker, are less predictive in the general population than in high-risk families.[12] Another set of prediction studies seeks to obtain blood from children in the general population prospectively from birth to see if a combination of genetic and immune markers can be more useful for predicting who will develop type 1 diabetes (e.g. NOBADIA, DAISY, AND PANDA).[13]

To date, most of the prediction/prevention trials have enrolled only children from high-risk families.[14] The interventions have been tested successfully in animal studies prior to the clinical trials in humans.[15] They include TRIGR, an examination of whether the avoidance of cow's milk in early childhood reduces the risk of developing type 1 diabetes in infants before any signs of the disease have manifested;[16] DPT-1, a randomized control trial of high-risk individuals assigned to close observation or twice-daily insulin injections to see if diabetes could be prevented or delayed in subjects with pre-clinical autoimmune changes;[17] and studies (e.g., DENIS, ENDIT)[18] involving high-dose nicotinamide (a B-vitamin anti-oxidant) because preliminary data found that it can retard the development of type 1 diabetes.[19]

The Diabetes Prediction and Prevention (DIPP) study in Finland is the only prediction/prevention study designed to enroll individuals in the general population.[20] DIPP is a secondary prediction/prevention trial that seeks to identify children with high-risk genetic markers at birth. These children are followed for the development of autoantibodies. Those who test positive to autoantibodies repeatedly over a period of time are eligible to participate in an intranasal insulin prevention program.[21] This intervention has been shown to be effective in suppressing the development of diabetes in non-obese diabetic (NOD) mice.[22] Intranasal insulin is not used in persons with diabetes due to problems in bioavailability and problems with nasal irritation and other side-effects.[23] A study to determine its safety in healthy volunteers was first undertaken in 1997, after the first children-subjects were already being randomized into the prevention component of the DIPP study.[24]

In summary, there are many studies, nationally and internationally, seeking to identify children who will develop type 1 diabetes. Some of these studies involve children from high-risk families; others involve children from the general population. Some involve a prevention strategy. Do all of these studies conform to research ethics standards?

4. Analyzing Prediction and Prevention Research under the Current Federal Regulations

As discussed in the previous chapter, research on the genetic predisposition to type 1 diabetes entails minimal physical risk but potentially more significant psychosocial risks. The federal regulations regarding the protection of human subjects do not specifically address the ethical aspects of prediction and prevention research, nor whether the phrase a 'disorder or condition' was meant to include children 'at risk' for a 'disorder or condition'. And yet, much important research being done in diabetes focuses on prediction and prevention of children at increased risk. As such, it is necessary to examine how such research should be classified in order to determine what research methodologies are ethically justifiable and whether they are permissible under the current federal regulations.

5. Minimal Risk Research in Children (45 CFR §46.404)

Can diabetes prediction research beyond the newborn period be classified as minimal risk research?[25] In most of the studies involving children, both those enrolling children from high-risk families (i.e., families with an affected first-degree relative) and those enrolling children from the general population, the researchers initially collected a single blood sample. If the researchers were only collecting prevalence data and were not disclosing the results to the family, many IRBs would classify a single venipuncture as minimal risk. However, all of the studies described above disclose the results in order to facilitate follow-up of those found to be 'at risk' (usually based on the presence of ICA although sometimes based on a high-risk genotype).

Follow-up was usually serial venipuncture, although sometimes it included an IVGTT.

Although there is wide variability on what minimal risk entails,[26] many institutional review boards [IRBs] would classify these procedures as involving minimal risk. But one must also factor in the psychosocial risks and benefits of testing children. Most children in the general population will test negative which can be viewed as a psychosocial benefit (reassurance), but in reality, there is little upside to this information. Without screening, most parents in the general population will not be worrying about whether their child will develop type 1 diabetes. Rather, it is the testing that induces the iatrogenic worry that the negative test dissipates. It is hard to call this a benefit. If the child tests positive and follow-up is offered, awareness of risk is introduced.[27] This can benefit the child in that early detection may avoid diabetic ketoacidosis (an extreme metabolic derangement due to large amounts of sugar in the blood that can result in death), and yet the child is now labeled as 'at risk' when, depending on the study, many if not most of the children will never develop the metabolic disorder. The result is that some of these children will spend a lifetime as 'at risk'.[28] When the subjects are children, this label may (1) have an adverse impact on parent–child relationships[29] and other intrafamilial relationships;[30] (2) lead parents to label their child as ill when he/she is merely at risk;[31] or (3) lead the parents to launch their child 'on an unbalanced, unproven or even frankly harmful programme of diet or exercise, resulting in paradoxical long-term physical and emotional harm to the child'.[32] Predictive diabetic research that reports the results of either genetic or antibody markers back to families entails more than minimal risk in the general population.

The psychosocial risks and benefits of screening newborns and children in high-risk families are different than these risks and benefits in the general population. As mentioned in the previous chapter, many of these children are considered to be at risk by their parents and they are monitored for signs of glycosuria (spilling sugar in the urine, a sign of clinical disease) or hyperglycemia (elevated blood sugar).[33] The exact percentage is unknown because physicians are often told about the monitoring only if the child develops diabetes.[34] Given the baseline anxiety that already exists within these families, the genetic and immunological testing do not induce the anxiety,[35] but rather, either confirm or refute these concerns. Unfortunately, the confirmation is only probabilistic and continues to leave the family in limbo. Because the results do not provide certainty, they often do not quell the anxiety.[36] As such, the reporting back of the results to these high-risk families involves more than minimal risk.

6.   *A Minor Increase over Minimal Risk (45 CFR. §46.406)*

If the diabetes prediction research entails more than minimal risk, the research can still be permitted under current federal regulations if the research entails only a minor increase over minimal risk and involves children who have a 'disorder or condition'. Do children being recruited for prediction studies have a 'disorder or condition'? Clearly they do not have type 1 diabetes as the goal is to identify those who are at risk for developing type 1 diabetes. Should 'at risk' children be included in the concept of children with a 'disorder or condition'?

In type 1 diabetes, the 'at risk' label can refer to two different populations: (1) individuals with a first-degree relative with type 1 diabetes; and (2) individuals who have certain genetic alleles or positive autoantibodies. Although most of the children classified as 'at risk' in both populations will not go on to develop diabetes, I believe that there are significant differences between the two populations. Children from high-risk families are appropriately labeled as having a 'disorder or condition' based on their at-risk status because their families frequently view them as high risk even if testing is not available. Testing these children for genetic or immune markers does not introduce risk but only confirms or refutes their presumed increased risk. In contrast, children in the general population with positive immune markers are only labeled as at risk after performing the research that identifies them. But the identification itself entails more than minimal risk and therefore cannot be done on healthy children under current federal regulations when the identification is not coupled with a therapeutic intervention.[37] What defines whether a child at increased risk for diabetes should be classified as 'at risk' for a 'disorder or condition' is not the child's actuarial risk, but their family's high-risk status. For the purpose of participation in research classified as CFR §46.406, only those children who are defined as high risk by virtue of their family history should be included in the umbrella of having a 'disorder or condition'.

There is some empirical evidence to justify distinguishing between those who do and those do not come from a high-risk family. Marteau has found that the receipt of positive test results has been associated with more negative effects than anticipated in population-based screening and less negative effects than anticipated in high-risk screening programs.[38] This can be explained in that the two groups have different expectations and motivations for testing, and different amounts of pre-test knowledge and information.[39]

In summary, then, predictive genetic testing for diabetes in which the results are reported back to the families entails a minor increase over minimal risk and should be restricted to those at risk children who are defined as having a disorder or condition because their risk status derives from their membership in high-risk families.

7.   *Research not Otherwise Approvable (45 CFR §46.407)*

The National Commission realized that the criteria based on risk and risk/
benefit for evaluating research on children were restrictive. It proposed
convening a national panel to review nontherapeutic research not approvable under CFR §46.404 or CFR §46.406. Given the increasing incidence of
type 1 diabetes in children, particularly in children younger than 5 years,
should a national committee approve research that identifies children with
diabetes markers in the general population and discloses this information to
their families?

A national committee should only approve diabetes population screening
and disclosure if it were convinced that the research was sound and important, minimized risks, and could not be done otherwise (CFR §46.407).
Although the research does address a major health epidemic in children, a
study in Sweden shows that such research can be done otherwise, that is, that
the research can be done without disclosure. In 1987, Swedish researchers
sought to recruit 1,185 schoolchildren to provide a blood sample to be
evaluated for ICA. Eighty-seven percent of children and parents consented.[40] But unlike the other population studies previously described,
the researchers did not contact children found to have positive autoantibodies. Rather, in 1994 and 1997, the clinical development of diabetes was
assessed by personal contact with the five pediatric clinics within the study
area, other health care units, and the Diabetes Incidence Study in Sweden
(DISS) registry. It found that ICA together with GADA (another autoantibody) are closely associated with the development of type 1 diabetes in the
general population.[41] Thus the study was able to show that autoantibodies
show high sensitivity in the general population without disclosing risk status
to the families. As such, the study only involved one venipuncture and is most
appropriately classified as minimal-risk research.

Was the non-disclosure ethical? If so, then a national commission is
unnecessary and population data can be obtained by minimal-risk research.
I would argue that non-disclosure was not only ethical but ethically mandatory for general population research in children when preventive therapies
have not been established. As discussed in Chapter 10, non-disclosure minimizes risk. Of course, families must be informed that they will not be given
risk information at the time of recruitment. Whether parents and children in
the US will consent under these conditions is unknown.

8.   *Prospect of Direct Benefit (45 CFR §46.405)*

Finally, diabetes prediction studies can be combined with a prevention trial
and be approved under CFR §46.405. To date, all the prediction/prevention

trials except those using intranasal insulin have enrolled only individuals from high-risk families. There are both pragmatic and ethical reasons for this. Practically, individuals from high-risk families are at greater risk of developing type 1 diabetes and so a smaller sample needs to be screened and enrolled.[42] The study design also minimizes the risks to subjects by avoiding the need to identify and inform unsuspecting parents that a child has an increased susceptibility to develop diabetes. Unfortunately, to date all of these prevention studies have been unsuccessful in human subjects.

The DIPP study in Finland identifies children at birth with high-risk genetic alleles. I do not support identifying these children at birth because the intervention is months to years later. As I argued in Chapter 10, newborns are a vulnerable population, and prediction of susceptibility should be done later in childhood unless an immediate intervention is planned. I also question whether a secondary prevention trial should enroll children with high-risk alleles from the general population rather than restrict enrollment to children with high-risk genetoypes from high-risk families. Restricting subjects to high-risk families beyond infancy is feasible as was shown by the success in recruitment in the DPT-1 trials which screened a large number of first-and second-degree relatives of persons with diabetes.[43] Even if enrollment in the general populations can be justified, the requirement to minimize risk would move genetic identification beyond the newborn period and recruitment of children may be difficult. The DIPP study is also problematic in that it began to randomize children into the nasal insulin prevention trial before a phase I trial to determine the safety of intranasal insulin in healthy subjects had been completed.[44]

9. A Re-Examination of Predictive and Preventive Diabetes Research in Children

In Chapter 10, I argued that prediction research should enroll children beyond the newborn nursery unless an immediate intervention treatment is proposed. Thus TRIGR can justify identifying newborns, but DIPP cannot. Although a number of prediction diabetes studies to date and in-progress enroll older infants and children, I have shown that very few can be morally justified using their current study designs. Given the psychosocial risks, prediction diabetes research studies in children should be designed not to require the disclosure of susceptibility results. If the susceptibility results are not disclosed, then the studies can be approved as minimal-risk research (CFR §46.404) and can be performed in both high-risk families and the general population. All predictive research in which parents are informed of their child's risk status for diabetes entails at least a minor increase over minimal risk, and can only be justified in children with a disorder or condition. I have argued that children who are members of high-risk families should be classified as having a 'disorder or condition', but children from the general population should not, even if they are discovered to have high-risk alleles.

The IOM committee rejected a very broad definition of 'disorder or condition' because it would make the distinction between research approvable under CFR §46.404 and CFR §46.406 meaningless.[45] In contrast, I argued in Chapter 4 that the amount of risk to which it is appropriate to expose children should be the same, regardless of whether the child has a disorder or condition. If my arguments are correct, then the arguments in this chapter about which at-risk children should be classified as having 'a disorder or condition' may seem unnecessary. It might seem that both children in the general population and children from high-risk families should be eligible for type 1 diabetes nontherapeutic research that exposes them to no more than a minor increase over minimal risk.[46]

This is a misunderstanding of my position. Even if the two guidelines (CFR §46.404 and CFR §46.406) are combined, the question of whether one has a disorder or condition may still be relevant for selecting the appropriate subject population. Population screening for genetic susceptibility in the low-risk pediatric population exposes these children and their families to potentially significant psychological distress of being labeled as at risk without much potential for benefit (reassurance of low risk). However, in families with a positive history, reassurance of low (or lower) risk may be beneficial or at least not harmful.[47]

I am not arguing that it is permissible to expose children from high-risk families to greater risks than their peers from low-risk families. Having a disorder or condition, or being at risk for a disorder or condition, should not change the level of risk to which it is appropriate to be exposed. I am arguing, however, that having a disorder or condition may change the appropriate subject population selection. Although the physical risks are the same, the psychosocial risks of participation in prediction diabetes research are generally lower for children from high-risk families than for children in the general population. However, even within the population of children from high-risk families, not all children should be treated as equally appropriate research subject candidates. As I argued in Chapter 10, newborns are at greater risk than older infants such that prediction research without a prevention strategy should only be done on older infants.

Prediction research coupled with primary or secondary prevention strategies should also begin in the high-risk community because that minimizes overall risks. Such research should extend into the general population only if the therapy is shown to be both safe and effective.

References

1. Heine, R. J., 'Diabetes in the Next Century: Challenges and Opportunities', *Netherlands Journal of Medicine*, 55 (1999), 265–70.
2. Siegler, M., Amiel, S., and Lantos, J., 'Scientific and Ethical Consequences of Disease Prediction', *Diabetologia*, 35 (Suppl. 2) (1992): S60–S68.
3. See EURODIAB ACE Study Group, 'Variation and Trends in Incidence of Childhood Diabetes in Europe', *Lancet*, 355 (2000): 873–6.
4. Department of Health and Human Services (DHHS) (45 CFR Part 46, Subpart D), 'Protections for Children Involved as Subjects in Research', *Federal Register*, 48 (8 March 1983), 9814–20; revised *Federal Register*, 56 (18 June 1991), 28032. The concern whether subjects have 'a disorder or condition' is specific to Subpart D of the federal regulations; hereinafter Subpart D will be cited in the text by CFR.
5. Buzzetti, R., Quattrocchi, C. C., and Nistico, L., 'Dissecting the Genetics of Type 1 Diabetes: Relevance for Familial Clustering and Differences in Incidence', *Diabetes/Metabolism Review*, 14 (1998), 111–28.
6. Dahlquist, G. G., 'Primary and Secondary Prevention Strategies of Pre-Type 1 Diabetes: Potentials and Pitfalls', *Diabetes Care*, 22 (2S Suppl.) (1999): 4B–6B.
7. Dahlquist, G., 'Potentials and Pitfalls in Neonatal Screening for Type 1 Diabetes', *Acta Paediatrica Supplement*, 432 (1999), 80–2.
8. Ibid.
9. Ibid.
10. For the German BABYDIAB studies, see, e.g., Ziegler, A-G., Hummel, M., Schenker, M., and Bonifacio, E., 'Autoantibody Appearance and Risk for Development of Childhood Diabetes in Offspring of Parents with Type 1 Diabetes: The 2-Year Analysis of the German BABYDIAB Study', *Diabetes*, 48 (1999), 460–8; Hummel, M., Fuchtenbusch, M., Schenker, M., and Ziegler, A-G., 'No Major Association of Breast-Feeding, Vaccinations, and Childhood Viral Diseases with Early Islet Autoimmunity in the German BABYDIAB Study', *Diabetes Care*, 23 (2000), 969–74.

    For the Australian BABYDIAB studies, see, e.g., Colman, P. G., Steele, C., Couper, J. J., Beresford, S. J., Powell, T., Kewming, K., Pollard, A., Gellert, S., Tait, B., Honeyman, M., and Harrison, L. C., 'Islet Autoimmunity in Infants with a Type 1 Diabetic Relative is Common but is Frequently Restricted to One Autoantibody', *Diabetologia*, 43 (2000), 203–9; and Couper, J. J., 'Annotation: Environmental Triggers of Type 1 Diabetes', *Journal of Paediatric and Child Health*, 37 (2001), 218–20.
11. For the Childhood Diabetes in Finland (DiMe) studies, see e.g., Tuomilehto, J., Lounamaa, R., Tuomilehto-Wolf, E., Reunanen, A., Virtala, E., Kaprio, E. A., and Akerblom, H. K., 'Epidemiology of Childhood Diabetes Mellitus in Finland—Background of a Nationwide Study of Type 1 (Insulin-Dependent) Diabetes Mellitus', *Diabetologia*, 35 (1992), 70–6; Kimpimaki, T., Kulmala, P., Savola, K., Vahasalo, P., Reijonen, H., Ilonen, J., Akerblom, H. K., and Knip, M., 'Disease-Associated Autoantibodies as Surrogate Markers of Type 1

Diabetes in Young Children at Increased Genetic Risk', *Journal of Clinical Endocrinology and Metabolism,* 85 (2000), 1126–32; and Veijola, R., Reijonen, H., Vahasalo, P., Sabbah, E., Kulmala, P., Ilonen, J., Akerblom, H. K., and Knip, M., 'HLA-DQB1-Defined Genetic Susceptibility, Beta Cell Autoimmunity, and Metabolic Characteristics in Familial and Nonfamilial Insulin-Dependent Diabetes Mellitus', *Journal of Clinical Investigation,* 98 (1996), 2489–95.

12. See Veijola *et al.,* 'HLA-DQB1-Defined'; Bingley, P. J., Bonifacio, E. Shattock, M., Gillmor, H. A., Sawtell, P. A., Dunger, D. B., Scott, R. D. M., Bottazzo, G. F., and Gale, E. A., 'Can Islet Cell Antibodies Predict IDDM in the General Population?' *Diabetes Care,* 16 (1993), 45–50; and Landin-Olsson, M., Palmer, J. P., Lernmark, A., Blom, L., Sundkvist, G., Nystrom, L., and Dahlquist, G., 'Predictive Value of Islet Cell and Insulin Autoantibodies for Type 1 (Insulin-Dependent) Diabetes Mellitus in a Population-Based Study of Newly-Diagnosed Diabetic and Matched Control Children', *Diabetologia,* 35 (1992), 1068–73.

    However, Schatz *et al.* in the US found ICA equally predictive in high-risk families and the general population. See Schatz, D., Krischer, J., Horne, G., Riley, W., Spillar, R., Silverstein, J., Winter, W., Muir, A., Derovanesian, D., Shah, S., Malone, J., and Maclaren, N., 'Islet Cell Antibodies Predict Insulin-Dependent Diabetes in United States School Age Children as Powerfully as in Unaffected Relatives', *Journal of Clinical Investigation,* 93 (1994), 2403–7.

13. The Norwegian Babies Against Diabetes (NOBADIA) study also seeks to identify at birth the infants in the general population with the highest genetic risk for developing type 1 diabetes. An allele found in 4% of the population accounts for 46% of future cases giving these infants a lifetime risk of 12% for developing type 1 diabetes. See, e.g., Ronningen, K. S., 'Genetics in the Prediction of Insulin-Dependent Diabetes Mellitus: From Theory to Practice', *Annals of Medicine,* 29 (1997), 387–92.

    In the US, two such studies are on-going. In Colorado, the Diabetes Autoimmunity Study in the Young (DAISY) began in February 1994. Infants with the highest genetic risk alleles (2.3%) are offered antibody screening at 9 months, 15 months, and yearly from age 2. See Rewers, M., Bugawan, T. L., Norris, J. M., Blair, A., Beaty, B., Hoffman, M., McDuffie, Jr., R. S., Hamman, R. F., Klingensmith, G., Eisenbarth, G. S., and Erlich, H. A., 'Newborn Screening for HLA Markers Associated with IDDM: Diabetes Autoimmunity Study in the Young (DAISY)', *Diabetologia,* 39 (1996), 807–12. A study of the general population is also on-going in Florida. The Prospective Assessment in Newborns for Diabetic Autoimmunity (PANDA) tracks genetically high-risk babies to discover the impact of possible environmental triggers such as breast feeding, immunizations, and viral infections. See Greener, M. 'PANDA Identifies Babies at Risk of Developing Type 1 Diabetes', *Molecular Medicine Today,* 6 (2000), 3.

14. Prevention studies can be divided into primary, secondary, and tertiary prevention strategies. Primary diabetes prevention is the attempt to prevent disease development before the self-perpetuating autoimmune destruction of the beta cells has begun by identifying those with a genetic predisposition and successfully avoiding environmental triggers. Secondary diabetes prevention involves inter-

vention after autoimmune destruction has begun (as identified by the appearance of circulating autoantibodies) but is still subclinical. The goal is to prevent, arrest, or delay further beta cell destruction. Tertiary diabetes prevention involves intervention after clinical disease has manifested by attempting to preserve or restore beta cell mass, and will not be considered in this chapter.

15. See, e.g., Gottlieb, P. A., Rossini, A. A., and Mordes, J. P., 'Approaches to Prevention and Treatment of IDDM in Animal Models', *Diabetes Care*, 11 (Suppl. 1) (1988), 29–36; Karges, W., Hammond-McKibben, D., Cheung, R. K., Visconti, M., Shibuya, N., Kemp, D., and Dosch, H-M., 'Immunological Aspects of Nutritional Diabetes Prevention in NOD Mice: A Pilot Study for the Cow's Milk Based IDDM Prevent Trial', *Diabetes,* 46 (1997), 557–64; and Beales, P. E., Burr, L. A., Webb, G. P., Mansfield, K. J., and Pozzilli, P., 'Diet Can Influence the Ability of Nicotinamide to Prevent Diabetes in the Non-Obese Diabetic Mouse: A Preliminary Study', *Diabetes/Metabolism Research Reviews,* 15 (1999), 21–8; and Daniel, D., and Wegmann, D. R., 'Protection of Nonobese Diabetic Mice from Diabetes by Intranasal or Subcutaneous Administration of Insulin Peptide B-(9–23)', *Proceedings of the National Academy of Sciences of the United States of America*, 93 (1996), 956–60.

16. The Trial to Reduce IDDM in the Genetically At Risk (TRIGR) is a primary prediction study. Paronen, J., Knip, M., Savilahti, E., Virtanen, S. M., Ilonen, J., Akerblom, H. K., Vaarala, O., and the Finnish Trial to Reduce IDDM in the Genetically at Risk Study Group, 'Effect of Cow's Milk Exposure and Maternal Type 1 Diabetes on Cellular and Humoral Immunization to Dietary Insulin in Infants at Genetic Risk for Type 1 Diabetes', *Diabetes,* 49 (2000), 1657–65. It was motivated by a small pilot study in 1992–3 that had promising results. See 'Prevention of Type 1 Diabetes Mellitus', Conference Summary from American Diabetes Association. On the web at Diabetes Forum. http://www.diabetesforum.net/cgi-bin/display_engine.pl?category_id=15&content_id=230.
However, other studies have failed to establish this link. See Norris, J. M., Beaty, B., Klingensmith, G., Yu, L., Hoffman, M., Chase, H. P., Erlich, H. A., Hamman, R. F., Eisenbarth, G. S., and Rewers, M., 'Lack of Association between Early Exposure to Cow's Milk Protein and Beta-Cell Autoimmunity: Diabetes Autoimmunity Study in the Young (DAISY)', *JAMA,* 276 (1996), 609–14; and Couper, J. J., Steele, C., Beresford, S., Powell, T., McCaul, K., Pollard, A., Gellert, S., Tait, B., Harrison, L. C., and Colman, P. G., 'Lack of Association between Duration of Breast Feeding or Introduction of Cow's Milk and Development of Islet Autoimmunity', *Diabetes,* 48 (1999), 2145–9.

17. The Diabetes Prevention Trial-1 (DPT-1) is a secondary prevention trial. Unfortunately, the subcutaneous low-dose insulin arm was found to be no more protective than placebo. See Diabetes Prevention Trial—Type 1 Diabetes Study Group, 'Effects of Insulin in Relatives of Patients with Type 1 Diabetes Mellitus', *New England Journal of Medicine,* 346 (2002), 1685–91, hereinafter cited as 'DPT-1 Trial'. A second arm of this study assigns individuals at moderate risk aged 3–34 years (25–50% risk) to either oral insulin or placebo. A press release on the National Institute of Diabetes and Digestive and Kidney Disease website dated

15 June 2003 reported on the negative results of this arm of the trial. See 'Oral Insulin Does Not Prevent Type 1 Diabetes'. On the web at http://www.nidd-k.nih.gov/welcome/releases/6–15-03.htm

18. Like DPT-1, both the Deutsche Nicotinamide Intervention Study (DENIS) and the European Nicotinamide Diabetes Intervention Trial (ENDIT) are secondary prevention trials. DENIS recruited children aged 3 to 12 years with a sibling with type 1 diabetes. Individuals either received high-dose nicotinamide or placebo twice daily. It was terminated early because it was unlikely to reach a statistically significant result. See Lampeter, E. F., Klinghammer, A., Scherbaum, W. A., Heinze, E., Haastert, B., Giani, G., and Kolb, H., 'The Deutsche Nicotinamide Intervention Study: An Attempt to Prevent Type 1 Diabetes', *Diabetes*, 47 (1998), 980–4.

ENDIT tested the more modest hypothesis of whether it is possible to decrease the incidence of type 1 diabetes by 40% over five years in high-risk first-degree relatives using nicotinamide. Final negative results were reported in 2004. See Gale, E. A., Bingley, P. J., Emmett, C. L., Collier, T., and the European Nicotinamide Diabetes Intervention Trial (ENDIT) Group, 'European Nicotinamide Diabetes Intervention Trial (ENDIT): A Randomised Controlled Trial of Intervention before the Onset of Type 1 Diabetes', *Lancet*, 363 (2004), 925–31.

19. See Gottlieb *et al.*, 'Approaches'; Beales *et al.*, 'Diet'; Schatz, D. A., and Bingley, P. J., 'Update on Major Trials for the Prevention of Type 1 Diabetes Mellitus: The American Diabetes Prevention Trial (DPT-1) and the European Nicotinamide Diabetes Intervention Trial (ENDIT)', *Journal of Pediatric Endocrinology,* 14 (Suppl. 1) (2001), 619–22; and Elliott, R. B., and Chase, H. P., 'Prevention or Delay of Type 1 (Insulin-Dependent) Diabetes Mellitus in Children Using Nicotinamide', *Diabetologia,* 34 (1991), 362–5.

20. The Diabetes Prediction and Prevention (DIPP) study in Finland seeks to identify all children with HLA-DQB1 genotypes that confer a high (~8%) or moderate risk (1.7–2.6%) of developing type 1 diabetes (compared with a national average risk of 0.7%, the highest in the world). See, e.g., Kimpimaki, T., Kupila, A., Hamalainen, A-M., Kukko, M., Kulmala, P., Savola, K., Simell, T., Keskinen, P., Ilonen, J., Simell, O., and Knip, M., 'The First Signs of B-Cell Autoimmunity Appear in Infancy in Genetically Susceptible Children from the General Population: The Finnish Type I Diabetes Prediction and Prevention Study', *Journal of Clinical Endocrinology and Metabolism,* 86 (2001), 4782–86.

21. See Hoppu S., Ronkainen, M. S., Kimpimaki T., Simell S., Korhonen, S., Ilonen, J., Simell, O., and Knip, M., 'Insulin Autoantibody Isotypes During the Prediabetic Process in Young Children with Increased Genetic Risk of Type 1 Diabetes', *Pediatric Research*, 55 (2004), 236–42, 237. There is also an Australian study that is using intranasal insulin to prevent or retard the development of type 1 diabetes. See the report on a trial by Leonard C Harrison, MD Director of the Burnet Clinical Research Unit and Professorial Associate at the University of Melbourne School of Medicine in Victoria, Australia. Skolnick, A. A., 'First Type I Diabetes Prevention Trials', *JAMA*, 277, (1997), 1101–2.

22. Daniel, D., and Wegmann, D. R., 'Protection of nonobese diabetic mice from diabetes by intranasal or subcutaneous administration of insulin peptide B-(9–

23)', *Proceedings of the National Academy of Sciences of the United States of America,* 93 (23 January 1996), 956–60; and Aspord, C. and Thivolet, C., 'Nasal Administration of CTB-Insulin Induces Active Tolerance against Autoimmune Diabetes in Non-Obese Diabetic (NOD) Mice', *Clinical & Experimental Immunology,* 130 (2002), 204–11.

23. See, e.g., Cefalu, W. T., 'Concept, Strategies, and Fesibility of Noninvasive Insulin Delivery' *Diabetes Care,* 27 (2004), 239–46; and Owens, D. R., Zinman, B. and Bollit, G. 'Alternative Routes of Insulin Delivery', *Diabetic Medicine* 20 (2003), 886–98.

24. Kupila, A., Sipila, J., Keskinen, P., Simell, T., Knip, M., Pulkki, K., and Simell, O., 'Intranasally Administered Insulin Intended for Prevention of Type 1 Diabetes—A Safety Study in Healthy Adults', *Diabetes/Metabolism Research Reviews,* 19 (2003), 415–20, 416.

25. Minimal risk is defined in the Common Rule (Subpart A) as 'the probability and magnitude of harm or discomfort anticipated in the research are not greater in and of themselves than those ordinarily encountered in daily life or during the performance of routine physical or psychological examinations or tests'. Department of Health and Human Services (DHHS) (45 CFR 46 Subpart A), 'Final Regulations Amending Basic HHS Policy for the Protection of Human Research Subjects', *Federal Register,* 46 (26 January 1981), 8366–91; revised *Federal Register,* 56 (18 June 1991), 28003–18; CFR §46.111; hereinafter Subpart A is cited in the text by CFR number.

26. See, e.g., Janofsky, J., and Starfield, B., 'Assessment of Risk in Research on Children', *Journal of Pediatrics,* 98 (1981), 842–6; and Shah, S., Whittle, A., Wilfond, B., Gensler, G., and Wendler, D., 'How do Institutional Review Boards Apply the Federal Risk and Benefit Standards for Pediatric Research?' *JAMA,* 291 (2004), 476–82.

27. Dahlquist, G. G., 'Primary and Secondary Prevention Strategies of Pre-Type 1 Diabetes: Potentials and Pitfalls', *Diabetes Care,* 22 (2S Suppl.) (1999), 4B–6B.

28. See, e.g., Davison, C., Macintyre, S., and Smith, G. D., 'The Potential Social Impact of Predictive Genetic Testing for Susceptibility to Common Chronic Disease: A Review and Proposed Research Agenda', *Sociology of Health and Illness,* 16 (1994), 340–71; and Kenen, R. H., 'The At-Risk Health Status and Technology: A Diagnostic Invitation and the "Gift" of Knowing', *Social Science and Medicine,* 42 (1996), 1545–53.

29. McNeil, T. F., Harty, B., Thelin, T., Aspegren-Jansson, E., and Sveger, T., 'Identifying Children at High Somatic Risk: Long-Term Effects on Mother-Child Interaction', *Acta Psychiatrica Scandinavia,* 74 (1986), 555–62.

30. Tymstra, T., 'False Positive Results in Screening Tests: Experiences of Parents of Children Screened for Congenital Hypothyroidism', *Family Practice,* 3 (1986), 92–6.

31. McNeil, T. F., Thelin, T., Aspegren-Jansson, E., and Sveger, T., 'Identifying Children at High Somatic Risk: Possible Effects on the Parents' Views of the Child's Health and Parents' Relationship to the Pediatric Health Services', *Acta Psychiatrica Scandinavia,* 72 (1985), 491–7.

32. Clarke, A., 'The Genetic Dissection of Multifactorial Disease: The Implications of Susceptibility Screening' in P. S. Harper and A. J. Clarke (eds.), *Genetics, Society and Clinical Practice*. Oxford: Bios Scientific Publishers, 1997, 93–106, 102, citations omitted. See also Johnson, S. B., and Tercyak, K. P., 'Psychological Impact of Islet Cell-Antibody Screening for IDDM on Children, Adults and Their Family Members', *Diabetes Care*, 18 (1995), 1370–2; and Roth, R., 'Psychological and Ethical Aspects of Prevention Trials', *Journal of Pediatric Endocrinology and Metabolism*, 14 (2001), 669–74.

33. See, e.g., Lucidarme, N., Donmingues-Muriel, E., Castro, D., Czernichow, P., and Levy-Marchal, C., 'Appraisal and Implications of Predictive Testing for Insulin-Dependent Diabetes Mellitus', *Diabetes Metabolism*, 23 (1998), 550–3; and Shepherd, M., Hattersley, A. T., and Sparkes A. C., 'Predictive Genetic Testing in Diabetes: A Case Study of Multiple Perspectives', *Qualitative Health Research*, 10 (2000), 242–59.

34. Lucidarme *et al.*, 'Appraisal'.

35. See Ziegler *et al.*, 'Autoantibody'; Hummel *et al.*, 'Psychological Impact'; Lucidarme, 'Appraisal'; and Nordenfelt L., 'Prevention and Ethics in Medicine: The Case of Diabetes Prevention', *Journal of Pediatric Endocrinology and Metabolism*, 9 (1996), 381–6.

36. Baum, A., Friedman, A. L., and Zakowski, S. G., 'Stress and Genetic Testing for Disease Risk', *Health Psychology*, 16 (1997), 8–19; and Croyle, R. T., and Lerman, C., 'Psychological Impact of Genetic Testing', in R. T. Croyle (ed.), *Psychosocial Effects of Screening for Disease Prevention and Detection*. New York: Oxford University Press, 1995, 11–38.

37. Even in those studies in which identification (prediction) is coupled with a therapeutic intervention (prevention), I believe that the earliest therapeutic research trials should only enroll children from high-risk families. See discussion in previous chapter at text corresponding to endnotes 80–1.

38. Marteau, T. M., 'Psychology and Screening, Narrowing the Gap between Efficacy and Effectiveness', *British Journal of Clinical Psychology*, 33 (1994), 1–10.

39. Ibid.

40. Samuelsson, U., Sundkvist, G., Borg, H., Fernlund, P., and Ludvigsson, J., 'Islet Autoantibodies in the Prediction of Diabetes in School Children', *Diabetes Research and Clinical Practice*, 51 (2001), 51–7.

41. Ibid.

42. And yet, even if one focuses on high-risk families, the number of subjects who need to be screened is still quite large. The DPT-1 trials screened approximately 89,827 individuals under 45 years of age with a first- or second-degree relative with type 1 diabetes for ICAs and 3.7% of the subjects were found to be positive. These individuals underwent further screening to determine whether they were at high or intermediate risk. See 'DPT-1 Trial'.

43. 'DPT-1 Trial'.

44. See Kupila, A., Sipila, J., Keskinen, P., Simell, T., Knip, M., Pulkki, K., and Simell, O., 'Intranasally Administered Insulin Intended for Prevention of Type 1

Diabetes—A Safety Study in Healthy Adults', *Diabetes/Metabolism Research Reviews*, 19 (2003), 415–20, 415.

45. Field M. J., and Behrman, R. E. (eds.), Committee on Clinical Research Involving Children, the Institute of Medicine (IOM). *The Ethical Conduct of Clinical Research Involving Children*. Washington DC: National Academies Press, 2004, 129; hereinafter this reference is cited as IOM, *Ethical Conduct*.

46. The actual degree of risk is the 'one in which the probability of physical and psychological harm is no more than that to which it is appropriate to intentionally expose a child for educational purposes in family life situations'. See Ackerman, T., 'Moral Duties of Parents and Non-Therapeutic Research Procedures Involving Children', *Bioethics Quarterly*, 2 (1980), 94–111 as cited in S. L. Leiken, 'An Ethical Issue in Biomedical Research: The Involvement of Minors in Informed and Third Party Consent', *Clinical Research*, 31 (1983), 34–40, 38. As I explained in Chap. 4, this risk is probably akin to a minor increase over minimal risk.

47. See Marteau, 'Psychology and Screening'.

12

Lead Abatement Research

1. Introduction

In August 2001, the Maryland Court of Appeals harshly criticized the Kennedy Krieger Institute of Johns Hopkins University for knowingly exposing poor children to lead-based paint.[1] The court's decision made national news[2] in part because it compared the studies to Tuskegee.[3] In this chapter, I address the court's ruling that parents cannot consent to nontherapeutic research that poses *any* degree of risk to children subjects.[4] I argue that the court was mistaken because parents legally can consent and morally should be allowed to consent to some nontherapeutic research. I also examine the research methodology to determine whether the research is approvable under the current federal regulations. In doing so, I will continue to refine what is meant by being 'at risk' for a 'disorder or condition'.

2. The Lead Abatement Research

The research conducted by the Kennedy Krieger Institute was an attempt to understand how successful different lead abatement programs were in reducing continued lead exposure to children. Previously Julian Chisolm and Mark Farfel, of the Kennedy Krieger Institute at John Hopkins University had disclosed the dangers of traditional dust-generating de-leading practices.[5] In the current study, Dr Farfel and colleagues sought to document the longevity of various lead-based paint abatement strategies.[6]

The research under review involved abating residences in Baltimore with known lead problems to one of three levels of lead abatement to determine how much abatement was necessary to prevent plumbism (lead poisoning). A fourth arm consisted of children who lived in new homes, free of lead paint. All the children would undergo serial venipuncture (less frequently in the control group). The study design was exceptional because prior research focused on children with plumbism and not on how to prevent plumbism. In fact, the results of this study and other studies by the principal investigators have been described as helping to 'provide the basis for federal health-based standards and prohibitions on unsafe practices'.[7] Although it was clear that the research under scrutiny had scientific merit, the court challenged the ethics of the study's methodology.[8] The researchers encouraged landlords to rent the repaired premises to families with children despite the fact that the researchers (1) suspected that some of these programs would not fully eradicate the problem; and (2) knew that the continued lead exposure was dangerous for the children.[9]

The researchers and their supporters have defended the ethics of the research. First, the project was one of the first primary prevention studies to perform lead-safety measures before children were exposed to lead paint. Most attempts to control lead hazards in Baltimore and other cities in 1993 were in response to already poisoned children.[10] Second, all the homes had some degree of lead abatement, and therefore all families benefited, even if the children in homes with more extensive repairs were expected to have less lead exposure.[11] Third, while the research provided for a control group (children living in modern housing that was built without lead paint), there was no placebo arm. Thus, no children in the research lived in housing with untreated lead hazards.[12] Fourth, the consent forms clearly explained that living in housing that had undergone renovation for lead abatement may not fully protect one's child from lead exposure: 'The repairs are not intended or expected, to completely remove exposure to lead.'[12]

3.   *The Court's Ruling*

The court argued that the research was nontherapeutic and that it was impermissible for a parent to consent for their child's participation in nontherapeutic research that poses any degree of risk: 'We hold that in Maryland, a parent, appropriate relative, or other applicable surrogate, cannot consent to the participation of a child or other person under legal disability in nontherapeutic research or studies in which there is any risk of injury or damage to the health of the subject.'[14]

Three distinct challenges can be made to this ruling. First, whether the court was correct to classify the lead abatement research as nontherapeutic. Second, if yes, did the research pose greater than minimal risk? Third, and more generally, do guardians have the moral and legal authority to consent on behalf of a child or other legally incompetent person to participate in nontherapeutic research that poses any risk of injury? The first two questions are important in determining whether this research can be approved under the current federal regulations. The third question was the focus of the motion for reconsideration filed in September 2001 by the Kennedy Krieger Institute with their *amici curiae*. The *amici* were concerned by the potential 'immediate and long-term consequences of the Court's broadly worded decision'.[15] The *amici* argued: A rule prohibiting 'nontherapeutic research or studies in which there is *any* risk of injury' would prohibit virtually all medical and public health research involving children and other persons under a legal disability.[16]

The *amici* pointed out that this ruling is not consistent with the federal regulations pertaining to the participation of children in research.[17] The regulations permit children to participate in nontherapeutic research (or, in the language of the regulations, research that does not offer the prospect of direct benefit) provided that it involves only minimal risk (CFR §46.404). Nontherapeutic research that poses greater than minimal risk is permitted if the risk is only a minor increase over minimal risk and the research offers the potential for generalizable knowledge of vital importance about the subjects' disorder or condition (CFR §46.406). If the nontherapeutic research poses more than a minor increase over minimal risk, it is permitted if the research presents an opportunity to prevent or alleviate serious health problems and it is reviewed and approved by a national panel of experts (CFR §46.407). In all cases, parental consent is required (CFR §46.408).

On 11 October 2001, the Court of Appeals denied the motion for reconsideration, but clarified its decision, stating '[a]lthough we discussed the various issues and arguments in considerable detail, the only conclusion that we reached as a matter of law was that on the record currently before us, summary judgment was improperly granted.'[18] With respect to the question of whether children can participate in nontherapeutic research that poses any degree of risk, the court replied, 'by "any risk", we meant any articulable risk beyond the minimal kind of risk that is inherent in any endeavor'.[19] Whether the research was nontherapeutic or entailed more than minimal risk was also qualified: 'As we indicated, the determination of whether the study in question offered some benefit, and therefore could be regarded as therapeutic in nature, or involved more than that minimal risk is open for further factual development on remand.'[20] Unlike the wide publicity for the court's earlier ruling, the court's clarification, and toning down of its condemnation, was covered only by the local media.[21]

4.   *Nontherapeutic versus Therapeutic Research*

Is this research nontherapeutic? In part, the court's assessment that the research is nontherapeutic is based on the fact that the research was being performed on healthy children.[22] But healthy children can benefit from therapeutic research (e.g., vaccination research to prevent infection). Furthermore, while the court describes the plaintiffs as healthy children, it may be better for the court to understand them as healthy but 'at risk'. At-risk children can benefit from therapeutic research that attempts to minimize risks of harm in their environment or in themselves (e.g., decreasing second-hand smoke to decrease ear infections in young children; treating infants exposed to HIV *in utero* with antiviral therapy to prevent them from becoming HIV-infected).

In the research under scrutiny, all the children (except the control group) lived in homes that had received lead abatement. Although the researchers intended to observe the children without treating them or providing further abatement, the three different levels of initial lead abatement were intended to reduce the children's exposure to lead. Therefore, all the children who lived in residences that received lead abatement could have potentially benefited from their participation,[23] even if the therapeutic interventions were performed on the homes and not the children directly.

If the research is therapeutic for those whose homes were abated, is this the case for the control group? The control group consisted of healthy children living in modern urban housing. Their houses were not treated because they were assumed to be lead-free. The research would not offer the prospect of direct benefit to the children as they were not expected to have high lead exposures. However, the Johns Hopkins University's IRB was concerned with calling this arm of the study the control group because federal regulations were, in its words, 'really quite specific' about using children as controls when there is no potential benefit. The IRB recommended that the researchers claim that the control group was not merely serving as 'a control', but was 'being studied to determine what exposure outside the home may play in total lead exposure; thereby, indicating that these control individuals are gaining some benefit'[24]

The court was quite disturbed with the IRB's attempt to make an end run around the federal regulations, and then extrapolated this concern to question the competence and ability of all IRBs.[25] Before condemning the IRB's recommendation, one must ask whether the IRB was correct in its assessment that a control group could not be morally justified.

To correctly review the ethics of pediatric research, the National Commission (for the Protection of Human Subjects of Biomedical and Behavioral Research) stated that an IRB must review each arm of the research methodology independently and the research protocol as a unified package.[26] For the children who lived in, or were moving into homes with lead paint that were partly abated, the research was a therapeutic trial and could be approved under CFR §46.405. For the healthy children who lived in modern housing, the research involved no prospect of direct benefit. If it entailed only minimal risk, then this arm could be approved under CFR §46.404. Thus, the IRB failed to appreciate that the study design could be ethical because it failed to consider that a review of each arm independently means that different arms can (and often must) be approved under different categories.

Contrast this study design with the traditional clinical trial that uses a randomized double-blind control methodology to ensure that any improvement in the treatment group is due to the therapy or prevention strategy being tested.[27] In recent years, there has been serious criticism regarding the use of placebos,[28] particularly the use of placebo-controlled research trials when a known treatment exists.[29] In this trial, however, the researchers did not choose to create a placebo arm of children who lived in houses with suspected lead problems whose homes would be randomized to receive no lead abatement. All of the homes that were suspected of having lead exposure were given some degree of lead abatement or had received a full lead abatement treatment prior to the study. As such, all of the at-risk children were enrolled in a therapeutic arm. The children whose homes were not perceived to be at risk for lead exposure were enrolled in an observational minimal risk control arm that required five phlebotomies over two years. Unfortunately, both the IRB and the court failed to appreciate that this was not a traditional placebo-controlled trial.

5.   Degree of Risk

Assume that the above analysis is wrong and that the court was correct in asserting that (all of the arms of) the research were nontherapeutic. If the research is nontherapeutic, then the federal regulations govern under what circumstances it is ethical to expose children to certain degrees of risk. The court rebuked the researchers for intentionally exposing healthy children to more than minimal risk in a nontherapeutic study. If their assessment is correct, this research would not be permitted under current federal regulations.[30] Thus, we need to clarify what degree of risk the research entailed.

Does the research qualify as minimal risk? 'Minimal risk' is defined in federal regulations as 'the probability and magnitude of harm or discomfort anticipated in the research [that] are not greater in and of themselves than those ordinarily encountered in daily life or during the performance of routine physical or psychological examinations or tests'.[31] The researchers argued that most poor children in Baltimore were living in housing with lead and, thus, the proposal to test the effectiveness of various abatement strategies by venipuncture and apartment sweeps did not expose the children to more than minimal risk or no additional risk beyond what they would have ordinarily encountered.[32] Specifically, the children would undergo eight venipunctures over a two-year period and the control arm would undergo five. Although universal lead testing was not the standard of care at the time of the studies,[33] in 1993 the American Academy of Pediatrics (AAP) recommended testing all children twice before the age of 2, with more frequent testing for those with continued exposure.[34] Thus, the children were subjected to no more than three to six additional venipunctures over a 2-year period. The minor discomfort, risk of ecchymoses (blotchy areas of hemorrhage in the skin), and the minuscule risk of infection are within the minimal risk standard.

Given the known variability in the interpretation of minimal risk,[35] the court might have concluded that the research exposed children to a minor increase over minimal risk. The research could still be permissible if it offered the potential for generalizable knowledge about the subjects' disorder or condition (CFR §46.406). As I have been discussing in the past three chapters, it is not clear whether a subject must actually have a disorder or condition to be eligible for research classified under CFR §46.406 or whether it is adequate that the subject is at high risk for having it. If 'disorder or condition' in CFR §46.406 of the federal regulations is defined to include at-risk children, then the research would be permissible, even if the risks posed a minor increase over minimal risk, at least for the children outside of the control arm (those in the control group were never considered at risk). However, if 'disorder or condition' is not defined to include healthy but at-risk children, then the research would only be permissible if the research posed no more than minimal risk (CFR §46.404).

In the last chapter, I argued that children 'at risk' for type 1 diabetes on the basis of family history should be considered as having a 'disorder or condition' for the purposes of the federal regulations. Here I propose that children who live in lead-contaminated homes because of socio-economic disadvantages are also 'at risk' and should be considered as having a disorder or condition. As discussed in Chapter 3, the National Human Research Protections Advisory Committee (NHRPAC) argued for such a broad understanding of 'disorder or condition',[35] the Institute of Medicine (IOM) committee was a bit more conservative. The IOM required that 'investigators who define a research population on the basis of social characteristics or "conditions", such as ethnicity, family circumstances, or economic status, must present a case that the condition has a negative effect on children's health and well-being that is relevant to the research question' and that the research will generate vital knowledge about the condition.[37] I believe these children would meet the IOM and NHRPAC criteria. Virtually all low-income housing in Baltimore at the time had lead contamination such that the socio-economic conditions of these families would have precluded them from living in urban Baltimore without lead exposure. The different lead-abatement programs were designed to produce vital knowledge about how to most efficiently reduce lead in these homes. The knowledge to be gained from the research, then, would help children at risk for plumbism by studying successful environmental lead-abatement practices.

If the risk of numerous phlebotomies is classified as a minor increase over minimal risk, then the control arm might still be problematic because these children are presumed not to have a condition nor to be at risk for the condition (plumbism). On the other hand, one could argue that although the children in the control group were not at risk in their home environment, there is no guarantee that they are not being exposed to lead in other settings (e.g., day care). Thus, they too may be 'at risk', albeit at lower risk. The problem with this interpretation is that it is overbroad and as the IOM committee feared, it makes the concept of 'at risk' so broad that it could include anyone as potentially at risk for anything.[38]

An alternative control arm would include children 'at risk' for plumbism: children who lived in homes at risk for lead—homes that would be abated only after the children were found to have been poisoned. While this would have represented the standard of practice at the time, it was specifically rejected by the researchers as unethical.[39] The researchers rejected this option because living in an unabated home would have exposed these children to significant amounts of lead. In addition, such exposure represents more than a minor increase over minimal risk, and should not have been permitted under CFR §46.406. To knowingly expose children to lead poisoning entails more than a minor increase over minimal risk and would require that the research be classified under CFR §46.407. Such research needs to undergo national review and approval, where hopefully the control arm would not be permitted because it would expose children to unnecessary risks.

If the research is classified as nontherapeutic research and the research methods are judged to pose more than minimal risk, then there is no satisfactory control arm. Legally, the federal regulations do not permit healthy children without a 'disorder or condition' to be exposed to more than minimal risk; ethically, the researchers would not enroll children 'at risk' and leave them in unabated homes. But this study would not have been scientifically valid without a control arm given that the best abatement procedure was not known. As such, if the research were nontherapeutic and exposed children without a 'disorder or condition' to more than minimal risk, then its methodology could not have been approved under current federal regulations.

It is clear, then, why the Court of Appeals ruled as it did. The court harshly criticized the research because it believed that (1) the research was nontherapeutic; (2) the children were healthy and did not have a condition or disorder; and (3) the risks were more than minimal, such that the research could not be justified. In contrast, I am arguing that the research was ethically permissible because (1) it offered the prospect of direct benefit to the children who lived in the homes with lead paint; and (2) albeit nontherapeutic for the children in the control arm, it entailed no more than minimal risk.

6. *Scope of Parental Authority*

The third issue that needs clarification is whether parents have the moral and legal authority to expose their children to any degree of risk in nontherapeutic research? The court argued that parents do not have the moral or legal authority to consent to the participation of their children in nontherapeutic research that poses *any* risk of injury. This question was the focus of the motion for reconsideration and several *amici* briefs.[40]

The court's ruling is contrary to the federal regulations which offer specific guidelines regarding parental authority to authorize their children's participation in research (CFR §46.408). The guidelines allow parents to consent to research at all levels of risk with certain stipulations. First, one-parent permission is required if the research poses minimal risk (CFR §46.404) or if there is the prospect of direct benefit (CFR §46.405). Second, children can participate in research with the permission of both parents if the research poses no more than a minor increase over minimal risk and offers the potential for generalizable knowledge of vital importance about the subjects' disorder or condition (CFR §46.406); or if the research presents an opportunity to prevent or alleviate serious health problems of children generally, regardless of degree of risk, and the research is reviewed and approved by a national committee of experts (CFR §46.407).

In Chapter 1, I argued why parents should have moral authority to authorize their children's participation in nontherapeutic research. I argued that Ramsey's position that parents cannot give informed consent for their child's participation in activities that do not benefit the child directly is based on the overly demanding belief that parents must always act to promote their child's best interest. In contrast, I believe that parents are not and should not be held to a best-interest standard because it would be too intrusive into the daily routine of most families.[41] Parents should have presumptive decision-making authority for their children and this parental autonomy should be questioned only if their decision is disrespectful of the child's developing personhood.[42] Parental authorization of their children's participation in nontherapeutic research can be morally legitimate.

7. *Denouement*

Many of the facts in the case are not publicly available because the case never proceeded beyond summary judgment, which the lower court granted in favor of the researchers. The trial court held that, even assuming all disputed facts in favor of the plaintiffs, the researchers did not have a legal duty to the parents to abate or eliminate hazards the researchers did not create. In a 96-page opinion that went far beyond this question, the Court of Appeals (Maryland's highest court) reversed the earlier decision, arguing that research can create 'special relationships', and remanded the case back to the lower court for trial.[43] The court's opinion, which calls the research unethical and compares it to the US Public Health Service experiments at Tuskegee, is the basis for much of the negative publicity surrounding the case.[44] Judge Raker, who concurred with the ruling only, stated that he thought the court might be acting unfairly by choosing to publish such a scathing opinion before all the evidence had been presented.[45] Of note, in October 2003, the case was dismissed with prejudice.[46] This was not covered by any newspaper.

The two children whose parents brought suit against the Kennedy Krieger Institute had peak levels of 21 ug/dL and 32 ug/dL.[47] Of note is that the former child lived in a home that had received the middle-level degree of lead abatement and that the latter child lived in a home that had received the comprehensive abatement.[48] Neither child required chelation therapy as the recommended course of treatment at the time was not to treat children with blood-lead levels of less than 45 ug/dL.[49] This is not meant to exonerate the researchers completely. During the last 30 years, the Centers for Disease Control and Prevention (CDC) have revised the definition of the blood-lead level at which lead poisoning occurs from 60 ug/dL in the early 1960s, to 30 ug/dL in 1975, to 25 ug/dL in 1985, and to 10 ug/dL in 1991.[50] As such, when the research was being done, the researchers should have known that both of these children had blood-lead levels that posed risks to them. At minimum, they should have repeatedly encouraged these families to perform lead-safety measures (e.g., cleaning the windowsills and mopping the floors).

While I believe that the research design was ethical and that the Kennedy Krieger Institute researchers met their ethical obligations, there are two collateral issues that also deserve concluding comments. First, the court's ruling must be publicly criticized lest it be used as a precedent in other cases. It led to the passage by the Maryland legislature of a statute that affirmed that all Maryland research be held to the requirements of 45 CFR 46,[51] but whether this is adequate has not been challenged. Second, the case raises concerns regarding the media's approach to the promises and perils of human experimentation. The publicity surrounding the court's initial condemnation was covered throughout the United States; its disclaimers were covered only locally, leaving the public falsely believing that its trust had been betrayed once again.

References

1. Grimes v. Kennedy Krieger Institute, Inc., 782 A.2d 807 (Md. 2001).
2. The court's harsh criticisms were covered by newspapers in many cities, both locally and nationally. See, e.g., Roig-Franzia, M., and Weiss, R., 'Maryland

Appeals Court Slams Researchers; Participants in Study on Lead Paint Weren't Informed of Risks, Judge Says', *Washington Post*, (21 August 2001), B01; Bor, J., 'Lead Paint Lawsuits to Go to Trial; Kennedy Krieger Accused of Putting Children in Danger; Research Deemed Risky; Appeals Court Finds Doctors Failed to Warn of Hazards', *Baltimore Sun* (17 August 2001), 1B; Lewin, T., 'US Investigating Johns Hopkins Study of Lead Paint Hazard', *New York Times* (24 August 2001), A11; 'Experiments and Ethics,' *Times-Picayune* (New Orleans), (27 August 2001), Metro Section; Robertson, T., 'Subjects in Baltimore Rue Lead-Paint Study; Hopkins Affiliate Faces Suit, Inquiry', *Boston Globe* (3 September 2001), A1; and Editorial, 'Stiffen Medical Research Rules', *San Francisco Chronicle*, (27 August 2001), A14.

3. Grimes v. Kennedy Krieger Institute, Inc., 782 A.2d 807, 816 (Md. 2001).
4. Ibid., 858, italics added.
5. Farfel, M. R., and Chisolm, J. J. Jr., 'Health and Environmental Outcomes of Traditional and Modified Practices for Abatement of Residential Lead-Based Paint', *American Journal of Public Health*, 80 (1990), 1240–5.
6. Grimes v. Kennedy Krieger Institute, Inc., 782 A.2d 807, 819 (Md. 2001) (citing deposition of Mark Farfel).
7. Ryan, D., 'Controversy over Kennedy Krieger Research', E-mail to the Children's Environmental Health Network list-serv (28 August 2001) (on file with author). Don Ryan is the executive director of the Alliance to End Childhood Lead Poisoning, an advocacy group based in Washington DC. An editorial offering some of the facts and opinions detailed on the list-serv was published in the *Baltimore Sun* on that same day. See Ryan, D., 'Research on Lead Hazards is Solution, Not Problem', Op-ed, *Baltimore Sun* (28 August 2001), 19A.
8. Grimes v. Kennedy Krieger Institute, Inc., 782 A.2d 807, 812–13, 819–24 (Md. 2001).
9. Ibid., 812–13, 820–2.
10. Ryan, 'Controversy over Kennedy Krieger Research'.
11. Bor, J., 'Kennedy Krieger Doctor Defends Lead Paint Study; Researcher Disputes High Court's Findings', *Baltimore Sun* (18 August 2001), 1B.
12. Ryan, 'Controversy over Kennedy Krieger Research'.
13. Grimes v. Kennedy Krieger Institute, Inc., 782 A.2d 807, 824 (Md. 2001) (citing the Consent Form, Purpose of Study).
14. Ibid., 858.
15. Brief of *Amici Curiae* Association of American Medical Colleges, Association of American Universities, Johns Hopkins University, and University of Maryland Medical System Corporation, 'In Support of Appellee's Motion for Reconsideration, Grimes v. Kennedy Krieger Institute, Inc., 782 A.2d 807 (Md. 2001) (No. 128)'. On the web at: http://www.hopkinsmedicine.org/press/2001/SEPTEMBER/briefs.htm, 1; hereinafter cited as Brief of *Amici Curiae*.
16. Ibid., 5, italics added.
17. Department of Health and Human Services (DHHS) (45 CFR Part 46, Subpart D), 'Protections for Children Involved as Subjects in Research', *Federal Register*, 48 (8 March 1983), 9814–9820; revised *Federal Register*, 56 (June 18, 1991), 28032; hereinafter Subpart D is cited in the text by CFR number.

18. Grimes v. Kennedy Krieger Institute, Inc., No. 128 (Md. 11 Oct. 2001) (order denying motion for reconsideration). On the web at: http://www.hopkinsmedicine.org/press/2001/October/CourtofAppeals.pdf, 1.

19. Ibid., 2.

20. Ibid.

21. A Lexis–Nexis search of general news and major US and international newspapers, using the key words 'Kennedy Krieger', 'lead paint', or 'lead poisoning', found that the initial story was covered by newspapers in many cities, including Boston, San Francisco, New York, and New Orleans. In contrast, the same Lexis–Nexis search found that only the *Washington Post* and the *Baltimore Sun*, both local papers, covered the court's 11 October 2001 decision to deny reconsideration despite the fact that the case raises major issues for pediatric research generally.

22. Grimes v. Kennedy Krieger Institute, Inc., 782 A.2d 807, 815 (Md. 2001).

23. This is not meant to say that all of the children were necessarily better off in terms of lead exposure than they would have been had they lived elsewhere or just not participated. Although most low-income rental properties in Baltimore at the time were old and heavily leaded, and steps to control lead hazards were almost exclusively in response to already poisoned children, some families may have moved into other homes with lower lead exposure, albeit unintentionally. In addition, it is not clear whether families who chose to move into these abated homes and participate in the research were better or worse off than those who moved into these homes but refused to participate. The former were encouraged to stay in their homes; the latter would not have been, and thus, unwittingly, they may have moved to homes with less lead risk.

24. Grimes v. Kennedy Krieger Institute, Inc., 782 A.2d 807, 814 (Md. 2001) (citing a letter dated 11 May 1992 from the Johns Hopkins University Joint Committee on Clinical Investigation to Dr Farfel).

25. Ibid., 817. The issue of the proper role of IRBs and whether they are fulfilling this role is discussed in the article published previously. See Ross, L. F., 'In Defense of the Hopkins Lead Abatement Studies', *Journal of Law, Medicine and Ethics,* 30 (2002), 50–7, 54.

26. National Commission for the Protection of Human Subjects of Biomedical and Behavioral Research, *Report and Recommendations: Research Involving Children.* Washington DC: US Printing Office, 1977, DHEW Publication No. (OS) 77–0004, 7. To that extent, the Johns Hopkins University deserves credit because it is not clear whether this was the standard of IRB review in the 1990s. The fact that this issue is still being addressed in medical journals today suggests that it is not. See, e.g., Miller, F. G., Wendler, D., and Wilfond, B., 'When do the Federal Regulations Allow Placebo-Controlled Trials in Children?' *Journal of Pediatrics,* 142 (2003), 102–7.

27. Brief of *Amici Curiae,* 'In Support', 6 (footnotes omitted).

28. See, e.g., Kaptchuk, T. J., 'The Double-Blind, Randomized, Placebo-Controlled Trial: Gold Standard or Golden Calf?' *Journal of Clinical Epidemiology,* 54 (2001), 541–9; Ellis, S. J., and Adams, R. F., 'The Cult of the Double-Blind

Placebo-Controlled Trial', *British Journal of Clinical Practice*, 51 (1997), 36–9; Cleophas, T. J., Van der Meulen, J., and Kalmansohn, R. B., 'Phase III Trials: Specific Problems Associated with the Use of a Placebo Control Group', *International Journal of Clinical Pharmacology and Therapeutics*, 35 (1997), 47–50. The biggest challenge to the use of placebos came with the revision to the Declaration of Helsinki in 2000 when it specifically addressed when placebos are ethical: 'The benefits, risks, burdens and effectiveness of a new method should be tested against those of the best current prophylactic, diagnostic, and therapeutic methods. This does not exclude the use of placebo, or no treatment, in studies where no proven prophylactic, diagnostic or therapeutic method exists.' (See Paragraph 29). In 2002, due to much pressure from the US, a note of clarification was added: 'a placebo-controlled trial may be ethically acceptable, even if proven therapy is available, under the following circumstances: Where for compelling and scientifically sound methodological reasons its use is necessary to determine the efficacy or safety of a prophylactic, diagnostic or therapeutic method; or where a prophylactic, diagnostic or therapeutic method is being investigated for a minor condition and the patients who receive placebo will not be subject to any additional risk of serious or irreversible harm (clarification of paragraph 29).' See 'Declaration of Helsinki, Ethical Principles for Medical Research Involving Human Subjects', adopted by the 18th WMA General Assembly, Helsinki, Finland, June 1964, and amended by the 29th WMA General Assembly, Tokyo, Japan, October 1975; 35th WMA General Assembly, Venice, Italy, October 1983; 41st WMA General Assembly, Hong Kong, September 1989; 48th WMA General Assembly, Somerset West, Republic of South Africa, October 1996; and the 52nd WMA General Assembly, Edinburgh, Scotland, October 2000. Note of Clarification on Paragraph 29 added by the WMA General Assembly, Washington 2002; and Note of Clarification on Paragraph 30 added by the WMA General Assembly, Tokyo 2004. On the web at: http://www.wma.net/e/policy/b3.htm. See the discussion of placebos in Chap. 13.

29. See, e.g., Miller *et al.*, 'When'; Lurie, P., and Wolfe, S. M., 'Unethical Trials of Interventions to Reduce Perinatal Transmission of Human Immunodeficiency Virus in Developing Countries', *New England Journal of Medicine*, 337 (1997), 853–6; Angell, M., 'The Ethics of Clinical Research in the Third World', *New England Journal of Medicine*, 337 (1997), 847–9. After the US complained vociferously about the new version of the Declaration of Helsinki, the World Medical Association restricted their objection to placebos to research on conditions for which a known treatment exists.

30. I argued in Chap. 4 that it should be permissible to expose *all* children to a research procedure in which 'the probability of physical and psychological harm is no more than that to which it is appropriate to intentionally expose a child for educational purposes in family life situations'. Ackerman, T., 'Moral Duties of Parents and Non-Therapeutic Research Procedures Involving Children', *Bioethics Quarterly*. 1980; 2: 94–111 as cited in S. L. Leiken, 'An Ethical Issue in Biomedical Research: The Involvement of Minors in Informed and Third Party Consent', *Clinical Research*, 31 (1983), 34–40, 38. Using this definition of minimal

risk, I concluded that it was not necessary to distinguish between minimal risk and a minor increase over minimal risk. Nevertheless, in this chapter, I will use current federal guidelines which would make it impermissible to perform nontherapeutic research on healthy children involving more than minimal risk.

31. Department of Health and Human Services (DHHS) (45 CFR 46 Subpart A), 'Final Regulations Amending Basic HHS Policy for the Protection of Human Research Subjects', *Federal Register*, 46 (26 January 1981), 8366–91; revised *Federal Register*, 56 (18 June 1991), 28003–18 at CFR 46.102(i); hereinafter, Subpart A or the Common Rule is cited in the text by CFR number.

32. Ryan, 'Controversy over Kennedy Krieger Research'. As discussed in Chap. 4, one problem with this argument is the ambiguity of the definition of 'minimal risk'. As such, the regulations could be interpreted to allow the probability and magnitude of harm to be defined against what the particular child in question encounters in his daily life. Since poor children are frequently exposed to lead, the research by the Kennedy Krieger Institute could be classified as minimal risk. Even if one used a more stringent notion of minimal risk, the issue is whether the research itself involved more than minimal risk. The research was a study of nature and entailed collecting lead data from the homes and blood of children. The methods used in the study itself did not expose the children to more than minimal risk, even if their environment did.

33. See, e.g., Anonymous, 'State Activities for Prevention of Lead Poisoning Among Children—United States, 1992', *MMWR* (*Morbidity & Mortality Weekly Report*), 42 (1993), 165, 171–2; Weismann, D., 'Lead Intoxication in Iowa Children', *Iowa Medicine*, 82 (1992), 119–22; and Kirchner, J. T., and Kelley, B. A., 'Pediatric Lead Screening in a Suburban Family Practice Setting', *Journal of Family Practice*, 32 (1991), 397–400.

34. American Academy of Pediatrics (AAP) Committee on Environmental Health, 'Lead Poisoning: From Screening to Primary Prevention', *Pediatrics*, 92 (1993), 176–83.

35. Janofsky, J., and Starfield, B., 'Assessment of Risk in Research on Children', *Journal of Pediatrics*, 98 (1981), 842–6; and Shah, S., Whittle, A., Wilfond, B., Gensler, G., and Wendler, D., 'How Do Institutional Review Boards Apply the Federal Risk and Benefit Standards for Pediatric Research?' *JAMA*, 291 (2004), 476–82.

36. National Human Research Protections Advisory Committee (NHRPAC), 'Clarifying Specific Portion of 45 CFR 46 Subpart D that Governs Children's Research', Undated. Found on the web at: http://www.hhs.gov/ohrp/nhrpac/documents/nhrpac16.pdf, 3.

37. Field M. J., and Behrman, R. E. (eds.), Committee on Clinical Research Involving Children, the Institute of Medicine (IOM), *The Ethical Conduct of Clinical Research Involving Children*. Washington DC: National Academies Press, 2004; hereinafter this reference is cited as IOM, *Ethical Conduct*.

38. Ibid., 129.

39. See Ryan, 'Controversy over Kennedy Krieger Research'.

40. Grimes v. Kennedy Krieger Institute, Inc., No. 128 (Md. 11 Oct. 2001) (order denying motion for reconsideration); Brief of *Amici Curiae*; and Brief of the University of Maryland Baltimore as *Amicus Curiae*, 'In Support of Motion for Reconsideration, *Grimes v. Kennedy Krieger Institute, Inc.*, 782 A.2d 807 (Md. 2001) (No. 128)'. On the web at: http://www.hopkinsmedicine.org/press/2001/SEPTEMBER/UMbrief.htm.
41. See also Ross, L. F., *Children, Families, and Health Care Decision-Making*. Oxford: Clarendon Press, 1998, 42–4. Others have argued against holding parents to a best interest of the child standard. See, e.g., Goldstein, J., Freud, A., and Solnit, A., *Before the Best Interests of the Child*, vol. II. New York: Free Press, 1979, 5–14; Schoeman, F., 'Parental Discretion and Children's Rights: Background and Implications for Medical Decision-Making', *Journal of Medicine and Philosophy*, 10 (1985), 45–62.
42. Ross, '*Children*', esp. Chap. 3, 'Constrained Parental Autonomy', 44–52.
43. Grimes v. Kennedy Krieger Institute, Inc., 782 A.2d 807, 858 (Md. 2001).
44. Ibid., 816.
45. Ibid., 861 (Raker, J., concurring).
46. Ericka Grimes v. Kennedy Krieger Institute, Inc. *et al.* Case No.: 24-C-99–00092. Stipulation of Dismissal with Prejudice, 12 May 2003 (on file with author).
47. Grimes v. Kennedy Krieger Institute, Inc., 782 A.2d 807, 825,828 (Md. 2001).
48. Ibid at 825, 826–7.
49. AAP, 'Lead Poisoning'.
50. Ibid.
51. Maryland Health-General Title 13. Miscellaneous Health Care Programs; subtitle 20. Human Subject Protection. Code Ann. 13–2002 (2003).

13

Clinical Asthma Trials

1. Introduction

In February 1999, the *Journal of Pediatrics* published a letter by Drs Ferdman and Church commenting on a study published in June 1998 by Shapiro *et al.*[1] Shapiro and colleagues found a dose-related effect of inhaled budesonide powder, an anti-inflammatory medication, in children with moderate to severe asthma.[2] Ferdman and Church did not question the findings, only the methodology. They asked why a placebo group was included in addition to the three different arms of budesonide, given that current guidelines require anti-inflammatory medications for all individuals with moderate to severe asthma.[3] They argued that the trial put a large number of children at unnecessary risk, using as evidence that 44% of the placebo group withdrew from the study compared with 15–18% in the three budesonide groups and that these withdrawals were primarily due to worsening asthma.[4] Shapiro *et al.* responded that it was critical to study the safety and efficacy of a new delivery device, the turbuhaler, using a placebo-controlled study design for Food and Drug Administration (FDA) approval.[5] They viewed the study as an ethical compromise in that they accomplished this protocol without incurring serious consequences in their subjects.[6]

The correspondence led me to undertake with colleagues an empirical study to examine four ethical issues raised by clinical asthma research involving children subjects: (1) to what extent are clinical asthma trials designed as placebo-controlled trials as opposed to active-drug controlled trials?; (2) do placebo-controlled trials (PCTs) in a condition like asthma place the research subjects at increased risk of harm?; (3) are the new guidelines promoting increased access of children to research changing the enrollment pattern of children in research?; and (4) are the new guidelines achieving their goal of garnering useful information about medication safety, efficacy, and dosing for children as a class?

2. Background on Asthma

Asthma is a lung disease with the following characteristics: (1) airway obstruction that is reversible either spontaneously or with treatment; (2) airway inflammation; and (3) increased airway responsiveness to a variety of stimuli.[7] Asthma is one of the most common chronic diseases in the United States, and its prevalence has been increasing since 1980.[8] In 1997 a total of 26.7 million persons reported a physician diagnosis of asthma during their lifetime.[9] It is estimated that people with asthma collectively have more than 100 million days of restricted activity and 470,000 hospitalizations annually.[10]

In the US pediatric population alone, asthma affects about 5 million children,[11] although there is evidence to suggest that a significant number of children with asthma remain undiagnosed.[12] Life-threatening attacks are more common in those with severe disease, but children with all degrees of asthma can have a life-threatening event. In children under 15 years, asthma accounted for 5.3 million outpatient visits, over 766,000 emergency department visits, 166,000 hospitalizations, and 189 deaths.[13]

In 1998, the cost of asthma in the US was estimated to be 12.7 billion dollars.[14] One of the largest expenses is for prescriptions accounting for 3.188 billion dollars in 1998.[15] Inhaled corticosteroids (ICS) are one of the two main classes of asthma drug therapy, the other treatment being β-agonists. Given the large potential market, it is not surprising that there are a large number of ICS: beclomethasone dipropionate (Beclovent, Qvar, Vanceril); budesonide (Pulmicort); flunisolide (AeroBid); fluticasone propionate (Flovent), and tramcinolone acetonide (Azmacort). Throughout the past two decades, numerous studies have been done to bring new ICS and delivery devices into the market. The study by Shapiro *et al.* was one such study being done to get data for FDA approval. After the drugs and devices are approved, there are large incentives to increase market share by showing superiority in post-marketing studies or by continuing to test for efficacy in different populations to meet drug labeling and advertising requirements.

3. Asthma Guidelines

In 1990 the US Department of Health and Human Services (DHHS) made the reduction of asthma morbidity a national health care objective.[16] In an effort to achieve improved asthma care outcomes and to 'bridge the gap between research and practice', the National Heart, Lung, and Blood Institute (NHLBI), a branch of the National Institutes of Health, published *Guidelines for the Diagnosis and Management of Asthma* in 1991.[17] These guidelines emphasized the importance of environmental control, objective lung function measurements, patient education, and the use of anti-inflammatory medications, specifically ICS. ICS were initially introduced to reduce the need for oral glucocorticosteroids in patients with severe asthma because chronic use of systemic glucocorticosteroids is associated with serious morbidity.[18] It was hypothesized that ICS would produce less systemic effects, and early evidence supported this hypothesis.[19]

The 1991 guidelines stated explicitly that ICS are first-line therapy for moderate and severe asthma in adults and for severe asthma in children.[20] In children with moderate asthma, the nonsteroidal anti-inflammatory drug cromolyn was regarded as first-line therapy, with ICS reserved to supplement or replace cromolyn if symptoms persisted. It was expected that cromolyn would be effective in 60–80% of children with mild and moderate asthma.[21] The guidelines did state, however, that ICS 'is an acceptable primary therapy for moderate asthma although a trial of cromolyn should usually precede its use because of the extensive clinical experience with and study of cromolyn sodium'.[22] These recommendations are similar to the international pediatric asthma guidelines published in 1989,[23] 1990,[24] and 1992.[25]

With the growing understanding of the inflammatory nature of asthma,[26] the ability of steroids to prevent or reduce inflammation,[27] and the safety of ICS,[28] there was a move to test ICS on individuals with less severe asthma.[29] In 1995, the NHLBI in conjunction with the World Health Organization (WHO) jointly produced a report entitled 'Global Initiative for Asthma'[30] which revised the current classification of asthma to include both mild intermittent asthma and mild persistent asthma. The report recommended that children and adults with moderate persistent asthma be treated with ICS.[31] Adults, children, and infants with mild persistent asthma could be treated with either inhaled corticosteroids or cromoglycate.[32] In 1997, the NHLBI issued revised guidelines that recommended ICS as first-line therapy for children and adults with mild persistent asthma,[33] and this recommendation was reaffirmed in 2002.[34]

The evolving guidelines reflect the accumulating evidence that ICS are safe and effective in both children and adults. The incorporation of ICS in the pediatric guidelines lags behind their inclusion in adult guidelines in part because of long-term safety concerns but also because of research policies and practices that encourage the testing of new therapies on adults first. Nevertheless, while ICS were not recommended as front-line therapy for children in the early 1990s, data from the UK revealed a much higher use of ICS than would have been expected if they were only used when cromolyn failed.[35] The prescribing pattern is more likely due to physician belief in the superiority of ICS and greater ease in administration (once or twice a day versus four times a day).[36]

The gap between policy and practice is one reason that critics bemoan the policy to test new therapies on adults first. The critics argue that the delays in pediatric testing place children at unnecessary and serious risk because practice changes are made before there are adequate pediatric data. In the case of ICS, safety and efficacy data in children were not complete in 1991, but physicians were already using ICS to treat children with asthma in their clinical practice based on adult data. This practice was occurring despite the fact that children, or certain classes of children, might have had a different benefit-risk from the medication than adults. In retrospect, ICS have been found to be effective and to have minimal side-effects in children, but that has not always been the case when extrapolating drug safety and efficacy from adult data.[37]

4. Empirical Data Collection Methodology

We performed a MEDLINE search to identify all clinical asthma trials (CAT) published between 1 January 1998, and 30 December 2001. Articles were excluded if they (1) did not include subjects under the age of 18; (2) did not include original data or involve active recruitment of subjects (e.g. pooled analyses or meta-analyses); (3) were nontherapeutic (e.g. pharmacokinetic studies or cost-benefit studies); or (4) focused on such related conditions as exercise-induced asthma, allergic rhinitis, or status asthmaticus. Articles were also excluded if they were conducted outside the United States because two of our goals were focused on whether recent US policies (1) influenced access of children to research; and (2) achieved the goal of advancing pediatric medicine. Of the initial 450 articles, over 200 (44%) were excluded as foreign studies. All US articles were reviewed to ensure that each study represented a separate population or a distinct research methodology. Seventy studies were included for further analysis. A full methodology is given elsewhere.[38]

The numbers of subjects who enrolled in, completed, and withdrew or were withdrawn from each CAT were recorded. To account for subject withdrawals during active and placebo phases of cross-over studies, each subject was counted once for every arm to which that subject belonged. The causes of withdrawals, including asthma exacerbations and adverse events, were recorded. Withdrawals due to unspecified reasons or reasons specified as 'other' often could only be determined in total, not for each treatment arm. We defined a subject as being harmed by his or her participation in research if he or she withdrew prematurely or was hospitalized for an asthma-related problem while participating in the research. More specifically, we focused on those subjects who were harmed specifically because they withdrew due to an asthma exacerbation.

Subjects' asthma severity and treatment prior to enrollment were recorded. Many studies prohibited concurrent use of any prescription or over-the-counter medication that might affect the course of asthma or its treatment. No inferences were made from these statements about what medications were prohibited, and we recorded only whether anti-inflammatory medications (AIM) were specifically allowed or prohibited.

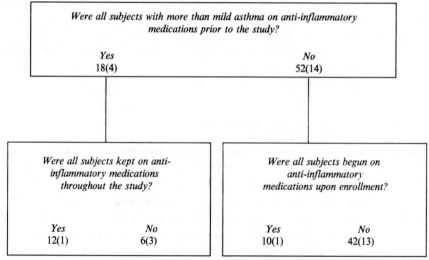

Total no. trials (number of trails including only children)
Figure 2. NHLBI Asthma Guideline Adherence in CAT Including Children (n = 70). Figure 2 is modified and reprinted with permission from Coffey, M. J., Wilfond, B., and Ross, L. F. 'Ethical Assesment of Clinical Asthma Trials Including Children Subjects', *Pediatrics*, 113 (2004), 87–94, 89, Figure 1.

Finally, we recorded whether all subjects with more than mild asthma in each study received AIM upon enrollment and throughout the course of their participation in the research as delineated in the 1991 NHLBI Guidelines,[39] unless the study specifically referred to the 1997 NHLBI guidelines to distinguish mild intermittent from mild persistent asthma.[40] If this distinction was made, we documented whether all subjects with more than mild intermittent asthma received AIM.

The University of Chicago IRB approved the research and waived written consent for the three researchers contacted to clarify data available in their publication. The NIH exempted the research from review.

5. Results from the Empirical Study

The characteristics of the 70 eligible studies are given in Table 12. All studies enrolled at least some subjects who would meet the criteria for daily AIM. Fifty (71%) studies used placebos. Most of these studies (*n*=45) compared an investigational treatment against placebo (PCT); the others (*n*=5) were add-on trials in which all subjects continued on AIM. The total number of studies enrolling only children was 18 (26%), 14 of which were PCT. The percentage

Table 12.   Study characteristics

Trials eligible	70
Trials using placebos	50
Placebo vs. experimental drug (PCT)	45
Placebo as add-on vs. experimental drug (add-on)	5
PCT	45
Trials involving children and adults	31
Trials involving only children	14
Trials involving children and adults	52
Trials differentiating between children and adults at baseline	8
Trials differentiating between children and adults in results	1
Average duration of trials in weeks (excluding run-in period)	26.8
Trials more than 6 months in duration	16
PCT	7
Trials documenting withdrawal information	62
PCT	40
Trials documenting source of funding	67
Pharmaceutical company	63
NIH with pharmaceutical-sponsored medications	3
Academic institution	1
PCT documenting source of funding	42
Pharmaceutical company	39
NIH with pharmaceutical-sponsored medications	3
Academic institution	0
Trials documenting IRB review and approval	67
Trials documenting procurement of informed consent	68
Trials performed by year – #(# including only children)	
1998	15(7)
1999	22(4)
2000	20(5)
2001	13(2)
Subjects available for analysis (# counted more than once)	30,101(218)
Subjects enrolled in 62 trials documenting withdrawal information	25,366(218)

Table 12   is modified and reprinted with permission from Coffey, M. J. Wilfond, B. and Ross, L. 'Ethical Assessment of Clinical Asthma Trials including Children Subjects', *Pediatrics*, 113 (2004), 87–94, 89, Table 1.

of studies that enrolled both adults and children increased from just over 50% in 1998 (8 of 15) to greater than 70% in the remaining three years.

Of the 52 studies that involved both children and adults, only two included children younger than 4 years of age, and only one included a subpopulation analysis of adverse effects according to age. Thirty-one of the studies were PCT. The duration of the trials ranged from 5 days to 6 years. Sixteen studies enrolled subjects for at least 6 months; seven of which were PCT. Sixty-seven documented IRB approval.

Thirty thousand one hundred one subjects were available for analysis from the 70 studies, including 218 subjects who were counted more than once because they were enrolled in one of the three cross-over studies. Our withdrawal analysis is based on the 62 studies (40 of which were PCT) documenting withdrawals and involves 24,953 subjects.

Figure 2 describes whether all the subjects enrolled in the 70 studies were treated in adherence with the NHLBI guidelines. In only 18 (26%) studies were all subjects with more than mild asthma on AIM prior to the study. In 6 (33%) of these studies, some of the subjects were taken off these medications during the trial. All of these studies were placebo-controlled trials. In the 52 studies in which all subjects were not on AIM prior to the study, only 10 (19%) were begun on appropriate treatment at the time of study enrollment. Only 1 of the 18 studies (6%) that enrolled only children-subjects ensured that they received appropriate AIM upon enrollment.

Table 13 shows the number of subjects who withdrew and the reasons for their withdrawal in all studies for which that data is provided ($n=62$). The first column describes the number and reason for subject withdrawals. Four thousand six hundred fifty-three (19%) subjects withdrew or were withdrawn from research participation. The most common reason for withdrawal was asthma exacerbation (34%). Adverse events accounted for an additional 11%. The remaining withdrawals were due to noncompliance, protocol violation, failure to return, and a loss to follow-up, etc. No reasons were given for 10% of withdrawals. The second and third columns compare the withdrawal number and reason for subjects in add-on and active-controlled trials (column 2) versus subjects in the PCT (column 3). The results show that subjects in PCT withdrew or were withdrawn more frequently than subjects in add-on and active-controlled studies ($p<.001$). A higher percentage of these withdrawals were due to asthma exacerbations ($p<0.001$). More subjects in PCT were withdrawn because of asthma exacerbations than subjects in other trials (1,247 of 13,263 or 9.4% vs. 358 of 11,690 or 3.1%, $p<0.001$). Very few studies reported any hospitalizations. Less than 1% of all subjects are documented as having required hospitalization.

Table 14 shows the number of subjects withdrawn and the reasons for their withdrawal in the 40 PCT for which withdrawal data are given. There is a

Table 13.   Subject withdrawals by trial design

	All trials (n=62)	Add-on & active-controlled trials (n=22)	Placebo-controlled trials (n=40)
Subjects analyzed –no.	24,953	11,690	13,263
Withdrawn –no.(%)	4,653 (19)	1,849 (16)	2,804 (21)#
Asthma exacerbations	1,605 (34)	358 (19)	1,247 (44)#
Adverse events	518 (11)	277 (15)	241 (9)#
Other	2,069 (44)	1,177 (64)	892 (32)#
Not discussed		37 (2)	424 (15)#
	461 (10)		
Hospitalized –no.(%)		108 (<1)	14 (<1)
	122 (<1)		

Significant difference between PCT and all other trials (p<0.001).
Table 13 is modified and reprinted with permission from Coffey, M. J. Wilfond, B. and Ross, L. 'Ethical Assessment of Clinical Asthma Trials including Children Subjects', *Pediatrics*, 113 (2004), 87–94, 90, Table 2.

separate analysis for the 12 PCT that included only children-subjects and for which withdrawal data are given. Two thousand eight hundred and four (21%) subjects withdrew or were withdrawn from all studies. One cannot determine from the available data whether adults or children withdrew as none of the PCT distinguished between children and adults in withdrawal data. Eight hundred and ten (20%) subjects withdrew in studies that only included children. These totals include 172 and 64 subjects (from 4 studies, 3 of which only enrolled children) who withdrew from unspecified study arms in columns 1 and 4 respectively and are not analyzed further. When all PCT data are analyzed, asthma exacerbations account for 44% of these withdrawals. Columns two and three specify the number of subjects who withdrew from active and placebo arms, respectively. The results show that subjects withdrew more frequently from placebo arms ($p<0.001$), and they mainly withdrew because they experienced an asthma exacerbation ($p<0.001$). These differences were also found in PCT including only children, as described in columns 5 and 6. Children withdrew more frequently from placebo arms ($p<0.001$), with the reason more likely being an asthma exacerbation ($p<0.001$). Overall, children in placebo arms of PCT were more than twice as likely to withdraw due to asthma exacerbations as children in active treatment arms (205 of 1,180 or 17.4% vs. 226 of 2,906 or 7.8%, $p<0.001$). Few studies reported hospitalizations, and those that did failed to specify whether the subjects were children or adults, except for one exclusively pediatric study in which one child was hospitalized from the active arm of a PCT.

Table 14. Subject withdrawals for each arm of placebo-controlled trials (PCT)

Study arms	All trials (n=40)			Trials including only children (n=12)		
	All arms	Active arms	Placebo arm	All arms	Active arms	Placebo arm
Subjects analyzed –no.	13,263	8,867	4,396	4,086	2,906	1,180
Withdrawn –no.(%)	2,804 (21)	1,422 (16)	1,210 (28)#	810 (20)	428 (15)	318 (27)#
Asthma exacerbations	1,247 (44)	580 (45)	667 (55)#	431 (53)	226 (52)	205 (64)#
Adverse events	241 (9)	136 (11)	105 (9)	44 (5)	28 (6)	16 (5)
All other reasons	1,316 (47)	571 (44)	438 (36)^	335 (41)	180 (41)	97 (31)#
Hospitalized–no.(%)	14 (<1)	9 (<1)	5 (<1)	1 (<1)	1 (<1)	0 (0)

Significant difference between placebo arm and active arms (p<0.001).
^ Significant difference between placebo arm and active arms (p<0.05).
Table 14 is modified and reprinted with permission from Coffey, M.J. Wilfond, B. and Ross, L.F. 'Ethical Assessment of Clinical Asthma Trials Including Children Subjects', *Pediatrics*, 113 (2004), 87–94, 90, Table 3.

6. Discussion: The Use of Placebos in Asthma Research

Placebo-controlled studies have been the 'gold standard' of research since their introduction half a century ago.[41] A study is placebo-controlled if it compares an experimental drug with an inert substance. It is a randomized controlled trial if the therapy given to the subject is chosen randomly and not by the physician-scientist. Randomized controlled trials are usually done in a double-blind fashion; neither the researcher nor the subject knows to which arm the subject is randomly allocated.

Placebo-controlled studies can be ethical. In 1977, the American Academy of Pediatrics Committee on Drugs enumerated five conditions in which the use of placebos is ethical in drug research in children: (1) when there is no commonly accepted therapy for the condition and the agent under study is the first one that may modify the course of the disease process; (2) when the commonly used therapy for the condition is of questionable or low efficacy; (3) when the commonly used therapy for the condition carries with it a high frequency of unacceptable side-effects; (4) when the incidence and severity of undesirable side-effects produced by adding a new treatment to an established regimen are uncertain; and (5) when the disease process is characterized by frequent spontaneous exacerbations and remissions.[42] These conditions were reaffirmed by the American Academy of Pediatrics in 1995.[43]

The first condition states that placebo-controlled trials are ethical when there is no standard of care and it is not clear that the new intervention is effective. In these cases, it is unknown whether the experimental drug is better than placebo. Such uncertainty at the beginning of a trial is known as 'clinical equipoise'.[44] However, by 1991, there was a standard of care for children with asthma clearly stated in several consensus statements.[45] The guidelines recommended that all children with moderate and severe asthma be given a daily anti-inflammatory of cromolyn or ICS respectively. Yet 45 of the 70 studies published in the years 1998–2001 compared a study drug to placebo. That is, in at least one of the arms, subjects were either discontinued from their current treatment or not begun on an anti-inflammatory agent despite the consensus for anti-inflammatories. All such studies, then, were unethical because (1) they failed to provide standard of care in the placebo-arm;[46] and (2) they lacked equipoise at the start of the trials. As one researcher admitted, 'Asthma symptoms would be expected to worsen in the placebo group during the treatment period because these patients were dependent on inhaled steroids but were not allowed treatment with inhaled steroids while in the study.'[47]

A second way that placebo-controlled studies can be ethical is if they compare a new study drug as an add-on (condition 4). In an add-on study, subjects continue to take their current treatment and are given an additional drug (or placebo) to see if the new drug improves their medical status. To be ethical, add-on studies require that the subjects' current treatment conform to standard of care. In other words, if one wanted to study the effectiveness of montelukast, a leukotriene inhibitor, as an adjuvant therapy for individuals with moderate persistent asthma, it would be necessary to ensure that all of the subjects were also on an anti-inflammatory agent. Alternatively, it would be ethical for an add-on study to compare an ICS against placebo for children with moderate persistent asthma provided that all the subjects were on cromolyn. Five of the 50 placebo-controlled studies were designed as 'add-on' studies in which all subjects continued on AIM and were ethically designed.

A third way that placebo-controlled trials in asthma would be ethical is if the commonly used therapy for the condition carries with it a high frequency of unacceptable side-effects. Although there were serious concerns regarding the potential side-effects of ICS, it is fair to say that by the early 1990s, most of these had been disproven,[48] even though research continues to look for long-term side-effects.

The final two justifications for a placebo-controlled trial are if the commonly used therapy for the condition is of questionable or low efficacy (condition 3), and if the disease process is characterized by frequent spontaneous exacerbations and remissions (condition 5). These conditions do not apply to the treatment of moderate to severe asthma in the 1990s: AIM were known to be effective in the long-term treatment of asthma, and asthma exacerbations require treatment.

From an ethics perspective, our data show that current placebo-controlled asthma trials are methodologically flawed. First, they lack clinical equipoise. The researchers expect the patient-subjects on placebo to do worse than those on the experimental ICS. Second, they fail to provide all subjects in the control arm with the current standard of care. In fact, in six studies, subjects were taken off their AIM to be randomized to either an experimental ICS or placebo. Not surprisingly, the subjects who received placebo withdrew more frequently and had more frequent asthma exacerbations. These children were also being placed at risk for chronic irreversible changes.[49]

The studies are also not scientifically valid. Miller and colleagues recently published an in-depth analysis of a 'typical' placebo-controlled asthma study.[50] The study they analyzed compared mometasone furoate (MF), an ICS, at two different doses versus beclomethasone diproprionate (BDP), another ICS, versus placebo in subjects with moderate persistent asthma.[51] Miller *et al.* note that the researchers did not articulate a specific scientific question to be answered by the trial, but that the researchers noted that MF has been found to be well tolerated and efficacious in previous studies.[52] Miller *et al.* argue: 'In view of the already demonstrated efficacy of MF in the treatment of persistent asthma, the scientific value of another trial designed to test the efficacy of MF as compared with placebo is dubious.'[53] Rather, Miller *et al.* argue, 'testing the equivalence or superiority of MF to BDP would have been scientifically and clinically valuable'.[54] If further testing of efficacy was unnecessary at the time of the study, then the study is not scientifically justifiable. If it is not scientifically sound, then it cannot be ethical because one of the fundamental principles of human subject protections is that the research must be scientifically sound to justify placing any human subjects at any risk.[55]

7. Discussion: Studies Involving Children and Adults

Of the 70 asthma studies, 52 included children and adults. The number of studies with children and adults was 8 (of 15) in 1998, 18 (of 22) in 1999, 15 (of 20) in 2000, and 11 (of 13) in 2001. The pattern of a greater number of studies including adolescents and adults may reflect the policy initiatives in the 1990s towards the increased participation of children.

What is the purpose of enrolling children, a vulnerable population, in clinical research? According to the National Commission's report, *Research Involving Children*, the purpose should be to enhance the well-being of the individual child or children-as-a-class.[56] As such, one would assume that any clinical drug trial that enrolled children would have as one of its goals an assessment of the safety and efficacy of the drug on children. Unfortunately, only one of the 52 studies that included children and adults did subset analysis to determine (1) if the treatment responses in children were the same or different than the responses in adults; or (2) whether the adverse events and withdrawals occurred more frequently in the pediatric subjects or in the adult subjects.[57] In response to two asthma studies that included subjects older than 12 years and were published in the same issue of *JAMA* in 2001,[58] I questioned the authors regarding the reason for including children if not enough subjects would be enrolled to make useful subset analyses.[59] While one principal investigator [PI] agreed that 'studies involving children must balance the generalizability of results against the risk of participation',[60] another PI responded that 'neither trial was designed specifically to evaluate if the response of children or adolescents differed from adults; rather patient selection was based on criteria that would permit the results to be generalized to the patient populations for which these medications were approved by the US Food and Drug Administration and routinely prescribed.'[61] Why were children enrolled if their were no plans to analyze the pediatric data separately? While it may help the researchers achieve their enrollment criteria more quickly, the participation of children or adolescents in these studies was unethical because it placed some at risk without plans to benefit each individual child or to benefit the class of children generally.

If clinical drug trials that enroll children do not benefit children as a class, the child-subjects in all arms of the study should at least be assured standard of care. Unfortunately, this was rarely the case.

8.   Why Such Research Designs?

It should be clear, then, that very few of the asthma studies published between 1998 and 2001 were done ethically, despite the fact that 67 of the 70 documented IRB review and 68 of the 70 documented that consent was procured. One could argue that the research was ethical because the subjects and/or their parents knew the aim of the research and its methodology and were free to consent or to refuse to consent to participate. Such an argument, however, fails to acknowledge the dual responsibility of IRBs: both to promote subject autonomy and to protect human subjects.[62] Consent is necessary, but not sufficient. The protection of human subjects requires that research risks are minimized.[63]

Why then did the researchers choose such study designs? In her response to Ferdman and Church, Shapiro explained that the study was being done to get FDA-approval for a new delivery device. Although the FDA does not require placebo-controlled studies, it is clear that it favors placebo-controlled trials.[64] Other researchers use placebo-controlled trials to be able to show significant results. Many of the review articles show that differences in efficacy and side-effects of the different ICS are not clinically significant.[65] Thus, any trial that compares an ICS against placebo shows greater differences than a trial that compares one ICS against a competitor ICS. To that extent, the research functions more as medical advertisement to increase market share than as groundbreaking research.[66]

Many of the ICS placebo-controlled studies published between 1998 and 2001 replicate results. Consider, for example, a paper by Baker *et al.* published in 1999 comparing budesonide inhalation suspension (BIS), an ICS, or placebo in 480 infants and children with asthma. The researchers noted that their results are similar to the findings of nine other studies that evaluated the efficacy of BIS in young children with asthma.[67] The numerous replications of asthma trials contrast sharply with the paucity of research done to replicate efficacy of innovative therapies lacking commercial value.[68] What distinguishes the asthma trials from these other therapies is that the asthma medications are quite profitable. The asthma trials studies are being funded by pharmaceutical companies that have a significant financial interest in them. Sixty-seven of the 70 studies reported funding source; and 63 of these were pharmaceutically funded; three were funded by the NIH with study drug supplied by the pharmaceutical company, and one was institutionally funded. Often these studies were being done to get 'me-too' drugs to market or to increase the brand's visibility and hence its market share.

One may argue that I am being too harsh. There is a need to replicate research results in order to ensure that the findings are correct and do not reflect a statistical anomaly. I agree. But before one can justify additional placebo-controlled asthma trials, one should examine the world literature. Many of the studies examining the efficacy of ICS against placebo between 1998 and 2001 merely duplicate research already performed by European researchers and published in the European literature.[69]

9. Further Anecdotal Support

An FDA ruling in 2003 exemplifies a problem with the current incentives to promote pediatric drug testing.[70] In June 1999, the FDA issued a Written Request to GlaxoSmithKline (GSK) which was amended in May and October 2001 for further study of fluticasone proprionate [FP] in numerous preparations.[71] Under the Best Pharamceutical for Children's Act [BPCA], companies that do the studies under the Written Request are eligible for an additional six months of patent protection on their drugs. Since FP has sales of around $1 billion dollars in the US,[72] the additional six months is worth a lot of money.

GSK completed numerous studies as required by the Written Request including (1) two clinical study reports; (2) in vitro CMC (chemical, manufacturing and controls) study of dose delivery from different US-marketed spacers (a chamber fitted to an inhaler which avoids the coordination necessary for direct inhalation from an asthma inhaler); and (3) a population PK [pharmacokinetic] evaluation of FP levels at the end of 12 weeks of therapy in the two requested clinical Flovent [the trade name for FP] studies.[73]

Both clinical trials were randomized double-blind placebo-controlled 12-week efficacy and safety studies using Flovent in two different doses given to children twice daily. The children with asthma were either 6 to 23 months (study 1) or 24 to 47 months of age (study 2). Overall 493 children were enrolled and 332 children were randomized from 77 centers into the first study. In the second study, 337 children were enrolled and 211 were randomized from 54 centers.[74]

The primary efficacy variable for both clinical trials was the parent rating of the patient's daytime and night-time asthma symptoms. Unfortunately, as the FDA review notes 'a meaningful interpretation of the efficacy results from these studies cannot be made because of detectable plasma levels of fluticasone seen in placebo treated patients. Therefore, efficacy data from the studies are not presented in the summary.'[75] The report noted that GlaxoSmithKline was not able to explain this finding although one possible explanation was a drug allocation error. The report continues that 'the problem [drug misallocation] may have been larger than stated...[s]ince many patients on active treatment did not have detectable FP levels'.[76]

The probable misallocation of study drug also meant that the safety data was 'uninterpretable as to the true extent of the safety risk.... Therefore safety data from the studies are not presented in the summary.'[77]

Despite the lack of meaningful data on either safety or efficacy, the FDA granted GSK six-month additional patent protection:

On the basis of the completion and submission of the studies requested in the Written Requests, including the two clinical studies, the CMC study report and the population PK report, GlaxoSmithKline (GSK) requested a Pediatric Exclusivity determination. The Pediatric Exclusivity Board met on February 25, 2003, determined that Pediatric Exclusivity requirements were met, and granted exclusivity.[78]

That is, GSK was rewarded, and not punished, for the poor quality of results from its pediatric asthma studies despite the fact that children were placed at risk and no useful generalizable knowledge was obtained.

10.   *Concluding Remarks*

Shapiro's response to Ferdman and Church fails both scientifically and ethically.[79] Scientifically, Shapiro and colleagues could have used active controls. Their ethical justification also fails. First, whether subjects were seriously harmed could only be known after the fact, and as Beecher noted two decades earlier, the ethics of a study are determined at its inception and not post-facto.[80] Second, Shapiro is wrong to say that there were no serious consequences.[81] Asthma exacerbations should not be taken lightly. Likewise, the GSK randomized controlled trials failed scientifically and ethically.

I do not mean to suggest that all pharmaceutically funded research is unethical or bad science. However, the source of funding changes what is studied, how it is studied, and what is published.[82] The implications are particularly significant because pharmaceutical spending currently accounts for over 50% of funding of clinical trials of new drugs.[83]

Children are a vulnerable population in clinical research and need additional protection. This means that we should maintain the former recommendations of the National Commission to perform research first on animals, second on adults, and only then on children. It also means that when we do involve children, we must ensure high scientific and ethical standards. There must be a plan to enroll enough children to perform subset analyses in order to benefit children as a class. The data we collected on recent CAT support the concern that the ideological shift from a focus on protection to a focus on access has exposed children to significant and unnecessary risks. The policies that promote pediatric participation in clinical trials are not necessarily being implemented in a way that promotes either the advancement of the individual child's health or the advancement of pediatric medicine more generally.

References

1. Ferdman, R. M., and Church, J. A., 'Ethical Issues of Placebo-Controlled Trials', *Journal of Pediatrics*, 134 (1999), 251.
2. Shapiro, G., Bronsky, E. A., LaForce, C. F., Mendelson, L., Pearlman, D., Schwartz, R. H., and Szefler, S. J., 'Dose-Related Efficacy of Budesonide Administered Via a Dry Powder Inhaler in the Treatment of Children with Moderate to Severe Persistent Asthma', *Journal of Pediatrics*, 132 (1998), 976–82.
3. National Heart, Lung, and Blood Institute, National Institutes of Health, *Global Strategy for Asthma Management and Prevention*, NIH Publication No. 95–3659 (1995) as cited by Ferdman and Church, 'Ethical Issues', 251.
4. Ferdman and Church, 'Ethical Issues', 251.
5. Shapiro, G., 'Reply', *Journal of Pediatrics*, 134 (1999), 251–2.
6. Ibid., at 252.
7. National Heart, Lung and Blood Institute (NHLBI), National Institutes of Health, National Asthma Education & Program, *Expert Panel Report, Guidelines for the Diagnosis and Management of Asthma*, DHHS Publication No. 91–3042 (1991), 1; hereinafter cited as NHLBI, *Expert Panel*.
8. Mannino, D. M., Homa, D. M., Akinbami, L. J., Moorman, J. E., Gwynn, C., and Redd, S. C., 'Surveillance for Asthma—United States, 1980–1999', *MMWR: Morbidity & Mortality Weekly Report: Surveillance Summaries*, 51 (29 March 2002), 1–13.
9. Ibid.
10. National Heart, Lung and Blood Institute (NHLBI), National Institutes of Health, National Asthma Education & Program, *Expert Panel Report-2, Guidelines for the Diagnosis and Management of Asthma*, DHHS Publication No. 97–4051 (July 1997), 1. On the web at: http://www.nhlbi.nih.gov/guidelines/asthma/asthgdln.pdf; hereinafter cited as NHLBI, *Expert Panel 2*.
11. American Academy of Allergy, Asthma, & Immunology (AAAAI), American Academy of Pediatrics, National Heart, Lung & Blood Institute, National Asthma Education & Prevention Program, *Pediatric Asthma: Promoting Best Practice, Guide for Managing Asthma in Children* (released in 1999, updated in 2002). On the web at: http://www.aaaai.org/members/resources/initiatives/pediatricasthmaguidelines, Epidemiology, 2; hereinafter referred to as the AAAI, *Best Practice*.
12. Crain, E. F., Weiss, K. B., Bijur, P. E., Hersh, M., Westbrook, L., and Stein, R. E., 'An Estimate of the Prevalence of Asthma and Wheezing Among Inner-City Children', *Pediatrics*, 94 (1994), 356–62; and Joseph, C. L., Foxman, B., Leickly, F. E., Peterson, E., and Ownby, D., 'Prevalence of Possible Undiagnosed Asthma and Associated Morbidity among Urban Schoolchildren', *Journal of Pediatrics*, 129 (1996), 735–42.
13. Mannino *et al.*, 'Asthma Surveillance'.

14. Weiss, K. B., and Sullivan, S. D., 'The Health Economics of Asthma and Rhinitis. I. Assessing the Economic Impact', *Journal of Allergy & Clinical Immunology*, 107 (2001), 3–8.

15. Ibid., Table 1.

16. US Department of Health and Human Services [DHHS], Public Health Service, *Healthy People 2000: National Health Promotion and Disease Objectives*. Washington DC: US Government Printing Office, DHHS Publication no. 91–50212; hereinafter cited as *Healthy People 2000*. Asthma continues to be a priority for *Healthy People 2010*. It can be found on the web at http://www.cdc.gov/nchs/about/otheract/hpdata2010/abouthp.htm.

17. Claude L'enfant, Director, NHLBI, Foreword to *Healthy People 2000*.

18. These side effects include suppression of the hypothalamic-pituitary-adrenal axis which can reduce adrenal response to stress, reduction in bone mass causing osteoporosis and an increased risk of vertebral and rib fractures, stunting of growth, thinning of the skin, easy bruising, cataracts, and psychiatric disturbance including emotional lability, aggressiveness, and insomnia. See Barnes, P. J., 'Inhaled Glucocorticoids for Asthma', *New England Journal of Medicine*, 332 (1995), 868–75, 871–3; and Pedersen, S., and O'Byrne, P., 'A Comparison of the Efficacy and Safety of Inhaled Corticosteroids in Asthma', *Allergy*, 52 (39 Suppl.) (1997), 1–34, 16–27.

19. The main side effects of long-term ICS are oral thrush, sore throat, and hoarseness. See Brogden, R. N., Heel, R. C., Speight, T. M., and Avery, G. S., 'Beclomethasone Dipropionate. A Reappraisal of its Pharmacodynamic Properties and Therapeutic Efficacy after a Decade of Use in Asthma and Rhinitis', *Drugs*, 28 (1984), 99–126, 121.

20. *Healthy People 2000*.

21. Murphy and Kelly cite several studies that report a success rate between 60% and 80%. See Murphy, S., and Kelly, H. W., 'Cromolyn Sodium: A Review of Mechanisms and Clinical Use in Asthma', *Drug Intelligence & Clinical Pharmacy*, 21 (1987), 22–35, 28 and references 109–15.

22. *Healthy People 2000*, 81.

23. Warner, J. O., Gotz, M., Landau, L. I., Levison, H., Milner, A. D., Pedersen, S., and Silverman, M., 'Management of Asthma: A Consensus Statement', *Archives of Disease in Childhood*, 64 (1989), 1065–79.

24. Hargreave, F. E., Dolovich, J., and Newhouse, M. T., 'The Assessment and Treatment of Asthma: A Conference Report', *Journal of Allergy & Clinical Immunology*, 85 (1990), 1098–111.

25. International Paediatric Asthma Consensus Group, 'Asthma: A Follow Up Statement from an International Paediatric Asthma Consensus Group', *Archives of Disease in Childhood*, 67 (1992), 240–8.

26. Barnes, P. J., 'A New Approach to the Treatment of Asthma', *New England Journal of Medicine*, 321 (1989), 1517–27, 1517. The evidence can be found in Chung, K. F., and Durham, S. R., 'Asthma as an Inflammatory Disease: Clinical Perspectives', *British Medical Bulletin*, 48 (1992), 179–89.

27. Barnes, 'Inhaled Glucocorticoids', 868.

28. See, e.g., Godfrey, S., 'The Place of a New Aerosol Steroid, Beclomethasone Dipropionate, in the Management of Childhood Asthma', *Pediatric Clinics of North America*, 22 (1975), 147–55; Clissold, S. P., and Heel, R. C., 'Budesonide. A Preliminary Review of its Pharmacodynamic Properties and Therapeutic Efficacy in Asthma and Rhinitis', *Drugs*, 28 (1984), 485–518; and Davies, B., 'A Comparison of Beclomethasone Dipropionate and Budesonide in the Treatment of Asthma', *British Journal of Clinical Practice*, 47 (1993), 87–93. Davies 'critically assesses the published literature from 1980 to August, 1992' (ibid., 87).

29. See e.g., Clissold and Heel, 'A Preliminary', 505; Chambers, W. B., and Malfitan, V. A., 'Beclomethasone Dipropionate Aerosol in the Treatment of Asthma in Steroid-Independent Children', *Journal of International Medical Research*, 7 (1979), 415–22; and Lorentzson, S., Boe, J., Eriksson, G., and Persson, G., 'Use of Inhaled Corticosteroids in Patients with Mild Asthma', *Thorax*, 45 (1990), 733–5.

30. National Heart, Lung, & Blood Institute, US Department of Health and Human Services, World Health Organization (WHO), *Asthma Management and Prevention: A Practical Guide for Public Health Officials and Health Care Professionals*, Based on the Global Strategy for Asthma Management and Prevention, NHLBI/WHO Workshop Report, NIH. Publication No. 96–3659A. December 1995. On the web at: http://www.ginasthma.com/practical/prac.html.

31. Ibid., 19–20 (Figures 10a and 10b).

32. Ibid.

33. NHLBI, *Expert Panel 2*.

34. National Heart, Lung and Blood Institute (NHLBI), National Institutes of Health, National Asthma Education & Program, *Expert Panel Report, Guidelines for the Diagnosis and Management of Asthma, Update on Selected Topics, 2002*. DHHS Publication No. 02–5074 (June 2003); hereinafter cited as *Update on Selected Topics*. On the web at: http://www.nhlbi.nih.gov/guidelines/asthma/asthmafullrpt.pdf.

35. Kaarsgaren, R. J., Zijlstra, R. F., and Helms, P., 'Asthma Medication in Children—1991', *Respiratory Medicine*, 88 (1994), 383–6; and Warner, J. O., 'Review of Prescribed Treatment for Children with Asthma in 1990', *BMJ*, 311 (1995), 66306.

36. Robins, A. W., and Lloyd, B. W., 'Most Consultants Deviate from Asthma Guidelines', *BMJ*, 311 (1995), 508.

37. See the examples cited by the Food and Drug Administration, 'Regulations Requiring Manufacturers to Assess the Safety and Effectiveness of New Drugs and Biological Products in Pediatric Patients, Part V, Proposed Rule', *Federal Register*, 62 (15 August 1997), 43900–16, 43901.

38. Coffey, M. J., Wilfond, B., and Ross, L. F., 'Ethical Assessment of Clinical Asthma Trials Including Children Subjects', *Pediatrics*, 113 (2004), 87–94.

39. NHLBI, *Expert Panel*.

40. Ibid., 2.

41. The first placebo-controlled trial was probably conducted in 1908 when W. H. R. Rivers compared alcohol and other drugs to an inert substance (not then referred

to as a placebo) in their effects on fatigue. See Shapiro, A. K., and Shapiro E., *The Powerful Placebo*. Baltimore MD: Johns Hopkins University Press, 1997, 137. The first *randomized* placebo-controlled trial to be conducted was a study of immunization against whooping cough done under the auspices of the Medical Research Council (UK). Medical Research Council Whooping-Cough Immunization Committee, 'The Prevention of Whooping-Cough by Vaccination', *BMJ*, i (1951), 1463–71. With the publication of classic papers by Wolf, Beecher, and others, the placebo control became an integral part of the randomized controlled trial. See Wolf, S. 'Pharmacology of placebos', *Pharmacological Review*, 2 (1959), 689–704; and Beecher, H. K., 'The powerful placebo', *JAMA*, 159 (1955), 1602–6.

42. American Academy of Pediatrics Committee on Drugs, 'Guidelines for the Ethical Conduct of Studies to Evaluate Drugs in Pediatric Populations', *Pediatrics*, 60 (1977), 91–101 at 99.

43. Ibid., *Pediatrics*, 95 (1995), 286–94.

44. The term 'equipoise' was coined by Charles Fried to refer to the state of uncertainty that must exist for a clinical trial to be justified. Fried, C., *Medical Experimentation: Personal Integrity and Social Policy*. New York: American Elsevier, 1974, 52–3. Benjamin Freedman suggested that the equipoise needed for a clinical trial to be ethical is 'clinical equipoise', which refers to a state of disagreement in the expert community about the merits of a particular therapy. See Freedman, B. 'Equipoise and the Ethics of Clinical Research', *New England Journal of Medicine*, 317 (1987), 141–5.

45. See, e.g., NHLBI, *Expert Panel*, 79–84; Warner *et al.*, 'Management of Asthma'; and Hargreave *et al.*, 'Assessment and Treatment'.

46. Not all ethicists would agree that all placebo-controlled trials are unethical when a standard of care exists. See, e.g., Brody, B. A., *Ethical Issues in Drug Testing, Approval, and Pricing: The Clot-Dissolving Drugs*. New York: Oxford University Press, 1995, 112–13, 116. Brody argues that if three criteria are met, placebo-controlled trials can be ethical in the face of a proven therapy: '(1) withholding the proven therapy for the period of the clinical trial is unlikely to produce any significant long-term losses for the patient; (2) the patient is aware that the therapy in question is proven to be efficacious and may be withheld as part of the trial and nevertheless agrees to participate in the trial; and (3) conducting the trial as a placebo-controlled trial rather than as an active-controlled trial produces considerable scientific gains and/or substantially lessens the cost of conducting the trial.' His position is that if these conditions are met, then 'the requirements of respecting patient autonomy and of protecting patients from excessive risks are met, and the research in question would be morally licit'. One major problem with Brody's argument is that the requirements are or ought to be not merely to protect patients from excessive risks, but rather to minimize risks. (This standard is found in many national and international research ethics documents as was discussed in Chap. 10 (see Chap. 10, endnote 63).) It is also not clear whether Brody would want his argument to be used for pediatric research where the emphasis on autonomy is of less significance and the role of protection is and ought to be much more stringent. See Ross, L. F., *Children,*

Families, and Health Care Decision-Making. Oxford: Clarendon Press, 1998, 89–93.

47. Shapiro, G., Mendelson, L., Kraemer, M. J., Cruz-Rivera, M., Walton-Bowen, K., and Smith, J. A., 'Efficacy and Safety of Budesonide Inhalation Suspension (Pulmicort Respules) in Young Children with Inhaled Steroid-Dependent, Persistent Asthma', *Journal of Allergy and Clinical Immunology*, 102 (1998), 789–96, 795.

48. Brogden *et al.*, 'Beclomethasone: A Reappraisal', 117–19; Clissold and Heel, 'A Preliminary', 511.

49. This danger was noted by one group of researchers who explained why they specifically chose not to do a double-blind study, even if the design would be criticized: 'a double-blind treatment protocol would have required that patients treated only with an inhaled beta-2-agonist would have had to be given a placebo for the inhaled corticosteroid for up to 2 years and then switched to the active corticosteroid treatment phase for an equally long period of time. The other group should have had active treatment with the inhaled corticosteroid from the beginning. With our current understanding of asthma as an inflammatory disease, such a study would certainly be considered unethical.' Selroos, O., Pietinalho, A., Lofroos, A. B., and Riska, H., 'Effect of Early vs. Late Intervention with Inhaled Corticosteroids in Asthma', *Chest*, 108 (1995), 1228–34, 1233. The risk of irreversible damage has been shown in several studies. See, e.g., Agertoft, L., and Pedersen, S., 'Effects of Long-Term Treatment with an Inhaled Corticosteroid on Growth and Pulmonary Function in Asthmatic Children', *Respiratory Medicine*, 88 (1994), 373–81; and Haahtela, T., Jarvinen, M., Kava, T., Kiviranta, K., Koskinen, S., Lehtonen, K., Nikander, K., Persson, T., Selroos, O., Sovijarvi, A., Stenius-Aarniala, B., Svahn, T., Tammivaara, R., and Laitinen, L. A., 'Effects of Reducing or Discontinuing Inhaled Budesonide in Patients with Mild Asthma', *New England Journal of Medicine*, 331 (1994), 700–5.

50. Miller, F. G., and Shorr, A. F., 'Ethical Assessment of Industry-Sponsored Clinical Trials: A Case Analysis', *Chest*, 121 (2002), 1337–42.

51. Nathan, R. A., Nayak, A. S., Graft, D. F., Lawrence, M., Picone, F. J., Ahmed, T., Wolfe, J., Vanderwalker, M. L., Nolop, K. B., and Harrison, J. E., 'Mometasone Furoate: Efficacy and Safety in Moderate Asthma Compared with Beclomethasone Dipropionate', *Annals of Allergy, Asthma, & Immunology*, 86 (2001), 203–10.

52. Miller and Shorr, 'Ethical Assessment', 1338.

53. Ibid.

54. Ibid.

55. This requirement can be found in many national and international codes of research ethics. See, e.g., Nuremberg Code. See Trials of War Criminals before the Nuremberg Military Tribunals under Control Council Law No. 10, vol. II. Washington DC: U.S. Government Printing Office, 1948, Principles 2, 3, and 6. On the web at: http://www.ushmm.org/research/doctors/codeptx.htm; hereinafter cited as Nuremberg Code; and the World Medical Association, World Medical Association Declaration of Helsinki, 'Ethical Principles for Medical Research

Involving Human Subjects', adopted by the 18th WMA General Assembly, Helsinki, Finland, June 1964, and amended by the 29th WMA General Assembly, Tokyo, Japan, October 1975; 35th WMA General Assembly, Venice, Italy, October 1983; 41st WMA General Assembly, Hong Kong, September 1989; 48th WMA General Assembly, Somerset West, Republic of South Africa, October 1996; and the 52nd WMA General Assembly, Edinburgh, Scotland, October 2000. Note of Clarification on Paragraph 29 added by the WMA General Assembly, Washington 2002; and Note of Clarification on Paragraph 30 added by the WMA General Assembly, Tokyo 2004, Principles 1, 5, and 6. On the web at http://www.wma.net/e/policy/b3.htm; hereinafter cited as Declaration of Helsinki.

56. National Commission for the Protection of Human Subjects, *Report and Recommendations: Research Involving Children*. Washington DC: US Printing Office, 1977, DHEW Publication NO. (OS) 77–0004. 1–2.

57. Tashkin, D. P., Nathan, R. A., Howland, W. C., Minkwitz, M. C., Simonson, S. G., and Bonuccelli, C. M., 'An Evaluation of Zafirlukast in the Treatment of Asthma with Exploratory Subset Analyses', *Journal of Allergy & Clinical Immunology,* 103 (1999), 246–54.

58. Lazarus, S. C., Boushey, H. A., Fahy, J. V., Chinchilli, V. M., Lemanske, R. F. Jr., Sorkness, C. A., Kraft, M., Fish, J. E., Peters, S. P., Craig, T., Drazen, J. M., Ford, J. G., Israel, E., Martin, R. J., Mauger, E. A., Nachman, S. A., Spahn, J. D., Szefler, S. J., and the Asthma Clinical Research Network for the National Heart, Lung, and Blood Institute, 'Long-Acting Beta-2-Agonist Monotherapy vs. Continued Therapy with Inhaled Corticosteroids in Patients with Persistent Asthma: A Randomized Controlled Trial', *JAMA,* 285 (2001), 2583–93; and Lemanske, R. F. Jr., Sorkness, C. A., Mauger, E. A., Lazarus, S. C., Boushey, H. A., Fahy, J. V., Drazen, J. M., Chinchilli, V. M., Craig, T., Fish, J. E., Ford, J. G., Israel, E., Kraft, M., Martin, R. J., Nachman, S. A., Peters, S. P., Spahn, J. D., and Szefler, S. J., Asthma Clinical Research Network for the National Heart, Lung, and Blood Institute, 'Inhaled Corticosteroid Reduction and Elimination in Patients with Persistent Asthma Receiving Salmeterol: A Randomized Controlled Trial', *JAMA,* 285 (2001), 2594–603.

59. Ross, L. F., 'Salmeterol and Inhaled Corticosteroids in Patients with Persistent Asthma', *JAMA*, 286 (2001), 3076.

60. Lazarus, S. C., 'In Reply, Salmeterol and Inhaled Corticosteroids in Patients with Persistent Asthma', *JAMA,* 286 (2001), 3077–8, 3077.

61. Lemanske, R. F. Jr., 'In Reply, Salmeterol and Inhaled Corticosteroids in Patients with Persistent Asthma', *JAMA,* 286 (2001), 3078.

62. National Commission for the Protection of Human Subjects of Biomedical and Behavioral Research, *Report and Recommendations: Institutional Review Boards.* Washington DC: US Government Printing Office, 1978, DHEW Publication No. (OS) 78–0008, 1–2. The language used by the National Commission is: 'to assure that the rights and welfare of human subjects are protected'. To protect the subjects' rights is to promote their autonomy to give an informed consent.

To protect the subjects' welfare is to protect them from undue or unnecessary risks.

63. See, e.g., Nuremberg Code and Declaration of Helsinki. A more complete list of national and international codes that enumerate the need for the risks to be minimized can be found in Chap. 10 (Chap. 10, endnote 63).

64. Brody does an extensive analysis of the FDA and its position regarding studies that use placebos versus active controls. See Brody, *Drug Testing*, 105–16.

65. Pedersen and O'Byrne argue that the methodologies of many of the studies do not allow a firm conclusion to be made about the relative advantages and disadvantages of the ICS. Pedersen & O'Byrne, 'A Comparison' at 28–9. Other factors can influence the efficacy of inhaled corticosteroids besides the compound and the dose including the devices used to deliver the drugs. There has been much research on different types of drug-delivery devices and propellants, in part, because the older formulations of ICS used chlorofluorocarbon (CFC) propellants that are now banned because of their harmful effect on the environment. Drug manufacturers have solved this issue by using either finely divided dry powders or by substituting a non-CFC propellant, both of which may be better for patients than the CFC-metered dose inhalers. It is worth noting that none of the guidelines prefers one ICS to another. Comparative daily dosages for inhaled corticosteroids are listed in the AAAAI, *Best Practice,* 73.

66. See, e.g., Weiss, G. B., and Winslade, W. J., 'Is Post-Marketing Drug Follow-Up Research or Advertising?' *IRB: A Review of Human Subjects Research,* 9 (July–August 1987), 10–1.

67. Baker, J. W., Mellon, M., Wald, J., Welch, M., Cruz-Rivera, M., and Walton-Bowen, K., 'A Multiple-Dosing, Placebo-Controlled Study of Budesonide Inhalation Suspension Given Once or Twice Daily for Treatment of Persistent Asthma in Young Children and Infants', *Pediatrics,* 103 (1999), 414–21, 418.

68. See, e.g., Silverman, W., 'Non-Replication of the Replicable', *Paediatric and Perinatal Epidemiology,* 10 (1996), 406–9. Similar discussions found in Haines, A., and Jones, R., 'Implementing Findings of Research', *BMJ,* 308 (1994), 1488–92.

69. Consider, e.g., that a review of budesonide in 1984 reported dozens of therapeutic studies, both short- and long-term trials, in children and in adults, using both active and placebo controls, at various dosages and time intervals. Clissold and Heel, 'A Preliminary', 499–506. Likewise, a review of fluticasone proprinate in 2000 reported dozens of studies involving more than 3,000 subjects prior to 1994. Again, these studies included both active and placebo controls. Holliday, S. M., Faulds, D., and Sorkin, E. M., 'Inhaled Fluticasone Propionate. A Review of its Pharmacodynamic and Pharmacokinetic Properties, and Therapeutic Use in Asthma', *Drugs,* 47 (1994), 318–31, 325–7.

70. I thank Skip Nelson for pointing out this case to me.

71. BPCA Clinical Summary of NDA 20–548, SE8–018. Applicant GlaxoSmithKline for Flovent® Inhalation Aerosol. On the web at: http://www.fda.gov/cder/foi/esum/2003/20548se8–018BPCArev2.pdf.; hereinafter cited as GSK, Written Request.

72. GlaxoSmithKline Annual Report, 2000. On the web at: http://www.gsk.com/financial/reports/ar/report/op_finrev_prosp/finrev_20/finrev_20.htm, 1.

73. GSK, Written Request, 1.

74. Ibid., 6.

75. Ibid., 7.

76. Ibid., 7.

77. Ibid., 8.

78. Ibid., 1.

79. Shapiro, 'Reply'.

80. Beecher, H. K., 'Ethics and Clinical Research', *New England Journal of Medicine*, 274 (1966), 1354–60, 1360.

81. Shapiro, 'Reply', 251.

82. Djulbegovic notes that industry-sponsored studies are more likely to be designed to compare experimental treatment against placebo or no therapy than did studies sponsored by public resources. See Djulbegovic, B., Lacevic, M., Cantor, A., Fields, K. K., Bennett, C. L., Adams, J. R., Kuderer, N. M., and Lyman, G. H., 'The Uncertainty Principle and Industry-Sponsored Research', *Lancet,* 356 (2000), 635–8. Davidson found that most published trials supported by pharmaceutical manufacturers favor the experimental therapy. Although some reasons may be legitimate (e.g., the selection of drugs for study that are likely to be proven efficacious), it may also reflect a decision not to publish negative results. *See* Davidson, R. A., 'Source of Funding and Outcome of Clinical Trials', *Journal of General Internal Medicine,* 1 (1986), 155–8.

83. In 2001, federal spending on biomedical science was slightly more than $20 billion, whereas drug companies spent $22.4 billion in 2000. *See* Hotz, R. L., 'Science File: Scientists Sharing Fewer Discoveries', *The Los Angeles Times* (11 February 2002), A12. Biomedical research is also sponsored to a lesser extent by not-for-profit philanthropies.

14

Research not Otherwise Approvable: A Look at One 407 Protocol

1. Introduction

CFR §46.407 of Subpart D of the federal regulations addresses research that is not otherwise approvable.[1] The research is not otherwise approvable because either (1) it seeks to enroll healthy children, but offers no prospect of direct benefit and entails more than minimal risk; or (2) it seeks to enroll children with a disorder or condition, but offers no prospect of direct benefit and entails more than a minor increase over minimal risk. According to CFR §46.407, such research can be permissible if it is reviewed and approved by a panel of experts convened by the secretary of the Department of Health and Human Services (DHHS). The regulations also require public review of the research.

Prior to the year 2000, only two panels of experts were convened.[2] However, in 2002, Dr Greg Koski, then director of Office of Human Research Protections (OHRP), stated that OHRP had received more than two dozen requests for 407 review in the previous year.[3] Seven panels were convened in August 2001.[4] In this chapter, I examine in detail the protocol on precursors to diabetes in Japanese American youth as a case study in the protection of human subjects. In Chapter 15, I provide a history of the 407 panels and discuss three of them in-depth to uncover the lessons of history.

2. Precursors to Diabetes in Japanese American Youth: Description of the Protocol

Researchers at the University of Washington designed the protocol to study the development of type 2 diabetes in childhood.[5] The researchers plan to enroll 450 healthy, nondiabetic children aged 8–10 years (prepubertal), 300 with some degree of Japanese ancestry and 150 Caucasian cousins, and to follow them for 2 years into puberty. They are interested in Japanese American children because Japanese American adults have a high rate of type 2 diabetes. The study is a longitudinal observation study of the metabolic and obesity-related factors that are associated with insulin resistance metabolic syndrome, an abnormal response to insulin, high blood pressure, and abnormalities of blood cholesterol and other lipids, and the changes in these factors as the children progress to puberty. The researchers also will describe how these factors are related to lifestyle factors (e.g., diet and physical activity) and to the proportion of Japanese ancestry.

Parents of enrolled children will be asked to provide demographic information and a family history of medical conditions and ethnicity. At baseline, the children will undergo a physical examination, including Tanner staging (an examination for sexual maturity), and a dietary and physical activity assessment. Approximately three tablespoons of blood will be taken for a variety of chemical, metabolic, and hematologic tests, although DNA samples are optional. All children will undergo an intravenous glucose tolerance test (IVGTT), dual energy x-ray absorptiometry (DEXA), and magnetic resonance imaging (MRI) to quantify regional fat mass in the abdomen.

According to the researchers, the physical risks are related to phlebotomy and intravenous catheter insertion as well as minimal radiation exposure. There is also the risk of embarrassment related to the examination for sexual maturity. The children and their parents may receive some educational benefit regarding type 2 diabetes, and they will receive the test results, which may be relevant to the child's medical care (e.g., blood pressure measurements and blood test results such as hematocrit and cholesterol). However, the researchers and the Institutional Review Board (IRB) of the Children's Hospital and Regional Medical Center of the University of Washington concurred that the research did not offer the prospect of direct benefit.

The study seeks a large number of subjects of Japanese ancestry, but the consent forms will not be translated into Japanese. Rather, lack of English proficiency is an exclusion criterion. The researchers justify this criterion on the grounds that the rise in diabetes among Japanese children coincides with the adoption of a westernized lifestyle, both with respect to diet (e.g., increased calories and increased animal protein) and a more sedentary lifestyle. They believe the studies will be relevant to other Asian populations in the United States.

Consent forms for children and parents are available for review on the OHRP website.[6] The permission of both parents is sought. The children will receive a gift certificate after each visit.

3. Does the Study Require 407 Review?

According to Subpart D, research involving children is permissible when the risks are minimal (CFR §46.404). If the risks are more than minimal, research is permissible only if (1) the research offers the prospect of direct benefit and the potential benefits justify the risks (CFR §46.405), or (2) the research, albeit nontherapeutic, poses only a minor increase over minimal risk and the research offers generalizable knowledge of vital importance about the subjects' disorder or condition (CFR §46.406). Research that offers no prospect of direct benefit and either (1) seeks to enroll healthy children and poses more than minimal risk, or (2) seeks to enroll children with a disease or condition and poses more than a minor increase over minimal risk, can be performed if it presents an opportunity to understand, prevent, or alleviate serious health problems, and is reviewed and approved by a national panel of experts convened by the Secretary of DHHS (CFR §46.407). The protocol requires national review only if it cannot be approved under CFR §46.404, CFR §46.405, or CFR §46.406.

The first question, then, is whether the risks of the research are minimal.[7] The research involves the placement of two intravenous (IV) catheters (one to infuse sugar water, the other to draw multiple blood samples) that will remain in place for approximately four hours, MRI and DEXA scans (each of which entails minimal radiation exposure), and Tanner staging. Although there is wide variability on what 'minimal risk' entails,[8] surely some centers would find these procedures fit the general description of minimal risk.

However, many IRBs would find that the *package* of procedures entails more than minimal risk, particularly in the age group being studied.[9] Since the research does not offer the prospect of direct benefit (CFR §46.405), such research can only be approved if it seeks generalizable knowledge of vital importance about the subjects' disorder or condition. The children, however, are described as healthy children and so do not have a disorder or condition.

If one believes that the medical procedures entail only minimal risk, the research could have been approved by the IRB of the Children's Hospital and Regional Medical Center of the University of Washington under CFR §46.404. If one believes that the procedures entail a minor increase over minimal risk, then the research would need 407 review under current regulations because the children are healthy. In actuality, the IRB of the Children's Hospital and Regional Medical Center of the University of Washington approved the study under CFR §46.406 in June 2000.[10] Doug Diekema, MD, the chairman of the IRB, quickly questioned the IRB decision because he was concerned that the control group did not have a 'disorder or condition' as required for research to be approved under CFR §46.406.[11] After consultation with OHRP in February 2001, the Children's Hospital IRB classified the research as requiring 407 review because the research involved a minor increase over minimal risk, offered no direct benefit, and sought to enroll healthy children.

4.   What Level of Risk Does the Research Pose?

To understand the degree of risk posed by the University of Washington proposal, another diabetes study in the literature is worth examining. The University of Iowa's IRB was asked to review a protocol to explore longitudinal changes in peripheral and hepatic insulin sensitivity in prepubertal and early pubertal children and to determine predictors for changes in insulin resistance and growth velocity (Insulin Sensitivity Study). The study sought to enroll healthy children of Tanner stage 1 and 2. Each group would be admitted overnight four times over 18 months, at which time the children would undergo a physical examination that would include sexual-maturity rating. Two IVs would be placed, one to infuse sugar (glucose) and the other to withdraw blood. The IRB members questioned the impact on the children of overnight admission and the accompanying tests. Consequently, they asked that pediatric psychologists advise the researcher about procedures for identifying subjects appropriate for inclusion and subsequently determine whether there were any post-study adverse effects.[12]

Twenty-eight children between the ages of 8 and 14 were psychologically screened. Twenty-four eventually participated in the study; four did not. Follow-up psychological data were obtained on twenty of those who participated; data were not available for the four who did not participate in the study.

Several interesting findings were reported. Prior to participation, none of the children reported concerns about being in the study. However, four of the children screened were found to have high levels of anxiety. These children and their parents were encouraged not to participate, and two children did not. One chose to continue but dropped out when feeling ill as IV insertion was attempted; the fourth completed the research. One other child who had tested normal on the psychological screening also dropped out because of difficulty starting the IV line.[13]

Following participation, children and parents were asked to rate the child's comfort level with four aspects of the research: (1) Tanner assessment; (2) IV insertion; (3) blood draws; and (4) staying overnight in the hospital. Although parents thought their children would find the IV insertion most difficult, children were most concerned about the Tanner staging. In fact, the majority of parents underestimated their child's discomfort across the four hospitalizations on all four aspects. All of the parents stated that they would allow their children to participate in future research and only one child reported not wanting to be in research in the future 'if there are IVs'.[14]

This research is quite valuable in trying to understand how research risks should be assessed and classified. The children had a different perspective from that of their parents. The children found the various elements of the research more disturbing than their parents expected, although none of the children or parents reported emotional or behavioral sequelae after participation in the study that they attributed to being in the study.[15]

5. *Other Diabetes Research Studies*

Despite their concerns about (1) the potential impact on the children of overnight admission and the accompanying tests, and (2) subject selection inclusion criteria, members of the University of Iowa IRB approved the insulin sensitivity study as a minimal-risk study.[16] The question of how much risk a related diabetes study posed to its subjects became a national issue in 2000 when OHRP halted a study at the National Institute of Child Health and Human Development (NICHD) of the National Institutes of Health (NIH).[17]

In 1996, NIH researchers began a study that enrolled obese children and normal weight children of obese parents into a longitudinal study to examine population differences in insulin sensitivity, resting energy expenditure, and body composition. The study included an euglycemic clamp study—a technique that involves two intravenous lines, one for the infusion of insulin and glucose and one for phlebotomy (blood-drawing). Jack Yanovski and colleagues had enrolled more than 190 children aged 6 to 10 years, when OHRP halted the study because it involved more than minimal risk, offered no prospect of direct benefit, and enrolled healthy children and therefore could not be approved without a 407 panel.[18] The IRB of the NICHD re-examined the protocol and argued that the research could be approved under CFR §46.406 on the grounds that the research entailed only a minor increase over minimal risk and that the children, who were either obese or normal-weight children of obese parents, were 'at risk for developing type 2 diabetes'.[19] OHRP accepted the interpretation that children 'at risk' for obesity could be classified as having a 'disorder or condition' as required for research to be approved under CFR §46.406.[20]

Although Yanovski *et al.*'s research was questioned, and temporarily halted, research on insulin resistance was and is on-going at the University of Minnesota. Beginning in 1996, researchers at the University of Minnesota have been recruiting fifth-through eighth-grade children in the Minneapolis public school system to undergo an euglycemic clamp study. The researchers recruit half of the children from the upper twenty-fifth and half of the children from the lower seventy-fifth percentiles of blood pressure to increase the percentage of children at potential cardiovascular risk.[21] Clearly the latter group of children cannot be classified as having or even being at risk for cardiovascular disease and insulin metabolic resistance syndrome.

In 1999, the Minnesota researchers reported on 357 children who had undergone the euglycemic clamp study. The authors note that the study was funded by NIH and approved by the University of Minnesota Committee for the Use of Human Subjects in Research and that informed consent was obtained from the parents and assent from the children. The children were paid $75 for their participation.[22]

The article does not say on what grounds the study was approved. Although there may be disagreement as to whether the placement of two catheters can be classified as minimal risk or a minor increase over minimal risk, the infusion of glucose and insulin justifies classification of more than minimal risk. Dosage errors could lead to hypoglycemia (low blood sugar) and resultant seizures. The research also did not offer the prospect of direct benefit. Thus, the research cannot be classified as CFR §46.404 (minimal risk) nor CFR §46.405 (prospect of direct therapeutic benefit). Nor could the IRB approve the research under CFR §46.406 because many of the children were normotensive (normal blood pressure) and not at increased risk for insulin metabolic resistance syndrome. Despite this, in January 2003, the team reported on data from 296 (of the original 357) children who underwent a second euglycemic clamp study two years later.[23] Furthermore, a University of Minnesota web page explains that the research is now in its second phase and that the goal is to study 1000 individuals over four years.[24]

Neither Yanovski and his colleagues nor the Minnesota researchers, however, are the first to perform euglycemic clamp studies on healthy children. A MEDLINE search confirms that such studies were being done in the 1980s and 1990s, both to understand insulin resistance and the impact of puberty on it, and as controls for studies on type 1 diabetes. One Pittsburgh study on type 1 diabetes is worth noting because it was the first research study approved after a 407 review.[25] The protocol was designed to examine the effect of hypoglycemia on cognition in children with type 1 diabetes. The issue that led to a 407 panel of experts was the plan of the researchers to enroll a control group. The Children's Hospital of Pittsburgh IRB thought that the research involved more than a minor increase over minimal risk and could not be approved in healthy children, unless supported by a panel of experts.[26]

6.   *National Review of the Japanese American Diabetes Study*

The Iowa, NICHD, and Minnesota studies are important for two reasons. First, they confirm the wide range of interpretation of the meaning of risks in the federal regulations.[27] Second, although OHRP determination letters are case specific, the series of letters between OHRP and NICHD[28] are important because they give some insight into (1) OHRP's interpretation regarding the degree of risk that an IV insertion and infusion of insulin and glucose entail, i.e., a minor increase over minimal risk; and (2) OHRP's willingness to consider those 'at risk for a disorder or condition' to be classified as having a disorder or condition.

With regard to the Japanese American diabetes study, then, one way to get around the need for national review is to argue that the children being recruited are 'at risk for a disease or condition', in this case, type 2 diabetes. Neither the federal regulations nor the National Commission's report from which they are derived, specify what is meant by having a 'disorder or condition'. In previous chapters, I argued that 'disorder or condition' should be defined to include at-risk children, a concept employed by the IRB at NICHD and accepted by OHRP.[29]

It is doubtful, however, that being of Japanese ancestry is in itself adequate to classify an individual as being 'at risk' for developing type 2 diabetes. The American Diabetes Association notes that being of minority race/ethnicity increases one's risk for diabetes, but they state that testing for type 2 diabetes should be restricted to those who are *overweight*, and have one of the following risk factors: (1) family history of type 2 diabetes in a first- or second-degree relative; (2) race/ethnicity of American Indian, African American, Hispanic, Asian, or Pacific Islander; or (3) signs of insulin resistance or conditions associated with insulin resistance.[30] Using this strict definition, it is not clear that Yanovski *et al.*'s research subjects, who are either overweight or normal-weight children of two obese parents, fulfill the criteria, as both groups have only one risk factor.

Although the risk of type 2 diabetes is higher in children of Japanese ancestry, fewer than 1% of Japanese children living in Japan have this condition.[31] Even if type 2 diabetes were tenfold more likely in Japanese American children because of their lifestyle,[32] the prevalence of type 2 diabetes would still be less than 2% of the Japanese American population under 18 years of age. The children to be recruited for the University of Washington study are non-obese. Ethnicity alone does not justify classifying them as at risk. In addition, the study seeks to enroll 150 Caucasian cousins who cannot be considered at risk based on ethnicity.

The expert panel for the Japanese American Diabetes project met on 13–14 August 2001. It found that the study entailed a minor increase over minimal risk, offered no prospect of direct benefit, and sought to enroll healthy children. As such, the majority of the panel of experts agreed with the IRB of the children's hospital and regional medical center of the University of Washington that the research was not approvable under CFR §46.404, CFR §46.405, or CFR §46.406. The panel believed that the proposed study offered a reasonable opportunity to further the understanding of an important health risk to children and as such could be approvable under CFR §46.407.[33]

One member of the panel did not recommend approval. He argued that there were serious design flaws. First, the two-year observational period meant that the majority of children would not have reached puberty and therefore the study period was too short. Second, the statistical probability is that only one subject ultimately would become diabetic and therefore the sample size was too small. Third, single test determinations might not prove representative of an individual's glucose metabolism or insulin resistance, and therefore the study would provide little if any knowledge about the problem it intended to address.[34] If correct, these scientific flaws would be dispositive as research must be both scientifically and ethically sound. The fact that an NIH review panel was willing to fund the project suggests that other experts did not agree with this panelist's assessment.

7.   *Children of Japanese Ancestry*

The subject selection criteria for the University of Washington study raises serious ethical concerns about the assumptions that the researchers make about race and ethnicity that suggest that these terms are more objective than they really are.

The concept of race was first introduced into the biological literature by Comte Georges Louis Leclerc de Buffon in 1749 as a convenient, albeit arbitrary, label and not as a definable scientific entity.[35] In 1977, Stephen Gould wrote: 'Many biologists are now arguing that it is not only inconvenient, but also downright misleading to impose a formal nomenclature on the dynamic patterns of variability that we observe in nature.'[36] Many who criticize the use of 'race' support the use of 'ethnicity'. Although often used interchangeably, they are not synonymous: 'race' refers to inaccurate differences of biology, whereas 'ethnicity' refers to differences of culture and geographic origin.[37] This is not to deny that ethnic boundaries are dynamic and imprecise, but that ethnicity is understood to be a multifactorial social concept.[38]

Ethnicity is important in part because there are allelic variations in haplotype frequency between ethnic groups. The GENIND (Genetics of Non-Insulin Dependent Diabetes Mellitus) study group found that linkages to diabetes or impaired glucose homeostasis were found on various chromosomes and that these variants often were clustered within particular ethnic groups.[39] From studies of other genetic conditions, rarely is there an absolute genotypic-phenotypic correlation, although some genotypes may be more benign than others and some genotypic-phenotypic correlations (e.g., pancreatitis in individuals with cystic fibrosis) are more consistent than others (e.g., pulmonary disease in individuals with cystic fibrosis).[40] Therefore, understanding insulin resistance and other aspects of diabetes in diverse populations such as Japanese American youth is important.

Studies in the Japanese American adult population using a variety of techniques including euglycemic insulin clamp studies and intravenous and oral glucose tolerance tests have shown that visceral adiposity (abdominal fat) increases the risk of impaired glucose tolerance, as does an increase in the consumption of animal protein.[41] These data support limiting the subject population to obese Japanese American children or to children of obese Japanese American parents.

The researchers are excluding families who do not speak English fluently on the grounds that English proficiency is a surrogate marker for westernization. They also note, however, that type 2 diabetes is becoming more frequent within Japan.[42] The justification to exclude non-English-speaking families, then, is not so obvious. If based mainly on ease and expense, it is not morally justifiable. The researchers should be asked to justify the exclusion of non-English-speaking Japanese Americans. If they want to focus their research on more westernized subjects, they could justify limiting the study to second- or third-generation Japanese Americans (who are more likely to speak English), but then they would lose the wide variation that a descriptive study might want to capture.

The researchers also claim that their data may provide useful information for all Asians, and the expert panel seems to accept this generalization in its summary.[43] I am not sure why. There are wide allelic variations in haplotype frequency and wide cultural differences within the Asian population.[44] The federal classification of race and ethnicity classifies under one heading individuals whose ancestry is Japanese, Chinese, Cambodian, or from one of more than two dozen other Asian countries.[45] The practice of combining Asian Americans and Pacific Islanders (AAPI) adds individuals from an additional 25 identified Pacific Island cultures and ethnicities.[46] Clearly there are wide differences both within and between each of these ethnic groups.[47] A white paper on the health status of AAPI concluded, however, that 'the paucity of systematic collection of disaggregated AAPI data leads to a lack of information of the health status, treatment and service delivery to various AAPI subgroups'.[48] For example, health indicators show that AAPI are one of the healthiest population groups in the USA with an average life expectancy of 80.3 years, but there is wide variability, with Japanese life expectancy at 82.1 years and Native Hawaiians at 68.3 years.[49] Therefore, the researchers ought to explain why they believe their data will be generalizable.

8. Was 407 Review Necessary?

A second ethical concern centers on whether an alternative study design could accomplish the same goals without imposing research risks that require

407 review. The methodology described in the University of Washington proposal includes the insertion of only one IV, the infusion of glucose (but not insulin), and Tanner staging. Clearly, then, the research is less risky than Yanovski *et al.*'s research at NICHD, and, as such, entails no more than a minor increase over minimal risk.

If the protocol is classified as minimal risk, then it would not matter whether the children are classified as having a disorder or condition as the research would be approvable under CFR §46.404. If, however, the research is classified as posing a minor increase over minimal risk, then the protocol's failure to focus on children with a 'disorder or condition' or at least 'at risk' for a disorder or condition means that it cannot be approved except under 407.[50]

Before seeking review by a national panel of experts, one should consider whether the protocol could be amended to include only 'at risk children' and thereby be approvable under CFR §46.406. In general, research ethics standards require that studies be designed to minimize risks (CFR §46.111). Research that can only be approved with 407 review should be a last resort and should only be approved if the information to be gained is important and cannot be obtained in any other manner. Consequently, if the University of Washington researchers could change their eligibility criteria and still answer their major research objectives, then this would be preferable. Currently, the University of Washington protocol seeks to enroll children of Japanese ancestry and their Caucasian cousins, subjects who do not necessarily fulfill the American Diabetes Association's criteria for being 'at risk'. Three different subject populations could be defined as having a 'disorder or condition' under the broader definition that I have been developing in previous chapters. Enrolling subjects from any of these three subject populations would obviate the need for 407 review. The three populations are: (1) Japanese American children whose parents have type 2 diabetes; (2) obese Japanese American children; or (3) Japanese American children of obese parents.

This proposed subject eligibility revision will miss some individuals of Japanese ancestry who will develop diabetes. But the primary aim of the research is to describe the metabolic and obesity-related factors that are associated with insulin resistance metabolic syndrome in the child longitudinally from pre-pubertal through puberty. Given the incidence of type 2 diabetes in children generally, even in Japanese American children, a sample of 300 healthy not at-risk children is unlikely to discover more than one or two children who will develop overt disease.[51] The researchers are more likely to find children who will develop type 2 diabetes if they use a stricter eligibility criteria. In fact, the researchers seem to realize this since they restrict their population to Japanese Americans who are fluent in English and therefore are more likely to have adopted a westernized diet and sedentary lifestyle, which will predispose them to obesity and type 2 diabetes.

The proposed subject eligibility revision would require that the research be performed without the control group (the Caucasian cousins). It is not clear, however, what additional information this control group offers given the large amount of information already available on insulin resistance in the Caucasian (and Black American populations).[52] I suggest that the University of Washington researchers should explain why the revised subject eligibility would be inadequate before the research is approved by a 407 panel. One answer may be the funding agency. The principal investigator (PI) for the type 1 diabetes protocol that underwent 407 review in 1993 stated that she and her colleagues had suggested elimination of the control group to NIH and were told that their funding would be rescinded.[53]

9. What Happens Next?

One year after the 407 panel met, notice was placed in the Federal Register soliciting public comments.[54] In December 2002, a second notice to solicit public comments was published,[55] in part due to comments from August stating that there was inadequate information about the protocol and too short a response time (two weeks). Parts of the protocol and the consent forms were made available on the OHRP web-site.[56] Those who wanted additional information could obtain it by a freedom of information act request (FOIA).[57] The public comment period was one month.

ORHP gave conditional approval to the University of Washington project in July 2003, three years after the protocol first underwent IRB review. By this time, the original PI had retired and the team that was established had been disbanded. In August 2004, a new PI had taken over the project, but the Children's Hospital IRB was still waiting for a few revisions before the project could get full approval and subjects could be enrolled.[58] On 1 March 2005, almost four years from the time the protocol was submitted to OHRP, the protocol had full approval.[59] To what extent the research questions are still valid, or whether an alternative study design would be appropriate given greater knowledge about insulin resistance raises additional questions about the 407 review process.

10. Critique of the 407 Process with Respect to this Protocol

The initial expert panel for the Precursors to Diabetes in Japanese American Youth convened in August 2001. The panel members were promised anonymity so the individual members' identity and background would not be known. Robert Nelson, MD, PhD of the University of Pennsylvania publicly states that he served as chair and that the expert panel included scientific, ethical, and regulatory experts and community representatives.[60] The panelists submitted written reports shortly after the meeting, although all that is publicly available is the summary report.[61] The panel was criticized for lack of transparency. Critics recommended that the name and affiliation of each member and a declaration of possible conflicts of interest be disclosed. Critics also recommended that the protocol and consent forms as well as the report of each panel member be available online to the public. As I will discuss in Chapter 15, all of these recommendations have been implemented.

The panel was also criticized for its slowness. Timeliness is important because research designs depend on the current state of knowledge, and a delay of two or three years may make the research questions or design obsolete. A slow or cumbersome process will discourage researchers and their institutions from applying for 407 review. The danger here is that some institutions may take an overly liberal interpretation of minimal risk or a minor increase over minimal risk in order to justify approving a research project, particularly one that is externally funded. To OHRP's credit, the process has been improved as will be seen in Chapter 15.

The University of Washington's experience with its protocol, Precursors to Diabetes in Japanese American Youth, serves as an important case study of the strengths and limitations of the 407 process in 2001. In the next chapter, I discuss three more recent 407 panels, and the strengths and weaknesses that persist in the 407 process. I conclude with several recommendations.

References

1. Department of Health and Human Services (DHHS), (45 CFR Part 46, Subpart D). 'Protections for Children Involved as Subjects in Research', *Federal Register*, 48 (8 March 1983), 9814–20; revised *Federal Register*, 56 (18 June 1991), 28032, CFR 46.407; hereinafter cited by its CFR number in the text.
2. These protocols were reported in the *Federal Register* in 1991 and 1993. See National Center for Research Resources, National Institutes of Health, Public Health Service, Department of Health and Human Services (DHSS), 'Proposed Protocol Entitled Myoblast Transfer in Duchenne Muscular Dystrophy; Recommendations', *Federal Register*, 56 (27 September 1991), 49189–190; and National Institute of Child Health and Human Development, (NICHD), National Institutes of Health, Public Health Service, Department of Health and Human Services (DHHS), 'Cognitive Function and Hypoglycemia in Children with IDDM', *Federal Register*, 58 (30 July 1993), 40819–820.
3. Koski, G., 'National Human Research Protections Advisory Commission Transcript 29 January 2002'. On the web at: http://www.hhs.gov/ohrp/nhrpac/ mtg01–02/0129NHR.txt.
4. Nelson, R. M., 'A Brief History of Protocol Reviews under 45 CFR 46.407'; presented at the American Society of Bioethics and Humanities, October 2003, Montreal, Canada.

5. The protocol, consent forms, and communications between OHRP and the University of Washington can be found on the web at http://www.hhs.gov/ohrp/children/japanese.html.

6. Ibid.

7. As discussed in Chap. 3, minimal risk is defined in Subpart A of the federal regulations as 'the probability and magnitude of harm or discomfort anticipated in the research are not greater in and of themselves than those ordinarily encountered in daily life or during the performance of routine physical or psychological examinations or tests.' Department of Health and Human Services (DHHS). (45 CFR 46 Subpart A), 'Final Regulations Amending Basic HHS Policy for the Protection of Human Research Subjects', *Federal Register*, 46 (26 January 1981), 8366–91; revised *Federal Register*, 56 (18 June 1991), 28003–18, CFR §46.111; hereinafter cited by its CFR number in the text.

8. See, e.g., Janofsky, J., and Starfield, B., 'Assessment of Risk in Research on Children', *Journal of Pediatrics*, 98 (1981), 842–6; and Shah, S., Whittle, A., Wilford, B., Gensler, G., and Wendler, D., 'How Do Institutional Review Boards Apply the Federal Risk and Benefit Standards for Pediatric Research?' *JAMA*, 291 (2004), 476–82.

9. National Commission for the Protection of Human Subjects, *Report and Recommendations: Research Involving Children*. Washington DC: US Government Printing Office, 1977, DHEW Publication No. (OS) 77–0004, 7; hereinafter cited as National Commission, *Research Involving Children*. The need to examine the research study both as a complete package and in its components (individual research arms) is also discussed with respect to placebo-controlled trials by Miller, F. G., Wendler, D., and Wilford, B., 'When Do the Federal Regulations Allow Placebo-Controlled Trials in Children?' *Journal of Pediatrics*, 142 (2003), 102–7.

10. Diekema, D., 'Precursors to Diabetes in Japanese American Youth: A 3-Year Odyssey in the Kingdome of 46.407', presented at the American Society of Bioethics and Humanities, October 2003, Montreal, Canada.

11. Ibid.

12. McCarthy, A. M., Richman, L. C., Hoffman, R. P., and Rubenstein, L., 'Psychological Screening of Children for Participation in Nontherapeutic Invasive Research', *Archives of Pediatrics and Adolescent Medicine*, 155 (2001), 1197–203.

13. Ibid.

14. Ibid., 1202.

15. Ibid.

16. Ibid., 1198.

17. Marshall, E., 'Enforcers Halt NIH Study Called Less Risky than Outdoor Play', *Science* 290 (2000), 1281.

18. Office for Human Research Protections (OHRP), Determination Letter, 3 November 2000. On the web at: http://www.hhs.gov/ohrp/detrm_letrs/nov00a.pdf.; hereinafter referred to as OHRP, Determination Letter, November 2000.

19. Office for Human Research Protections (OHRP), Determination Letter, 15 August 2001. On the web at: http://www.hhs.gov/ohrp/detrm_letrs/aug01o.pdf de-

scribing the NICHD Institutional Review Board (IRB) review on 23 May 2001; hereinafter referred to as OHRP, Determination Letter, August 2001; and Uwaifo, G. I., Parikh, S. J., Keil, M., Elberg, J., Chin, J., and Yanovski, J. A., 'Comparison of Insulin Sensitivity, Clearance and Secretion Estimates Using Euglycemic and Hyperglycemic Clamps in Children', *Journal of Clinical Endocrinology and Metabolism*, 87 (2002), 2899–905, 2900.

20. OHRP, Determination Letter, August 2001.

21. Moran, A., Jacobs D. R., Jr., Steinberger, J., Hong, C-P., Prineas, R., Luepker, R., and Sinaiko, A. R., 'Insulin Resistance During Puberty: Results from Clamp Studies in 357 Children', *Diabetes*, 48 (1999), 2039–44.

22. Ibid.

23. Murtaugh, M. A., Jacobs, D. R., Jr., Moran, A., Steinberger, J., and Sinaiko, A. R., 'Relation of Birth Weight to Fasting Insulin, Insulin Resistance, and Body Size in Adolescence', *Diabetes Care*, 26 (2003), 187–92.

24. Protocol 488 (not dated). On the web at http://www.gcrc.umn.edu/gcrc/ proto.php?p488.

25. See DHHS, 'Cognitive Function'.

26. Ibid.

27. See Janofsky and Starfield, 'Assessment'; Shah *et al.*, 'How Do Institutional Review Boards'.

28. OHRP, Determination Letter, November 2000; OHRP, Determination Letter, August 2001; and Office for Human Research Protections (OHRP). Determination Letter 30 October 2002. This letter refers to a letter sent by the NICHD on 7 February 2001. Found on the web at: http://www.hhs.gov/ohrp/detrm_letrs/ YR02/oct02g.pdf.; hereinafter cited as ORHP, Determination Letter, October 2002.

29. OHRP, Determination Letter, August 2001; and OHRP, Determination Letter, October 2002.

30. American Diabetes Association, 'Type 2 Diabetes in Children and Adolescents', *Pediatrics*, 105 (2000), 671–80.

31. Kitigawa, T., Owada, M., Urakami, T., and Yamauchi, K., 'Increased Incidence of Non-Insulin Dependent Diabetes Mellitus among Japanese Schoolchildren Correlates with an Increased Intake of Animal Protein and Fat', *Clinical Pediatrics*, 37 (1998), 111–5.

32. Troiano, R. P., Flegal, K. M., Kuczmarski, R. J., Campbell, S. M., and Johnson, C. L., 'Overweight Prevalence and Trends for Children and Adolescents. The National Health and Nutrition Examination Surveys, 1963 to 1991', *Archives of Pediatrics and Adolescent Medicine*, 149 (1995), 1085–91.

33. 'Report on Expert Panel Review under Subpart D of 45 CFR 46, Precursors to Diabetes in Japanese American Youth Grant Number 1 RO1 DK 59234–01.' On the web at: http://www.hhs.gov/ohrp/pdjay/expert.pdf; hereinafter cited as 'Report on Expert Panel'.

34. Ibid., 5.

35. Montague, A. (ed.), *The Concept of Race*. New York: Collier-MacMillan 1964, 3–4.

36. Gould, E. J., *Ever Since Darwin: Reflections in Natural History*. New York: W. W. Norton Company, 1979, 233.

37. Caldwell, S. H., and Popenoe, R., 'Perceptions and Misperceptions of Skin Color', *Annals of Internal Medicine*, 122 (1995), 614–17.
38. Witzig, R., 'The Medicalization of Race: Scientific Legitimization of a Flawed Social Construct', *Annals of Internal Medicine*, 125 (1996), 675–9.
39. See Raffel, L. J., Robbins, D. C., Norris, J., Boerwinkle, E., DeFronzo, R. A., Elbein, S. C., Fujimoto, W., Hanis, C. L., Kahn, S. E., Permutt, M. A., Chiu, K. C., Cruz, J., Ehrmann, D. A., Robertson, R. P., Rotter, J. I., and Buse, J., 'The Gennid Study: A Resource for Mapping the Genes that Cause NIDDM', *Diabetes*, 19 (1996), 864–72; and Ehm, M. G., Karnoub, M. C., Sakul, H., Gottschalk, K., Holt, D. C., Weber, J. L., Vaske D., Briley, D., Briley, L., Kopf, J., McMillen, P., Nguyen, Q., Reisman, M., Lai, E. H., Joslyn, G., Shepherd, N. S., Bell, C., Wagner, M. J., Burns, D. K., and the American Diabetes Association GENNID Study Group. Genetics of NIDDM, 'Genomewide Search for Type 2 Diabetes Susceptibility Genes in Four American Populations', *American Journal of Human Genetics*, 66 (2000), 1871–81.
40. See, e.g., The Cystic Fibrosis Genotype-Phenotype Consortium, 'Correlation between Genotype and Phenotype in Patients with Cystic Fibrosis', *New England Journal of Medicine*, 329 (1993), 1308–13; and Zielenski, J., 'Genotype and Phenotype in Cystic Fibrosis', *Respiration*, 67 (2000), 117–33.
41. See, e.g., Liao, D., Asberry, P. J., Shofer, J. B., Callahan, H., Matthys, C., Boyko, E. J., Leonetti, D., Kahn, S. E., Austin, M., Newell, L., Schwartz, R. S., and Fujimoto, W. Y., 'Improvement of BMI, Body Composition, and Body Fat Distribution with Lifestyle Modification in Japanese Americans with Impaired Glucose Tolerance', *Diabetes Care*, 25 (2002), 1504–10; McNeely, M. J., Boyko, E. J, Leonetti, D. L., Kahn, S. E., and Fujimoto, W. Y., 'Comparison of a Clinical Model, the Oral Glucose Tolerance Test, and Fasting Glucose for Prediction of Type 2 Diabetes Risk in Japanese Americans', *Diabetes Care*, 26 (2003), 758–63; and Hayashi, T., Boyko, E. J., Leonetti, D. L., McNeely, M. J., Newell-Morris, L., Kahn, S. E., and Fujimoto, W. Y., 'Visceral Adiposity and the Risk of Impaired Glucose Tolerance: A Prospective Study among Japanese Americans.' *Diabetes Care*, 26 (2003), 650–5.
42. See Kitigawa, 'Increased Incidence'.
43. 'Report on Expert Panel'.
44. See, e.g., Williams, H. C., 'Have You Ever Seen an Asian/Pacific Islander?' *Archives of Dermatology*, 138 (2002), 673–4; Louie, K. B., 'White Paper on the Health Status of Asian Americans and Pacific Islanders and Recommendations for Research', *Nursing Outlook*, 49 (2001), 173–8; and Kim, B. S. K., Yang, P. H., Atkinson, D. R., Wolfre, M. M., and Hong, S., 'Cultural Value Similarities and Differences among Asian American Ethnic Groups', *Cultural Diversity and Ethnic Minority Psychology*, 7 (2001), 343–61.
45. See Louie, 'White Paper'.
46. Ibid.
47. Ibid; and Kim *et al.*, 'Cultural Value'.
48. See Louie, 'White Paper', 176.
49. Ibid., 176.

50. A 407 review could also be avoided if the federal regulations were modified to permit exposing healthy children to a minor increase over minimal risk. Freedman *et al.* argue for this position on the grounds that the current standard of minimal risk is overly restrictive. See Freedman, B., Fuks, A., and Weijer, C., '*In Loco Parentis:* Minimal Risk as an Ethical Threshold for Research upon Children', *Hastings Center Report* 23 (March/April 1993), 13–9. They compare asking a parent to agree to the child's participation in research that entails a minor increase over minimal risk with asking a parent to allow a child to participate in any new situation with its attendant risks. For example, they compare a child's research participation with his/her participation in an overnight camping trip for the first time: 'the parental decision to permit exposure to new risks is not itself governed by, but rather anchored to, the risks of everyday life. ... A prohibition on such research involvement would be to the long-term detriment of this child and other children, just as a prohibition on new experiences is harmful to children over the long term' (ibid., 17). This could help avoid numerous 407 reviews in the future. I argued for a similar position in Chap. 4, 'Should We Provide Healthy Children with Greater Protection in Medical Research?'

51. 'Report on Expert Panel', 5.

52. See e.g., Uwaifo *et al.*, 'Comparison'; Moran *et al.*, 'Insulin Resistance'; Murtaugh *et al.*, 'Relation of Birth Weight'; Sinaiko, A. R., Jacobs, D. R., Steinberger, J., Moran, A., Luepker, R., Rocchini, A. P., and Prineas, R. J., 'Insulin Resistance Syndrome in Childhood: Associations of the Euglycemic Insulin Clamp and Fasting Insulin with Fatness and Other Risk Factors', *Journal of Pediatrics*, 139 (2001), 700–7; Arslanian, S., and Suprasongsin, C., 'Differences in the In Vivo Insulin Secretion and Sensitivity in Healthy Black vs. White Adolescents', *Journal of Pediatrics*, 129 (1996), 440–3; and Arslanian, S., Suprasongsin, C., and Janosky, J. E., 'Insulin Secretion and Sensitivity in Black versus White Prepubertal Healthy Children', *Journal of Clinical Endocrinology and Metabolism*, 82 (1997), 1923–7.

53. Personal communication from Dorothy Becker, MD, University of Pittsburgh, October 2003.

54. Department of Health and Human Services (DHHS) 'Proposed Recommendation Regarding Support of Research Protocol: Precursors to Diabetes in Japanese American Youth', *Federal Register*, 67 (7 August 2002), 51283–4.

55. Department of Health and Human Services (DHHS), 'Proposed Research Protocol: Precursors to Diabetes in Japanese American Youth', *Federal Register*, 67 (18 December 2002), 77495–6.

56. See endnote 5 supra.

57. DHHS, 'Proposed Research Protocol'.

58. Doug Diekema personal communication, August 2004.

59. Ibid., March 2005.

60. Nelson, 'A Brief History'.

61. 'Report on Expert Panel.'

15

Evolution of the 407 Process

1. Introduction

In the more than two decades since passage of Subpart D, fourteen 407 panels have been convened. The first two were in the early 1990s; the remainder since 2001. In this chapter, I provide a brief history of the first ten 407 panels, and then consider in more depth three of the last four panels.[1] I conclude with several observations that can be gleaned from an historical and ethical analysis of the 407 process: observations that may be instructive for future 407 panels and for the protection of pediatric research subjects.

2. The 1990s: The First Two 407 Panels

There is scant public information about the first two protocols except their reporting in the Federal Register. The first, 'Myoblast transfer in Duchenne muscular dystrophy [DMD]' was disapproved in June 1991.[2] There are no public records that explain why the research was disapproved by the 407 panel. Despite this, at least five human trials were conducted in the early 1990s.[3] Four of the five studies found no improvement.[4] The fifth claimed benefit,[5] but it has been widely discredited.[6] All these studies involved boys with DMD (mid-childhood to adolescence).

In order for a local institutional review board (IRB) to approve this research, it would have to decide that the research either (1) had the potential to provide direct benefit and the benefits justified the risks (CFR §46.405), or (2) had no potential to provide direct benefit, but the risks were either minimal (CFR §46.404) or a minor increase over minimal risk (CFR §46.406). The five studies were probably approved under CFR §46.405 because the animal data may have suggested some potential for at least transient benefit.[7] Yet it is not clear why an IRB would have approved the first myoblast transfer trials using children-subjects. In 1977, the National Commission (for the Protection of Human Subjects of Biomedical and Behavioral Research) recommended that children not be used in research if the scientific question could be answered using adults,[8] and the National Commission's reports are the basis for most of our federal regulations on research protections. The scientific question of these studies was to understand the toxicity of myoblast transfer. While adults with DMD may have been too weak and less responsive to transplant, there are adults with Becker muscular dystrophy (a milder non-lethal form of muscular dystrophy) who could have been the subjects of the initial studies.[9]

The second 407 panel was convened to review research on 'Cognitive Function and Hypoglycemia in Children with IDDM (Insulin Dependent Diabetes Mellitus now known as Type I Diabetes)'.[10] As discussed in Chapter 14, it was brought to the Office for the Protection of Research Risks (OPRR now OHRP) because the research design involved insulin clamp studies to be performed on both children with diabetes and healthy controls. Although there are no public records, it is clear that the IRB that sought 407 review clearly believed that the research risks were more than minimal or they could have approved the research locally under CFR §46.404. If the research risks entailed a minor increase over minimal risk, then the research could be approvable for children with diabetes (a condition) [CFR §46.406], but given that insulin clamp studies entail more than minimal risk, the healthy children could only serve as controls if the research were reviewed nationally [CFR §46.407]. If the research risks were found to entail more than a minor increase over minimal risk, then the research would require national review for all the subjects [CFR §46.407]. In speaking with the principal investigator (PI), the panel was convened only for the healthy controls.[11] It was approved by OPRR (now OHRP) in July 1993. It is noteworthy, however, that numerous studies involving an insulin clamp technique have been (and continue to be) performed with healthy children without 407 review.[12]

3. The Re-Emergence of National Panels

Between August 2001 and June 2003, eleven 407 panels were constituted. The panels included scientific, ethical, and regulatory experts and community representatives. The first seven panels were convened in August 2001, and the panelists were promised anonymity and they submitted 'unstructured' written reports shortly after the meeting. The reports were unstructured in the sense that the panelists were not given guidelines about what issues to consider.[13] No votes were taken. Of these seven protocols, three were retracted after the panels met because they found them to be approvable under CFR §46.404–406 and two were withdrawn because they had closed to enrollment. OHRP produced a written summary of panel deliberations from notes and individual reports of the other two. One of these, 'Precursors to Diabetes in Japanese American Youth', planned to study Japanese Americans and their Caucasian cousins using an insulin clamp procedure. As discussed in Chapter 14, it was approved conditionally by the 407 panel although it does not yet have full IRB approval from its own institution. The other study 'Alcohol, Sleep and Circadian Rhythms in Young Humans, Study 2 -Effects of Evening Ingestion of Alcohol on Sleep, Circadian Phase, and Performance as a Function of Parental History of Alcohol Abuse/Dependence' involved adolescents and adults. The part of the grant requiring 407 review was a study that sought to examine the effect of a moderate evening dose of alcohol on sleep and waking performance in adolescents (aged 15–16) and young adults (aged 21–22). In December 2003, OHRP sent a letter to Rhode Island Hospital stating that the study was disapproved and that the researchers should defer the enrollment of adolescents until the research has been done and analyzed in the adult sub-population,[14] a recommendation consistent with the National Commission's position to begin with adults first. After the adult data are analyzed, 're-review would be warranted'.[15]

In October 2002, a panel was convened to consider a research study on Dryvax (smallpox vaccine) in children. Although the panel never physically met, they submitted individual signed reports. The protocol was eventually withdrawn because bioterrorism preparedness plans had evolved such that diluted Dryvax in children would not be used, and therefore there was no justification for the particular clinical investigation to proceed.[16]

In May-June 2003, three additional panels met to review the following three protocols: (1) 'Characterization of mucus and mucins in bronchoalveolar lavage fluids [BALF] from infants with cystic fibrosis (CF)'; (2) 'Sleep Mechanisms in Children: Role of Metabolism'; and (3) 'Human Immunodeficiency Virus (HIV) Replication and Thymopoiesis in Adolescents'. The panelists were asked to consider specific questions regarding risks and benefits, consent, and other aspects of research ethics review. Structured signed reports were submitted to OHRP. Given the development and refinement of the process over the past 2.5 years, it is these three proposals and the expert panel reports that I examine in depth. Relevant aspects of the protocols, IRB minutes, communication with OHRP, and the individual panelist reports are available on the OHRP web-site.[17]

4A. BALF from Infants with CF: Study Description

CF is a genetic condition that presents with pulmonary (lung) disease and gastrointestinal problems including meconium ileus (colonic obstruction) in the newborn, pancreatic insufficiency, and failure to thrive. The purpose of this study is to investigate the initial pathogenesis of airway disease in CF. The researchers plan to examine the relationship between hypothesized abnormalities in airway surface liquid and chronic infection and inflammation by performing three nontherapeutic bronchoscopies (examination of the lower airways of the lung with a special lens at the end of a long tube) and bronchoalveolar lavage (BAL). Bronchoalveolar lavage involves inserting a thin tube through the nose into the lungs (airways). A small amount of sterile salt water (2 teaspoonfuls) is placed into the airways through the tube, and then suctioned out. The researchers propose to perform BAL three times over a 12-month period on infants diagnosed prior to or just after birth with CF (either because they have meconium ileus or a family history that leads to early diagnosis),[18] and to compare their data with control data from children without CF who are undergoing BAL for clinical indications.

Two-parent consent is sought for the children with CF who will undergo the BAL for research purposes; no assent is sought because the children are too young. The children will be paid $100 for each bronchoscopy and a $50 bonus if they undergo all three (total of $350). The parents will be paid $50 for filling out a questionnaire at the time of the child's bronchoscopy and a $50 bonus for the completion of the study (total of $200).

Although the researchers tried to suggest that there was some possible benefit to the individual children, the University of North Carolina (UNC) IRB disagreed and found that the research exposed children with a condition to more than a minor increase over minimal risk without the prospect of direct therapeutic benefit which meant that the research could only be done with a 407 review.

4B.   BALF from children with CF: Ethical Issues

All of the 407 panel members agreed that the research could potentially yield important generalizable information, but that the research did not offer the prospect of direct benefit. They also agreed that the research needed to be done on children as no adequate animal model exists and most individuals with CF are symptomatic by one year of age. This may or may not be scientifically accurate. A review article in 2001 describes eleven different mouse models of CF including one that is studying 'the role of CFTR [the gene] in determining either the volume or the ionic concentration of the airway surface lining in the lung epithelia'.[19] The review also notes that the various influences including the role of distribution of submucosal glands can be controlled for, and altered, in future studies.[20] These are some of the factors that this study seeks to examine in infants. Thus, although expert 5 was convinced that the question 'Why children now?' could be justified,[21] it could be argued that the research team needs to explain whether advances in animal models should be pursued further before using this most vulnerable population (infants with a life-threatening condition) in invasive research.

The panel members raised two methodological questions regarding the protocol. The first was the need for greater clarification about sedation. The second was whether at least one of the bronchoscopies could be piggy-backed onto clinical care. The panel members agreed that the research risks to the control children was negligible given that the children would be undergoing BAL for clinical indications and could be approved under CFR §46.404. To minimize the risks to the children-subjects with CF, the panelists asked the researchers to propose time-frame windows rather than specific dates during which each bronchoscopy needed to be done to possibly allow one or more of the BAL samples to be collected simultaneous with clinical care (e.g., if the infants were to undergo a bronchoscopy or intubation during that time period).

As currently designed, the panel members disagreed about how to classify the level of risk that three unnecessary bronchoscopies would pose to infants with CF. Two panelists thought that given the experience of the researchers at the UNC, the risks could be classified as a minor increase over minimal risk and that the research could be approved as CFR §46.406. Four of six panelists, however, thought the risks were more than a minor increase over minimal risk and required 407 review. Nevertheless, a literature review reveals that research performing BAL without clinical indications has been a part of pediatric research throughout the world for years,[22] without 407 review for those done in the US.[23] Like the myoblast transfer research and the insulin clamp studies a decade earlier, this is further evidence that there is wide variation in interpreting what a minor increase over minimal risk entails.

Some concern was raised by panel members regarding the consent process. Two panelists expressed the need for a separation between the clinician caring for the child and the individual who presents the research opportunity to avoid both parental perception of undue pressure to enroll and parental misperception of therapeutic benefit. This is particularly important given the vulnerability of families with young children with a life-threatening condition.

Concerns were also raised about costs and payments. Several panelists were concerned that in the event of research-related injury, the consent form stated that the investigators would assist in obtaining appropriate medical treatment, but the cost would be borne by the family. As one panelist noted (5): 'Although compensation for research injury is not required by regulation, virtually all federal human research advisory committees have recognized it as a moral duty owed by the sponsors of the research.'[24] A second concern was about the payments. If the infants completed all three bronchoscopies, the children would earn $350, the parents $200 which included a bonus payment. Although the panelists appeared to be comfortable that the amount of money was commensurate with the inconveniences (parental time and child discomfort) that the families were being asked to undergo, there was some discomfort, regarding the bonus payment.[25].

Despite these concerns, the expert panelists unanimously agreed that the research could offer important generalizable knowledge and approved the research. One year later, OHRP concurred although it requested over twenty modifications to the protocol and consent forms.[26]

5A.   Sleep Mechanisms in Children: Study Description

The purpose of this study is to measure metabolic function of adolescent children cycling in wakefulness and sleep using nuclear magnetic resonance (MR) spectroscopy. The researchers also propose to study a subset of children with MR spectroscopy after sleep deprivation. Their ultimate goal is to study all age groups, as it is known that the sleep processes of children and adults are different, but in this research project, they will start with five adults and then focus on adolescents (aged 13–17 years).

The research entails three sessions. The first involves a complete medical history, physical exam, and blood and urine tests. The next two sessions involve admission to the clinical research center of the hospital (duration between 24 and 56 hours). The first night entails polysomnography to exclude undiagnosed sleep disorders. During the hospital admissions, two intravenous lines are placed, one for infusions of ^{13}C-acetate or ^{13}C-glucose and the other for blood sampling for up to 12 hours, and MR studies (duration up to 90 minutes). One group receiving acetate and glucose will be studied after normal activities; the other after sleep deprivation (52 hours). The adolescent will be paid up to $100 and the parent(s) up to $350. One parent consent and the adolescent's assent are sought. Although the researchers describe the risks as minimal in the consent form, the Einstein Committee on Clinical Investigations found it to involve more than minimal risk. Since the research is proposed on healthy adolescents, the IRB requested 407 review.

5B.   Sleep Mechanisms in Children: Ethical Issues

In this case, all of the expert panelists agreed that the risks were more than minimal and that the subjects were healthy. The main issue for the 407 panel was the decision to enroll children when the researchers explain in the grant application that 'none of these studies proposed have been done in adults or children. Indeed, only a small part of what is proposed here has been done in animals with the use of invasive techniques.'[27] The researchers chose to begin with children at least in part because the NIH grant proposal was written in response to a Grant Request For Application (RFA) that stipulated the inclusion of adolescent subjects.[28]

The primary justification to perform research on adults first is to ensure safety. An adult-first policy results in less research being done on children because (1) sometimes the adult data are sufficient to answer the research question, or (2) sometimes the adult data show greater safety risks or less therapeutic value than were anticipated changing the benefit risk calculation. While the researchers give adequate reasons to show that the research will need to be done on children, they do not give any arguments to justify why children should be studied first. One panelist felt five adult-subjects were adequate to ensure safety whereas one panelist was not sure and asked for review by a data safety monitoring board (DSMB) before enrolling adolescents. A third panelist felt that knowledge on adults won't make it safer and therefore did not see the lack of adult data as problematic. The other two panelists believed that greater studies in adults were needed first. They expressed two concerns: (1) the safety of the MR spectroscopy—not in the amount of radiation, but in its performance while using polysomnography (concern that the wires could become heated during the study that could take as long as 90 minutes), and (2) the tolerance of sleep deprivation. Since some adults are to be recruited, the two panelists argued that they should undergo the procedure first to clarify the anticipatable risks and to potentially unveil other unanticipated risks.

There was also concern regarding the payment. As stated in the protocol, the parents would receive more money than the adolescent even though only the adolescent would undergo the procedures. While one panelist was able to justify this on the grounds that money may have greater 'undue influence' on adolescents who have less opportunities to earn money, the others were concerned that this would lead to parental pressure to participate and to remain in the study even if the adolescent wanted to withdraw. This is made even more problematic by the consent document which describes payment before stating the risks and benefits of the research.

Another issue is whose consent needs to be obtained. Although not raised by the panelists, the consent forms only seek the permission of one parent. The federal regulations allow IRBs to decide whether one-or two-parent consent is needed for research classified as CFR §46.404 and CFR §46.405, but research covered under CFR §46.406 and CFR §46.407 requires permission of both parents.[29] Whether the second parent's consent adds much in a culture in which almost half of all children will spend at least part of their childhood in a single-parent home is debatable. In this case, however, a large amount of money is being offered to the parents. If one believes that two parents would place additional pressure on the adolescent to participate, then the second parent's permission offers no protection. If one believes that by seeking the permission of both parents, one parent might look beyond his or her self-interest and focus on the child's best interest, then the second parent's permission may offer protection. There are no data. However, whether the second parent's consent provides additional protection cannot and should not be solved at the individual protocol level, but would require a revision of the regulations.

The panelists also expressed concern about how the researchers would exclude adolescents with a history of infection, hepatitis, or drug abuse and pregnancy. It is unclear whether this information will be obtained only by history (as suggested in the protocol) or by blood and urine testing (to be performed at the first visit). If testing will occur, the consent should discuss to whom this information will be disclosed.

Although no vote was taken, at least two if not three of the five panelists recommended against approving this research (one panelist was willing to consider approval after a DSMB reviewed the safety of the research done on adults). In March 2004, OHRP concluded that the studies on children should be disapproved until the adult data were collected and analyzed.[30]

6A.   HIV Replication and Thymopoiesis in Adolescents: Study Description

The purpose of the study is to examine several aspects of the function of the thymus (an organ that plays a key role in the body's defense against infection and cancer) in subjects aged 13–24 who acquire HIV at birth versus subjects who acquire HIV through sexual activity or drug abuse versus subjects who are HIV negative. All of the potential subjects are followed at the University of California at Los Angeles (UCLA) hospitals. All would undergo medical histories and physical exams as well as computed tomography (CT) exams of the thymus.

The researchers seek to include a substudy in their research in which the subjects are given deuterium (heavy water) labeled glucose over 24 hours, either intravenously or by mouth during a 24 hour stay in the General Clinical Research Center, and to continue to take heavy sugar water by mouth over the next month. If the subjects are over 18 years, they will consent or refuse to participate themselves. Otherwise, the researchers will seek one parent consent and the assent of the child. For participation in the substudy, the subjects will be paid $75 for the overnight stay and $35 twice for the two blood collections that seek to examine the amount of labeled glucose that enters their white blood cells. The UCLA IRB thought that the research could answer an important research question, but they thought it posed more than a minor increase over minimal risk in a healthy (HIV negative) population and could not be approved without 407 review.

6B. HIV Replication and Thymopoiesis in Adolescents: Ethical Issues

Although the UCLA IRB was mainly concerned about the risks in the substudy,[31] the 407 panelists were more concerned about radiation exposure from the non-contrast spiral CT of the thymus which was being proposed to measure the gland's volume. This involves radiation exposure to a gland that is known to be sensitive to radiation.[32] Although the amount of radiation is low, there is debate whether even this amount of radiation may increase the risk of cancer.[33] The main study also includes Tanner staging which is the determination of the level of sexual development in adolescents from stage I (pre-pubescent) to stage V (mature adult phenotype). While Tanner staging is not physically risky or invasive, some adolescents may find the process more stressful than one might anticipate.[34] This issue was not raised by the UCLA IRB nor any of the 407 panelists.

The panelists concurred that the study and substudy did not offer the prospect of direct benefit. Some panelists believed the research involved no more than minimal risk and suggested that the research be approved under CFR §46.404. The others believed it involved at most a minor increase over minimal risk such that the enrollment of HIV-positive adolescents could be approved under CFR §46.406 but the enrollment of healthy controls would require national review (CFR §46.407). One panelist considered whether the HIV-negative controls could be considered 'at risk for having a condition' (expert 7).[35] The researchers state that they will recruit the HIV-negative adolescents from their HIV clinic. These adolescents and young adults are being followed because of their high-risk activities. If these 'at risk' adolescents are included in the category of children having a disorder or condition (like the obese or normal-weight children of obese parents in the NICHD diabetes study described in Chapter 14),[36] then even those panelists who thought that the research involved a minor increase over minimal risk could approve the research under CFR §46.406 without the need for 407 review.

Another important issue is that of consent. Again, the researchers seek the adolescent's assent and permission from only one parent despite the requirement in the federal regulations for two-parent permission for research covered under CFR §46.407 'unless one parent is deceased unknown, incompetent, or not reasonably available, or when only one parent has legal responsibility for the care and custody of the child' (CFR §46.408(b)).

Two other consent issues were also raised. First, concern was expressed regarding the possibility that a subject would be found to be pregnant, and its impact on her right to confidentiality. Clearly this needs to be addressed in the consent form and in the consent process. Second, some of the adolescents will become 18 years of age during the course of the study, and they should consent for continued participation for themselves.

In summary, four of the eight expert panelists believed that both the HIV main study and the substudy entailed at most minimal risk and could be approved as CFR §46.404. The others believed that the risk was a minor increase over minimal risk, such that the research on the HIV-positive adolescents could be approved under CFR §46.406 but that 407 review was needed for the HIV-negative patients. If a broader interpretation of 'condition' were adopted, one could argue that adolescents at 'high risk' for HIV should be considered within the purview of 'adolescents with a disorder or condition', and the research could be approved under CFR §46.406 for all the subjects. However, in March 2004, OHRP approved this research project under CFR §46.407 [37] which means that the at-risk HIV-negative controls were not considered to have a condition relevant to the research.

7.   Lessons Learned

The first observation is the evolution in the 407 process since the first cases in the 1990s. The process has become more transparent. OHRP sponsors a web-page where it makes numerous documents available on-line to the public including relevant parts of the research protocol, the communication between OHRP and the institution that requested the review, and the comments of the expert panelists. Transparency is valuable because the wider community needs access to the panel meetings to be confident that the process to ensure the protection of human subjects was legitimate and that children, a vulnerable population, are not being placed at unnecessary risks. It also facilitates greater public comment. Such research should be evaluated publicly and supported by the diverse communities that are stakeholders in the research or who may be affected by the results that may emanate from it.[38] Nelson, the chair of many of the recent 407 panels, recommended that these panels become a FAC[39] which are required to be open to the public. The recent IOM report also recommended a standing committee because a continuing panel would accumulate experience and insights.[40] In March 2004, the Secretary's Advisory Committee on Human Research Protections (SACHRP), established after the National Human Research Protections Advisory Committee (NHRPAC) was disbanded, endorsed a non-FAC open panel model.[41]

A second process change is the disclosure of the panelists' identity. This is important because it allows the wider community to judge for itself whether the panels had appropriate expertise and diverse representation. A third process change is the speed in which protocols are reviewed. There was a two-year lag between the submission of the protocol, Precursors to Diabetes in Japanese American Youth, for 407 review and OHRP's decision. In contrast, the three cases discussed in this chapter took approximately one year. It is hoped that the time can be shortened even further now that OHRP has greater experience with convening such panels and the back-log of protocols has been cleared up.

Although the process has evolved, the issues raised have not changed. Two 407 panels, one convened in 1993 [42] and one in 2001 [43] examined the risks of the insulin clamp technique on healthy children. Although each protocol was approved by its 407 panel, one cannot deduce that the insulin clamp technique is always approvable in healthy children. However, one could imagine other research techniques or procedures for which the level of risk would decrease with time and experience such that later studies using them would not require 407 review.

A second observation from the 407 process is the wide variability between panelists about the level of risk these protocols entail, a variability already reported between pediatric chairpersons, researchers, and IRB chairpersons.[44] NHRPAC attempted to provide greater detail regarding which procedures should be judged to belong to each of the three categories of risk,[45] but NHRPAC was disbanded before its suggestions were debated and adopted. The IOM committee also examined the categories of risk and concluded that SACHRP 'should be encouraged to continue its predecessor's work to develop consensus assessments about the risk of common research procedures'.[46]

By making the expert panel reports public, IRB members, researchers, and the public at large can comment on the panelists' recommendation regarding risk classification. This is particularly important in the studies in which there was wide variability on the level of risk that the research entailed. Dialogue may lead to a body of cases described as minimal risk, a minor increase over minimal risk, and more than a minor increase over minimal risk. The data could serve as guidance for other IRBs about how such research is being classified by comparable institutions, and will provide a forum when serious disagreements arise. It could help reduce the number of referrals to OHRP for protocols that do not require 407 review and increase the number of referrals for research that does merit 407 review. In fact, it would be useful if OHRP decided to make publicly available all protocols that it receives for 407 review for which it convenes a 407 panel review, even those in which the 407 referral is voided, to give further guidance to IRBs about what research can be approved at the local level.

A third observation is that the research projects under review had already received federal funding. This means that they had been peer-reviewed and found to have significant scientific merit. IRB review earlier in the process could prevent the funding of ethically unapprovable research, or at least warn researchers when the project as designed will require 407 review. This is important because research designs are dependent on the current state of knowledge, such that a delay of two or three years may make the research questions obsolete, and yet the funding mechanism might not permit or encourage revision of the research design. A cumbersome process, then, will discourage researchers and their institutions from applying for 407 review, and may lead institutions to employ an overly liberal interpretation of minimal risk or a minor increase over minimal risk in order to justify approving a research project, particularly one that is externally funded.

The downside of earlier IRB review is that it significantly increases the workload of IRBs by requiring review of many projects that are never funded and therefore not executed. If researchers were to seek 407 review before funding was secured, it could mean 407 review of many projects that are never realized. If revisions that are ethically desirable may potentially affect the grant score of the protocol adversely, some researchers may choose to delay ethics review until after the funding decisions are made. The comment from the PI of the study examining hypoglycemia and cognitive function provides anecdotal evidence for this concern. When she offered to remove the healthy control arm, she was informed that her funding depended upon comparing data in children with diabetes and healthy controls.[47]

A fourth observation is that despite IRB and expert panel review, two of the consent forms sought the consent of only one parent which is inconsistent with the federal regulations requiring two-parent consent for all research approved under CFR §46.407. This may have been oversight, or it may been the belief that the second parent would not add much protection. This suggests that, at minimum, the current policy be re-examined.

A fifth observation is the issue of payment. Payment was offered in all three studies. They varied in how much was paid to the child versus the parent as well as the actual amount paid. The public process of 407 review may help create guidelines by community consensus regarding the legitimacy of paying pediatric research subjects. If payment is deemed to be legitimate in research that requires 407 review, then one still needs to determine how much the children and their parents could be paid.[48] Compensation for injury, another topic not addressed in the federal regulations, was also discussed in some of the 407 reviews. Many ethics advisory panels have supported the proposition to compensate all research subjects injured directly by their research participation.[49] The arguments in support of injury compensation are even more compelling in the case of research requiring 407 review.

8. Recommendations

Some important research questions on children will entail more than a minor increase over minimal risk and not offer the prospect of direct benefit. While an Institute of Medical Ethics working group (UK) concluded that such research should never be performed, [50] the National Commission (US) voted to permit such research (with two commissioners dissenting).[51] The concurring commissioners argued that such research should be permitted but restricted in its use.[52] They recommended a process involving national review to ensure greater scrutiny of both the scientific merit and the ethical concerns.[53] While 407 panels can offer this additional scrutiny, I have tried to show that the current structure needs reform. The panelists cannot vote or attempt to achieve consensus, lest they act as a committee without authority to do so.[54] Although public comments are solicited by OHRP as required for research to be approved under CFR §46.407, the public can only attend and participate if the panel is convened as a FAC. While a standing panel may resolve many of the procedural problems, it does not resolve all of the substantive problems such as (1) whether all research approved under CFR §46.407 ought to require two-parent consent; (2) whether and how much payment to children or parents is morally legitimate for research that requires 407 review; and (3) whether research approved under CFR §46.407 should be required to have an injury compensation plan. The 407 process may help elucidate how the regulations should be revised for research that is classified under CFR §46.407 as well as for research involving children more generally.

References

1. The most recent protocol, 'Effects of Single Dose of Dextroamphetamine in Attention Deficit Hyperactivity Disorder: A Functional Magnetic Resonance Study', was reviewed in September 2004. The protocol was different because it involved the use of a drug on healthy children and therefore both the Food and Drug Administration (FDA) and the Office for Human Research Protections (OHRP) participated in the 407 review. See Department of Health and Human Services, Food and Drug Administration, 'Pediatric Ethics Subcommittee of the Pediatric Advisory Committee; Notice of Meeting', *Federal Register* 69 (4 August 2004), 47157.

    The Panel that convened to discuss the research consisted of the Pediatric Ethics Subcommittee of the Pediatric Advisory Committee of the FDA. This committee is a federal advisory committee and therefore the meeting was open to the public in contrast with all the other 407 panels which were not established as a FAC. The pediatric ethics subcommittee recommended approval of the protocol with modifications. The consensus position of the committee (and not individual comments from each panelist) is available on the FDA website at http://www.fda. gov/ohrms/dockets/ac/04/minutes/2004-4066m1_summary%20minutes.pdf. However, OHRP has not yet made the committee's report nor its recommendations publicly available on its website (4 February 2004).

    Whether the 407 committee was different because it involved both OHRP and the FDA; or whether it has set a new precedent is not known at this time. In light of the lack of available documents and the other procedural unknowns, this protocol will not be considered further in the text.

2. Department of Health and Human Services (DHSS], Proposed Protocol Entitled 'Myoblast Transfer in Duchenne Muscular Dystrophy; Recommendations', *Federal Register* 56 (27 September 1991), 49189–90.

3. See Law, P. K., Bertorini, T. E., Goodwin, T. G., Chen, M., Fang, Q. W., Li, H. J., Kirby, D. S., Florendo, J. A., Herrod, H. G., and Golden, G. S., 'Dystrophin Production Induced by Myoblast Transfer Therapy in Duchenne Muscular Dystrophy', *Lancet*, 336 (1990), 114–15; Gussoni, E., Pavlath, G. K., Lanctot, A. M., Sharma, K. R., Miller, R. G., Steinman, L., and Blau, H. M., 'Normal Dystrophin Transcripts Detected in Duchenne Muscular Dystrophy Patients after Myoblast Transplantation', *Nature*, 346 (1992), 435–8; Huard, J., Roy, R., Bouchard, J. P., Malouin, F., Richards, C. L., and Tremblay, J. P., 'Human Myoblast Transplantation between Immunohistocompatible Donors and Recipients Produces Immune Reactions', *Transplantation Proceedings*, 18 (1992), 3049–51; Karpati, G., Ajdukovic, D., Arnold, D., Gledhill, R. B., Guttmann, R., Holland, P., Koch, P. A., Shoubridge, E., Spence, D., Vanasse, M., Watters, G. V., Abrahamowicz, M., Duff, C., and Worton, R. G., 'Myoblast Transfer in Duchenne Muscular Dystrophy', *Annals of Neurology*, 34 (1993), 8–17; and Mendell, J. R., Kissel, J. T., Amatao, A. A., King, W., Signore, L., Prior, T. W., Sahenk, Z., Benson, S., McAndrew, P. E., Rice, R., Nagaraja, H., Sephens, R. I., Lantry, L., Morris, G. E., and Burghes, A. H. M., 'Myoblast Transfer in the Treatment of Duchenne's Muscular Dystrophy', *New England Journal of Medicine*, 333 (1995), 832–8.

4. See Gussoni *et al.*, 'Normal Dystrophin'; Huard *et al.*, 'Human Myoblast'; Karpati *et al.*, 'Myoblast Transfer'; and Mendell *et al.*, 'Myoblast Transfer'.

5. See Law *et al.*, 'Dystrophin'.

6. See, e.g., Hoffman, E. P., 'Myoblast Transplantation: What's going on?' *Cell Transplantation*, 2 (1993), 49–57; and Cho, M., 'In Reply to Misrepresentation Conspires against Potential Treatment for Muscular Dystrophy', *IRB: Review of Human Subjects Research*, 17 (March/April 1995), 4–8.

7. See Law, P., 'Beneficial Effects of Transplanting Normal Limb-Bud Mesenchyme into Dystrophic Mouse Muscles', *Muscle & Nerve*, 5 (1982), 619–27; and Law, P. K., Goodwin, T. G., and Li, H. J., 'Histoincompatible Myoblast Injection Improves Muscle Structure and Function of Dystrophic Mice', *Transplantation Proceedings*, 20 (1988), 1114–19.

8. National Commission for the Protection of Human Subjects, *Report and Recommendations: Research Involving Children*. Washington DC: US Printing Office, 1977, DHEW Publication No. (OS) 77–0004, DHEW Publication No. (OS) 77–0004, 2–3; hereinafter cited as National Commission, *Research Involving Children*.

9. Cho, M. K., 'Are Clinical Trials of Cell Transplantation for Duchenne Muscular Dystrophy Ethical?' *IRB: Review of Human Subjects Research*. 16 (January–April 1994), 12–15, 14.

10. Department of Health and Human Services (DHHS], 'Cognitive Function and Hypoglycemia in Children with IDDM', *Federal Register* 58 (30 July 1993), 40819–20.

11. Ross, personal communication with Dorothy Becker, MD, October 2003.

12. See, e.g., Amiel, S. A., Sherwin, R. S., Simonson, D. C., Lauritano, A. A., and Tamborlane, W. V., 'Impaired Insulin Action in Puberty. A Contributing Factor to Poor Glycemic Control in Adolescents with Diabetes', *New England Journal of Medicine*, 315 (1986), 215–19; and Arslanian, S., Nixon, P. A., Becker, D., and Drash, A. L., 'Impact of Physical Fitness and Glycemic Control on In Vivo Insulin Action in Adolescents with IDDM', *Diabetes Care*, 13 (1990), 9–15; University of Minnesota, General Clinical Research Center. Protocol 488 (no date). On the web at http://www.gcrc.umn.edu/gcrc/proto.php?p488; and Weiss, R., Dufour, S., Taksali, S. E., Tamborlane, W. V., Petersen, K. F., Bonadonna, R. C., Boselli, L., Barbetta, G., Allen, K., Rife, F., Savoye, M., Dziura, J., Sherwin, R., Shulman, G. I., and Caprio, S., 'Prediabetes in Obese Youth: A Syndrome of Impaired Glucose Tolerance, Severe Insulin Resistance, and Altered Myocellular and Abdominal Fat Partitioning', *Lancet*, 362 (2003), 951–7.

13. Nelson, R. M., 'A Brief History of Protocol Reviews under 45 CFR §46.407', presented at the American Society of Bioethics and Humanities, October 2003, Montreal, Canada.

14. Office for Human Research Protections (OHRP) Determination Letter, 23 December 2003. On the web at http://www.hhs.gov/ohrp/children/407–01pnl/lrih.pdf.

15. Ibid., 9 December 2003 On the web at: http://www.hhs.gov/ohrp/children/407–01pnl/cact.pdf, 9.

16. Office for Human Research Protections (OHRP) and US Food and Drug Administration (FDA) Determination Letter, 24 January 2003. On the web at http://www.hhs.gov/ohrp/dpanel/determ.pdf.

17. HHS Reviews Under 45 CFR §46.407. On the web at: http://www.hhs.gov/ohrp/children/.

18. Another way to diagnose CF early is via newborn screening. The study is being proposed by researchers in North Carolina where CF is not part of routine newborn screening.

19. Davidson, D. J., and Rolfe, M., 'Mouse Models of Cystic Fibrosis', *TRENDS in Genetics*, 17 (2001), S29–S37, S34.

20. Ibid., S35.

21. Marshall, M. F., 'Panel Review of Research Involving Children under Subpart D: 'Characteristics of Mucus and Mucins in Broncheolar Lavage Fluids from Infants with Cystic Fibrosis'. On the web at: http://www.hhs.gov/ohrp/panels/407–02pnl/exp5.htm, 1.

22. See, e.g., Armstrong, D. S., Grimwood, K., Carzino, R., Carlin, J. B., Olinksy, A., and Phelan, P. D., 'Lower Respiratory Infection and Inflammation in Infants with Newly Diagnosed Cystic Fibrosis', *BMJ*, 310 (1995), 1571–2; Dakin, C. J., Numa, A. H., Want, H., Morton, J. R., Vertzyas, C. C., and Henry, R. L., 'Inflammation, Infection and Pulmonary Function in Infants and Young Children with Cystic Fibrosis', *American Journal of Respiratory and Critical Care Medicine*, 165 (2002), 904–10; Nixon, G. M., Armstrong, D. S., Carzino, R., Carlin, J. B., Olinksy, A., Robertson, C. F., and Grimwood, K., 'Early Airway Infection, Inflammation, and Lung Function in Cystic Fibrosis', *Archives of*

Disease in Childhood, 87 (2002), 306–11; Burns, J. L., Gibson, R. L., McNamara, S., Yim, D., Emerson, J., Rosenfeld, M., Hiatt, P., McCoy, K., Castile, R., Smith, A. L., and Ramsey, B. W., 'Longitudinal Assessment of Pseudomonas Aeruginosa in Young Children with Cystic Fibrosis', *Journal of Infectious Diseases*, 183 (2001), 444–52; and Balough, K., McCubbin, M., Weinberger, M., Smits, W., Ahrens, R., and Fick, R., 'The Relationship between Infection and Inflammation in the Early Stages of Lung Disease from Cystic Fibrosis', *Pediatric Pulmonology*, 20 (1995), 63–70.

23. See Burns *et al.*, 'Longitudinal Assessment'; and Balough *et al.*, 'Relationship'.

24. Marshall, 'Panel Review', 5.

25. See the panel reviews by Ronald C. Rubenstein, MD, PhD (panelist 1) and by Rosemary B. Quigley, JD, MPH (panelist 6). On the web at: http://www.hhs.gov/ohrp/children/mucus.html.

26. Office for Human Research Protections (OHRP), Determination Letter, 4 June 2004. On the web at: http://www.hhs.gov/ohrp/children/fund2.pdf.

27. 'IRB Protocol Application: Sleep Mechanisms in Children: Role of Metabolism'. On the web at: http://www.hhs.gov/ohrp/panels/407–03pnl/gappl.pdf, 1.

28. 'RFA: HL–01–006: Sleep and Sleep Disorders in Children'. On the web at: http://grants.nih.gov/grants/guide/rfa-files/RFA-HL-01-006.html.

29. Department of Health and Human Services (DHHS), (45 CFR Part 46, Subpart D), 'Protections for Children Involved as Subjects in Research', *Federal Register*, 48 (8 March 1983), 9814–20; revised *Federal Register*, 56 (18 June 1991), 28032, CFR §46.408; hereinafter cited by its CFR number in the text.

30. Office of Human Research Protections (ORHP), Determination Letter, 23 March 2004. On the web at: http://www.hhs.gov/ohrp/children/407–03pnl/hhhsdet.pdf; hereinafter cited as OHRP, Determination Letter, March 2004.

31. Correspondence from UCLA to OHRP requesting HHS review pursuant to 45 CFR §46.407. (20 June 2002). On the web at: http://www.hhs.gov/ohrp/panels/407–04pnl/review.htm.

32. Frush, D. P., Donelly, L. F., and Rosen, N. S., 'Computed Tomography and Radiation Risks: What Pediatric Health Care Providers Should Know', *Pediatrics* 112 (2003), 951–7.

33. Ibid.

34. McCarthy, A. M., Richman, L. C., Hoffman, R. P., and Rubenstein, L., 'Psychological Screening of Children for Participation in Nontherapeutic Invasive Research', *Archives of Pediatrics and Adolescent Medicine*, 155 (2001), 1197–203.

35. Quigley, R. B., 'Re: Expert Review of Research under 45 CFR §46.407 of Protocol "HIV Replication and Thymopoiesis" ', On the web at: http://www.hhs.gov/ohrp/panels/407–04pnl/exp7.htm, 2.

36. See Chap. 14, section 5, 'Other Diabetes Research Studies'.

37. OHRP, Determination Letter, March 2004.

38. An anonymous reviewer for a peer-reviewed journal asked me to justify my position in favor of public meetings for 407 panels. The reviewer noted that NIH study sections meet in private to improve candor and the quality of the reviews. I responded that I believe the two processes are different enough to

justify different treatment. Study sections are committees of scientists and researchers convened by NIH to evaluate the scientific merit of numerous research proposals. 407 panels are convened by DHHS to decide whether we as a society believe that the potential benefits of the research are of sufficient magnitude to justify exposing children to greater risk than that allowed by the standard regulations (CFR §46.404–46.406). Although both types of evaluations involve value judgments, study sections address technical questions that can be better answered by scientific experts, who are more likely to give a candid evaluation if promised confidentiality. In contrast, 407 panels address moral and political questions regarding the degree of risks to which we as a society think it is permissible to expose children, and must balance individual child well-being with societal benefits. The answer to these moral and political questions cannot be determined by scientific experts alone, but depends upon wide community consultation about what type of society we are and want to be. Such issues can be addressed most effectively when all the stakeholders are included in the dialogue. Public meetings provide an opportunity for this dialogue to occur.

39. Nelson, R. M., 'Comments on OHRP Announcement of 407 Review Panel.' Nelson's comments were published on IRB Forum, the Institutional Review Board-Discussion and News Forum. 23 August 2002. On the web at: http://www.irbforum.org/forum/read/3/10181/10181Vt. Reprinted with author's permission.

   The panel that met in September 2004 regarding Dextroamphetamine in Healthy Children consisted in part of the Pediatric Ethics Subcommittee of the Pediatric Advisory Committee of the FDA which is a federal advisory committee (FAC). Because it is a FAC, the members attempt to achieve consensus rather than submit individual panelist reports. Whether this process will continue, and whether it will continue for all 407 reviews and not just those involving an experimental drug, has yet to be determined.

40. Field, M. J., and Behrman, R. E. (eds.), Committee on Clinical Research Involving Children, the Institute of Medicine (IOM) *The Ethical Conduct of Clinical Research Involving Children.* Washington DC: National Academies Press, 2004, 272–3; hereinafter this reference is cited as IOM, *Ethical Conduct.*

41. Summary Minutes of the Secretary's Advisory Committee on Human Research Protections, 29–30 March, 2004. On the web at: http://www.hhs.gov/ohrp/sachrp/mtgings/mtg03–04/min0329.pdf.

42. DHHS, 'Cognitive Function'.

43. Department of Health and Human Services (DHHS), 'Proposed Recommendation Regarding Support of Research Protocol: Precursors to Diabetes in Japanese American Youth', *Federal Register* 67 (7 August 2002), 51283–4.

44. See Janofsky, J., and Starfield, B., 'Assessment of Risk in Research on Children'. *Journal of Pediatrics*, 98 (1981), 842–6; and Shah, S., Whittle, A., Wilfond, B., Gensler, G., and Wendler, D., 'How do Institutional Review Boards Apply the Federal Risk and Benefit Standards for Pediatric Research?' *JAMA* 291 (2004), 476–82.

45. Final Report to NHRPAC from Children's Workgroup (undated). On the web at: http://www.hhs.gov/ohrp/nhrpac/documents/nhrpac16.pdf.

46. IOM, *Ethical Conduct*, 135.
47. Ross, personal communication with Dorothy Becker, MD, October 2003.
48. The 2004 protocol, 'Effects of Single Dose of Dextroamphetamine in Attention Deficit Hyperactivity Disorder: A Functional Magnetic Resonance Study', offered $570 (US) to the potential healthy subjects who would undergo functional magnet resonancing imaging studies after taking one dose of dextroamphetamine, a drug commonly prescribed for children with attention-deficit disorder, but not approved for use in healthy children. The amount of payment was only discussed briefly in the transcripts of the meeting. On the web at: http://www.fda.-gov/ohrms/ dockets/ ac/04/transcripts/2004–4067t1_01.pdf, 34. However, the research and the amount of money being offered to the children were covered by an Associated Press story that was republished in many newspapers. See Henderson, D., 'FDA committee considers ethics of giving experimental stimulants to healthy children'. On the web at: http://www.detnews.com/2004/health/0409/04/health-263336.htm. It was also covered in the journal *Science*. Couzin, J., 'Human Subjects Research. Pediatric Study of ADHD Drug Draws High-Level Public Review', *Science*, 305 (2004). 1088–9. Both articles questioned whether the amount of money being offered the children and their families was too large and whether it would be an 'undue influence'.

   In Chap. 8, I argued that one of the reasons payment to children can be justified is that the federal regulations restrict the amount of risk to which children can be exposed. The risks of research approved under 407 review may be greater and may make payment more suspect. This means that the research must be scrutinized for safety and scientific importance; it does not mean, however, that the research cannot be done or that payment is unethical.
49. See, e.g., President's Commission for the Study of Ethical Problems in Medicine and Biomedical Research, *Compensating for Research Injuries: A Report on the Ethical and Legal Implications of Programs to Redress Injuries Caused by Biomedical and Behavioral Research*. Washington DC: US Government Printing Office, 1982; Advisory Committee on Human Radiation Experiments (ACHRE), *Advisory Committee on Human Radiation Experiments: Final Report*. Washington DC: US Government Printing Office, 1995; and Federman, D. D., Hanna, K. E., and Rodriguez, L. L. (eds.), Committee on Assessing the System for Protecting Human Research Participants, Institute of Medicine, *Responsible Research: A Systems Approach to Protecting Research Participants*. Washington, DC: National Academy Press, 2003, 193–4; and IOM, *Ethical Conduct*, 227.
50. Nicholson, *Medical Research*, 234.
51. National Commission, *Research Involving Children*, 139.
52. Ibid., 139–41.
53. Ibid.
54. Nelson, R. M., Prentice, E. D., and Hammerschmidt, D. E., 'The Process of Federal Panel Review of Research Protocols Involving Children', *Medical Research Law & Policy*, 1 (2002), 613–15.

Epilogue

The National Institute of Child Health and Human Development (NICHD) was established by US Congress in 1962. It was, in the words of then-president John F. Kennedy, the first 'Institute to promote studies directed at the entire life process rather than toward specific diseases or illnesses'.[1] Initially its mission was 'to investigate broad aspects of human development as a means to understanding developmental disabilities, including mental retardation, as well as events that occurred during pregnancy'. Forty years later, its mission has expanded to include 'all stages of human development, from preconception to adulthood, and addresses topics related to the health of children, adults, families, communities, and populations'. [2] To accomplish these goals, NICHD supports and conducts research.

Pediatric research is also funded by pharmaceutical companies, not-for-profit companies, and other philanthropic organizations. Some of the new policies have led to an increase in money spent on pediatric research, or at least to the inclusion of children in research.

Intellectually, research is a good in itself, but the real moral justification for performing research on children is its value in the translation of bench and clinical research into clinical practice. To the extent that the new policies promote this translation, they ought to be affirmed. To the extent that these polices are increasing participation without achieving greater knowledge and improved practice, these policies are in need of reform.

However, even if these new policies are promoting pediatric knowledge and advancing practice, one must still ask whether they are doing so in a way that minimizes risk to children. One way to minimize the risk to children is to follow the National Commission's principle that 'when possible, research should be done first on animals, then adults, and then older children'.[3] To date there is no moral argument to justify overturning the principle, although exceptions can be found (and should be permitted). As such, the principle of minimizing risk needs to be enforced by IRBs when they review a research study involving children, and the practice of minimizing risk needs to be incorporated into the methodology of every research study designed to include children. As many of my case studies showed, this is not always occurring.

Pediatric research is important, but it must be performed in a way that protects children, as individuals and as a class. The federal regulations for human subject protections are a good starting point. There are some issues regarding the protection of human subjects, however, that were not addressed; some policies that need to be modified; and even some that need to be overturned. In this book, I have tried to enumerate a number of recommendations. Some may remove unnecessary obstacles (e.g., removing the two-parent consent requirement, permitting fair payment); others may retard progress (e.g., must begin research on newborns only when the intervention permitting in the newborn period).

But in the end, human subject protections requires the integrity of the researcher and the research community. We need to be honest with our patients and human subjects about both the motive and goals of phase I research; and we need to respect the parents and children who agree to participate by seeking parental permission (or in rare circumstances, a substitute mechanism) and the children's assent (when their dissent will be dispositive). We need to be willing to challenge our colleagues who may be placing their careers above the safety and well-being of the volunteers who agree to be co-adventurers. In this era of high-profit science, we need to remember that our primary goal is our own humanity:

Let us also remember that a slower progress in the conquest of disease would not threaten society, grievous as it is to those who have to deplore that their particular disease be not yet conquered but that society would indeed be threatened by the erosion of those moral values whose loss, possibly caused by too ruthless a pursuit of scientific progress, would make its most dazzling triumphs not worth having.[4]

References

1. Kennedy, J. F., Ribbon-Cutting Ceremony, 17 October 1962. On the NICHD website at: http://www.nichd.nih.gov/40th/.
2. The two mission statements are also found on the NICHD website at http://www.nichd.nih.gov/40th/.
3. See National Commission for the *Protection of Human Subjects of Biomedical and Behavioral Research. Report and Recommendations: Research Involving Children.* Washington DC: US Government Printing Office, 1977, DHEW Publication No. (OS) 77–0004, 2 & 3; and National Commission for the Protection of Human Subjects of Biomedical and Behavioral Research, *The Belmont Report: Ethical Principles and Guidelines for the Protection of Human Subjects of Research.* Washington DC: US Government Printing Office, 1978, DHEW Publication No. (OS) 78–12. On the web at: http://ohsr.od.nih.gov/guidelines/belmont.html.
4. Jonas, H., 'Philosophical Reflections on Experimenting with Human Subjects' in P. A. Freund (ed.), *Experimentation with Human Subjects.* New York: Braziller, 1970, 1–31, 28.

Index